THE IDEAL LOVERS

Dima Lubov, reveling in the sweetness of success, the riotous pleasures of the flesh. **Jennifer Hale,** fragile, dedicated, immensely talented, trembling on the threshold of love and fame. Amid the intrigues and corruptions of the ballet world, among the moneyed manipulators and celebrity hunters, they created an enchanted world of their own.

AND THE FRIENDLY ENEMIES

Dave Loughlin, an over-the-hill CIA agent. **Ivan,** his Russian counterpart, grown worldly and cynical in his trade. Now these two are thrust together —operating without the knowledge of the countries they are supposed to serve and the people they hope to save—in a desperate race against time and an international grand master of murder.

In the spotlight, a breathtaking pas de deux of passion. In the lengthening shadows, the most nerve-twisting suspense ever to keep you reading far into the night. . . .

BALLET!

Big Bestsellers from SIGNET

If you wish to order these titles,
please see the coupon in the
back of this book.

BALLET!

❦TOM MURPHY❦

A SIGNET BOOK

NEW AMERICAN LIBRARY

TIMES MIRROR

This book is for my mother,
Margaret Louise Fitzgerald Murphy.

Acknowledgements

Many kind people have helped with this book, and I'd like to thank them for their patience and enthusiasm.

Joe Davis, dancer, choreographer and teacher of ballet, undertook the enormous task of educating me in what happens behind the scenes, and also served as technical advisor for the book. Anne Tolstoi Wallach invited me to my first *Giselle,* and thus set the whole thing in motion. Helen Wieselberg, as true a Friend as Covent Garden ever had, has been generous with advice, as have Sally Patterson and Frank Cucci.

My editor at NAL, Joanie Hitzig, and my agent, Al Zuckerman, have both been helpful and supportive far beyond the call of duty: thank you all, very much.

TM

CHAPTER
⌘ 1 ⌘

New York City, 1975

Jennifer Hale stood in the shadow of a plywood flat at the
left of the great stage; in one hour and ten minutes exactly
she would go mad and die. *If I last that long,* she thought, *if
they don't actually get up and leave the theater.* Jenny Hale
was about to face the most demanding ballet audience in the
world in the most demanding role ever created for a ballerina. Jenny Hale was about to become the youngest American girl ever to dance *Giselle.* And she felt all the great
Giselles in history crowding the audience, one hundred and
thirty-five years' worth of beauty and talent and perfect technique gazing disdainfully at the presumption of this Yankee
child, more critical than any critic. Jenny shuddered and continued her exercises.

This, she thought, bending her slim legs in demi-plié,
straightening, bending again, *is for Pavlova.* She continued
the exercise, at the same time lifting her arms in graceful arcs
over her head, port de bras: *And this is for Fanny Elssler
. . . and this, for Carlotta Grisi. . . .* The litany went on,
from Grisi, who had created Giselle in 1841, through all the
great ones: Markova, Ulanova, Fracci. Jenny had never been
a religious girl, and she certainly wasn't in the habit of pray-
ing to great ballerinas, past or present. But it was a way to
pass the time, a way not to think. Jenny knew, instinctively,
that she could dance the role and dance it well. She'd be fine
when she got onstage, when the music took her, when she'd
have Dimitri to flirt with, to help weave the spell. But in the
meantime, the most promising young ballerina of the famous
New York Civic Ballet Company was just another twitchy
nineteen-year-old with a stomach full of angry butterflies and
a head filled with unanswered questions. Where, Jenny wondered, was her father on this night, of all nights? A huge bou-

quet of long-stemmed white roses had appeared in her
dressing room with Clifford Hale's name on the card: phoned
in from where? And probably not paid for, either.

Jenny wore an old blue shawl and the crazy-quilt crocheted
woolen leg warmers Privy had made for her last year, her
lucky leg warmers she called them, because she'd had them
on the day Alexander de Lis told her he wanted her to dance
Giselle. After that she'd practically slept in them.

Under the shawl and leg warmers was Giselle's delicate
fairy-tale country-girl costume. At the very last minute Jenny
would throw off the shawl, shuck off the leg warmers and appear in Giselle's sky-blue bodice with its scoop-necked ivory
blouse, puff-sleeved, embroidered with small flowers, and the
skirt of palest blue with seven cream petticoats. Her long hair
was swept into a classic bun, fastened with more flowers, but
arranged to fall in a cascade of chestnut to her waist in the
mad scene. Giselle's tights were traditional, the palest pink,
with matching pale pink pointe shoes, the ribbons tied
smoothly around her slim ankles and glued with Elmer's Glue
to make sure they stayed that way. The canvas-and-glue-
boxed toes were bent and slammed six times each against her
dressing-room wall to make them a little more giving, the
toes of her pointe shoes carefully darned to make them less
slippery, quiet for running, less dangerous. Jenny as Giselle
would look like the soul of delicacy, but in fact, no pro foot-
ball linebacker ever girded more carefully for the fray.

Jenny kept up her exercises, oblivious to the sea of activity
that swirled around her backstage in the immense New York
State Theater at Lincoln Center.

The flat, whose raw plywood back gave no clue to its art-
fully painted front, was, to the audience, the facade of
Giselle's cottage. The dark rectangle of wood in the middle
was the door, and in a very few minutes Jenny Hale would
step through that door and emerge as Giselle, love-struck
maiden, Queen of the Harvest, doomed fairy-tale heroine.
Doomed, thought Jenny, *is the right word for it*. There were
times when she felt every bit as doomed as Giselle, times
when she wondered what it would have been like to have had
a normal girlhood, a real home, to have led a life that was
not bound on all sides by rehearsals, classes, footlights and by
the iron discipline of Alexander de Lis.

All around Jenny Hale, the several kingdoms of backstage
ballet hummed with increasing activity.

Here was the great hidden mass of the iceberg whose smallest part was the performance itself, just as the performance was the smallest part of Jenny's long day. She ran out of ballerinas to invoke and thought about that day. Breakfast with Privy at seven, class at nine-forty-five for two hours of intensive warm-up and drill with the whole company, stars mixing with kids from the corps de ballet and she, Jenny, not really at home anywhere among them, unfledged as a principal dancer, resented by many of the kids her own age—and older—who had been passed over by de Lis when he elevated Jenny.

All differences, all individuality, all competition disappeared in class. Every one of them became cogs in the same giant gear, functioning as one, working for one goal, precision, elegance of line, effortlessness in movement—no matter what effort it cost them. Two hours of that, and anyone would be ready for a nice long nap. Not Jenny Hale. It was off to a costume fitting with no time for lunch, then finally, the much-needed rest, a few hours in the afternoon during which Jenny tried in vain to relax but worried, not about Giselle but about a modern piece she was scheduled to do next week. *If I'm among the living next week*, she thought, bending, straightening, extending first her left leg and then the right. Then it was back to the theater for an hour's warm-up, to get dressed, to be here, ready, still warming up at a few minutes before curtain time, eight P.M. Jenny's working day was twelve hours old, and the performance hadn't even begun yet.

It was almost time. Weird, unmusical squeaks and moans floated up from the orchestra pit. The stage manager sat at his big console of a desk, issuing commands into two red telephones like some space-age general. Two hundred feet overhead the enchanted forest of Act II hung invisible but ready in the darkness. Hushed movement filled the big drafty spaces. The girls and boys from the corps de ballet were pouring out of the backstage elevators that came down from their dressing rooms three floors above the main stage. Like Jenny, they were fresh from their warm-ups, hurrying in a race to beat the backstage chill. Cold is the enemy of all dancers; one chilled muscle can seize up and literally cripple a dancer for days. Cold is the enemy. Age is the enemy. Lack of exercise is the enemy. "The ballet stage," the perceptive journalist Joseph Mazo had said, "is a combat zone." Too true.

Iris Dowling emerged from a group of village maidens and came up to Jenny. *She's going to stab me.* Iris was Jenny Hale's only real rival among the younger girls in the Civic Ballet. Jenny looked at Iris now and thought: *She's taller than I am, she's prettier, and God knows she's sexier. I wonder why de Lis chose me?* Jenny Hale wasn't the only member of the company who wondered. But the word of Alex de Lis was just slightly more compelling than direct word from God. You didn't question the word of Alexander de Lis, not if you intended to continue a career in the Civic Ballet Company.

Iris didn't stab Jenny Hale. Instead, the taller girl kissed her own fingertips and touched them to Jenny's bare shoulder.

"*Merde!*" said Iris, smiling. A ritual.

"*Merde,* Iris." Jenny repeated the odd gesture and smiled. *Her eyes are too bright,* thought Jenny; *she's on something again. But it was nice of her to wish me* merde. *She didn't have to do that. Merde meant luck. The touch on the shoulder was to avoid smudging makeup. No one quite knows how the French word for shit got turned into the dancer's way of wishing other dancers well. On Broadway they say, "Break a leg." In ballet, in the combat zone, injuries aren't funny. So, somehow, it got be *merde.* Jenny turned to watch Iris Dowling disappear farther backstage with the other kids from the corps. *She might have been my friend.* It was as though Iris Dowling had been left on some far-off shore and Jenny only now was beginning to notice her absence.

Jenny had had no real friends in the Civic Ballet: no real friends, no real enemies, one lover. Not a very crowded program for a girl of nineteen. Jenny thought about this, dismissed the thought. Her life was crowded enough. Her life was filled with dancing, and dancing was enough. At least, it always had been.

There was a kind of buzzing from out front, then a wave of applause. The conductor had taken his place. *I won't think about Iris.* Jenny hugged the worn terry-cloth robe tighter around her thin shoulders. But the chill she felt was not in the air, it was inside her. *I'll think about Giselle. I'll think about Dimitri.* That would do it. She'd think about Dimitri

Lubov. It was really Dimitri the crowd out there had come to see anyhow.

Dimitri's workout was more strenuous than Jenny's. He worked out at nearly full-performance strength because he wanted his first entrance onstage to be the seamless continuation of a momentum already building rather than a simple beginning.

Already the young Russian was sweating.

Dimitri Lubov wore the elegant fake-peasant costume of Albrecht, Duke of Silesia, posing as a bumpkin in order to win the heart of Giselle. Over the fawn-colored tights was a pair of faded gray baggy cotton sweat pants. A bright-red sweat shirt, much too large, covered Albrecht's suede vest and cream-colored loose-sleeved shirt. On the front of Dimitri's red sweat shirt was a huge engraving of Ludwig van Beethoven, printed in black, frowning. Beethoven frowned harder as Dimitri twisted his torso and extended first one leg, then the other, moving to a rhythm only he could hear, humming softly under his breath an old Cole Porter show tune. No wonder Beethoven was frowning. *"Night and Day"* hummed Dimitri Lubov in his not-yet-perfect English, *"you . . . are . . . the one."* Kick, extend, bend into demi-plié, up, tour en l'air: the routine went on, and Ludwig got ever more wrathful.

Backstage was the same everywhere, thought Dimitri: the same smells, the same rush, the same building tension, the same electricity jumping from the crowd to the performers and—with luck—back again.

At twenty-four Dimitri Lubov had been dancing the male lead in *Giselle* for six years. Albrecht was not news to Dimitri Lubov, the way *Giselle* was a beginning for Jenny Hale. Still, he looked forward to this night. The backstage loudspeaker warned everyone, "Five minutes to curtain, please . . . five minutes to curtain." It was a countdown as precise as the launching of any rocket. "And what," Dimitri asked himself, "will we be launching tonight?" Dimitri grinned, the grin of a street urchin, which was just what he had been not very many years ago. *Follow the impulse, Dimitri.* Impulse, gut instinct, crazy urge, call it what you will: Dimitri Lubov had been following his heart practically from the cradle. He never questioned it or ever thought very much about how or why he did what he did. Impulse had led him to slip away from the Kirov tour in Amsterdam two years ago, to disappear into a crowd of German tourists, hail a cab and head straight for the American Consulate.

Impulse had brought him here, tonight, to this big strange theater in this big cold city, dancing before the most demanding crowd in the world with an untried little girl. It wasn't the safest way. But safe ways had never beguiled Dimitri Lubov. If they had, he'd still be the bureaucrat's delight in Leningrad, dancing maybe twice a month at some commissar's whim, growing old in the classics, stuck like a fly in amber in the unchanging Kirov choreography that had been frozen irrevocably before Dimitri Lubov or Jenny Hale first saw light of day.

He thought of Jenny. Strange creature. There was a wild, haunted, ethereal quality about Jenny Hale that puzzled Dimitri and attracted him. She did not have the openness of most American girls: Jenny had secrets and kept them. The other American girls he knew were uncomplicated as sunrise—and, ultimately, as boring.

With Jenny Hale, Dimitri always sensed a reserve beneath the graceful technique. He had seen, at once, why de Lis had chosen her for Giselle. He knew as did de Lis that the elusive haunted quality would carry right across the footlights.

Still exercising as the seconds ticked toward curtain time, Dimitri thought of all the Giselles he'd partnered: first old Draknovna, in the Kirov, famous but over the hill at forty-five. She'd personally requested Dimitri, a huge honor for a boy just turned sixteen. He had been flattered, he'd danced well, Draknovna was pleased, but when all was said and done, it was an exercise in artifice, a triumph of the illusion created by Draknovna's skill over the reality, of the difference of more than twenty years in their ages. There had been other Kirov Giselles, many of them, and then the guest appearances after he defected. And of them all, Dimitri knew with his sure dancer's instinct, this would be the great one. This one would have magic in it. He couldn't say why if his life depended on it; these things were chemistry, as simple and as infinitely complicated as love or hate. Sometimes you could pair two great dancers and get . . . nothing. In other cases, some unlikely pairing worked a special alchemy and one of the great teams would be born. This had happened to another defector; when Nureyev first danced with Margot Fonteyn, they struck sparks that illuminated the whole world of ballet.

There was no way to legislate such magic, to make a formula of it, to put it in a bottle. It came as a blessing from capricious gods, and when it came, the only thing to do was accept the gift and try to do it justice. "Whether near to you . . . or far. . . ." Dimitri pulled off the red sweat shirt and carefully patted his made-up face with a tissue from the ever-present box of Kleenex. Then he peeled off the sweat pants. De Lis came by to wish him *merde*. He grinned and flexed his toes in Albrecht's boots. It was going to happen. He could feel it. Magic. There came a whirring. The huge golden curtain was going up.

Alexander de Lis prowled his kingdom like some legendary guardian panther. He moved across the empty stage, checking, touching, making absolutely sure all was in order. The curtain would not go up until de Lis gave the signal. He looked at Giselle's cottage and frowned; the flowers in the windowbox were wrong. He'd asked for silk geraniums in pink and scarlet. These were plastic, and the scarlet wasn't scarlet but more like the shade of an old fire hydrant. The stage designer had to be watched every minute. He must remember to check the invoices; if anyone thought he could bill Alex de Lis for silk and deliver plastic, he would be made to think again.

He worked across the set and came upon young Lubov exercising, and wished him *merde*. Lubov had been a gamble. Not for his ability as a dancer, which was well enough known even now. But in inviting Dimitri Lubov to be a guest artist in the Civic Ballet, de Lis had defied one of his own fundamental policies: to have a working repertory company without "stars." Dimitri arrived a star, and a star he would no doubt remain, whatever the policy of the Civic Ballet.

What de Lis was gambling on was that Dimitri would become a permanent part of the working company. His guest-appearance contract ran only three months, and the first month was nearly up already. Alex de Lis watched the boy working out, and smiled. You could spot the Kirov training anywhere. No one was better qualified to judge this; de Lis himself had trained in the venerable Maryinsky Theater. Had it been sixty years ago? De Lis had no patience with calendar time; calendars had been invented by historians and insurance companies and tax collectors. Time itself was boring. Only events mattered, people, lovers, performances, beginnings and endings.

At seventy-two, Alex de Lis could recall a Petipa ballet

he'd danced in Petrograd in 1918 down to the last detail of the headdresses in the corps de ballet. Yet he probably couldn't say what he'd had for lunch yesterday.

He left Dimitri Lubov and wandered around behind the deep stage, joking with the grips, wishing *merde* to a whole flock of village maidens and youths, adjusting the green ribbons on one girl's bodice—they were too long; they might catch on something. He made his quiet way from stage right all the way around to stage left in a giant U, looking, checking, making minor adjustments and mental notes about other adjustments too elaborate to go into five minutes before curtain time.

De Lis was stalking Jenny Hale, but no one backstage that night would have suspected it.

Finally, he could see her. For a moment de Lis stood back in the shadows, watching his other gamble of the evening, this strange, intense little girl, his unfledged Giselle. Jenny had cast off the robe now and pulled off the leg warmers. She reached out with one slender arm and used one of the supports for the facade of Giselle's cottage as a barre, continuing her exercises, oblivious to the mounting activity around her. Unseen, unheard, de Lis could feel the strength of Jenny's concentration. And as he had a hundred times before, Alex de Lis marveled at the power of Jenny Hale's dedication.

This was not a beautiful girl. Heads did not turn when Jenny Hale walked into a room. But the girl invented herself as she danced, and de Lis could only think of two, possibly three ballerinas in all his long memory who could create so much beauty just by moving: their names were Pavlova, Fonteyn, Plisetskaya.

De Lis walked up to Jenny, grinned and waved. Maybe he had gambled with the morale of the Civic Ballet by promoting this nineteen-year-old over the heads of all the corps. But choosing Jenny Hale to dance Giselle had not been a gamble. De Lis would have bet his life on it. In fact, he thought, and grinned his foxy grin again, he had bet something much more important on this skinny nineteen-year-old: Alexander de Lis had bet his reputation. Still smiling, he moved on to the stage manager and gave the signal for the curtain to go up.

The night was cold, and the solitary woman in black had walked four blocks from the crosstown bus. She made her way through the idlers outside the New York State Theater and paused for a moment in the big foyer. The sudden warmth fogged her gold-rimmed eyeglasses. The ivory travertine lobby was a blur of color and movement as people thronged toward the ticket takers and the twin travertine staircases that led to the mezzanine level. Slowly the scene faded into focus as the mist cleared on the woman's eyeglasses. Practical as ever, she used the interlude to remove her soft black kidskin gloves, mended these last ten years with stitches so fine they might have been Chinese, invisibly mended and looking very much like what they had once been: quietly splendid.

There was a kind of splendor about the woman herself. She was a bit taller than medium, built solidly without being fat, with dark brown hair attractively streaked with gray and the kind of fine-grained pink-and-white complexion that is often associated with nuns. Her eyes behind the slightly professorial spectacles were blue and merry, and her unrouged lips had the color of good health and a tendency to smile. You knew at once that here was a person of character, a personality of force and independence.

She frowned slightly, seeking the magic yellow ticket in her silk-velvet evening purse.

The ticket was magic because it had come to her through the efforts of Jenny Hale.

And it was magical, too, because tonight marked the first time in years that the ticket's proud owner had sat in the orchestra section of a New York theater. She found the ticket, smiled and made her way past the ticket taker and in to the orchestra. Almost everyone else was in pairs or in groups. The excitement building in this sophisticated audience was so intense it gave off rays. The rays of anticipation warmed the lone woman as she stood patiently at the back of the aisle waiting for the usher. She had waited for many things in her time. A few minutes more wouldn't hurt.

Miss Jessica Privet smiled graciously at the tired-looking lady usher, a woman near her own age more likely than not, pushing sixty. Privy took the program, thinking: *At least it hasn't come to that. I may be pushing sixty, but sixty isn't pushing me.* The seat was perfect, orchestra, fifteenth row and dead center. Privy carefully draped her black sealskin coat over the chair back. The coat was the last sign of Clifford Hale's flush period; it must be twelve years ago now, just about the time little Jenny had first entered the Civic Ballet Children's School, hardly suspecting where that would lead. Privy looked at the coat through her gold-rimmed eyeglasses. She'd had little enough occasion to use it these last few years. More than once she'd thought of selling the damned thing or anyway hocking it. Now she was glad she hadn't.

The orchestra was filling up. Jenny said the huge theater was hardly ever really sold out, not all the way up to the fifth tier. But from where Privy sat it looked enough like a sellout. She settled back into the comfortable plush seat, thinking that the theater was well-designed architecturally but decorated straight out of Woolworth's. Really, those giant rhinestones masquerading as lighting fixtures, strung all around the fronts of the balconies, looked like a tart's fake engagement ring multiplied by hundreds. It would get better when the lights went down. Most things did.

Slowly, savoring the moment, Privy opened her program. And there big as daylight were the words *"Giselle . . . Jennifer Hale."* Three words in not very large type on a cast listing. Twelve years of struggling to keep Jenny in the ballet school, of shielding her from Clifford Hale's increasingly erratic behavior, of juggling bills and improvising meals, of knitting leg warmers, feeding the child vitamins, of doing without and hiding the fact because Jenny would never have allowed it, would have chucked the dancing and got some tacky job somewhere just to eat, to pay rent.

The twelve years had gone by in what seemed like minutes. Privy felt the silken fur of the sealskin coat touch her hand and thought how little the years showed on her coat. And she wondered how much they showed on her face. No matter. It was worth it. Her Jenny had a life now. Tonight would just be the beginning. And, she realized with a little sigh, it might also be an ending.

Tonight would mean the start of a new phase for Jenny Hale. Even Privy, who was no expert about dancing, realized that. And she wondered just where, if anyplace, she, Jessica Privet, would fit in that new life. *Ye gods! A few minutes more in this vein, Miss Privet, and you'll end up in tears. Chin up, girl. The Empire wasn't won by whimpering.* Miss Jessica Privet giggled and sat back in the folds of her elegant coat just as a wave of applause rippled up out of the auditorium to greet the conductor.

It was another working night for Simon Bridge. The big, lumbering, round-bodied man had his timing down just about perfectly. Well he should have, considering the practice he got, six nights out of seven, and plenty of matinees thrown in to boot.

Tonight was one of the quieter nights. He had only *Giselle* to see. There were nights when he'd rush from theater to theater, catching fragments of two or even three performances. Simon Bridge was a conscientious man; he hated to send in a stringer if he could possibly cover something himself. Over the years he had become more and more adept at timing. Now, puffing just a little, he made his way down the aisle of the New York State Theater just as the first bars of the overture were struck. His seat, of course, was right on the aisle, as befitted the most influential ballet critic in the world. Simon Bridge of *The New York Times*. Of some performances, Simon Bridge knew all too well what to expect. Others were completely new, filled with surprises, and not always pleasant surprises. But tonight was the kind of night that made his job worth doing. Here was a great classic ballet danced by two young people who had never before appeared in New York in major roles.

Simon had, of course, seen Dimitri Lubov. He'd seen Dimitri as a teenager in the Kirov, seen him in Copenhagen just after his defection and again in London, in the summertime. Bridge's job, and his immense thirst to see the best of the best in ballet, took him all over the world in search of new talent. This gave his opinions extra weight, for Simon Bridge really had seen it all. And he had no doubt that Lubov was a major talent, another Nureyev and—sacrilege!—possibly destined to be more interesting when he reached his peak. As for the little Hale girl, Simon had seen her, too, although never in anything major.

He knew de Lis had picked the girl out of his own school and put her directly into solo roles with the Civic. That was last spring. And she had done well, very well. But an occasional pas de deux is only a hint. The real excitement tonight would be in seeing if the girl could bring it off. If she could, there was no limit to where she might go, to what she might achieve. There were already American ballerinas of unquestioned world-class talent; Suzanne Farrell, Cynthia Gregory, Melissa Hayden, Gelsey Kirkland, and Patricia M... came instantly to mind. But as good as those girls un edly were, America had yet to hatch its Pavlova, its Fonteyn, its Plisetskaya.

If and when that moment came, Simon Bridge would be ready to record it for all posterity. He slipped into his seat and settled back, looking neither left nor right. And as he adjusted himself and got out his famous green leather notebook and his slim gold pencil, the great critic permitted himself a little smile. It was the kind of night he liked best, a night crowded with infinite possibilities.

Jenny felt, rather than saw, a familiar presence at her elbow. She turned to look into the smiling fox face of Alex de Lis. He blew her a kiss. *"Merde, little Jenny."*

"Merde," she said, blushing. It was his performance as much as anyone else's. There was a muffled whirring as the great golden curtain rose into infinity. The first familiar bars of the Adolphe Adam music filled the air backstage. *He wrote this in a week,* thought Jenny irreverently, *and that's just what it sounds like.*

The score to *Giselle* wasn't really bad music, but it wasn't good either. No one ever left a theater humming a theme from *Giselle.* It was classic background music, perfectly adequate, filled with little trills and climaxes that lent themselves to dramatic choreography, exactly the same caliber of music that underlined the overwrought goings-on in a hundred 1930s three-handkerchief movie melodramas. And what else was *Giselle* but a melodrama spiced up with a few touches of the supernatural?

It had always struck Jenny as sad that the great era of ballet never managed to get its best composers together with its best librettists—with the single exception of Tchaikovsky, whose *Swan Lake* and *Sleeping Beauty* were both flops first time out, she remembered. Most of the great ballets had mediocre scores, just as most of the great operas had indecipherable librettos. There was a message in that, but Jenny had never been sure what it was.

Now she heard Hilarion's music. She'd be on in two minutes.

Hilarion was the boy next door, well meaning but dumb. On the other side of the plywood flat Hilarion would be doing his big mime number, showing his love for Giselle, even going so far as to hang a brace of dead rabbits on her door. *He should have tried emeralds,* she thought, waiting for Hilarion to unload his rabbits so that Albrecht could come on.

Albrecht. That was the real stuff. Jenny stepped back a few paces and faced the door. It wasn't just a square of raw plywood now. It was the door to her house, and she was going to step out of that door a simple, daydreaming country girl and have her life changed forever.

Unconsciously Jenny touched her hair, smoothing it, checking to see that the flowers were still in place. There was nothing of the coquette in Miss Jennifer Hale. But Giselle was another matter, and in those few seconds Jenny became Giselle. *I am the prettiest girl in the village. All the boys are crazy about me. And I tease them. I lead them on. Especially Hilarion. But it's all a game. Because I really love Albrecht—Dimitri—as who wouldn't, with that face, those eyes, that fire?* The pace of the music changed abruptly, became more intense. There was a wave of applause. Dimitri was on now. Jenny waited for her cue; it came.

Jenny Hale had waited for the cue, but Giselle stepped through the door.

Giselle stepped into a perfect Transylvanian morning. The village square was deserted. Yet she'd heard a knock. He must be hiding somewhere. She looked around, saw no one and went into a little dance. She danced alone, greeting the day, a dance of hope and innocence, short and beguiling as innocence itself, a dance for the morning but really for Albrecht. Wherever he might be. And before the dance was over, she'd lured him from his hiding place. He went to the girl. She saw him, stopped the dance, pretended to be alarmed. Albrecht reached out, touched her hand in a simple gesture more eloquent than a scream. *If he would look at me like that.* thought Jenny as she reacted with Giselle's response. *If he'd touch me with that much yearning.*

Dimitri's interpretation of the role of Albrecht was a new one, and typically daring. In the past Albrecht had always been portrayed as a callous aristocratic seducer, intent on nothing more than having a bit of *droit de seigneur* with Giselle, who is, after all, his subject.

Dimitri's Albrecht was another man altogether, genuinely in love with Giselle, trapped in an arranged marriage to the princess. Dimitri's reasoning was dramatically sound and simple: only if Albrecht's love for Giselle in Act I is real does his great remorse in Act II become credible. After Dimitri's insight into this role, no dancer would ever be able to use the traditional interpretation again without wondering. The audience believed the sincerity of his love from the beginning.

The ballet went on, and the lovers were caught up in their inevitable love, their inevitable doom. Albrecht led the hesitant Giselle to a little bench, reassuring her. She picked a daisy and played the ancient game: "He loves me . . . he loves me not." The petals spelled out "Not!" and Giselle became alarmed, half believing it the way a superstitious country girl might. Again Albrecht reassured her, for the moment believing his own romantic lie. *He acts so very well,* thought Jenny, looking timidly at Albrecht with Giselle's trustful eyes. *I wonder if he's to be trusted offstage, how I'd know if he was acting or if he wasn't.* Well. She might never have a chance to find that out. A new theme from the orchestra signaled Albrecht to lead Giselle into a dance, their first big pas de deux.

He took her hand, and they floated through the complicated choreography so simply and naturally they might have been doing it for the first time, inventing the steps as they went along. It was a pas de deux with the steps and gestures fixed in time as formally as any Catholic mass. But Dimitri Lubov and Jenny Hale turned it into a spontaneous expression of first love. They spun and leaped and floated through the dance, trailing music like stardust, caring for nothing on earth or in heaven but being together now, here, in this golden morning beyond time.

The audience sat dead silent. They'd seen it all before, they knew every move, every nuance, every beat of the score. But what happened onstage now was happening for the first time. A shock wave of discovery filled the huge auditorium. The audience saw that elusive moment when two beautiful doomed youngsters are actually falling in love. Such was the intensity of Dimitri Lubov's acting; such was the freshness of Jennifer Hale's response.

Jenny and Dimitri knew the famous choreography so well it was as natural to them as breathing, and between them they made it not just a complicated pattern of movements but a living relationship.

It would have been enough just to dance perfectly. These two gave it something much more. There was a tension between them that had a force far greater than anything built into the mime or the music or the dance steps of Giselle.

Even as he held her, Dimitri relaxed and allowed his practiced dancer's smile to become Dimitri's smile. "Beautiful!" he whispered through the smile as he turned her. All Jenny could do was smile back, but she felt it, too. They looked at each other, and the stage vibrated with longing. He touched her, and people in the fifth tier squirmed.

There was magic in the air that night, and it was contagious. The audience felt it, and the other dancers felt it, too. The corps danced better than they knew how; the village boys and girls came back from the harvest, and suddenly the stage was a festival. The prince and his entourage appeared, and the festival took on new momentum. Giselle danced another solo: brilliantly. Iris was spectacular in the peasant pas de deux.

The first act built to its climax, and the moment came when Albrecht's dilemma was revealed: he was not a commoner at all but the Duke of Silesia and betrothed to the princess. There was never a chance of his actually marrying Giselle. Giselle collapsed, fainting, was comforted, awoke . . . mad.

The role of Giselle is to ballerinas what Hamlet is to actors: the ultimate challenge. And Giselle's mad scene is unusually challenging for a ballerina because it is almost all acting, with very little dancing.

Jenny had rehearsed it for weeks in public and in private, read about it, agonized over it, acted it out, gesture by gesture in her dreams.

This was the one part of *Giselle* that she dreaded, and the reason was something she shared with no one but Privy: Jenny's own mother had been hopelessly insane for almost twenty years, plunged into a deep, permanent depression by the fact of Jenny's birth. Mrs. Hale had been kept hidden and unvisited at great expense in a fancy Connecticut asylum all these years. Jenny's deepest and most secret dread was for her own mental stability, with who-knew-what genetic time bomb lying in wait for her, ticking off the seconds until the time was ripe to explode. *Fiddlesticks*, she told herself, *it's just a bloody fairy tale*. It was much more than that to Jenny Hale.

Jenny's mad scene in *Giselle* would one day be in textbooks. But this night there was no time for analysis; the experience of watching her was too intense.

Giselle rose slowly from her faint, looked about, seeing nothing. She drifted toward Albrecht. Paused, reached out,

forgot why she wanted to touch him, smiled with gentle
madness, turned away.

She bent to pick an imaginary daisy and once again played
the fatal game, wandering brokenly about the stage, pulling
out petal after invisible petal, leaving a trail of dying dreams.
But her attention wandered. She dropped the imaginary
daisy, paused, discovered a sword lying on the ground. It was
the sword of the Duke of Silesia, Albrecht's sword. En-
tranced, she picked up the silvery blade with both slim hands,
the fatal point aiming at her breast, and slowly swung it
about in a mystical circle. Then she lifted her head, smiling
at some unheard message, and fell on the swordpoint!

The crowd gathered close around her. But it wasn't fatal—not yet. Giselle rose, staggered to her mother, pointed in
astonishment at Albrecht as though only now did she realize
that he had betrayed her. Albrecht, unable to bear the weight
of guilt that suddenly landed on his carefree shoulders, came
to her side and took her in his arms as she collapsed. He
knelt to cushion her fall. Giselle looked up at him, smiled
sadly, lifted one pale hand as if to touch his cheek. It might
be a gesture of forgiveness. It might be an accusation. But
the gesture was never completed. Giselle fell back, dead.

There was an involuntary gasp from the audience.

The curtain fell on silence. Then, from every corner of the
huge theater came a gathering roar, a roar not so much of
hands clapping but of an avalanche, of building thunder,
crashing surf. The noise built and built in great waves of
sound, and the sound seemed to batter at the thick gold curtain with force enough to shred it.

At last the curtain came up. Giselle and Albrecht and the
whole company stood there, drinking it in, basking in it,
hoarding this treasure of praise the way a miser hoards gold.
Here was the reward beyond money, the addictive drug, the
ultimate glory and final pleasure of their lives. The roar increased, defying all laws of acoustical physics. And while curtain calls are as rigidly programmed and rehearsed as any
other part of the ballet, the stage manager, whose finger is on
the button that raises and lowers the curtain, has in his head
a built-in applause meter. Stage managers are conditioned to
expect the unusual, for it almost always happens. So, while the
curtain calls had been programmed for a standard-enthusiastic
response—five calls, the last two for the principals—this was
an exception.

Up and down went the great curtain. And still the roar increased, building still. "Bravo, brava!" They were shouting their praise now. Giselle and Albrecht stood alone. He took her hand, looked into her eyes, bowed on one knee and kissed her hand. The audience were on their feet, cheering. Jenny and Dimitri bowed, tried to leave, were called back. It might have gone on for half an hour except that Jenny had to rush backstage and change for the second act. So the curtain finally came down and stayed down.

For a moment the two of them just stood there in the shadows. Then Dimitri squeezed her hand—she had forgotten he was still holding it. He said just two words: "Thank you." Then he kissed her.

Jenny Hale walked quickly back to her dressing room, but her way was blocked by clouds of praise, by thickets of compliments. She smiled, still dazed, not really thinking about it. *The praise isn't what matters; praise is cheap, dancing matters. And the real dancing in* Giselle *doesn't happen until Act Two, so cool it, Jennifer Hale.*

It wasn't until the curtain had fallen for the last time on a gravely smiling Dimitri and a more than slightly dazed Jenny Hale that Miss Privet realized the empty seat on her left was still empty. It was to have been Clifford Hale's seat. *Trust Clifford Hale,* thought Privy, her hands smarting from applause; *he never fails to disappoint.* Drunk and witty, no doubt, in some expensive bar. Smiling his charming smile to some superannuated debutante who still remembered the Clifford Hale Style, one of the catchphrases of architectural criticism of the 1950s.

Jessica Privet knew the Clifford Hale Style all too well, publicly and privately. The spectacular buildings she found cold and flashy. And the man's talent for self-destruction was nothing short of genius.

For eighteen years now, Jessica Privet had been picking up the pieces of Cliff Hale's shattered life. The man himself had long since lost his considerable ability to charm her, to persuade her, to make her believe his empty promises even as he always believed them himself in the instant he spoke them.

The promises of Clifford Hale had the beauty and endurance of smoke. They hung on the air in all their undeniable splendor and then vanished while you watched, leaving no more than a memory. Only for Jenny did Jessica Privet endure in the ruins that now surrounded Clifford Hale.

It was somehow fitting, Privy felt, that the famous Clifford Hale Style had always been a style of facades. At the top of his form he could conjure up acres of stone lacework with the wave of a hand, applying plastic surgery to the bulk and the bones of a building before the first spadeful of dirt had been turned over for its construction. Cliff Hale was obsessed with surfaces. He wanted them to glitter and deceive, to screen what was behind them, to give something squat the illusion of grace, to graft on distinction over clichés. It was in its essence a theatrical talent more than a structural one. The Clifford Hale Style aged badly, like the man himself. There was always something shallow about the Style; it had the air of false fronts, like some back-lot street owned by a bankrupt movie company, a little seedy now, inhabited by second-rate ghosts.

Miss Privet gathered her sealskin coat about her and rose to go eavesdropping in the lobby. She wanted to hear all she could that might be said about her girl.

The First Murder

Switzerland, 1974

It was raining, as usual, in Geneva. Maybe that was why so few people showed up for the poetry reading. Gregor Berisov accepted this disappointment philosophically, as he had accepted many things, both good and bad, in his long life.

There were perhaps thirty-five people in the big shabby room. A mixed lot. The usual clot of wild-haired students, all bones and solemnity, sat in front dressed in the rags and tags of five armies. *How little*, thought the poet, *do they know about armies, about fighting, about life or death.* Behind the students were the serious culture-seeking ladies, plump as partridges as if in some genetic attempt to insulate themselves from these raw Swiss winters. Then there were some older people with the look of real scholars. Berisov especially no-

ticed one tall, elegant, gray-haired gentleman in a worn gray
tweed overcoat that had seen better days. The man sat
meekly at the back, following the poet's every word.

The Swiss, thought Gregor Berisov with malice, *have
sucked the dullness out of every country around them and
turned it into an art form.* Was it for this that he'd risked everything to defect? Then Berisov's un-Russian sense of humor
got the best of him, and he grinned at his own melancholy.
Well he knew why he had left behind his friends and family
and very possibly his soul. Berisov had fled Russia because
for him the only alternatives were madness or death or both.
And although he had suffered much, Gregor Berisov had not
been ready to suffer that. His fame, within Russia and without, was based on two epic poems. The first, *Winter, 1943,*
was a tribute to the spirit of the Russian people in their gallant struggle against Hitler. It became, de facto, the great patriotic epic of the war. Then, much later, came *Questions in
the Night.* That was another matter entirely, bitter, knowing,
subversive in intention and effect, an instant scandal and an
equally instant underground success. Berisov, in absentia, had
won the Nobel Prize for *Questions.* Which only made matters
worse. To make a very long—twelve years long—story short,
Gregor Berisov became the first major Soviet artist to defect
to the West. This had been in the winter of 1964.

Ever since, Berisov had made his home in Switzerland,
barely making ends meet by his poetry and his lectures.

He read three new sonnets and a fragment of the epic-in-
progress and was met with the usual polite applause. There
were a few questions, mostly banal, and then the lecture was
over. It left Berisov with an empty feeling, even though, by
this time, he knew what to expect. The gray-haired man got
up, hesitantly, and with a slight limp approached the burly
poet. The man in gray held a first edition of the Paris printing of *Questions in the Night.*

"I wonder, Gregor Gregorovich Berisov," said the stranger
in flawless Russian, "if I might impose on you to sign this
book." The gray-haired man smiled, a tentative, professorial
smile. Berisov took the book.

"But of course. Your name?"

"Reynard. François Reynard."

Berisov wrote: "To François Reynard with my best wishes.
Gregor Gregorovich Berisov. November 1974."

"Your work has meant . . . very much to me, Mr. Berisov."

"Thank you."

"I wondered, if it might not be too presumptuous, if you
might be free to take a little supper with me."

"Thank you. I'd like that." The stranger looked kind. And
the price of a meal saved was the price of a meal earned.

Berisov got his coat, and the two men walked out into the
dark and wet Geneva night. Gregor Berisov's body was found
floating in Lake Geneva three weeks later, near the town of
Versoix. The body was badly disintegrated, but the coroner
found no signs of foul play. It was ruled "Death by misad-
venture" and presumed to be suicide. No one remembered
the man in gray, and it was impossible to fix the time of
death with any real precision. The tragedy was duly noted
and quickly forgotten.

———————◆———————

CHAPTER
❧❦ 2 ❧❦

Dimitri threw a clean towel on the floor of his dressing room
and lay on his back with his feet high overhead, resting
against the wall. He closed his eyes and kept perfectly still. In
this yoga trance he could condense an hour's rest into five
minutes. Felice had taught him that. He smiled, breaking the
trance.

Felice de la Tour-Fontaine had found a Russian bumpkin
had taught him many things, things that forty-year-old, old-
rich French countesses are probably born knowing but that
little boys growing up in tumbledown huts on the Volga do
not suspect. Dimitri had seen Paris and indeed most of Europe through Felice's perceptive eyes. Felice had taught him
about clothes, that food was not merely to eat, that making
love could transcend biological necessity into art. And in the
end Felice had used him up and grown bored and demanding. Having tamed her barbarian a little, she was no longer so
enraptured, and having smoothed away some of Dimitri's
rough edges, she began to display a few rough edges of her
own. It had never been meant to last, and they parted with
only the most superficial regrets, for each had given and each
had taken and the slate was clean between them.

"Five minutes to curtain, please . . . five minutes." The
loudspeaker gave its familiar warning. Dimitri stretched his
legs, then his arms, tucked up his knees and did a perfect
gymnast's backward flip, landing on his toes.

A bunch of deep-purple violets had appeared on his
dressing table sometime during the first act. He looked at the
card. Judith Winchester had taken the trouble to discover his
favorite flower. Judith Winchester was expecting him for supper after the performance. And in some way he couldn't
quite crystallize, Judith Winchester frightened Dimitri. He

was flattered at the attention from one of the most powerful
women in America—in the world. He was well aware that
Judith Winchester was the heavy patroness behind the International Ballet Theater, the only rival to the New York Civic.
Dimitri smelled an offer coming. Well, let it come. And come
big.

In the meantime, there was Act II to consider, and how it
would compare to the impression he and Jenny had already
made in Act I. Dimitri looked closely at his reflection in the
mirror, frowned, and added a touch more shading around his
eyes. Albrecht was to be grief-stricken, distraught. Albrecht
should look as though he hadn't slept or eaten for days.
There. That was better. Dimitri practiced looking distraught.
Then he made a very naughty Russian schoolboy's gesture at
the Albrecht in the mirror and walked, laughing, into the corridor.

Her name was Mavis St. John, and she was not altogether
without brains and charm. Yet to Alexander de Lis, Mrs. St
John was no more and no less than the Sunset Motel fortune
on the hoof, seventy-odd millions of dollars, some of which
might possibly be diverted into the perpetually empty coffers
of the Civic Ballet Company. So Alex himself was taking
Madame St. John on a personal backstage tour of the theater
during intermission. This tour had started with a glass of
champagne in the costume department, good champagne, not
the domestic nonsense purveyed at the public bar. Mrs. S.
John had met Princess Alexa Descharovna, for in de Lis' experience ladies with recently acquired fortunes are often
impressed by ancient titles.

The princess, eighty-four years old and de Lis' own tame
dragon, was charming and slightly demented-looking as she
played with costume sketches and a thousand swatches of
fabric.

"This lace," said the princess, holding up an old ivory-
colored fragment, "is given to my dear mama by the Czarina—
may-she-reign-in-heaven. Venice. Seventeenth century. Does
not exist. We try to have this copied for the new *Sleeping
Beauty*, but they are fools." The princess peered through her
spectacles at Mrs. St. John as if to imply that Mrs. St. John
might be the agent of the fools.

Mrs. St. John smiled timidly. "It's lovely."

"All fools." The princess turned to rummage in a large

cardboard box laden with rainbows of silk. Alex de Lis gently took his guest's arm and led her away.

Why the new *Sleeping Beauty* required real lace, seventeenth century or not, especially when the Civic was reeling with debt, was a question no cost accountant would ever understand. That, as de Lis often reminded his board of directors, was why cost accountants were cost accountants and not genius choreographers.

Like an Indian scout in the deep forest, de Lis guided his guest through the backstage wilderness to stage right, where he knew Dimitri Lubov would be preparing his entrance. With his slender hand still on Mrs. St. John's elbow, de Lis actually felt the quiver that went through her when she spotted Dimitri. "Come," said de Lis in a voice that implied the possibility of many such encounters in store for friends of the Civic, "you must meet Dimitri."

Dimitri, lost in Albrecht's grief, blinked, smiled, bowed. This parading of sacred cows was standard, he knew, in all the poor, unsubsidized ballet and opera companies of America. And even in Russia it happened, if the truth were to be told, only there the fatted calves were pompous bureaucrats and their wives or mistresses, fully as capable of giving or withholding favors as any capitalistic heiress.

"I hope," said Dimitri with a formal bow that sent shivers down the well-upholstered torso of Mrs. Sunset Motel, "that you enjoy the performance."

"It's just thrilling, Mr. Lubov."

"Please. Dimitri. It is a pleasure to dance for you." The familiar burst of applause came from the audience as the conductor took his place. Alex de Lis and his guest whispered their good-byes and disappeared into the darkness. And with the instinctive radar of a successful pawnbroker scanning a tray of dubious emeralds, de Lis could tell from the gleam in her eye that Mrs. St. John was well on her way to becoming a patron of the Civic Ballet. Silently he prayed that every bed in every Sunset Motel would be filled this night and every night thereafter.

Jenny Hale looked critically at Giselle's ghost in her dressing-room mirror.

Dressed all in the purest white, her naturally pale little face powdered even whiter, her eyes made immense and tragic with a glaze of pale-violet eye shadow, hair coiled tightly into a bun, her classic nineteenth-century midcalf ballerina's skirt of white tulle foaming out from her tiny waist like the cold breath of mourners in winter, Giselle was perfectly dressed for her initiation as the newest Wili in the club.

For the revenge of the Wilis is the form and substance of Act II, and in less than five minutes Giselle would rise from her lonely grave to join them.

Only a German, thought Jenny as she made one last pass with her powder puff, *could have invented the Wilis.* The Wilis, emerging from some specially murky corner of the Teutonic myth machine, are those deadliest of creatures, women scorned. They're all girls who have been betrayed and unrequited. Jenny wasn't sure down which garden paths the Wilis had been led, or by whom, and in any case those girls are ice-cold and ready for a very special revenge. The way they achieve this is to trap young men and force them to dance until they drop dead, in a true danse macabre.

Hilarion would be the first to get it, poor jerk. Then they'd try for Albrecht.

But Giselle, her love reaching out even from beyond the grave, would not allow that to happen. *At least,* thought Jenny, frowning, *not if she makes it through that first big pas de deux.* For a moment Jenny stood still, looking at the girl in the mirror. Then she kissed her own fingertips and touched them to the pale shoulder of Giselle's ghost in the mirror. *"Merde, Giselle!"* she whispered as the apparition in the mirror silently mouthed the lucky word.

Onstage it was night in the forest. The palest blue moonlight sifted down through the trees, turning everything bright as silver, hard as steel.

Giselle's lonely grave was marked by a rough wooden cross at stage right.

Jenny stood in the wings, quietly, exercising lightly, touched by the blue light. Hilarion walked on, deep in mourning. He stood transfixed. Suddenly, in a flash of white, a ghostly shape came flitting smoothly across the stage: a white-veiled woman en pointe, her toes scarcely seeming to touch the stage. Hilarion sensed something wrong, looked up, saw nothing. Flash!

The apparition darted back across the stage once more, unreal, menacing. And without even trying to force herself, Jenny was caught up in the mystery and magic.

The veiled lady was Myrtha, Queen of the Wilis. She went

into a cold, brilliant solo, radiating arrogance, cruelty, revenge. Myrtha paused, waved her hand, and suddenly the stage was filled with Wilis, dozens of them, all dressed alike, all in white, all ghosts. They moved effortlessly, with the coolness of drifting ice, with the grace of angels, yet despite the beauty of their dancing, there was something terrifying about them.

Hilarion, trapped like one of his own rabbits, was forced to dance between two unyielding formations of Wilis. Jenny watched Hilarion's dance, fascinated. The boy dancing Hilarion was David Devereaux, and Jenny hardly knew him at all. *He dances well,* she thought, *but not well enough.* Like so much of *Giselle,* this was an acting dance, not merely a run through a prescribed routine. Hilarion had to convey the desperation, the injustice, the misplaced gallantry of his situation. It wasn't a big role, but in the right hands it could have been a showpiece. In the hands of David Devereaux it was only adequate. *He's doing the best he can,* she thought, and it was true. Every step was well placed, all his movements were graceful, yet there was no excitement in it. He danced, collapsed, danced again, died.

Jenny tensed. Now it was Albrecht's turn—and hers. She walked onstage veiled like a bride, a shimmer of white silk gauze masking her head. Myrtha lifted the veil and touched Giselle with cold affection, welcoming. Giselle danced. *I'm showing them I have what it takes to be a Wili. I can be as cold and perfect and mechanical as anyone. Maybe more so.*

Jenny Hale launched herself into the great solo, and where in the first act she had been all innocence and trembling with joy, the girl now showed her audience a startlingly different Giselle, swift as death itself and just as cold, moving in moonlight like a knife through water, trapped in the bloodless waste—land between life and the strange eternal nonlife of the Wilis. Jenny whirled, balanced en pointe, traced arabesques so graceful they burned themselves into the minds of her audience and stayed there long after Giselle herself had spun on to other, even more remarkable feats. The theater was so quiet it seemed no one dared to breathe. Finally, the dance ended. Giselle stood near the Queen of the Wilis, waiting for her approval. The approval of all the audience was signaled by a great roar of applause.

Then the music struck a new chord, and Albrecht entered to meet his fate. Grief had changed Albrecht every bit as

much as death had changed Giselle. Gone was the dashing
courtier of the first act. This Albrecht considered himself a
murderer. He was filled with a guilt and remorse so heavy it
weighed on him visibly, affecting the very way he walked, the
angle of his head. Slowly he walked across the stage to lay a
sheaf of white lilies on the grave. Suddenly, in the treetops,
there was a flash of white. He looked up, startled: Giselle!
But no, he told himself. He must be imagining things.

Giselle came onstage while Albrecht knelt at her graveside,
deep in mourning. She stood behind him for a moment, then
reached out and touched his shoulder. This was a gesture of
longing and regret, of joy that he'd come and sorrow that it
was too late, of fear that the Wilis would get him and hope
that they wouldn't. All these emotions could be read into one
simple extension of Jenny Hale's arm. In the audience the
silence was deep as midnight.

Albrecht turned, rose, astonished. Was this happening, or
was it a cruel dream? They floated into each other's arms on
the wings of longing, moving through the blue bewitched
moonlight with a grace that seemed not to be born of music
but rather to trail music behind it.

Dimitri and Jenny Hale were creating the music with their
bodies as they moved. Their pas de deux was all that their
love might have been: lyrical and perfect and doomed. For
just as it ended, the Wilis appeared, moonlight guerrillas, pale
angels of vengeance. Albrecht was trapped, and it was Giselle
who had trapped him.

Giselle pleaded with an implacable Myrtha: let him live!
But no, the Queen was adamant. He must die. The lovers
took refuge behind the cross marking Giselle's grave. But
then Myrtha commanded the girl to dance, a command
Giselle had no power to resist.

I'm doing this for him. For once Jenny's private thoughts
and Giselle's scripted ones matched perfectly. She began her
dance solo brilliantly. The dance was so beautiful that Albrecht couldn't resist leaving his sanctuary to join in. They
danced from Wili to Wili, all down the line, pleading—in
mime—with each Wili in turn. But the Wilis are beyond all
feeling, drugged on revenge.

Now Albrecht danced alone, pleading his case before the
Queen. He approached her wildly, half-pleadingly, half-defi-
antly; executing a series of brisés volés with his feet beating
so quickly before him they looked like hummingbird's wings.

It became not a series of dance steps but a glorious blur of movement in which Lubov scarcely seemed to touch the ground at all.

Myrtha was not impressed. Still, Dimitri showed the full fire of his dancing, the astonishing rogue-stag leaps with that rare quality of ballon that made him seem literally to hang in the air at the highest arc of his jump, spread-eagled and with the angry grace of a young eagle, a spirit beyond the reach of gravity, born of the air itself.

The dance went on, with Albrecht growing ever wilder, more defiant and the Queen remaining unmoved. Finally, exhausted, he fell, struggled to rise and fell again. At last he did manage to struggle up, danced, fell again. To distract the Queen, Giselle began a new dance. And Albrecht gathered all his strength to join her.

In this, their final pas de deux, it was Giselle's love for Albrecht that sustained them both. Slowly, as they danced, the light changed from the blue of midnight to the first warm rays of dawn. A distant clock chimed four. It was dawn, and the Wilis must go. Giselle and Albrecht had won. And Giselle, having defied the Wilis, had won eternal peace. They rejected the dead girl and bade her return to her grave. It was an invitation she was more than willing to accept.

Every great dancer plays his own variations of a role, and Dimitri had worked long and hard at his version of the curtain scene at the end of *Giselle*. He knelt at the grave, paused, scooped up the white lilies and buried his face in them. Then, slowly, as the final melodramatic bars of the music came crashing down to a finish, he stood up and backed away from the cross, moving diagonally across the stage and strewing the stage with the flowers. Finally, unable to control himself, he knelt once again, trembling, and buried his face in his hands as the curtain fell.

This time there was no moment of silence. The applause came quickly and loud and went on longer than anyone in the house could remember. There were eighteen curtain calls in all, the last six for Jenny Hale and Dimitri, together and alone.

The crowd rose to its feet, but not to leave. An usher appeared with a big bouquet for Jenny, and other, smaller bouquets came flying out of the darkness in the ancient, if illegal, tradition. Jenny picked one rose from her bouquet and handed it to Dimitri, who bowed, smiling. The audience roared again. There was no movement to the exits; the audience had assisted in giving birth to a legend this night, and no one wanted to be first to break the spell that touched the whole theater with a special grace. A chapter had begun in the history of dance tonight, and everyone out front and backstage could sense it.

Jessica Privet, who loved dance only because Jenny made it real to her, could feel the electricity crackling in the air around her.

Simon Bridge, who had seen more ballet in more parts of the world than any man living, could feel it, too. He folded his green leather notebook. The page marked for this performance was as it had been two hours ago: empty. He knew the performance would live in his memory, and maybe forever. For tonight the most powerful dance critic in the world, creator and destroyer of reputations, arbiter of taste, Bridge of the *Times*, had been reduced to that lowest of common denominators: Simon Bridge became a fan again.

Alexander de Lis felt the rush of expectation fulfilled from his silver-white hair to his Gucci-encased toes. He smiled the smile of a gambler who knows he's onto a sure thing. In a life filled with triumphs there had been two, perhaps three others on this scale.

And it was, surely, his triumph as much as the girl's. Had he not spotted Jenny Hale as the merest tadpole in the Children's School? Had he not led her by the hand up and up through all the years of training, of school productions, class after class? Had he not given her a scholarship three years ago, when that dissolute father could no longer pay the bills? And, only last spring, had he not made one of his famous instinctive plunges and promoted this shy, timid, dedicated little Jenny right out of the school and into featured roles in the regular company, right over the heads of the entire corps de ballet? He, Alex de Lis, had created Jenny Hale as much—more so!—as if he had been her own father. He had invented the Jennifer Hale the world saw tonight, whereas Clifford Hale had merely fathered her. It was an act of creativity versus an incident of biology, and for Alexander de Lis there was no comparison. Jenny Hale was his creature; her glory was his, and her future. He stood backstage, kissed her as she came off and smiled. *We must*, thought de Lis as she thanked him, *not let it go too much to her head.*

Dimitri Lubov hardly ever walked. He darted, skipped, jumped, spun and sometimes simply flew through the air propelled by his own raw animal energy. This was disconcerting to earthbound mortals, but for Dimitri, flying came naturally as breathing, and he never thought twice about it.

When the curtain came down for the last time, he was past the crowd of well-wishers and into his dressing room and into a hot shower before the sweat got a chance to dry and chill him. Even in the tiny shower he moved, stretched, sang in the shrapnel of six languages, soaped himself lavishly with Roger & Gallet (another habit learned from Felice) and in general kept up the high spirits that had been building all during the performance and that would keep right on building until sometime in the first hours of the new day. Only because his agent had suggested it was Dimitri accepting the formal invitation of Judith Winchester. What he had intended to do was go to de Lis' party and take Jenny out dancing afterward. And after that? He grinned his imp's grin, the grin of a boy who often hoped and was often rewarded. Tonight it might not be possible. Well enough; there would be other nights. Jenny Hale would not forget him, any more than he would forget her. The magic had happened, right on schedule, and it would build, he felt it. What, precisely, it might build to, no one could say. But Dimitri Lubov felt the promise of it, and what Dimitri felt, Dimitri made happen.

Jenny had always been quick in her movements, and she worked quickly now, transforming the ghost of Giselle back into Miss Jennifer Hale. It was good to have something specific to do. It was good not to have to think too much.

The shoes came off first, slender finely made pink satin instruments of torture. She rubbed her throbbing toes. The shoes would have to be worn again, not for a performance but in rehearsal. They were always being badgered for using up too many pairs of shoes. Jenny averaged ten pairs a week, and so did everybody else. The rumor was that Civic Ballet was in hock to Capezio's for a quarter million dollars. If that were true, for so much money they ought to be able to make more comfortable shoes. No one out front could imagine the sheer pain of it.

The Spanish Inquisition never in its darkest hour invented a torture so exquisitely painful as what happens to a girl balancing her full weight on the pointed toes of one foot. Jenny rubbed her toes. At least they weren't bleeding. Then she stood and slipped out of the full-skirted white dress. The left strap was beginning to fray.

Jenny wondered how many other Giselles had worn the dress and how much longer the magical fingers of old Princess Descharovna would keep it intact. From out front the dress looked fresh as morning mist, but close up you could see the fine patching and basting that held it together. Nothing, but nothing, was ever wasted in the costume department of the Civic Ballet. The costumes were well made, sewn on a couture level, and Descharovna expected them to last. Last they did, sometimes too long. The princess saw to that, mother hen—"Mother Vulture" Iris called her—and to do the old hag justice, she did save the Civic thousands of dollars every year.

Jenny stripped with an athlete's absolute lack of consciousness of her naked body and put on the old blue robe only to keep from getting a chill. Then she sat at her tiny dressing table and dipped a Kleenex into the huge jar of cheap cold cream and began erasing the ghost's white makeup. The face underneath was white, too, but with a saving blush of pink. Alex de Lis was definitely anti-suntan, and tans were avoided, not that there was time to acquire one in any case. She had early got the habit of looking at her mirrored reflection with critical detachment. Dancers move in a world of mirrors; they rehearse before mirrored walls, and for every good dancer there comes a moment when the reflection is more real than what it reflects. Slowly the ghost of Giselle faded into Jenny Hale. Jenny Hale's huge gray eyes looked gravely out of the mirror as if to say, "Who are you? By what right are you in my dressing room?" Jenny sat for a moment and stared back at the rude reflection. "I earned it, damn it!" Then she got up and took a shower.

Her one extravagance was the hair dryer, the fancy twenty-nine-dollar-ninety-five-cent model, and to get it she'd eaten yogurt for lunch for a month. But without a dryer her waist-long chestnut hair took forever to dry, and if you went around New York with wet hair, you got colds, vitamin C or no vitamin C.

Tonight, for the de Lis party, she'd wear the hair long. Jenny put on the newest of the four dresses she owned, a long-skirted, high-necked nineteenth-century farm-girl-looking creation in periwinkle blue cotton splashed all over with

small bunches of white flowers. Privy had found it somewhere on sale. The blue dress pleased Jenny. She liked its
simplicity and the fact that it hid her feet. Like most dancers,
Jenny Hale felt that her feet were very ugly, tools of the
trade to be hidden when not in use. She slipped an old
twisted rope of gold over her head; it had been her mother's.
She touched the rope. It gleamed dully against the blue of her
dress, but the important thing about it was the sense of contact it gave Jenny Hale with the mother she had never
known. Jenny stood and made a comic-horrible face at herself in the mirror. "*Merde,* indeed!" Privy would be coming
soon; Jenny had insisted, over her protests, that her best
friend come to the de Lis party. That was as it should be. She
refused to think about Dimitri, but he popped into her mind
uninvited. *Face it, dummy,* Jenny thought grimly, *he'll be famous now, more famous than he was already. Even if he
ever did think of you, he'll have plenty of other things to
think about now.*

Jenny had known Dimitri Lubov just three weeks, and in
those weeks they'd spent part of nearly every day together,
but always in a crowd, in class, or rehearsing and re-rehears-
ing *Giselle.* Dimitri was polite, charming, a generous partner, patient with Jenny and a miracle to dance with. Period.
Jenny had none of the wiles or charms that came from long
practice in flirting. She'd never had time to flirt, or the inclination. Iris Dowling could arouse the stone lions in front
of the Public Library just by looking at them a certain way,
but not Jenny Hale. And well she knew, Dimitri had plenty
of other fish in his net.

The gossip columns were filled with reports and speculations about Dimitri's love affairs. Jenny didn't read gossip
columns or any other parts of the newspapers; she hadn't the
time or the money or the interest. But others did, and she had
heard about the French countess who had "befriended" Dimitri after his defection. She knew about the actress who
threatened suicide, the soft-drink heiress who offered Dimitri
his own theater, about his unlisted phone and secret address
that de Lis had imposed on the young Russian to foil the
mobs of young ballet groupies who followed him everywhere,
risking death by stampede just to get a touch of him. It was
all too rich for Jenny Hale. Yet Dimitri showed up every day
for rehearsals, clear-eyed and full of energy and even a little
bit shy. Maybe it was the language problem. Ballet, thank

God, is conducted everywhere in French; this was lucky for Dimitri, whose English was still unsure of itself. *The only part of him*, thought Jenny with a grin, *that is*.

Yes, Dimitri would be famous after this night. He could go Hollywood if he wanted to. She remembered the resentment that had swept through the Civic Ballet when they learned he was coming, trailing glory all the way from Leningrad. It was typical of Jenny Hale that it never occurred to her how the performance that certified the star quality of Dimitri Lubov might make her famous, too.

There was a knock on the door. Privy had come to escort Jenny to the party. The older woman hugged Jenny and gave her a big kiss. "It was lovely, my dear, just lovely." Privy was not a small woman. Both physically and emotionally, she seemed to fill the tiny dressing room. She glanced about disapprovingly. "Obviously," said Privy in tones of high disdain, "there has been some sort of misunderstanding." She sniffed, as if there might be something long-dead concealed on the premises. "These quarters were designed for the star . . . of a circus midget act."

"But, Privy, I love it. It's a palace compared to what I used to share with—"

"That hussy Iris? You're well out of it then."

"Privy, *please*. She might be anywhere."

"Well, then." Miss Privet sat gingerly down on the one small dressing-room chair and cast a piercing look at Jenny through the gold-rimmed bifocal glasses. "You were remarkable, my love. Quite remarkable. Even Privy felt it." Privy, like Queen Victoria before her, had long grown accustomed to referring to herself in the third person. "That Communist isn't all bad either."

"Darling, you know he's not a Communist. He *fled* the Communists. Dimitri's an artist. Art has no politics."

"I do hope that to be the case." Dimitri's blond hair was still a little damp from the shower. He poked his head into the little room and grinned like an eight-year-old. "Excuse me." Then he stepped in, still grinning, bowed deeply at Privy and presented Jenny with Judith Winchester's expensive violets. "For Giselle," he said, kissing the hand she put out to take them.

"Dimitri, they're lovely. I'll wear them to the party. Thank you." There was always a small dish of pins and needles on Jenny's dressing table. She pinned the flowers to the front of her blue dress and remembered her manners. "Miss Privet, this is Dimitri Lubov. Dimitri, my friend Miss Jessica Privet."

"I am very pleased." Dimitri bowed again and kissed her hand, a movement so quick and so graceful he might have been any fairy-tale prince paying court to a queen. It may have been the heat in the tiny room, but Jenny was sure she caught Privy blushing.

"You danced beautifully, Dimitri."

"Is not I. Is *we*." Dimitri made a small enclosing gesture that bound Jenny Hale to him as if with chains.

"Are you coming to de Lis' party?" Jenny tried to make it sound casual.

"I have first an . . . appointment?" He searched for the word, and Jenny wondered with whom. "Perhaps I come later." He bowed again and left them.

"I take it back," said Privy. "He's a nice boy after all."

"All the girls are crazy about him, and all the boys hate him."

"I'm sure." Jessica Privet looked at the girl she had reared from infancy and stopped the question that was ready on her tongue: And you, Jenny, how do you feel? Instead, she rose and said, "Perhaps we should be going."

Alexander de Lis confined his improvisations to the ballet stage; everything else he did had a reason, usually more than one reason. Tonight's party was no exception. He'd smelled a triumph, and the party would be a setting where the whole inner circle of ballet could share the triumph with him. It would boost the morale of the company; to be invited by de Lis was a great honor. It would flatter the critics and encourage the patrons. Mrs. St. John would not be the only ripe prospect in the mix.

He stood in his empty apartment and waited for the first ring of the bell. The party, like the ballet, would be a success. His parties always were. De Lis smiled and thought of Jenny. Another de Lis phenomenon! Another, in a long and famous line. That was a thing to contemplate. The doorbell rang. He was on. As always.

The Second Murder

California, 1974

Peter Chablesky loved strawberries. He loved them in all their many varieties and degrees of sweetness, loved them fresh in the meadows of his boyhood home outside Minsk, loved them in ice cream and sauces and syrups and jams. Strawberries and thermonuclear physics had long been an obsession with Peter Chablesky, and he made no attempt to conceal either fact.

Now, in the opalescent California twilight, with the ghost of the sun hovering wistfully above the endless Pacific, Peter Chablesky sat on his small but beautifully situated terrace in Santa Barbara and thought that he was a remarkably lucky man. To have all this! His good fortune was all the more magical for him because, well he knew, it was a gift as accidental as the color of eyes or the curve of a jaw.

His talent for pure physics had come out of nowhere, early, and taken root. And it had been encouraged; one must never deny that. If Russia did anything well it was to cultivate—not to say, force—such talent. So little Peter Chablesky became a privileged character at age nine, a minor phenomenon at eleven, an acknowledged wizard at eighteen.

Numbers spoke to Peter Chablesky, and something within him answered back until a kind of formal dialogue took place in which questions were asked and answered, theories proposed and expanded and proved, secrets revealed. He could not explain how this happened any more than he could explain the wind or the beauty of flowers. Or the taste of strawberries. It happened, and regularly, and Peter was grateful for the gift.

Only when he began to think of defecting did the gift present problems for him. By then Peter was thirty and known everywhere. His luck continued; no one suspected that the youngest full professor at Moscow University harbored unwholesome thoughts on the subject of democracy versus communism and the freedom of individuals. And with his academic status came certain suspiciously capitalistic privileges. One was his little car. Another was the ability to take interesting holidays, holidays not permitted to, for example, factory workers.

So it was that one fine hot September found Peter Chablesky basking like a seal on the beach at Dubrovnik. He'd given a week of lectures at the university in Belgrade, and this was his reward: another week at the seaside home of a widely respected and, fortunately, senile professor of advanced physics. The old professor kept a little fishing dinghy with a very small outboard motor. Peter stole it one moonlit night and made his way to Venice, where he turned himself in to the American consul.

That was the beginning of his good luck.

The scandal was immense. There were protests, threats, rattling of arms, shaking of fists. But Peter Chablesky was safe in a well-hidden mountain cabin in Kentucky two days after he landed in Venice, undergoing a friendly but intensive debriefing by the CIA.

Chablesky was too famous, too talented to hide. A job was found for him in the Randall Institute in Santa Barbara, and a house, all within a few weeks. He became a kind of test case: would the Russians dare try to hurt him in any way or perhaps kidnap him? They dared not.

Peter Chablesky defected in the fall of 1969. He had done valuable work for the institute and been well paid for it. And best of all, his strawberries had thrived in the perfect California weather. Peter had seven varieties growing in and around his terrace, and plans for more.

And just today a beautiful package had arrived by express truck: a huge, expensive terra-cotta strawberry jar well planted with a variety Peter did not have, real French *fraises des bois!* And with it a card from the students and faculty of the University of California at Berkeley, where he'd just finished a week-long graduate seminar. How kind these Americans were. And, more than kind, they were really very thoughtful. Peter Chablesky smiled, and walked over to the strawberry jar, where it stood in the fading light at the edge of the terrace. Perfect! Each small, well-shaped plant had both tiny white flowers and small, elongated berries at the same time. It would be twice an ornament, something to see,

something to eat. Feeling just slightly naughty, he bent and
picked one perfect *fraise*.

For a moment he simply looked at the berry, gently
squeezing its firm but yielding flesh between two fingers. Chablesky sniffed its fragrance with the reverence that might
more properly belong to a fine vintage wine. Then he popped
the little sweet into his mouth.

He sat down to relax in the white wrought-iron chaise
longue that looked out over the ocean. The taste of the berry
filled his mouth, and it was all he expected: both sweet and a
little tart at the same time. He crushed it on his tongue, prolonging the moment, watching the final coral-colored light
wash out of the darkening sky.

Peter Chablesky felt perfectly relaxed. Did his leg seem a
bit numb, or was he just tired? He tried to get up. It was an
enormous effort, like swimming in cement. Chablesky decided
not to make that effort. His head sank back on the pad of the
chaise longue, and he slowly closed his eyes.

That was how the cleaning lady found him the next morning.

The Santa Barbara coroner had seen plenty of heart attacks. This one had been sudden and massive. Pity, not only
was the guy just pushing forty, but he'd apparently been a
big-deal physicist.

On Peter Chablesky's terrace, the strawberries slowly
withered in the persistent sunshine of his adopted country.
Soon there was no trace of them at all but for a few withered
stems and mummified fruits. In the bushes, unseen, a small
brown swallow lay dead. It, too, had a fondness for strawberries.

———◆———

Dimitri Lubov looked at his hostess and thought: *The
Queen of the Wilis is after me yet!* Then he smiled a small
boy's smile. Maybe she wasn't the Queen of the Wilis, nothing so grand. Judith Winchester was more like something that
swam in dark waters, some clever, instinctive man-eating fish,
bright and quick, more barracuda than shark. There was a
tight thin slash where her mouth should be; it was a face
designed as a cutting tool. Without knowing why, he shuddered. There was no doubt Judith was after him. She had
made this absolutely clear from the first.

Judith Winchester was fifty-nine, but she might have been any age from forty to eighty. Her face was tight, unwrinkled, the mask of either hysteria or plastic surgery, depending on which of her enemies you listened to. She had no shortage of enemies. Judith's was a face you didn't forget and didn't want to remember. Her hair was dyed a convincing shade of dark brown, and her small bright eyes gleamed with a curious amber light as though illuminated by fires inside. It was a predator's face, the face of a very powerful woman. She gave Dimitri the creeps.

Born rich, Judith had little use for money or the trappings of wealth except insofar as her wealth could be used to gain power, to manipulate people and events. This was her one drive, her one source of pleasure: to be the biggest spider in the web, to pull the strings, to make things happen exactly how and when she wanted them to happen. Judith got this drive, as she had inherited many other things, from her father.

Judith was Luke Calvert's only child and he never bothered to hide his disgust at the fact that she hadn't been born male. Luke had started his career in the lumber camps of Oregon, a loud, brawling giant who was feared at nineteen and bossing twelve camps before he was twenty-five. But the camps couldn't hold Luke Calvert. Soon he was in Portland, charming his way into the bank loan that let him buy his first small lumber outfit. Shrewdness and guts and sometimes simply the persuasive crack of Luke's fist against a recalcitrant jaw soon turned one lumber company into three, a dozen, the best and the biggest in Oregon and then beyond, and most of the profits going back into timberland and more land and more after that. The logging operation spawned a paper mill, and that bred a newspaper, and before he was forty, Luke had a string of papers and was thinking about a magazine.

It was that year he married Lydia Pentland, the twenty-eight-year-old wispy but well-bred daughter of Portland's founding family, a sweet but dreamy spinster whose London-tailored father had just about given up on her. To old Judge Pentland, Luke, with all his drinking, whoring and rough edges, seemed a godsend. They were married extravagantly that spring, and Judith was born less than a year later. It was the end of her mother's life as a functional woman.

The birth was difficult, and Lydia's recovery lasted until the day she died of a liver ailment thirty years later. Lydia

Pentland Calvert retreated into a mauve world of lace and
sherry and romantic novels, and more sherry. Luke hardly
noticed, or cared, so long as his wellborn wife continued to
show up reasonably sober at the bigger parties and public
events that more and more often now seemed to center on
Luke Calvert. Judith barely remembered her mother. She
remembered her father very clearly.

Judith remembered the noise of him, the bay-rum-and-
cigar smell of him, the huge size, the raw physical force of
this astonishing creature who swept in and out of her life like
some random tornado, sometimes with a flash of guilty affection, more often with a sense of surprise, as if he had forgotten her existence, and sometimes with the uncontrollable
drunken outrage of a man betrayed by the gods, who had
sent this pale excuse for the sons he wanted more than anything.

They lived in an enormous oak and mahogany house at the
top of a hill, all turrets and verandas, marble and brass, Persian carpets and fringe. Tutors came to instruct Judith and
certain of the servants' children, which meant that Judith was
always at the head of her class, always the leader of games.
This was her first taste of power, and one taste was all she
needed.

Before she was ten, Judith had learned the extent to which
she could manipulate her mother and therefore the entire
backstairs of the household. "Wouldn't that palm be more attractive to the left of the staircase, Sturges?" she'd remark in
a lighthearted way that the shrewd old butler knew full well
to be an implacable command. The servants shrugged and let
her have her way. It amused the child, she meant no harm
and in any case there was no one to complain to; Luke was
never there, and the Mrs. just smiled her sweet smile and
asked for more Amontillado.

In Judith's fifteenth year Luke started his first magazine,
The Oregon Gazette. By this time she was bored with rear-
ranging the furniture and inventing menus. She'd become a
journalist! Since no one had ever really checked up on her tutors and since Judith herself was nothing of a scholar, her
education was a spotty thing. The essay she wrote on Civic
Virtue reflected this; it was equal parts of high-flown plaga-
rism and ungrammatical pretension. Nevertheless, Judith sub-
mitted it to the *Gazette* under a pen name and when it was
promptly rejected, took it to her father in person.

She knocked on his study door after breakfast one Sunday and heard his gruff "Come in!" The door was tall and thick, dark mahogany, as heavy and intimidating as the man himself. It felt like entering a prison. Luke Calvert had put on weight with his power and money; always tall, he now loomed behind the great green-leather-topped desk like some tailored but untamed grizzly wandered in from the forest. He was sleek, but there was a sense of building violence about the man. His voice was a storm cloud rumbling, and even his deep laughter held unstated threats.

"I wrote this." Judith had a speech rehearsed but forgot it now, here in the Presence. Her six white pages looked tiny on the waxed green leather battlefield that was her father's desktop. He reached out for them, squinted—too vain for reading glasses—and gave each page his consideration. Then he finished, stacked the pages neatly together and set them on the desk.

Luke Calvert examined his daughter as though she were some insect the exterminator had carelessly allowed to live. And as he looked at her, Luke's hand snaked across the desk for a great round ashtray carved from some green stone. When the ashtray was in front of him, he carefully picked up the essay and tore it in half from top to bottom. Then he tore the half in half, then quartered that, tearing and tearing in silence until a pile of white shreds was all that remained of Judith's effort. Then Luke Calvert struck a big wooden match on the sole of his shoe and lit the fragments of paper.

And while they smoldered and blazed in the ashtray, he said, in a voice that was more frightening for being quiet, "You little damned fool. You're a girl, Judith, and not a very talented one either. Forget writing. Get yourself a man who'll look after you—and see to it make him a better wife than your mother did me. There's but one kind of business women are good at, and I'll see you dead before you take to whoring even though"—he laughed a terrible laugh—"about the only businesswoman I ever did admire was old Lily Cigar down in Frisco. So stick to your needlework, girl, and your fussin' with the cooks and maids. Someone's got to. And forget this." He waved at the ashes in the big ashtray, writhing now like black worms from their own heat.

Judith looked at him, trembling, the strange amber light building in her eyes. "I wish you were dead." She said it quietly, then walked out of the room and never spoke to her father again.

Luke Calvert died of a stroke before Judith was twenty. It was then that the world found out how well she had spent the five years since that interview in his office. Judith, it turned out, knew her father's business better than he ever had; she knew who was strong and who was weak and how to make the most of the strengths and weaknesses. Judith's mother was the sole heir, but before the funeral flowers had wilted, the girl had her mother's signature on a power of attorney and was in full effective control of the Calvert empire.

The empire prospered. Judith absorbed herself in it completely, working eighteen-hour days, hiring expertise where she lacked it, consolidating here, expanding there, sharpening her managerial skills, biding her time, but always taking care to remain absolutely in control.

The time came when the Pacific Northwest was too small an arena for the Calvert empire. Judith moved her headquarters to Chicago and eventually to New York. She hired a bright young man whose vision of a weekly newsmagazine quickly became her vision, and long after the bright young man became a sad middle-aged drunk researching obituaries, *Scope* remained a worldwide success, bringing Judith money she hardly noticed, fame she cleverly exploited and what she wanted most of all: power. *Scope* bred other successful magazines: *Cash,* for the semipro investor; *Competitors,* all about sports; and lately *Audience,* a complete theater arts magazine.

In Chicago it had come to Judith's attention that husbands were useful accessories. She set about acquiring a suitable example. Larry Winchester was tall and distinguished-looking, the third son of old Chicago money, a research scientist of quiet habits and few demands. Judith stalked him, snared him and married him all within a year and then got back to business. The most visible feature of her husband was his name; she had never liked her father's name, and outside the Northwest the name Calvert had no special currency. So she became Judith Winchester to the world.

Judith Winchester made herself into a publishing genius with a desperate single-mindedness that had been forged in the flames of her first attempt at writing, burned by Luke Calvert in Judith's fifteenth year. Sole head of a huge publishing empire, she was still notoriously inept with words. So Judith hired writers and reporters as a builder might hire bricklayers: they were a necessary part of her plan, the artisans of her fantasy. Her talents were manipulative, learned by instinct and out of a Latin primer: "Divide and conquer." Judith had an almost surgical instinct for anyone's weakness. She would find these weaknesses and expose them and use them. She would pit people against each other—or against themselves—and sit back observing until they all but tore themselves apart; then and only then would she step in armed with knowledge and power, and straighten things out building more power. That manipulation was the force that ran the Winchester publishing empire, and if it was cruel, it was also effective.

A time came when her advisers hinted that it might be politic for a woman in Judith's situation to become a patroness of the arts. To Judith's mind and eye and ear no art had meaning: art was a decadent invention, handmaiden to leisure, and Judith had no leisure, no unfilled hour. But her advisers were the best money could buy, and Judith listened carefully. She set up a team of reporters to study the various museums and theaters and ballet companies. Their assignment, subtly put but unmistakable, was to find a weak spot, a place into which the Winchester wedge might most effectively be driven. Their project was huge and took six months. It resulted in the famous "State of the Arts" issue of *Scope*. It also resulted in Judith's sudden interest in the International Ballet Theater.

The study revealed two interesting facts. The first was that ballet was growing enormously faster than any other theatrical entertainment and that the center of great dancing, for all the world, was suddenly New York. The second fact was that the famous International Ballet Theater, one of New York's two most prestigious companies, was suddenly lacking a major patron, its previous big-money backer having lately died.

Judith Winchester became a patron of the International Ballet Theater. It seemed an ideal combination: her money and ability to create publicity in four major magazines combined with the ballet's constant need for patronage. Judith's patronage could have remained a matter of writing checks and making an occasional phone call to one of her editors. But Judith was no more capable of remaining quietly in the background of an enterprise than a ravening shark is capable of nibbling. If she were to be involved at all, it had to be completely. She had to pull the strings, to manipulate, to control. In less than one year she had achieved a startling measure of control. She was on the board now and saw a time when she might be chairman of that board. If Judith could add Dimitri Lubov to the galaxy of stars already dancing with the International, it would be a major victory in her drive toward absolute power.

Dimitri looked down the long table from his place of honor at Judith's right. The room had a special New York kind of ugliness, coldly and professionally decorated in a style that made him feel he was in some department-store window, on display. There was nothing personal in it, no object anyone loved. The food, too, was excessively opulent. Dimitri's first memories were of hunger. There had been days in the little shed in Saratov when two stolen potatoes had had to do for three Lubovs, and even now the sight of food destined to be wasted made him uneasy; to this extent he was, indeed, a Communist.

It was Dimitri's fate to be naturally gentle and polite. The melodramatic reports of his temper were exaggerated. Dimitri had a temper, and when it flared, it flared high and hot. But such storms came rarely and quickly passed. The everyday Dimitri was a gentle and humorous boy.

He sipped the excellent wine and listened to Judith on his left and Greg Holden across from him. Holden was the business manager of the International Ballet, a pleasant man of a type Dimitri thought typically American, easygoing, relaxed, quick to smile, somehow a bit rough with all the ease. A man, Dimitri thought idly, who might be trusted. And thinking that, he wondered what this man was doing at Judith's table, eating Judith's food, drinking her wine. For Greg Holden and Judith were not alike. Well, it hardly mattered.

From time to time Dimitri retreated into his ignorance of English, although his English got better every day. His smile was enough for these people, so mostly he smiled, and nodded, and mimed agreement.

And while he did these things, Dimitri daydreamed. He thought of Jenny, of Jenny dancing, of tonight's triumph, of many things. This never showed on his face.

The party was black-tie, an item of costume that Dimitri had never owned or wanted to own. He wore, instead, black velvet jeans, tucked into black cowboy boots, and a soft black cashmere turtleneck. His fine, pale head floated upon that slender column of black like some Donatello sculpture awaiting its base. He heard praise for his dancing, and it washed off him like rain; there were perhaps four people in the world whose praise or criticism made sense to Dimitri, and two of these were in Russia.

He looked at the two dozen guests. With the exception of Greg Holden all the men were a little too heavy, a bit too sleek. They looked like rich seals. By contrast, as if they had come in matched sets, most of the women were a little too thin, strung out on piano wires. *If you fell on them from any height,* he thought, *you'd be cut in two.*

Dessert was perfect, fresh, out-of-season peaches spinning in huge crystal goblets of champagne. Dimitri contemplated his peach and smiled, thinking of Saratov and potatoes. He turned to Judith.

"What is it you want of me?"

"I want you to leave de Lis and come to us." No one, in all the world, was going to win a contest with Judith Winchester when it came to laser-beam directness.

"And why should I do that?"

"Because you will have more of everything."

"Money?" He was close to being rude. They really thought they could buy and sell everything, these sleek Americans.

"Yes, money. But more than money. With us, you will be a star. A real star. De Lis will bury you. He buries everybody. And he has no money." This was true; Dimitri knew it. If a de Lis dancer wanted to make any real money, he or she had to do a lot of dancing outside the company.

"What I want. . . ." Dimitri spoke slowly, picking up each word as if with silver tongs.

"I will give you a ballet. Do you want Tudor? Twyla Tharp? Just name it. De Lis never made a real ballet on a man; he couldn't. He only likes women." This, too, was true.

Dimitri speared the huge peach out of the goblet and set it dripping on his plate. He looked at Judith Winchester. "What you say is interesting. I must think . . . for some time."

"We'll be waiting, Dimitri."

"We talk again."

"Of course. And soon." Judith smiled her best imitation of a warm and welcoming smile. She had found a tiny crack and inserted the steel wedge. It was only a matter of time now. Something would happen to upset Dimitri at the Civic

Ballet. Judith took this as gospel. Something always happened to upset dancers of Dimitri's caliber. The trick was to get them in an ironclad contract so the upset didn't matter. But Dimitri, she well knew, had only a limited contract with de Lis. Her time would come, and she had spies in plenty to tell her when it did come. She lifted her glass. He lifted his. She had won, then, although Dimitri would not know it for some weeks.

Jenny's eyes widened as she got her first glimpse of the de Lis apartment. He lived in four huge rooms high up in the old Dakota apartments on Central Park West. Jenny had never been in the famous building before. The apartment, she thought, was like de Lis himself: a fascinating mixture of elegance and shabbiness, of mystery and wit, of yesterday and tomorrow. Jenny Hale knew furniture and art because in better times her father's apartment had been filled with excellent examples of both, all long gone now, bringing what they could upon the cold altar of the Parke-Bernet auction block. The big rooms were filled with people and things, and Jenny was hard put to think which were more interesting, which more strange.

Three black cats struck poses on a priceless French prie-dieu covered in its original Louis XIV silk needlepoint. A set designer's sketch for the new production of *Coppélia* was crudely pinned to the oak-paneled wall next to an original Franz Hals pen drawing of peasants dancing. One room of the apartment was fitted out for ballet practice with a mirrored wall and a barre.

Tonight that huge mirror reflected the wild gypsy camp that is a ballet company at play. *They look*, thought Jessica Privet, sticking close to Jenny as if in fear the girl might be kidnapped, *like a field of daffodils*. And so they did, poised and slender with the ramrod backs and elevated necks that are the sure sign of ballet training everywhere. Only the cats slouched, and they did that gracefully. *I'll bet*, thought Jenny mischievously, *de Lis sits up here all alone and choreographs them hour after hour!*

Jenny was shy at facing the crowd. She knew it was only natural for the kids in the corps to resent her. And while she tried to ignore the jealousy, to rise above it, pretend it wasn't there, it was there, day after day, steady and often cruel. She knew they said she slept with de Lis. They knew who her father was, and some of them said he'd promised de Lis a theater of his own, which was funny if you came right down to it, sad-funny because if Cliff Hale had been sober long enough ever to bother even meeting de Lis, he might have promised that, and on the moon, too, and made of gold. Jenny looked around the crowded room. *They hate me. They'd really love it if an earthquake came right this minute and swallowed me up.* A maid came by, carrying a tray filled with wineglasses. Jenny got one for Privy and one for herself. "Cheers."

"Cheers, Giselle."

Everywhere there were photographs. Jenny had never seen so many; whole towns and cities of photos populated tables, the top of the grand piano, consoles, shelves. Anna Pavlova stood forever en pointe, framed in Cartier silver, signed in fading ink: "Pour mon cher Alexis." There was Nijinsky as the Faun, Markova as the Sylphide, Danilova, Massine, Marie Rambert, Margot Fonteyn in blue jeans, Sergei Diaghilev in a Keystone Kop bathing costume and a big cigar. Unrecognizable men in white tie stared gravely out of the past at whole corps de ballets, empty but impressive stage settings, and a framed musical score signed by Stravinsky (Jenny looked close; it was *Firebird*), and ballerinas and ballerinas and ballerinas. The whole history of ballet crowded these rooms. Jenny felt she was sipping legends with her wine.

And through it all moved the living legend, Alexander de Lis. "Ballet," a critic had written, "has a soul. Its name is Alex de Lis." He wore an old blue sweater, an open shirt with a casually tied silk scarf, beautifully cut gray flannel trousers that surely were not new and Gucci loafers. Alex de Lis moved among his hundred guests like the great dancer he had been, like the great host he was. Backstage at the Civic Ballet, de Lis seemed to be everywhere at once. He had a talent for materializing at unlikely times in unlikely places, observant, clever, altogether formidable. And so it went at his party: de Lis was everywhere at once, joking with the youngest girl in the corps, making her feel at home, taking a coat, feeding a star, scolding a critic, soothing a patron, tasting the wine, charming, sparkling, never missing a beat, never missing a trick.

All the cast was there but Dimitri. And they all were bursting with energy, still high on the adrenaline they had generated for the performance. Jenny, like all of them, felt starved. Well she should have; she'd hardly eaten all day.

The big old mahogany table had been pushed against one wall of the dining room and transformed into a buffet. Here were great mounds and vats of food, most of it Russian, all of it delicious. Jenny looked at the feast and thought how much Dimitri was missing. A mountain of the little cheese tarts called khachupuri bravely withstood the onslaught of the crowd. Platoons of golden pastries filled with meat, pirozhki, flanked a well of steaming beef Stroganov. There were noodles flecked with caraway seeds, fresh green peas with mint, a beet-and-herring salad, fat round loaves of bread so dark it looked black, sweet butter and goblets half filled with an excellent young Beaujolais. Tall candles gleamed and flickered from old bronze wall sconces and from candlesticks on every table. The room was filled with laughter and warmth and beauty, and Jenny Hale felt absolutely alone there. *Where was Dimitri?* Someone played hot, incongruous ragtime on the concert grand piano. De Lis materialized out of the crowd and bowed to Privy—whom he knew—then took Jenny's hand. *She's frightened,* he thought. *We must do something about that.* He looked at Jenny and smiled, but the words he spoke were for Privy.

"Tonight we have seen a kind of miracle . . . a birth. Tonight we have seen a new Giselle. I think, little Jenny, that it may be the first of many such." He lifted his wineglass in a toast. Their glasses clinked.

"In the first part of Act Two, the solo, my left hand. . . ."

"I know. Just slightly. We know, little Jenny, you and I. But think what they saw out front tonight. The magic of it. Tomorrow, we work on the hand. Only a little. There must be freedom. Tonight? We play!"

"Thank you, Mr. de Lis." Jenny wondered if there would ever come a time when she—or anyone—dared call him by his first name. Probably not.

Jenny Hale and Privy braved the party for an hour, then for half an hour more. Privy loved it all; she hardly went out anymore and had few party-giving friends in any event. Jessica Privet had learned to admire these young dancers—all but Iris Dowling, who was a hussy no matter how well she danced. As the level of wine in people's glasses went down, the level of noise at the party rose ever higher. Happy noise, thought Jenny, but noisy noise all the same.

Suddenly the quality of that noise changed, became muted. It was like being alone in a pine grove on a breezy day when all at once the breeze dies down. People looked at each other expectantly without knowing quite what to expect.

Then the crowd parted like the Red Sea before Moses, and Simon Bridge came ambling down the room. The big, rumpled, professional-looking critic headed straight for Jenny Hale. At first she thought de Lis or some other important person must have been standing behind her. Bridge took her hand. "I," he said unnecessarily, "am Simon Bridge. You'll have to wait until tomorrow, Miss Hale, to find out what I wrote. But it won't be spilling any beans to say I found you absolutely enchanting tonight." He gave her a great smile. Jenny knew praise from Simon Bridge could not be bought or begged; it was worth its weight in rubies. But more than for what his praise might be worth on the barrelhead, Jenny appreciated its caliber. Bridge was more than just a famous critic; he was a devoted enthusiast of ballet in all its forms. The man took his job as seriously as she took hers. That said a lot to Jenny Hale.

"Thank you, Mr. Bridge." She smiled her sweetest smile, wishing deep inside that she felt more. *You should be feeling something, dummy,* said an urgent voice inside her. *Do you think you're going to have a night like this every night for the rest of your life?* Jenny smiled harder, a dancer's fixed smile, and tried to think of something passably intelligent to say. Alex de Lis rescued her by taking Simon Bridge off to the buffet.

Jenny looked around the room, suddenly tense, very aware that she was adrift in uncharted waters. She could sense the currents bubbling around her. The room was filled with beauty and sex, with excitement and promise. The very air itself seemed to quiver with its burden of unimaginable possibilities. Even Privy felt it. Then, suddenly, Jenny guessed the real trouble.

I have no one to share this with. The glory was there, the hard work rewarded, the promises hovering all gilded and impossibly beautiful just ahead of her, and not even de Lis could understand how she felt. *Dimitri.* Dimitri would know. How he'd know or why he'd know wasn't really clear to Jenny. But she accepted it as fact, and as fact it was written in her heart. For Jenny Hale had never known love. Yes, sure, Privy loved her with a kind of supermaternal love, a watchdog love, a love that would go out and die for her without even thinking about it. But even dear Privy couldn't share the feelings that were suddenly bubbling up inside Jenny Hale. *Dimitri.* She said it to herself, unconscious of the fact that her lips moved just a little as she rolled the thought of him around and around inside her. He'd never come. It was hopeless. Even now, without looking at them, she could feel his violets wilting. *Who gave him those violets anyway?* He bloody well didn't grow them during intermission.

Jenny looked up with a start to notice that Privy was staring at her oddly. "You're tired, my love." Privy smiled at this odd changeling girl she'd known for almost twenty years and hoped it was only tiredness that made Jenny look so forlorn.

"I am that." They got their coats, thanked de Lis and left. It was after midnight. They took a taxi across Central Park, rare extravagance, to Clifford Hale's old apartment on Fifth Avenue. They had hot chocolate in the big, drab kitchen.

The kitchen was huge and inconvenient, designed for servants when servants were glad to have a job, any job. Jenny had sat like this with Privy ever since earliest childhood, just the two of them at the chipped white-enamel kitchen table, drinking the steaming hot chocolate that Privy knew how to make better than anyone else. The apartment was silent. Jenny had stopped trying to keep track of her father years before. Sometimes Clifford Hale would be in and out of the apartment every day for weeks; sometimes he'd vanish for consulting jobs overseas or in faraway parts of America. The maintenance bills on the apartment were paid through Cliff Hale's law firm, and not always regularly at that.

Jenny wondered for the second time where her father was tonight and then stopped wondering. Cliff Hale had faded out of her life into a pool of alcohol, into a haze of tarnished hopes and unkept promises. It might have been easier, she sometimes thought, if he were dead and buried instead of drifting in this living death of his own devising. She looked into her half-empty chocolate cup and said nothing.

Privy was chatting merrily about the de Lis party. Jenny's responses were polite but unenthusiastic. She was tired physically, but tiredness had nothing to do with the heaviness she felt inside. Finally, she pushed back her chair, forced a little smile and bent to kiss Privy. "I'm beat, darling. Good night."

"Sleep well, Giselle. It was beautiful." Jessica Privet looked at Jenny's thin back as the girl walked down the hallway. She frowned. What was eating the girl? Jenny had always been quiet, intense, but never moody. It was a night of triumph, a night of dreams come true for Privy and for Jenny Hale. But the girl seemed hardly to notice.

The long hallway was mercifully dark. The cracked, faded paint was hidden by the shadows. Jenny opened the door of her little room, flicked on the light and slowly, mechanically unpinned the violets. They were wilting, but maybe a glass of water would revive them. Seeing the flowers made her think of Dimitri again, although to tell the truth she'd been thinking of Dimitri all along.

Jenny reached behind her neck to unclasp the gold rope, but her mind was back onstage at Lincoln Center, dancing a pas de deux with Dimitri. She saw that golden head more clearly than life, smile flashing, eyes gleaming bright as the brute spotlights that obliterated the audience, that created a magic hot-crystal cage in which the two of them spun and leaped and flew together and were touched with glory. Love must be something like dancing with Dimitri Lubov.

She saw his face, joyous, bathed in sweat now, drenched with the raw energy it took to stoke the searing fires inside him. Dimitri smiled and went into an incredible spin, whirling, a wild and glorious blur. The sweat flew off him in a great shower like the summer sprinklers on rich people's lawns, and since Jenny was there beside him, some of the sweat splashed on her, and she didn't mind—it was from him and therefore precious, the sweat, any word, a smile, any contact at all. She could feel it, his sweat, hot on her cheek.

Jenny reached up and touched her cheek. Wet. She looked up, for the first time, looked in the mirror. Only then did she know that the wetness was her own tears, that she was crying as she could never remember crying. And sobbing still, Jenny slipped out of her dress and into the narrow bed. The violets, unwatered, died fragrantly in darkness.

Dimitri Lubov felt their eyes on him and paid no attention at all. Let Judith Winchester's friends drink their fill of him. It might be their last chance to do that. They were in the drawing room now, sipping bad coffee from cups so thin it was an astonishment they didn't melt. Mostly it was the women who looked at Dimitri; the men stole a glance from time to time, uncomfortable with the dancer because where they came from, all male dancers were fairies and to be wary of, and why were their wives and mistresses going so hot and heavy for this skinny Commie kid who could hardly speak the language and didn't even have a tie on, for chrissakes?

Dimitri had been the object of many stares and glances for half his twenty-four years, and by now he simply ignored them. The women looked at Dimitri, and their looks held many different messages if the boy had bothered to read them. He did not. Some of these looks were stark invitations to sex; some were the desperate seeking of lion-huntresses who, vampirelike, lived only in the glow reflected from the famous, the notorious, the powerful men and women with whom they fought to surround themselves.

Dimitri's boredom had grown and hardened at this party until it made a shell thicker than any turtle's. So these were the powermongers, the people who pulled strings and made the world jump. No wonder the world was in such rotten shape. He thought of two things that were really the same thing. How soon could he get out of here? How soon could he get to Jenny Hale?

All night, through the ballet, through the amazing response in the theater, response that even to Dimitri Lubov was a shock, a great unexpected blast of pure glory, all through this agonizing party and the unsettling maneuvers of Judith Winchester and the vulgar food and the good wines, one thought had grown and blossomed in Dimitri's head. The thought was of Jenny. *Jenny!* Even the name was different, delicious. A very American name, Jennifer. It might be the name of a spice, of a small wild flower that grows only on certain mountain slopes and blooms where only eagles see it. *And I,* he thought, smiling in a way that made a lady's demitasse rattle halfway across the room, *and I shall be that eagle.*

CHAPTER
ᴄᴏᴏᴄ 3 ᴐᴏᴏᴏ

Dave Loughlin had the rough bulk of a longshoreman and the ambling shuffle of a geriatric bear. Dave was thirty pounds heavier and more than thirty years older than he'd been in the Army OSS days, the last happy time he could remember. And now, as Dave made his way down the long green-asphalt-tiled corridor that always reminded him of a hospital, of death, he felt every minute of those years, and every extra ounce weighing on him like an unserved sentence. And he felt the effects of last night's boozing, which didn't help any either. He passed the blind lunch counter and shuddered, even though he'd known it would be there, creepy as ever, even if it was the Old Man's idea, even if it did make some kind of perverted sense.

Where else in the world would you have blind men and women cheerfully handing out wrapped sandwiches and cartons of coffee so bad it could have been made only by the blind? Where else but in the ever-vigilant atmosphere of CIA headquarters out in dear old Langley, Virginia?

The goddamned corridor was never going to end. The long, waxed, buffed, clinically clean passage was nearly empty and very quiet indeed. Now and then a brisk, beautifully tailored young man would glide swiftly by, avoiding Dave with the casual ease of a good car dodging a bad pothole. The new breed.

But Dave had other things on his mind, and he didn't take the time to consider the way the agency was changing or the way he wasn't changing with it. Dave was thinking about death, about three deaths, to be precise, which was just what he'd better be if he expected to sell his cockeyed theory to the Old Man. Three deaths. It was early October now, October 1975, going on a year since the first one. The first murder?

Any snowball in hell had more of a chance than Dave did of
proving murder with the evidence he had on him. That was
why he'd gone to all this trouble, of waiting three weeks until
the Old Man could free half an hour of his precious time.
Well, Dave told himself in tribute to the old days, Sam was
busy. You didn't get to be the deputy director of the Central
Intelligence Agency by twiddling your thumbs. Three weeks
to set up an appointment, half an hour—if that—to state his
case, to beg some time, to plead for the green light so maybe
he could start a full-scale investigation of his harebrained
theory.

It did sound harebrained. And the more he had to go
through channels, to play this gut hunch by the numbers, the
crazier it seemed. Dave sighed and wished for the old days.
In the old days hunches were hatched and tossed back and
forth and acted on in minutes because minutes—seconds
maybe—were all they had. Somehow everything had worked
better in the old days.

The hallway seemed to get longer as Dave walked down it,
past all the identical-looking numbered doorways with their
peepholes and buzzers and carelessly hidden intercoms. A
Communist cockroach would have his work cut out for him,
trying to get inside the wrong door in this crazy joint. Dave
walked down the hallway, trying to remember the number on
Sam Purcell's door without looking at the scrap of paper in
his pocket. But his mind kept pulling back to a foggy town in
Switzerland, on an early winter afternoon just over a year
ago. What would he give, Dave wondered, to know exactly
what happened on that bleak night? The night Gregor Berisov came into Geneva to give a lecture and ended floating
belly up in the lake, first of the famous defectors to die unna-
turally, but surely not the last.

Dave squinted a little to see the number more clearly.
Forty-six. Right. The Old Man's new number. It seemed every time Dave visited Langley, the Old Man had a new office.
New and fancier. There was no doubt about it, Sam Purcell
had come a long way since the old days.

The Old Man. If Dave was fifty-three, and he most surely
was, then how old was Sam Purcell? Had to be near sixty.
Well, there was only one kind of premature retirement in this
line of work, and it usually came unexpectedly and wrapped
in lead.

Dave wondered how the Old Man would be, how he'd take

to Dave's visit, but in fact, he knew. The Old Man was always the same, cool and smart, making it look easy. Only once had Dave seen Sam Purcell lose his cool, and that had been in the old days and under circumstances that would turn Gibraltar to dust. Dave pressed the buzzer. Maybe he shouldn't harass the Old Man.

Sam had been good to him all these years. And why? From a sense of duty? Friendship? You couldn't call the Old Man a friend, exactly, even though he always acted friendly, always asked for Effie and the kids, sent Christmas cards while Mrs. Sam was still living, all that. No. You couldn't really call someone like Sam a friend. Still, he'd kept Dave on in a soft assignment, right where he wanted to be, in New York, and permanently, with just enough to do to justify a not very big salary and an even smaller expense account, with very little danger and even less excitement. But close to Staten Island, close to home, to Effie and the kids and the church and bingo nights and young Davey's Little League games. Very cozy stuff for someone in Dave Loughlin's line of work. He pressed the buzzer again. They took their fucking time, did Sam's minions. Which was one more way that the present was very unlike the old days.

One thing about the old days, you could trust them. They always stayed the same. You never had to worry about what was coming at you next because you knew. You'd been there. Sometimes, especially after the Jack Daniel's went to work on a man's head, the old days even got a little bit better. Dave guessed that Sam Purcell had probably left the old days pretty much behind him. Not Dave. Not good old dumb, trusty Dave Loughlin.

A cool voice came over the buzzer, asking his business, doubting his right to breathe the rarefied air of CIA/HQ. *"I saved your candy ass, damn it."* He had, too. Well, fair was fair. The Old Man never forgot that. Dave would at least get a hearing. He identified himself. The cool voice checked with another cool voice. The buzzer sounded, and the doorknob clicked, and Dave walked into the first of Sam Purcell's two antechambers.

It was always night in the old days. They moved in darkness like bats, and if it happened to be raining or misty, so much the better. Their hastily acquired French got better at night. Grunts were more to be expected at night. Being caught by the Gestapo was not expected.

The Gestapo caught up with Sam Purcell on a suitably dark and misty night in Aix-la-Chapelle in 1944. *Don't ask the details,* Dave always said, and for good reason, because the details sickened even him and by now he'd pretty much blocked them out, buried them where even the whiskey couldn't find them, buried them nearly as deep as the three German officers who had decided to carve up Sam Purcell like Granny's Christmas goose before they let him die.

It was a very sure thing the Old Man wouldn't have got to be the Old Man, or even an hour older than whatever his age was in '44, but for the convenient fact that Dave had smelled something fishy and wandered over to the old nunnery they used as a message drop, where, through the open window he'd seen what you aren't supposed to ask about and quickly stopped it with three muffled but very accurate leaden surprises from the OSS to the Gestapo with no love at all.

Dave Loughlin's hand had been very steady in the old days.

He'd done what he could to stop the bleeding and hefted Sam in a fireman's carry through four-odd miles of patrolled woodland to the safe house, where by some miracle Sam pulled through. Barely. *Thirty years,* thought Dave as he was escorted into the second antechamber, *is a very long time.*

In the thirty years since that night at Aix, Sam Purcell and Dave had traveled on very separate roads. Sam's, typically, had been the high road. Dave never begrudged his old boss the success Sam had worked so long and cleverly to achieve. The Old Man was by no means universally beloved in the CIA, but fast-rising leaders seldom are.

Dave shifted his weight as the thin-lipped secretary murmured into an intercom on her desk. He was too worried to get mad at the delay. He thought of the second murder—if it was murder. He thought of Santa Barbara, and how tough it was going to be, even with Sam's blessing, to pick up the raveled threads of his wild-assed theory. Santa Barbara! Maybe Peter Chablesky had died of a heart attack after all. Maybe. Maybe the deaths were accidents. Maybe. Dave sighed and opened the door.

Sam Purcell sprang to his feet on well-conditioned muscles, a lean, fit man with rather short steel-gray hair and gold-wire eyeglasses. He might,   ave thought, have been a Boston banker or a professor of something fancy at an Ivy League university. "Davey!" Sam's voice registered surprise and pleasure.

Dave knew the surprise had to be fake, diplomatic surprise. He hadn't, after all, after three weeks of trying, and two anterooms, dropped down the fucking chimney. But Dave hoped the pleasure was real. At least some of it. He shook the Old Man's tanned, manicured hand and checked out the new office. It had the same quiet, elegant, old-money look that Sam had somehow assumed over the years: Persian carpets, well-waxed mahogany, big, comfortable Chippendale chairs covered in soft suede, studded with brass nailheads. "How are you, Sam?"

"Keeping fit—barely. How's yourself? And Effie?"

"Effie's fine. Sends her regards. I'm OK, I guess."

Purcell walked around the big desk and put his arm around the younger man's shoulder. *He looks like the devil,* thought Sam; *he's letting himself go.* There was a point when people who let themselves go also let themselves become security risks. Sam wondered, as he smiled, if that time had come for Dave Loughlin. Sam motioned his guest to a chair by the big plate-glass window that looked out over the autumnal Virginia landscape and pressed a small ivory button, one of four identical buttons set into a mahogany case on the desk. Secretary Number Two marched into the room. "I think we'd like some tea, Miss Pritchard. Or would you rather have coffee, Davey?"

"Tea's fine." *Tea yet,* thought Dave; *my, my but we're getting fancier by the minute.*

"The Lapsang-Souchong, then. Thank you." Sam moved silently over the thick carpet to the window and pressed another button. The heavy draperies of ivory raw-silk came gliding shut, throwing the big office into premature twilight. Sam switched on a lamp. "There are such things," he murmured, "as telescopes and lip readers." Dave felt a small but determined flush of anger rising from his gut. So now the Old Man was giving out free security lessons with his fucking tea. But Dave said nothing.

"What's up, Davey?" Sam's voice was harder to read than it had ever been. There was warmth in it, but there was something else, too, maybe an edge of impatience, maybe something a bit patronizing. Here was the deputy director being kind to his old buddy, indulging his sad little Staten Island fantasies.

Dave had rehearsed his argument, had organized what facts there were, and now he felt like a fool, and more the fool because he'd made such a point of stalking the Old Man to his lair. If only he knew what really happened on the west coast of Ireland last summer. If only he knew what really happened to Gaia Muldovska, whose death had convinced him that there was a pattern, that it had to be something more than just coincidence.

The Third Murder

Ireland, 1974

Gaia Muldovska was one of those people who can be transformed by fast cars. On the concert stage, gracious but hardly dashing in understated black velvet, Gaia sat at her grand piano like the monument she was and tossed off the most elegant renditions of Bach and Mozart and, occasionally, the romantics. But get her behind the wheel of her flag-red MG in the hills around her little hideaway cottage overlooking Galway Bay near Kilfenora, and the legendary pianist was a woman changed.

For to Gaia the little convertible meant freedom more than all the money she earned or the novel experience of being able to cross any border she wished, whenever she wished to. So Gaia Muldovska drove her little car fast, some would say recklessly, and she drove it as often as she could invent excuses to do so.

The cottage in the quiet green hills was a kind of freedom, too, a small white blessing to one whose career demanded long tours in grand hotels, comfortable enough, to be sure, but never like home. The cottage had been fixed up, fitted with what the British liked to call "MOD CONS," but it was still a cottage, simple, all on one floor and very peaceful. There was one big room where her piano looked too elegant no matter where she placed it or how she draped it, two bedrooms, one bath and a small but happy kitchen. It was the kitchen Gaia thought of now as she guided the red MG nim-

bly down the narrow road to Ballyvaughan. For in Ballyvaughan was the only decent greengrocer for miles, and in
Ballyvaughan Gaia would buy fat beets and onions and a few
bones for broth. Her manager was due in the evening, and he
would find a pot of her beautiful borscht perfuming the cottage when he got there.

One did not, thought Gaia as she downshifted fluently
through a turn, actually leave Russia by defecting; her music
was with her always, in her head and her fingers, and so were
the recipes of her motherland, a permanent, if invisible, part
of her baggage. The borscht proved it. From Irish beets and
Spanish onions Gaia could compose a soup her own blessed
grandmother might deem authentic.

It was ten in the morning, and the sun shone bright. The
road snaked its way through the hills and close by the cliffs
of Moher, with Galway Bay glistening below and beyond. A
wild, lovely land, with police few and friendly to the famous
concert artist. Gaia's happy thoughts were rudely interrupted
by an unfamiliar sputtering noise from the car's engine. Yet
surely the gas was half-full? She slowed the MG and stopped
it by the side of the road. A fine thing! Sometimes these
roads were untraveled for hours. And who knew where the
nearest telephone might be? She could imagine her manager,
the impatient Freddie Reiner, having apoplexy, unmet and
unpaged at Shannon. And she with the beets yet to buy, the
borscht yet to make!

Gaia got out of the red convertible and stood for a moment with her slender white hands on her ample hips, looking
like any outraged peasant woman. She didn't even know how
to open the hood of the car, let alone how to determine what
might be the matter with it.

Then a wave of Russian philosophy overcame Gaia's indignation. Who knew? There might be no beets at Ballyvaughan.
Freddie might have missed his plane. And at the very worst it
was a glorious day, and here she was, alive and free in these
lovely hills, warmed by the sun, blessed by the view. Good
heavens. She could walk to Ballyvaughan if it came to that.

In the midst of this fragile consolation the miracle happened, and before Gaia had even had a chance to pray! The
expensive hum of a perfectly tuned motor rose above the gull
shrieks and the distant rumble of the sea. And a big old
Bentley touring car, dark-green and gleaming, came around

the corner with a grace and speed that belied its forty-odd
years of age.

Gaia waved, and the big green car slowed to a halt. The
driver was alone, your typical upper-class Englishman, she
thought, noting the old but expensive tweeds, the almost
metallic shine on his thick amber-colored boots, his lanky
build, discreet gray hair, his perfect manners.

"May I help?" Such voices had won at Waterloo. His voice
had the unmistakable languid ease of Cambridge. She told
him her problem, and in no time he'd taken off his jacket,
rolled up his bespoke shirt sleeves and was burrowing under
the MG's hood. He fiddled, stood up, frowned, fiddled some
more and finally went to the trunk of the Bentley and came
back with an elaborately fitted tool case. Tinker, tinker; he
obviously knew exactly what he was about, thought Gaia
with admiration. There was a surgeon's expertise in the quick,
precise manner in which he approached the tangle of wires
and valves and other mysterious objects that lived, usually in
harmony, under the MG's hood.

Finally, this elegant gray-haired stranger stood up, grinning
like a schoolboy on prize day. His beautifully manicured fingers held a small tangle of what looked like matted hair stuck
together with grease. "Clogging up the fuel pump, wouldn't
you know? Happens to the best of them." He clambered into
the MG, started the engine, got out and listened to the engine
with that uncannily surgical attitude. He really must be a
doctor, she was sure of it. Then the man wiped his hands on
an immaculate linen handkerchief and bowed. She thanked
him warmly and invited him to supper if he happened to be
in the neighborhood. But the man just looked at his watch
and smiled inscrutably and said no, he was just passing
through.

There were beets in Ballyvaughan! Gaia bought two fat
bags of them; she'd make double the amount and freeze it.
She had a quick teashop lunch and hurried back to the car.
She'd just have time if she made haste.

The red MG seemed to know its way home. It sped up the
road from Ballyvaughan into the hills, up higher and higher
to the very cliff top itself. And there, as the road leveled off a
bit, Gaia Muldovska really stepped on the gas. And she
started singing. The needle crept higher and higher on the
round black speedometer dial. The low, well-balanced sports
car poured itself flat around these familiar curves with never

a screech of tires. Gaia sang and sang, a happy Strauss Lied. Three more big curves and then the turnoff for her cottage. The first curve flew by, and the second angled out hard by the edge of the cliff itself. Gaia was still singing when the steering wheel went limp in her hands.

The singing turned to a screaming as the red MG sailed off the road at nearly ninety miles per hour. The car shot down a small gully, bounced once, then sailed up and out over the clifftop. It landed two hundred and seventy-three feet below, on the boulders where the surf broke. The car burst into flame.

When they found her three days later, the fire and the sea and the rock crabs had done their work, and there was very little to see of the world's most famous Russian concert pianist.

———◆———

There was a pause while Dave tried to find the right words. Sam was not a man to waste time, not his own time, not anyone's time. So he nudged a little. "You understand," said Sam gently, patiently, "that I haven't the foggiest idea why you're here."

"It may sound crazy, Sam, but hear me out." Dave leaned forward in the big wing chair by the window. "I think someone's knocking off a bunch of Soviet defectors, and it looks like a high-level operation that's doing it."

"Who, precisely, has been killed?" Sam might have been asking the details of Dave's ride in a flying saucer.

"Last November the poet Berisov was found belly up in Lake Geneva. They wrote it off as suicide. Maybe it was."

"But maybe it wasn't?"

"I didn't pay much attention to the Berisov thing. After all, he was a poet, and who knows what goes on in their heads? And shit, he'd defected nearly eight years before. But then, in July, Peter Chablesky—you know, the physicist—was found dead of a heart attack in Santa Barbara."

"Heart attacks—"

"Can be induced, or so some folks believe."

"Very few people have that capability, Davey." There was a slight but noticeable change in Sam's tone.

He's getting interested, thought Dave. *This is where I make it or break it.*

"Ivan does." Ivan was their nickname for the Soviet equivalent of the CIA, the KGB. "And," Dave went on, gaining confidence with every word, "so do the Limeys, and the Frogs, and quite a few other folks."

"It could be a coincidence." Sam sounded as though he were arguing with himself. "I mean, if Ivan wanted to—let us say, discipline—these people, wouldn't he have done it much, much sooner?"

"That," said Dave, "is just what I thought. Until the third one." The tight-lipped secretary came in with a silver tray containing a large, antique-looking blue-and-white china teapot and two delicate cups. *We might,* thought Dave, *be at Miss Fuckup's Academy for Young Ladies of Genteel Breeding.* Dave had trouble resisting a sudden impulse to slide his hand up the secretary's skirt. He said nothing until she left. "Then, wouldn't you know, Gaia Muldovska, the pianist, just happened to drive her little sports car off a cliff in Ireland. That's three in less than a year. That's some big coincidence, Sam."

Sam stirred his tea and raised the cup to his lips. There was a pause while he tasted the brew, and Dave realized how very quiet it could be in a well-insulated room in Langley, Virginia. The warm lamplight glinted off Sam's eyeglasses, and Dave couldn't quite see what kind of expression might be forming in Sam's eyes. Not that Sam was ever easy to read. Sam sipped the tea with the respect some men might give a rare vintage wine, then put down his cup with the smallest possible click of porcelain on silver. He spoke softly. "I think, old sport, that you might just have stumbled on something."

Now Dave smiled in earnest for the first time that morning. The "old sport" was a good sign. Sam used to call him that in the old days. In fact, Sam's first words when he finally came to in the safe house outside Aix had been a hoarse but unforgettable whisper: "Thanks . . . old sport."

Now Dave was glad he'd made the effort. The trip from New York had been worth it after all. Now maybe the Old Man would look at him a little differently, with a little more respect, not just as a tired workhorse in a safe pasture.

Dave had a plan, and he outlined it. Dave had a theory about the kinds of defectors who were being knocked off. Whoever was doing it picked celebrities. People who were prominent in the arts and sciences. Dave had made up a list of more than a dozen others: writers, the chess master Poussine, Rosoff, a diplomat, maybe Nureyev, or maybe this flashy kid who'd just come over, Dimitri Lubov.

Sam's advice, as ever, was excellent. There would be a quiet—but full-scale—investigation. Dave would head it up, under Sam's personal supervision. That was as good as it ever got. He'd work secretly, saying nothing to anyone until sufficient evidence was gathered. This was, after all, the most sensitive possible area of suspicion; the entire balance of Soviet-American relations could be shattered if word got out prematurely. What would happen if Dave's suspicions proved true, and could be documented, they hardly dared consider.

But at least it was a start, and a better start than Dave had hoped to achieve. The seed had been planted. Something big was about to happen, and Dave would be part of it, right up there with Sam again, right in the thick of it. This was a good feeling to Dave's tired bones, to his weary spirit. It was a very good feeling. It was almost like the old days.

CHAPTER
⌘ 4 ⌘

It had all started with Gloria Bruce.

Jenny lay in the narrow white bed of her childhood and tried to wish away the unwelcome tears. She thought of Gloria, of what Gloria had done to her life in the casual, offhand way that had been part of Gloria's famous chic. Gloria, who had wafted into Jenny's existence in a rustle of silk, in a mist of perfume, on Daddy's arm, all smiles, Daddy's new wife.

Jenny, aged eight, looked up, stood for the lightest of kisses, squirmed under Gloria's appraisal, lost her tongue, looked to her father for help only to find that Clifford Hale had eyes for Gloria and for Gloria alone, a man bewitched. So Jenny stood in silence looking at her new stepmother, her father's third wife, the beautiful Gloria. And in that moment Jenny knew exactly who Gloria Bruce had to be. She was Snow White's cruel, beautiful stepmother. Gloria even looked like the pictures in Jenny's Snow White book; it was in the arch of the eyebrow, the sculptured red-cherry lips, the disdainful cheekbones. Never, never would Jenny accept an apple from this one!

But if Gloria was wicked, it didn't show. She treated Jenny in an offhand way and went on with her busy life, with her career as a fashion model, with her cocktail parties and fittings and low, mocking laughter. From time to time Gloria indulged in a sudden rush of interest in Jenny. There was a moment of museumgoing, a stab at getting the child interested in riding, a few inconclusive attempts at children's parties.

What Gloria really wanted, Jenny decided early on, was to get Jenny out of the way. There was a hint of boarding school in Switzerland. *"Très chic!"* cried Gloria, using her fa-

vorite words of praise. But for once Cliff Hale put his foot
down, and Jenny stayed safely in the warm custody of Miss
Privet.

The next thing Gloria tried was ballet.

"Surprise, darling!" Gloria never just walked into a room.
She entered, gesturing, smiling—or not smiling, which was
worse—but forever riding a chic little whirlwind of her own
devising. Jenny was reading on her bed, this same narrow
white bed. Gloria swooped and delivered another of her famous butterfly's-wing kisses on Jenny's cheek, a kiss so light
it had no weight or warmth at all. "We"—Gloria paused to
underline the effect—"are going to the ballet! And not just
the ballet, my love, but the *Royal Ballet* at that."

"Will Daddy be there?" Jenny had only the vaguest notion
of what a ballet was, but if Daddy was going, it would be all
right.

"No, sweetie, that's just it. He's got to go to Cleveland or
some godforsaken place. It'll just be us girls together."

"Sure." Jenny felt the way she did when Privy announced
a trip to the dentist.

"Ask Privy to get you ready by six, darling; we're dining
out."

"OK."

"You might say, 'Thank you,' Jenny."

"I'm sorry. Thank you, Gloria."

"Wear the red velvet, darling. You look so pretty in it."
Jenny hated the red velvet. It had a lace collar that made her
feel as if she had a rope around her neck, about to be
hanged. And she didn't like that deep red very much either.
But Gloria assured her it was *très chic.* Jenny watched her
stepmother sweep out of the room. Well, it was better than
being completely an orphan. Or a leper. She went back to her
book, and soon her imaginary playmate, a French boy named
Gustave, came to visit. Then Privy appeared to help her get
dressed. Gustave went away then. He didn't like other
people's being there, even Privy. Reluctantly Jenny got
dressed, never thinking this day would end in a miracle.

Jenny, stiff in her red velvet dress and uncomfortably
aware of the matching red velvet ribbon holding back her
long chestnut hair, tried not to show how much she hated the
experience of having supper out with the glorious Gloria.

It was a small French restaurant with red velvet walls that

clashed with Jenny's dress. The restaurant, according to Gloria, was also *très chic*. Jenny began to suspect these were the only two words of French Gloria knew. It didn't seem to matter, though; everyone in the *très chic* restaurant knew *très chic* Gloria. Jenny had to bob up and down so many times, being introduced to people, she felt like a yo-yo. Finally, the waiter came and spoke to Jenny in French. When she instantly answered in French, a large, false smile split his long French face in two. He looked, Jenny thought, like the wolf in "Red Riding Hood" masquerading as the grandmother. The food was very good. Gloria even let Jenny have one glass of red wine. Jenny didn't like the taste, but she supposed it, too, was chic. Suddenly Gloria looked at the tiny platinum wristwatch Cliff had given her and gave a small shriek. They left the restaurant in a flurry of check signing and blown kisses and disappeared into the blustery fall night.

Jenny had never been in the old Metropolitan Opera House.

They flew out of the taxi and joined a stream of latecomers pouring into the theater. Jenny held Gloria's hand with the intensity of a drowning person. She was sure she'd be swept away in this mob, never to be seen again. Then they were inside the auditorium.

The sheer vastness of the opera house stunned Jenny. Their seats, of course, were in the orchestra, row 12, center. The house was filled, and many of the men and women in the orchestra were wearing evening clothes. There was a sparkle of what Gloria called "serious jewels," but the greatest sparkle came from the Metropolitan Opera House itself, where the old gilding shimmered bravely through its cloak of dust and the immense waterfall of diamonds that was the central chandelier hovered above them, levitating on the force of its own splendor. Jenny looked up and up until counting the great golden horseshoes of the balconies made her seasick with reverse vertigo. There was a squeaking and peeping and twanging from the orchestra pit. It sounded like feeding time at the zoo.

But what struck Jenny most about all this was the sense of anticipation. It was one thing for her to be looking forward to the ballet. But here were thousands and thousands of grown-ups, whispering and laughing and excited. She could tell; there was a special feeling to the audience, a feeling of

Christmas Eve, of mysterious but sure-to-be-thrilling presents to be unwrapped, and right here, and soon! It was contagious. Jenny forgot her father wasn't with them, forgot that she didn't really like Gloria very much, forgot even Gustave, her imaginary friend. A wave of applause burst over the audience, and Jenny had to ask why. She hadn't seen the conductor taking his place on the podium.

Jenny wiggled back in her seat. Something was happening to the lights. She looked up, and up, and up; the great cloud of crystal drops high overhead seemed to be vanishing in a dark mist, like a movie fade-out. The lights dimmed. The music began. Jenny sat up now, as tall as she could make herself. This night was special, she could feel it inside her.

It was the best fairy tale ever, *The Sleeping Beauty.*

Margot Fonteyn was the Princess Aurora, and Jenny had never seen anything so beautiful. Princess Aurora smiled, and it was a magical smile, reaching right into Jenny's heart. How different, she thought from the *très chic* smiles of Gloria Bruce, smiles which even when they appeared on the real-life Gloria only a few inches away looked as if they were meant to be frozen forever on the cover of *Harper's Bazaar,* as indeed they often were. The music caught a spark in Jenny's imagination, and the production fanned that spark into flames that would never go out.

Even now, almost twelve years later, Jenny could remember it all: Princess Aurora, radiant in pink and silver, dancing the rose adagio. Jenny remembered the bad fairy's curse, the Prince's kiss, the Lilac Fairy guiding the Prince into the sleeping palace of the Sleeping Beauty. Then the wedding! The procession, the gifts, the Bluebird pas de deux in which an awestruck Jennifer Hale learned for the first time that people could fly without wings. But what she would remember most was the pure magic of it.

For here was an enchanted world where everything was beautiful and even the bad fairies weren't all that bad, a world that lived happily ever after and young girls didn't wonder where their fathers were or who their next stepmother would be or whatever was going to become of them.

Jenny Hale made up her mind then and there to become part of this world. It was much better than the world she knew. Anyone could see that.

"Gloria?" Jenny turned to her stepmother in the speeding taxi.

"What, darling?"

"Do you think Daddy would let me take ballet lessons?"

"Well, sweetie, we can sure ask him." Gloria smiled in the darkness and squeezed Jenny's hand. It was working after all. "Personally, Jenny, I think they're a great idea. I mean, darling, they'll be good for you even if you decide not to become a dancer."

"I'm going to be one."

"A dancer?"

"Yes! I want to be like Princess Aurora."

"When I was your age, Jenny, do you know what I wanted to be?"

"What?"

"I wanted to be a cowboy." Gloria laughed her low, thrilling laugh.

"Why didn't you?" Jenny knew the answer. Cowboys were not *très chic*.

"I guess I was fickle. For a while there I wanted to be everything."

"I won't be fickle."

Even in the darkened back seat of the taxi, Gloria Bruce could feel the intensity of Jenny's stare like a physical thing. She looked at the girl thoughtfully. "No," said Gloria, "probably you won't be."

Clifford Hale came back from Cleveland to find his daughter had become a ballet junkie. In this, Gloria was a willing conspirator. "But it's a must, Cliffie," she said in her famous low, throaty whisper that was used with great effect on everyone from lovers to grocery clerks. "It'll give the child poise, a sense of her body." *And,* she said to herself, *it'll get the little bastard out of my way in the afternoons, if there's any justice in this world.* Jenny made Gloria Bruce feel oddly guilty. This would be Gloria's way of helping the child. And like most things Gloria Bruce did, it would also do a little something for Gloria. Cliff Hale, flush with money and always an easy touch for a pretty woman, agreed immediately.

If Clifford Hale's child were going to ballet school, it would have to be the best ballet school. And in New York, in 1964, that could only mean the Children's School of the Civic Ballet.

You did not merely pay money and go there; you were auditioned.

Gloria Bruce, who had met everyone worth meeting at least twice, arranged for a private audition. And it was Gloria, ravishing in the artificial simplicity of afternoon tweeds by Chanel, who led a very nervous Jenny Hale up three flights of clanging cast-iron stairs to the huge loft that was the home of the Children's School, on West Fifty-seventh Street in Manhattan.

With every step Jenny withdrew deeper and deeper into her fears. Suppose she flunked? Suppose she didn't answer the questions right? Suppose they wanted her to have seen more than one ballet? Suppose she fainted dead away? Jenny wondered if it hurt to drink poison. And all of a sudden they were at the top of the stairs. Gloria looked at Jenny and smiled. "Just be yourself, darling. It won't be hard at all."

Never, never, never, thought Jenny Hale, *will they take me if I'm myself.* But Jenny didn't know how to be anyone else.

The Children's School of the Civic Ballet was run by a very old lady with a long Russian name and the bright predatory eyes of a squirrel. Everyone called her Madame. Madame sat in an old bentwood chair next to a battered concert grand piano in the otherwise-empty studio. She did not rise as Gloria and Jenny approached. "Yes, yes, Hale." The old woman sized up Gloria in an instant and gestured her to a row of chairs halfway down the enormous room. Then Madame reached out and touched the trembling shoulder of Jenny Hale and smiled.

It was a smile, Jenny thought, that had no age to it, only warmth, only interest. Yet Madame was the oldest person— or thing—Jenny could remember, so old that somehow she wasn't scary anymore, only fascinating. *She is two hundred years old if she's a day.* Jenny thought irreverently and nearly smiled. It was like being introduced to a cathedral. She wondered how this ancient creature could teach dancing, wondered, in fact, if the old lady could move at all.

"Now," said Madame in a voice that had the dark resonance of a growl, startling in such a delicate-looking creature except that nothing could startle Jenny at this moment. "Now take off your coat, child. Let me see what we have here." Automatically Jenny took off her best winter coat and laid it on the piano. She looked at Madame with her enormous gray eyes, eyes far too large for an eight-year-old.

So this was the dragon who guarded the magic kingdom. The lively old eyes, Jenny thought, were not unkind. Halfway down the studio, a bored Gloria Bruce extracted a black-wrapped, gold-tipped Russian cigarette from a slim gold case.

"Before we dance, child, we must walk. So walk for me, Jennifer Hale. Walk away from me, all the way to the end of the room, straight as you can—standing tall—and then turn and run back to me. Pretend when you run that you are the wind itself." Jenny Hale walked. She ran. "Now. Can you jump?" Jenny jumped as high as she could. "Raise your left arm slowly . . . slowly, until it is straight over your head." Jenny's hand went up. "Now the other." Jenny's thin arm described a shallow arc. "Now, slowly, slowly, bring them down again." Jenny did this, her eyes never leaving Madame's face. It seemed crazy. Jenny couldn't for the life of her figure out why the old lady was having her do these silly things, but if this was the way you got into the classes, then this was what Jenny Hale would do. The trouble was, she had no idea whether she was doing it right.

The old lady looked at Jenny Hale. How many such little ones had she seen, thus, in all her years? Thousands, surely. She looked at Jenny through the filter of more than sixty years of constant training in the dance, starting when she had been no older than this child, in the drafty classrooms of the Maryinsky Theater in Petrograd. And how could one tell, looking at an eight-year-old, what the years would make of her?

There were certain physical proportions that must be right, to be sure. A straightness of leg, an elegance in the line between hip and knee, the carriage of the head, the length of a neck. Madame preferred shoulders and collarbones to be straight, parallel to the floor, but this was not absolutely necessary. Pavlova, for instance, had shoulders so sloping they almost didn't exist. There had, too, to be a promise of beauty, a hint of natural grace. Yet for all this, there was no guarantee the student might not grow too tall, or injure himself, or simply lose interest.

Madame knew, too well, that for every hundred children beginning in a serious class, perhaps five might keep on with it and get good enough to join professional companies. Of these five, two might achieve some real distinction. One might—just might—become a principal dancer or, better, a star. One in ten thousand! And still, she did it. Still, she saw them all and tried to screen out the clumsy ones and the bored ones, the ones with no real interest. And over the years Madame had learned to seek out another, less obvious quality in the students she auditioned for her school. This quality was not a physical thing but rather an intensity of emotion, a special concentration without which all the strength and grace and beauty that might be born into a dancer would fall by the wayside. The concentration was the key to it all, the driving force, the gas for the engine without which the engine would be just so many inert pipes and pistons, however nicely polished. It was this dedication that Madame thought she saw in Jenny Hale. Madame smiled and reached out with a surprisingly tiny hand to touch Jenny on the shoulder. "And tell me, child, why you think you want to be a dancer."

"I want to be a dancer," said Jenny, who had never thought about why until this very minute, "because dancers make people happy."

"An excellent reason." The million wrinkles in Madame's sparrow face arranged themselves into a smile. "Most excellent. But you should know, little Hale, that dancers do not always make themselves happy."

"If I could dance well, Madame, then I would be happy."

"I hope that may be, child." With unexpected grace the old lady rose to her feet and once again touched Jenny on the shoulder, a benediction. Jenny sensed acceptance without being told of it. She would be one of them now! The gates to the magic kingdom had opened just wide enough to let in one skinny eight-year-old. Yes. She'd be one of them now. She would be a dancer.

The first day of class was two weeks later. Jenny made Privy leave her at the door of the big old loft building on West Fifty-seventh Street. The little girl knew that, whatever the magic might be inside those doors, it was hers alone, magic to make her own or to fail—maybe die!—in the trying. But it must be alone, a sacred quest. She opened the door.

It was the same studio where she'd had her interview with Madame, but vastly changed now, alive with movement and voices. Children of all sizes and both sexes seemed to be everywhere, most of them already dressed for class in leotards and sweaters and leg warmers. They did warming-up and stretching exercises that looked to Jenny's wondering eye

painful and awkward and unlike anything she'd expected.
There was none of the recess-at-school merriment that Jenny
was used to. The kids talked, called greetings, listened to
what Madame and her two assistants had to tell them. Jenny
stood there, expectant, clutching the Air France flight bag
that Gloria had given her, the bag holding a new leotard and
dance slippers and a towel and still smelling of Gloria's heavy
perfume. One of the assistants came over and showed Jenny
to the girls' changing room. It was a shabby version of the
girls' locker room at school. Jenny dressed quickly, glad that
she'd practiced and practiced for more than a week at home,
cheered on by Privy and once by Gloria herself. The little
slippers were a disappointment. She wanted toe shoes from
the start. But even the news that girls weren't allowed to go
up en pointe until their leg muscles were more developed, until twelve or thirteen at the earliest, failed to discourage
Jenny.

She came out of the dressing room into the big studio.

For a moment Jenny simply stood there, taking it all in.
There was a lot to take in. Some of the kids had the
scrubbed, sleek look of rich children: they might have come
from Jenny's own school, and in fact, two of the older girls
did. Others looked and talked as though nameless slums had
spawned them, and Jenny would learn that this was true, that
they were on de Lis scholarships. There were kids who spoke
French more easily than English, UN kids and kids who lived
the rich-gypsy life of big-time show business. There were four
black children and two girls from India. Jenny wondered if
she'd ever fit in. Then the class began, and she had no time
to wonder.

Madame divided them into groups by age and experience.
Jenny's group was the biggest: the beginners. She soon
learned that the dropout rate was high; the school was expensive and hard, and it soon weeded out the ones whose interest
was a fickle thing or imposed by parents who didn't really
know what dance was all about. The assistant who taught the
class was quite young, and she smiled a lot and had a brisk,
let's-get-on-with-it manner that reminded Jenny of Privy. The
first thing the instructor said, after one loud handclap to get
their attention, was: "These are your feet." There was a
ripple of giggles. The lesson went on, and after a few moments of very basic theory they began to practice the basic
positions and movements. To do this, they were lined up

against the wall, with one hand on the fat wooden railing called the barre.

One of the first things Jenny learned was that she'd be getting lessons in French on top of lessons in dance. Classical ballet, the instructor told them, originated at the court of Louis XIV, in France, and dance classes everywhere were conducted in French to this day. It was a convenience, because it enabled a Russian, for instance, who spoke no English, to take a class anywhere and still understand the dance part of it. Before long they learned to recognize the instructor's commands: "Plié!"—that was a bending of the knees and basic to just about everything. Or "Port de bras!" which was a—they hoped—graceful upsweep of the dancer's arm. Soon the air was filled with French commands and flying limbs and the basic repetitious exercises that build the foundations of a dancer's technique. But it wasn't all simply exercises. They did center-floor work, too, almost from the start. This developed a sense of rhythm, an ability to link even the most fundamental movements into a graceful series of steps that might, in time, actually become a dance.

Jenny loved it all, even the tedious parts. She loved the fact that here was something that could be learned, perfected, that, once learned, would be hers forever, that no one would be able to take her dancing away from her, not a wicked stepmother or a careless father, not anyone.

Jenny became a sponge for learning. She came early. She stayed late. She practiced at home until it taxed even the patience of Privy. For hours, on a Sunday, when there was no class, Jenny would stand in the living room, holding the arm of a chair for a barre, doing her tendus and pliés and battements. The extra work showed; when her instructor first praised her progress, Jenny didn't know what to say. It wasn't for praise that she worked. It was so that she wouldn't lose any time, on her way to becoming a dancer. "Thank you," was what she said, very quietly, to the instructor, and then went back to the barre.

The moment came when Jenny realized her imaginary friend Gustave hadn't visited her for months.

After the first year Jenny skipped a class, was promoted to dance with the eleven-year-olds. Madame taught this class herself, and Jenny hung on her every word. "Ballet," Madame said one day, "is a line drawing. Think! The highest leap, the longest balance en pointe, the quickest pirouette mean nothing if the line is not complete. We want one elegant, unbroken line from the tip of your finger to the tip of your toe. It should be possible to take a moving picture of a good ballet dancer and stop that film at any one frame and see—always—a perfect line."

When Jenny first heard those words, she wondered precisely what Madame meant. But Jenny wasn't an architect's daughter for nothing. She asked her father for examples. First he said, "Botticelli." Jenny looked in the Botticelli picture book and began to see what Clifford Hale was getting at, the languid curlicues of hair, the boneless arms of Venus surfing in on her scallop shell, yes, there was line.

Jenny asked Gloria about line, and Gloria said, "Balenciaga!" instantly, and gave examples.

When Jenny asked Privy, Privy took her to the zoo and brought her to the panther's cage. "That," said Miss Privet, pointing to the elegant cat that seemed to flow, rather than walk, even in a cage, "that is line, darling, and in motion. A swan has line, but swans don't really move, they're frozen, if you take my meaning." Jenny began to understand about line.

Madame was stern, but fair, and sometimes had a kind word for Jenny.

Some of the kids made fun of Madame, but Jenny paid no more attention to the kidding than she did to her father's increasing fits of drunkenness. Someone in dance class told Jenny in all seriousness that Madame had cloven hooves, that Madame was forever *non grata* in Monaco, that Madame had been the mistress of a king; these legends were part of the mythology of the school, and many of the kids accepted them as fact. Jenny didn't accept them or reject them; they simply didn't matter.

She had never been a gregarious child. If Jenny was lonely, in fact, she somehow never felt lonely, never thought about the possibility of having a circle of friends, of larks and parties and giggling and the other kinds of fun young girls seem to thrive on.

Dancing became more and more the center of her life. The intensity that Jenny devoted to her dancing was startling in a girl approaching ten years of age, but it wasn't startling to anyone who had a chance to see the girl in class. Without ever becoming aware of it, Jenny Hale eclipsed all the girls her age. She never thought of class as a competition. Except in questions of choreography, of matching figures and partnerships, she hardly thought of the other children at all. They simply didn't exist for her.

At home, things were going from bad to worse. Jenny would never know how hard Privy worked to shield her from Cliff Hale's escalating drunkenness and irresponsibility. Jenny loved her father, but she was used to the sight of him drunk now, to his unfocused speeches and unfulfilled promises. Her response was to retreat ever further into her dancing.

In the winter of Jenny's tenth year Gloria Bruce moved on to greener pastures.

Jenny knew things hadn't been going well for Daddy and Gloria. There had been loud arguments, ever-more-frequent trips out of town for both of them, more drinking for Daddy. She thought about that one icy December evening as she walked back from Madame's class. She thought of a way to cheer him up.

Madame was stingy with praise and famous for the stinginess. But today, and for the first time this year, and in front of everybody, Madame had praised Jenny! Madame was a fiend for reverences, the classical ballerina's curtsy. And today, after an hour at the barre doing grands rounds de jambes jetés, had come an interlude of practicing the reverence. Even the older girls went at it—as Madame remarked—like so many geese. Finally, exasperated, she said, "Only Jennifer looks as if she is *not* suffering from some incurable disease. Please, please, children, try to do it like Jennifer." There were giggles and mutterings, and Jenny blushed deep red. But she was thrilled to her toes. She'd tell Daddy all about it.

Jenny had her own key to the apartment now. She sensed something wrong as she opened the front door. There was music playing loudly. Privy never played music loudly. The music itself was dark and cold as the night outside: Sibelius. Jenny put her dance bag on the bench in the hall and followed the music into the living room. Privy was nowhere to be seen.

"Hi, Daddy." One look told her what to expect. Clifford Hale was slouched in a Louis XVI wing chair by the fire, and only firelight illuminated the big high-ceilinged room. On the floor next to Daddy's chair was a silver ice bucket, and in the bucket were two bottles of Dom Pérignon champagne, *très chic,* Gloria's favorite. "If I am not mistaken," said Cliff Hale

thickly, "it is my daughter, the fair Miss Sugarplum Pirouette." That was their private game, inventing funny names.
Only it wasn't funny when Daddy was plastered. Nothing
was, even though he often seemed to think so. He looked into
his glass, not at her. "Shall I tell you how I spent my afternoon?"

"Sure, Daddy. How?" Jenny didn't really want to know.
She also didn't know how to change the subject when he was
like this.

"It is a great mystery," Daddy said to no one in particular
as he stared into the half-filled champagne glass. "They come
from nowhere, and to nowhere they shall return." His voice
was heavy with its weight of bottled wisdom.

"What, Daddy? What comes from nowhere?"

"Bubbles." He sipped thoughtfully, and a small spasm of a
smile flicked on and off his lips. "Wives. Money. Pleasure.
Ideals. Champagne, Jennifer Rond de Jambe, brings the gift
of instant wisdom. Through the pure gemlike clarity of its
bubbles one sees all the future, all the past, all . . . all. . . ."
His voice trailed off.

"What did you do today, Daddy?"

"Ah." He shook his head like a big dog shaking off water.
"We digress. Today I traded in Gloria, your wicked stepmother. She belongs to the ages now, Jennifer Pas de Chat.
I am afraid her facade was cracking a little. They just don't
make 'em like they used to, kid. But, never fear. A search
is on for the new, improved model. Teams of experts have
been alerted. Some of the finest minds in the country will be
applied to the question."

"Daddy?"

"Just ask it, my sweet Fouetté, and it is yours."

"Why do you have to marry them?"

"Such a philosopher, and yet so young." Cliff Hale reached
for the bottle and refilled his glass nearly to the brim. He put
the bottle back, gently, and raised his glass toward his daughter, who sat on the ivory-and-blue Persian carpet by the fire.
She had wanted to ask this question for years and never
dared. And now, even before he answered, Jenny knew it was
too late. "Why do I marry 'em? Let me count the ways." He
fixed her with a stare of mock ferocity.

"You aren't the first female to ask me that one, kid. I
marry them, Jenny-Jennifer, because I am an optimist. All artists are optimists, or they'd never lift a brush or a pen or a

brick. I marry the wretches in the face of all the evidence of my not-yet-entirely-decayed mind because my heart wants silver linings and the Easter bunny and gold at the end of the rainbow. I marry them, little Jenny, because the way some people thirst for water I thirst for something to believe in. And after a certain point it isn't enough simply to believe in Mozart or the cathedral at Chartres or twelfth-century Khmer Buddhas. I want to—have to—believe in the perfectability of the human spirit, in the possibility of love. . . ." At this moment the record got stuck in a groove; Clifford Hale set down his wineglass and lurched to his feet to fix it. He walked across the big room as though it were a minefield. Gently, with a draftsman's touch, he corrected the stuck needle. Then he turned back toward his chair, slipped on the waxed floor and fell with a crash. He lay silent for a moment, then looked up at Jenny. "I fell."

"Are you all right, Daddy?" Jenny was trying to remember if they'd finally paid the doctor's bill, if it would be possible to call him now.

"Hunky-dory. A-one. Acme-Peerless. Hand me my glass, honey. I'm getting to like the view from down here." She did that.

"Good night, Daddy."

"Jenny?"

"What, Daddy?" She was frightened now. He'd never been this bad before.

"I've had a pretty rough day."

"I know. I'm sorry." Jenny thought: *Now I'll tell him.* Then she looked at her father and knew his mind was somewhere else; somewhere it had floated on the small, expensive bubbles of Gloria's *très chic* champagne, somewhere, maybe, where women who looked as perfect as Gloria Bruce on the outside were equally beautiful on the inside. Jenny couldn't tell him now. She might not ever be able to tell him. He lay where he had fallen, sprawled on the old Persian rug in front of the fireplace, his glass lifted to catch the reflected glow. She turned.

"Good night, Jenny Pavlova."

"Good night, Charlie Chartres." Jenny hoped he didn't hear the sobs building in her voice.

Fame crept up on Jenny like a thief. She never dreamed of glory, not even this night, the night of the first *Giselle*, when there had been glory all around her, by her and for her. Jenny lay in the narrow white bed and watched the shadows of branches dancing on her ceiling. These were expensive shadows. The tree that threw them grew on Fifth Avenue near the corner of Seventy-fourth Street. Jenny wondered how much longer they'd be able to keep the apartment. It had been paid for long ago, in cash, when cash was no problem. But the upkeep kept going up, and her father's income kept going down. The place was too big anyway. It would cost a fortune to refurnish it properly. And even if she could afford to do that, Jenny wasn't sure she wanted to. The memories inside these walls were not happy ones. Maybe it would be better if she and Privy took a smaller place on the West Side, closer to the theater. She was determined that no matter what, Privy would be with her forever.

Jenny turned from her back to her side, knowing as she did it that sleep was far away. As far as Dimitri. But she'd thought too much about Dimitri.

Dimitri, so far, was an incident. He might never be more than that. It was pure chance that de Lis had broken his own long-standing rule by inviting the young Russian to be guest artist. And it was even more of a chance—a miracle!—that de Lis had chosen her to be Dimitri's partner.

The one predictable thing about Alexander de Lis was unpredictability. He struck like lightning, and no one knew why. Not even, Jenny often thought, de Lis himself. Yet from the age of ten, his had been the major influence on her life. More than Privy, much more than her father, more than Madame, who was, after all, merely his deputy in the Children's School, de Lis had woven a tight golden net around Jennifer Hale. And as the years sped by, Jenny never once stopped to think just what a snare it had become, and how tightly spun, and how very comfortable.

Jenny cherished her memory of the day when de Lis had first seen her dance with all the care another girl might give some fragile family heirloom.

It was spring, April, and time had mellowed even this to the symbolism of a new beginning. Jenny was eleven now.

Three years had passed since a frightened eight-year-old sparrow of a child had first set foot in the big shabby room. Jenny had grown, and she was no longer frightened. But there would always be something more of the air than of the

earth about her, the look of a creature poised for flight. It
could be disconcerting across a dinner table, but it was pure
magic onstage. They were rehearsing *The Nutcracker*. This
was the Civic's famous Christmas production, but rehearsals
started in the spring of the year before. Madame had cast
Jenny as one of the Dew Drops. It would be her first time in
a real production, on a real stage. And even now, more than
half a year ahead, she could feel the excitement building.

So far it had been like every other class: an hour of drill
at the barre with the tempo set by the piano, then center-floor
work in groups, now a short rehearsal. Just after the rehearsal
began, Jenny sensed a ripple of excitement in her group.
Some of the girls giggled; some grew suddenly more serious
and haughty-looking; some made mistakes. Then Jenny knew.
"De Lis!" someone hissed through clenched teeth.

One of the assistants was conducting the class now. In the
shadows at the back of the studio Jenny could see Madame
standing close to a man, a stranger, whispering. The stranger
must be de Lis, the Wizard of Oz, the power behind the entire Civic Ballet.

Jenny would not turn from her assigned choreography to
stare at the man who might hold the secret of her future.

Only when the music and the movement turned her head
in that direction would she look. Alexander de Lis, in the distance and the shadows, looked slight, gray, unprepossessing.
He wasn't much taller than Madame, slim, graying, with a
high forehead and an eagle's beaked nose and an eagle's
bright eyes.

The other girls, thought Jenny, were being silly. So what if
Madame had an important visitor? Madame often had visitors, and many of them were well known: dancers, former
pupils, other teachers, musicians. Jenny, as always, concentrated on improving her line. She had been having a problem
with a certain movement of her wrist: how to make it flow
more gracefully in port de bras. She concentrated on that and
the music, and soon she almost forgot the visitor. They were
rehearsing the groupings for *Nutcracker* now. Madame had
placed one of the older girls at the head of the line of Dew
Drops, and Jenny was third from the front. The familiar
Tchaikovsky tune came tinkling from the piano. Out from
behind an imaginary set of stage wings came the Dew Drops.
Jenny knew her steps well, had known them from the second
day. The choreography was de Lis' own, simple but charm-

ing. The Dew Drops were glad to be part of the Sugar Plum
Fairy's festival; Jenny smiled to show it. She was wearing
a ratty practice leotard left over from last year. Privy said
they'd have to make it last as long as possible. There was a
patched spot on the leotard. Jenny wondered if de Lis noticed
things like that. There was no point in wondering. It was the
only leotard she had.

From the back of the studio Alex de Lis watched the little
dancers. He seldom came to Madame's classes until the children were thirteen or fourteen, when you could get a clear
picture of what they'd be like in a year or two when they'd
be ripe for the Civic. Madame's message had been simple.
"There is one," she had said on the telephone, "that you
should see now."

He stood with her now in the classroom, and it was as if
they were in a world beyond time. How often had they stood
thus, judging, hoping, guiding!

They went back a long way, de Lis and Madame, back
fifty years and more, back to the Maryinsky before Pe-
tersburg became Petrograd, let alone Leningrad, back to a
time when the Winter Palace blazed with candles and rang
with laughter and the rattle of ropes of jewels.

They had seen it all, had de Lis and Madame. Times might
change, empires might crumble, Europe and all the Russians
might splash the chameleon map with the blood of two un-
speakable wars, and still, de Lis would make dances and
Madame would make dancers to dance them. So it had always been, so it would be until one day they died backstage
or onstage, which was their fondest dream. And in the meantime, there was so much to do! Their heads teemed with
dreams, plans, hopes. No teenagers saw the future in such a
rosy light. This was what kept them alive, kept them young,
fed the creative fires. He stood silent for a few minutes and
then touched her arm. "And this prodigy is. . . ."

"You tell me." It was an old game between them.

"There. The Dew Drop. With the eyes."

"Exactly. Jennifer Hale."

"Yet you hide her in the line."

"She is eleven, Alexis. She has time."

"As always, Madame is right." His mockery was light, the
earned privilege of ancient friendship.

"You were always a rogue, Alexis Lisczhensky." Madame
claimed never to have forgiven him for Frenchifying the

name when they'd all fled to France with Diaghilev in the
twenties.

"But never with you, Katerina Fyodorovna."

"Which is whose loss?" She laughed, and de Lis heard the
young girl in it, eager, just up from the chorus in Maryinsky.
It had never been a romance between them. It was something
beyond that. Alex de Lis had had five wives and who could
count how many lovers, and where were they now? This had
endured, and the dance.

"We may never know, Madame. In any case, you are right.
We will keep an eye on that one, that. . . ."

"Jennifer Hale."

"It will do." He meant the name. Already de Lis was imagining that name on theater programs, on marquees. More
than once he had persuaded a girl to change her name when
it was unsuitable. He looked at Jenny, who did not look
back. Then he kissed Madame's hand and vanished. The class
became just a class again. Madame never mentioned de Lis
to Jenny Hale. There would be time enough for that.
Madame looked at the girl in the full knowledge of all that
might lie in store for her. *I want to be a dancer because
dancers make people happy.* Even now Jenny Hale's eyes
loomed huge and tragic in her small face. Madame sighed
and resumed control of the rehearsal. What would be would
be.

The shadows still danced on Jenny's ceiling. The fat hands
of her old Big Ben alarm clock greenly announced three-
thirty. She usually went to bed early, by eleven at the latest,
and slept, as Privy put it, "Like a toad in winter." But not
this night. What, she wondered, was her heart turning into
that she didn't feel the excitement? Count sheep. Count fou-
ettes. Count Dimitris.

Other first nights, not starring Jennifer Hale, had sent electricity through her until she thought it'd make her hair stand
on end. That first *Nutcracker!* Even the first time with Gloria
Bruce, at *Sleeping Beauty.* At this rate she'd be a disaster by
morning. And morning was coming; that was one thing you
could count on, even if you were Jenny Hale.

Morning was coming, and so was class, and after that rehearsal. And, of course, Dimitri. *Good morning, Dimitri. Oh?
You missed the party? I hardly noticed.* What would she say
to him? How could she look at him? Let alone dance with

him. You were supposed to be professional. You were supposed to be able to work with your worst enemy, if you had a worst enemy. *Are you going to be my worst enemy, Dimitri Lubov?*

What would I give, Jenny asked herself, *for one drop of Iris Dowling's sex appeal?* It all came so easily to Iris. Even the boys who were gay flocked around her. And Jenny? She'd never wanted a friend, and she'd almost never had one. Iris was as close to a girlfriend as she'd ever known, and that wasn't saying much. Iris was naturally warm and friendly to everyone. Even if it meant going to bed with him.

You couldn't really call Machito a friend. He was friendly, even now. He had been more than that. A lover. Right in this bed, too. At least she could smile when she remembered the loving. At least she didn't hate him. How could you hate Machito? It would be as silly as hating rainbows. Or building your future on a rainbow. Maybe Machito was right: *Life is short, don't take it so seriously, don't cry over the spilled milk, Jenny, go fill your glass again, and maybe with wine.* But she couldn't be like Machito any more than she could be like Iris. At that moment Jenny wasn't even sure she could be like Jenny, whatever that was. She relived *Giselle,* step by step, gesture by gesture. Somewhere about halfway through the second act, sleep finally caught her.

Dimitri's cab racketed up the empty streets of two A.M., making haste toward the Dakota. If he knew his dancers, the de Lis party would still be going on. If God was good, Jenny would still be there. Dimitri perched on the edge of the seat, tense, straining forward. The night's energy bubbled in him still, barely repressed all through Judith Winchester's dull party. He needed to dance, to sing, to make love, and all with Jenny Hale. He left the driver blinking at a five, sprinted past the nodding doorman and prayed on his mother's icon, all the way up in the lurching elevator, that she'd still be there.

The party Dimitri walked in on was not the party Jenny left. The mood was quieter now, more intense. Those who stayed were there because they were too immersed in wine or sentiment to venture out into the unforgiving night. Smoke and guttering candles thickened the atmosphere. The piano had stopped and someone was picking out half-remembered gypsy ballads on a balalaika. Dimitri found de Lis, made his apologies and was handed a glass of red wine. "Thank you,

Mr. de Lis," he said, lifting the glass, "you have given me a wonderful Giselle."

"No, Dimitri." Alex de Lis smiled his fox's smile. "God has given both of us a wonderful Giselle. And surely the finest Albrecht of this generation." De Lis couldn't bring himself to expand the compliment; had he not, after all, danced the role himself, and nobly well?

"Jenny has gone?"

"An hour ago. Have you eaten?"

"Thank you. Yes."

"Then play a little, young Lubov. It's good for the bones." They exchanged smiles across the shortening distance of nearly fifty years between them and became in that moment simply two Russian dancers, alone, who shared some of the same secrets. *Five wives,* thought Dimitri, *and all of them ballerinas. There has to be one bone it's good for, at any rate!* Alex de Lis patted the boy on the shoulder and thought, *He might possibly be managed, but he will never be tamed.* And even though de Lis knew too well what havoc that might bring to the Swiss-watch perfection of the Civic Ballet, he couldn't help admiring young Lubov. No one had ever tamed Alex de Lis, either.

Dimitri left his host and wandered about the big apartment, smiling, mingling, but not really feeling part of it. Why hadn't she waited? He'd told her he'd be there. Was there someone else? Could a girl like Jenny fail to have dozens of suitors? Had she been faking onstage? Not possible. If Dimitri knew anything, he knew that. She wouldn't know how. Still . . . where was she?

Iris Dowling appeared out of the shadows and kissed him, long and wet and coated with wine. It was more than a kiss. It was an invitation. "Hi." The creamy skin of her face was flushed, and there was a fine film of sweat on her upper lip. The long black hair streamed out behind her as if stirred by some unfelt but wild wind. She was the soul and image of a strumpet, and it suddenly occurred to Dimitri that a strumpet might be just what he needed.

"Hi." He grinned the famous urchin's grin.

"You were nifty tonight, Dimitri."

"What means nifty?"

"Great, terrific, classy, sensational."

"You danced well also."

"Thanks. I do a lot of things well." She squeezed his hand,

and a wave of heat surged through him. Dimitri looked into her eyes and returned the pressure of her hand. If the plums were going to drop off the tree on you, it would be pitiful not to taste them. Especially such a juicy plum. "Come," he said. She never took her eyes off his, but only nodded.

Dave Loughlin liked the weight of the blue manila folder. When the Old Man gave the nod, headquarters jumped. The folder, packed with the promise of action, was the first result of the Old Man's belief in Dave's crackpot theory. Somewhere, buried in red Virginia clay under CIA/HQ at Langley, was a vast computer named FRED. FRED's owner was the Records Integration Division. Integrated was hardly the word for it. It had everything about everything, and FRED could spit it out in minutes, when the right buttons were pressed. With, needless to say, the right authorization.

It took more self-control than Dave Loughlin was used to practicing not to tear open the folder and read its contents right there in the corridor. Inside was a mound of raw information that might contain the clue to the plot. If it was a plot. He had to keep telling himself "if." In the folder were several dossiers, one each for the three dead defectors, and others, from Dave's own random list of similar defectors who might be targets for Ivan's revenge.

The Old Man had given Dave the green light. There would be an official investigation now, and with Dave at the head of it. Police cooperation would be requested, locally and internationally: Switzerland, Ireland and California. Maybe there'd be a little freebie traveling. But anyway, there'd be action, a chance to get the old juices flowing one more time.

Dave looked at his watch. It was almost lunchtime. He walked out past the blind lunch counter, shuddering a little, as always. For the first time in a long time, he didn't care if he had a drink with lunch. He walked briskly down the polished green hallway and checked himself out. Dave felt like someone seriously ill who'd been given a new lease on life. He'd read that folder tonight. Tomorrow he'd have a plan, some plan, who knew what? Dave pushed open the impressive glass door and walked down the granite steps to the visitors' parking lot. He sniffed the air like an inquisitive rabbit. There was rain in that gray Virginia sky. Then, for the first time that day, Dave Loughlin grinned, ear to ear. He was back in the saddle again!

CHAPTER
❧ 5 ❧

Dimitri woke smiling. The girl must have let herself out sometime in the night. He stretched in the big bed, deliberately prolonging the moment of opening his eyes. The sheets, cool on his skin, were one of Dimitri's luxuries. He allowed himself many small indulgences, and most of them were traceable back to his dirt-poor boyhood on the outskirts of a town named Saratov, on the bank of the Volga.

Dimitri Lubov had been twelve before he knew the touch of clean sheets on his skin, and even they had been the coarse and mended linen of the Kirov Ballet School in Leningrad. And if, today, at twenty-four, his sheets came from Porthault and cost more than a hundred dollars each, who was to complain? Certainly not the girls who shared them so willingly. Surely not Iris Dowling. He grinned, opened his eyes, surveyed the big room.

Alex de Lis had helped Dimitri find the apartment. De Lis was interested in every aspect of his dancer's lives, from the balance of the newest girl in the corps de ballet, en pointe, to the balance of a principal dancer's diet. Given half a chance, the saying went, de Lis would run your life from dawn to dawn, everyone's mother hen. Some of the dancers loved it, not having to make decisions. Dimitri, for the moment, found it amusing. And he appreciated the help; de Lis knew what strings to pull and how to pull them.

If Dimitri stayed with the Civic—and he knew de Lis wanted him to stay—he'd see if the old fox could get the Soviet to liberate his mother. That, to be sure, would take some doing. Still, in the meantime, the lady was well taken care of; Dimitri's sister had done herself well. Kyra Lubov was a researcher in pediatric medicine with her own spacious flat in Moscow, and there his mother lived in more comfort than she had ever known. It might be too late. Dimitri realized, for the old woman to learn new ways, a new language. He wondered what she'd make of this apartment, this fabulous city, his new life here.

The entire top floor of a brownstone on West Seventy-fourth Street had been gutted to make Dimitri's apartment. It had a huge living room with skylights and a fireplace, one big bedroom and a kitchen in an ell. He had been in New York three months, and the place was still mostly unfurnished. There was the big bed, some plants, a fat brown leather couch in front of the fireplace and a few red canvas director's chairs. Still, Dimitri loved it as much as any palace. His first real home! He would furnish it, in time, and he'd furnish it well. Interesting, to see how de Lis lived. The creator of some of the most modern choreography the world had ever seen kept his private life in a sort of museum of eighteenth-century Europe. That would not be Dimitri's style. He wasn't sure what his style would be, but it wouldn't be that. And in the meantime, he could use a cup of tea.

Simon Bridge permitted himself a smile. As he reread the *Giselle* review, he had to admit it was one of his better efforts.

DETENTE DANCES

Jennifer Hale and Dimitri Lubov excel in Civic Ballet's "Giselle"

What politicans have struggled to do, in vain, for years, Alexander de Lis has achieved in a few short weeks on the stage of the New York State Theater. His production of "Giselle" unites the USSR and the USA in one artistic entity that shows every sign of becoming a landmark in the history of American ballet.

In Jennifer Hale, de Lis has come up with a young talent who redefines this great classic role. Too often, we see ballerinas skillfully pretending to be Giselle. Miss Hale convinces us she *is* Giselle. Her technique, to be sure, is all but impeccable. But greatness begins where technique leaves off, and it is here that the 19-year-old native New Yorker astounds us. Jennifer Hale infuses the 134-year-old warhorse of a role with a freshness and vitality that instantly invite comparison with the greatest

Giselles of the past and the present. We not only admire her, but we believe her. It was a pleasure to be present at the debut (in a major role) of a blazing new talent. Miss Hale brought the house down, and deserved to.

Dimitri Lubov, deservedly famous for his Albrecht, his Romeo, his Corsaire and his Bayadère in the Kirov versions, amply justified his reputation as Albrecht to Miss Hale's Giselle. Here, too, one sees masterful dancing fused to equally masterful acting. Lubov's Albrecht is alternately bold and tender, defiant and repentant, and always, always a glorious specimen of Russian athleticism at its finest.

The quality of ballon has been discussed to death, yet every time we see it carried to its utmost it astounds us all over again. It is said that Nijinsky could leap high into the air with no apparent preparation and hang there like a hummingbird. Nureyev used to do this. Lubov does it, too, with an offhand, casual-seeming grace that is literally breathtaking.

Yet his performance is not merely fireworks. Lubov reacts, he listens, he loves, he is involved. Where many of our principal male dancers display all the emotion of a felled tree, Dimitri Lubov radiates passion. Lubov's Albrecht is no trifling Transylvanian playboy. He cares, and he makes us care with him. We share the joy of his courtship, the triumph of his love, his grief at Giselle's death, his mad defiance of Myrtha's death sentence and, in the final sequence, a poignant and truly melancholy regret. In other words, Lubov milks the part for all it's worth, does it magnificently, and does it all while dancing Albrecht as well as I, for one, have ever seen it danced.

Miss Hale and Mr. Lubov may come from different worlds. But together, onstage, they create a new and better world. Mr. de Lis and his dancers are to be congratulated. They are making history.

The review went on. Simon Bridge had kind words to say about the entire production. It was what producers like to call a money review, the kind of glowing notice that makes stars overnight and, better yet, makes lines at the box office. Suddenly *Giselle* would be a hot ticket. New forces would be set in motion. Nothing for Jenny and Dimitri would be quite the same again.

Jenny saw the review at breakfast. Privy read it aloud, and then Jenny read it all over again, and still, she couldn't guess the impact it would have.

"I can't remember," said Privy, "ever reading a better ballet review. It will be the making of you, my pet."

"Oh, Privy. It's just one review. Next week or the week after, no one will even remember it." Jenny knew a review this good was not an unmixed blessing. It meant she'd have to be even better the next time she danced, and the time after that. The level of expectation was being raised on her, just the way a high jumper's bar is raised in competition, raised higher and higher until inevitably the moment comes when even the best, highest jumper misses, falls, his reputation falling with him.

The Simon Bridge review meant the dancers in the Civic Ballet who resented Jenny a little for getting the plum part would now resent her even more. And even de Lis himself might not be pleased. Maybe the review was too extravagant. Jenny knew de Lis was death on "stars." And this was definitely a star-making review. And how would Dimitri react, Dimitri who was already famous, to have this upstart young girl so well reviewed, as though she were already his equal?

"I guess," said Jenny in a small voice, "we ought to save it for Daddy." Privy looked at the girl. There was nothing Privy could say about Cliff Hale anymore, and nothing she could do. It was a lucky thing, thought Jessica Privet, that Jenny had her dancing.

"We'll save it, my girl, for *posterity!* Today I'm going out and getting a big, beautiful new Jennifer Hale scrapbook. I have a feeling the old one is too small for what may be coming." Privy poured more tea. "Then you'll have it to show your grandchildren one day."

"If Mr. de Lis found me getting pregnant," said Jenny with a giggle, "he would personally murder me."

"Mr. de Lis may not always be the most important man in your life, Jenny."

"You mean some other man is going to come along and sweep me off my poor, aching feet? You think that's possible?"

"The beautiful thing, my poppet, about being young," said Privy in her best Woman of the World imitation, "is that everything is possible."

"I'll take your word for it. But don't hold your breath."

Jenny got up from the table. If she didn't hurry, she'd be late for class. And review or no review, de Lis could get furious when his principal dancers showed up late.

Alexander de Lis also read the Simon Bridge review over breakfast. He read it twice and smiled a thin and foxy smile. Better and better! He trusted his instinct with a fine fanatical belief, but even so, it was a good thing to have his instinct so elaborately confirmed, and by the most influential ballet critic in the world. Was it nine years ago that Madame had summoned him to her studio?

As always, before coffee, de Lis had done his half hour of warm-up at the barre. Now he sprang up from his breakfast and circled the practice room in a great thrusting series of *jetés en tournants par terre en manège,* spread-eagled leaps and pivoting turns linked one after the other in a breathtaking chain. Laughing, he stopped when he had circled the room back to the little table where he started. Seventy-two years old and hardly out of breath. The exercise helped him think. There were times, he knew, when he could think only in motion. The choreographer's curse. His body more articulate than his mind. De Lis sat down again and sipped his tea. He was going to have to do some serious thinking about Miss Jennifer Hale.

Judith Winchester had the review read to her during her massage. Every morning at seven-thirty the famous blind Japanese masseur Waldo Ninimaya spent twenty minutes stretching and pounding and stroking Judith's piano-wire muscles and tendons into shape.

Waldo was the ballet dancer's favorite masseur. He worked on Nureyev, on Dame Margot when she was in town, on all the great ones. He was a short, muscular man, completely bald, who might have been almost any age. Waldo was booked months in advance at fifty dollars per session. He was worth it. Magic flowed through Waldo Ninimaya's strong fingers. He could untie a knotted muscle, relax a strained tendon, soothe and pummel and pamper all the aches and stresses dancers are heir to.

Judith Winchester used him because he was one more entrée into the world of ballet. Waldo was reputed to know everything about everyone in ballet. So far he had been absolutely discreet with Judith. But instinct told her that sooner or later Waldo Ninimaya would be useful, and her instinct rarely failed. In the meantime, it felt good. And the time was far from wasted, for a private secretary read through *The New York Times* during the session.

"Mr. de Lis and his dancers," read the secretary, "are to be congratulated. They are making history."

"That's enough of that." Her voice, dealing with servants, was like a rasp. Judith closed her eyes. Pages turned. The secretary was a fool, but a well-connected fool, the not-terribly-bright nephew of the current ambassador to France. The uncle was useful to the Winchester publishing empire, so the nephew was kept on. He read a financial item that Judith had caused to be planted. She smiled. Waldo's hands worked on her back. The review was dazzling. What fun it was going to be, taking Lubov away from Alex de Lis! What havoc it would cause in the International, bringing in a new star right in the midst of the season. Maybe this way she could get Greg Holden mad enough to quit and put in her own man.

The secretary's voice droned on. Judith thought of stopping him but didn't. Instead, she thought of Dimitri Lubov, not of his dancing, but the boy himself. There must be a way to get to him. It was only a question of time. Waldo was working on her calf muscles now. He was nearly done. Next she'd spend fifteen minutes in her sauna, dictating the morning's memos into a built-in tape recorder. Then a bath. Then to the office. She allowed her mind to drift a little. It was a good feeling, knowing her plans for the International Ballet were taking shape at last. She could feel the power building, just as she could feel the strength flowing from Waldo Ninimaya's magic hands. The International Ballet needed to be shown who was boss. And Judith Winchester was exactly the person to do it. And soon.

Dimitri's English was still in a formative stage. He could speak it with some difficulty, although, being a natural mime, he had no trouble getting himself understood. But reading was another matter. So Dimitri, alone of all the principals in the ballet, did not read the Simon Bridge review with his breakfast. He read nothing at all, but merely put an old Beatles album on his expensive hi-fi system and drank tea to "Lucy in the Sky with Diamonds." Dimitri's mind ranged far and wide, but always it came back to Jenny Hale.

He would be seeing Jenny in less than an hour. And he

must finish what he had started last night, with that bunch of
violets. Jenny must be made to know what feelings were
building in him. Jenny must be made to fall in love! Dimitri
wasn't sure how that could be accomplished, but for the moment wanting it was enough. After all, wanting a role, or a
girl, or almost anything had always been enough and would
be this time. Dimitri the man might not know that for sure,
but Dimitri the street urchin knew it by heart.

He cut a ripe pear into neat wedges and ate it with his tea.
The Beatles played and sang. Dimitri was ten years old again,
always in rags, always a little hungry, running in the hills
outside Saratov, stealing apples, poaching rabbits, grabbing
stray lumps of coal from the railroad tracks and always, always running. He ran like the wind, and the wind was his
friend.

The wind had messages for young Dimitri that no one else
could hear. He would run, after school, to the top of a barren
hill behind town and lie on his belly on a big rock, the warm
rock pressing into him, solid and reassuring. He'd lie on his
rock and look down across the distant town to the river, to
the barges and freighters that were always coming and going,
and the wind would talk to him then, with stories of places
far away, where it was never cold and there was always
enough to eat.

Dimitri looked at the river and knew that it was a liquid
highway that might take him anywhere, anywhere at all. And
he knew a time would come when he would go out of this
poor little town, out of the falling-in shack they were forced
to call home, away from the hunger and the fear that worse
things might happen than had already happened, things like
having no father and never enough work for his mother, and
never enough potatoes to steal, or shoes that fit or soap to
wash with. In those days, alone on his rock, listening to the
wind, Dimitri never knew what shape his future would take.
But he did know, and with a knowledge sure as dawn, that he
had a future, that he would make it happen, that it would
take him away from Saratov, away from hunger, maybe even
away from the wind itself. And happen it did.

The voice of the wind stirred music in him. The energy
from running and hiding and poaching exploded in the school
folk-dance classes where no one had ever seen the like of
little Lubov, all fire and part bird. He was winning dance
competitions at twelve and in the same year found himself

before a grave-faced committee that offered him the rare
chance of a scholarship at the Kirov Ballet School in Leningrad. Leningrad! Dimitri had never seen a classical ballet,
but he would have gone to Leningrad to dig ditches. It was
happening, as he knew it would happen. And something
would happen with Jenny Hale, too. Dimitri knew that where
it counted: in his heart, in his bones.

Diana Leighton was never bored. If there was one basic
drive in her life, it was outwitting boredom. This battle took
time, energy, money, brains and determination. And Diana
had enjoyed all these things, to the hilt, from childhood. Diana Leighton was never bored. But as she woke this morning
in her big late-Tudor four-poster bed and looked at what lay
sleeping beside her, she thought, *The road to boredom is
paved with men like Jeremy Holt.*
   There lay Jeremy, blue of blood, cleft of chin, clubman,
sportsman, incipient bore. Jeremy made love with all the passion of a computer readout. It must be something they taught
at the Harvard Business School. Jeremy was perfect in almost
every way. He even wanted to marry her. Fat chance. But
Jeremy was the most eligible of all New York's eligible
bachelors, sought after, prized, displayed like a trophy.
   Diana shrugged, grinned and slipped out of bed. She
walked to the window and drew the pale apricot silk curtains,
opened the tall French windows and stepped out onto the
little balcony. It was seven A.M. All the gardens of Turtle Bay
lay below her, New York's most desirable secret garden,
walled on all four sides by some of New York's most fashionable brownstone town houses. Diana's house was in the
middle of the block on the north of Turtle Bay, the Forty-
ninth Street side. This meant all her back windows got the
southern sun, and the sun blessed her own section of the
walled garden. Her bedroom was on the top floor of the town
house. Diana rang for Inez, her gifted Costa Rican cook-
housekeeper, and in fluent Spanish discussed breakfast and
the menu for tonight's dinner party. Then she took a shower,
yawned and walked down to the library for breakfast and to
plan the day. Diana breakfasted on honeydew melon with
lime, China tea, and *The New York Times.* Jeremy, God
knew, could find his own way out when he recovered from
his hangover.
   Diana tasted the melon. Not bad, for November, in New

York. She leafed through the paper, which was filled with local politics. Local politics were interesting, she thought, only to local politicians. International politics were sometimes interesting.

It was interesting, for instance, that the United States was opening up negotiations with Red China. This meant that sooner or later the market for Chinese antiquities would open up in its turn, and that meant new opportunities for Diana Leighton, Ltd., New York's most exclusive private interior-decorating consultants. She must ask Uncle Alf to see about a visa. Diana didn't need the money, and everybody knew that, and that was one of the reasons why her decorating firm had had such success from the first. But there were other reasons. Diana was an art scholar, had majored in art history at Radcliffe, worked at Parke-Bernet, appraising French seventeenth- and eighteenth-century furniture, and was gifted with a painter's eye and an architect's sense of proportion. Diana Leighton, Ltd. had social cachet to match its artistic reputation. She took on very few clients, which naturally made her much more desirable. Diana had two young art students, girls, and an architect on full-time retainer. She spoke five languages and roamed the world at whim looking for works of art and rare fabrics to give the unique effect her clients expected. She accepted only carte blanche commissions from the very rich.

To have a Diana Leighton-done house or apartment was more of a status symbol than owning Rolls-Royces or racehorses, for Rolls-Royces and racehorses can be bought by anyone who has the price; Diana's services were a sign of social acceptance. It wasn't bad, she thought, squeezing more juice from her lime, for a girl not yet thirty.

Diana poured more tea. She frowned, and pulled the thin silk kimono tighter around her, and shivered, but not from cold. Her hair was honey blond and thick, loosely pulled back and tied with a brown velvet ribbon. Her eyes were gray, wide-spaced, appraising. Diana was five-six, a skier, broad-shouldered and graceful, an outdoor woman whose New York life kept her too much indoors. She thought of Jeremy and of other men. There had been too many Jeremys in her life, she decided. Not that she wasn't adventurous.

Diana had married at eighteen, against everybody's advice, a beautiful boy from Colorado, from a family nobody knew. Charlie turned out to be brutally jealous, sadistic; the marriage was annulled within a year. Thank God for no children. It had taken years to get over Charlie. And you could say this for the Jeremys of the world: they were safe. Too safe. Too predictable. Too close to boring. She turned the page. There was Simon Bridge's review, illustrated with a big dramatic picture of Dimitri Lubov, staring passionately at Jenny Hale.

Diana held the paper quite still, and sipped her cooling tea. There was a face. There was a man. There was no Jeremy. She knew just a little about Dimitri Lubov, not because of his dancing, but because of the sensation he'd caused last year— or was it the year before?—by skipping out of the Kirov tour and into the waiting arms of Felice de la Tour-Fontaine.

Felice and Diana sometimes moved in the same orbit, and Diana well knew that when Felice took a lover, he must be some lover. And now Dimitri Lubov was in New York, without Felice. She could hardly imagine a face like that, a talent like that, a reputation like that being lonely. But you never knew. She looked at her wristwatch, the familiar rectangle of Cartier's Tank Watch, but with a special soft patina. For unlike the glossy fakes that suddenly seemed to be everywhere, Diana's watch had come to her from her grandfather, who had actually worn it in a tank, in the trenches of World War I. It was only eight-thirty. Too early to call her ticket broker. Still, Diana Leighton had come to a decision. The next time Dimitri Lubov danced in *Giselle,* she was going to be in the audience. In the meantime, there was the Parke-Bernet catalogue to study. The auction began at ten, and there was a celadon vase of the Sung Dynasty that would look just right against the pale-apricot velvet of her bedroom walls. With a little luck, she might be able to get it for under ten thousand dollars. Diana smiled. She would get the Sung Dynasty vase. And anything else she put her mind to.

Jenny went to rehearsal in blue jeans, an old sweater and a Navy-surplus pea jacket, carrying her worn canvas dance bag and a sandwich in a brown paper bag. It was eight-forty-five. Class began at nine. Jenny hurried across the big empty plaza that was framed on three sides by three palatial tributes to the musical life of New York: the Metropolitan Opera, the Philharmonic, and the New York State Theater, home of the Civic Ballet, the City Opera, and whatever ballet and opera companies could squeeze in when the resident companies

were away. It was cold. The Simon Bridge review was wonderful, but it hadn't cheered Jenny out of the gloom left over
from last night. She'd heard about women who went into
deep depressions after having babies. Maybe this was some
crazy version of the same thing. Jenny walked faster.

Suddenly she jumped. There was a hand on her arm! All
set to scream, she turned and confronted the owner of the
hand. Dimitri's grin warmed the chill morning. "Good morning, Mademoiselle Giselle." Was there a mockery in his
voice?

"Dimitri. Hi. Have you read the review?" He, too, was in
blue jeans, and old sweater, a kind of ski jacket. Shabby re-
cruits in the same underpaid army.

"I am reading ultimately only Russian and a little in
French. But last evening de Lis says Bridge likes us."

"You bet he did. You made it to the party after all?"
Jenny wanted to flirt, to tease, to say something provocative.
She didn't know how.

"Late. I am sorry. I . . . wanted to see you." He took her
hand, and it seemed the most natural thing in the world.

Jenny thought: *Some one'll see us holding hands. The
tongues will wag; they'll have us in the sack when he hasn't
even kissed me. Yet.*

"I'm sorry, too. I didn't stay long. I was tired after all
that."

"Jenny, could we be having supper tonight?" They were at
the stage door. *Giselle* would run for a week, but tonight and
tomorrow night other dancers would replace Jenny and Dimitri.

"I'd love to. Thank you. Pick me up around seven." Jenny
always carried some of her father's cards. She found one in
her worn purse and gave it to Dimitri.

"You are not married?"

She laughed. "That's my father. No, Dimitri. I am a spinster."

"What means spinster?"

"Old maid . . . unmarried lady . . . female bachelor."

"You are not those things." He said it quietly, the blue
eyes searching for hidden meanings.

"Not yet anyway." She smiled and squeezed his hand,
friend to friend. I'll see you at seven then." Jenny was
thrilled. She forgot the tears and the sleepless night and her
doubts. Quickly, if just for a moment, Jennifer Hale became

every young girl in the world looking forward to a big date.
What would she wear? What would she say? Was he just
being polite, or was he really interested? She rushed in to
change, and to class, and had no more time to think that day.

They were in the same class, but so were seventy-three
other dancers. All lined up at the barre, all doing the same
repetitive exercises to the same familiar beat. Freddie Momontov ran the big classes for de Lis. If the dancing bear of
old Russia had a sense of humor, he might have looked like
Freddie. Fyodor Momontov was in textbooks. He had been a
Kirov dancer, a Diaghilev mime, and the dance master for de
Lis ever since there had been a Civic. Freddie was every
young dancer's confidant, the den mother of them all, gruff
on the surface and melted butter within, a perfect foil to the
implacable, inscrutable and all-powerful Alexander de Lis.
Freddie called the steps, kept them trying their hardest,
drilled the corps and principals and soloists alike, until they
felt their feet would drop off then and there.

Every dancer at the long barre did the same steps in much
the same way. To a casual stranger, it might have been a picture of symmetry. But every dancer at the barre was an island unto himself, unaware of what went on around him,
working out his own special problems in his own special way.

Every dancer was on trial, and the incorruptible mirror
was judge. For two hours, seventy-five of the world's most accomplished ballet dancers worked side by side with their
images in the huge cold mirror. Jenny could have worked at
the barre all day, and right next to Dimitri, and had no more
communication with him than if he'd been in China. They
strained. They made faces at the mirror. They sweated, and
they sweated. The old rehearsal piano banged on, playing
classic after classic, and through it all Freddie Momontov
kept them going, warmed them up, set new exercises, moved
up and down the line, correcting a leg here, the angle of a
neck there, a dancer's phrasing someplace else. No one was
immune: a kid in the corps might be singled out for praise, a
famous principal dancer mocked for being lazy or self-indulgent or too fat. There was no place, Jenny thought, so dem-
ocratic as a ballet class.

After an hour at the barre Freddie let them do some center
work. Still, Jenny and Dimitri were at opposite ends of the
big hall, paired with other dancers, doing other things. In the
afternoon she had a rehearsal, not with Dimitri. How many

years till tonight? Jenny smiled at her partner and went into
the pas de deux.

Privy, as always, did miracles. Jenny called her at
lunchtime in a panic; she had nothing to wear! It couldn't be
the dress of last night, not in a public restaurant. And Jenny
owned only three other dresses, one definitely for summer,
the other two just not right. Jenny wasn't sure what she'd find
when she got home, but knowing Privy, there would be something. And sure enough, on sale and in the teenage section of
Saks, the dauntless Miss Privet unearthed an emerald-green
woolen wrap skirt that just fitted Jenny's twenty-inch waist.
That, with an ivory turtleneck and boots she already had and
her mother's gold rope, made Jenny feel suddenly grown up.
She rushed home from rehearsal, showered, washed her hair
and wore it long, brushed straight back, falling halfway down
her slim back.

"You look lovely, darling."

"I'd die if Dimitri knew I own exactly four dresses."

"Nonsense. How many dresses do you think people own in
Russia? If he likes you, my pet, it won't be because of your
wardrobe. And, if he has any sense at all, he will like you."
Privy warmed herself in the reflection of Jenny's happiness. It
had been some time since the girl had looked forward to a
date with this much expectation.

"You should see the way girls throw themselves at him. It's
disgusting."

"He might not think so." Privy laughed, and soon had
Jenny laughing with her.

"It's hard to know what he's thinking. That face—it can be
expressive, yet also a mask, and both at the same time."

"You sound as though you've spent some time looking at
it."

"Of course I have. We've been rehearsing for three weeks.
I see him in class every day. I see the way other girls—and
even some of the boys—look at him." Jenny was setting out
some cheese and crackers on a tray. Privy always had one
bottle of good sherry put by. They could offer Dimitri that at
least. Or tea.

"It would be interesting to see," said Privy, "how they look
at you."

"Oh, nobody pays much attention to me." Jenny believed
that. She never paid any special attention to herself, as a pri-

vate person, and it always took her by surprise when someone else did. To Jenny, the real Jennifer Hale was the girl in the mirror, the girl behind the footlights, something made of muscular discipline and magic. This new private Jenny was someone she had to discover, and soon. The private Jenny Hale had twenty years of catching up to do. The doorbell rang.

There stood Dimitri in a cowboy's sheepskin coat and a cowboy's Stetson hat, bowing low and presenting a huge sheaf of peppermint carnations. She laughed at his costume, although it looked strangely right on him. Anything, Jenny thought, would look right on Dimitri Lubov. Or nothing. Jenny stood in the doorway for a minute that seemed like a year, smiling foolishly at her guest, thinking that there were a million girls in New York tonight who'd probably do a better job of charming Dimitri, wondering if he'd notice her fears, if he'd see the peeling paint or the places where the good pictures used to hang, wondering if he'd like Privy on second meeting, if Privy would like him, wondering if she, Jenny, would die right here and now. Maybe that would be easier. "Come in," she said, and he did.

Dimitri followed her down the big hallway to the even bigger living room where a small fire flickered bravely in the old pink-marble fireplace. Here, not filling the room, were the few good pieces of furniture that hadn't yet been auctioned. To Jenny they looked sad, lonely. To Dimitri, it seemed splendid, a home. They sat by the fire. Privy went to make tea.

"I did not know," he said quietly, "that you were rich." Jenny looked at him and at the room, seeing it for the first time through his eyes. She giggled. "Sorry, Dimitri, but it's funny. You see, we're flat broke all the time." She got up, impulsively, suddenly proud of the poverty she'd hoped he wouldn't notice. She pointed to a spot on the wall. "See this? That was a pretty good Matisse watercolor. We had to sell it last year. And over there, that empty wall, that was a Flemish tapestry. It went two years ago. The only reason we still live here is it's paid for. My father has been very sick for quite a long time."

"I am sorry."

"We live with it." Jenny wondered, desperately, how to change the subject. Privy saved her, coming in just then with a pot of fragrant tea and a plate of her special ginger cookies. Privy poured for them, declined a cup for herself and left them alone. Dimitri ate a cookie, sipped his tea and for a moment looked over Jenny's head at some dim and distant ghost. Then he spoke.

"I," said Dimitri quietly, "have no father." He sipped the hot tea. "As children we are told our father is dead, but in reality he ran away from us."

"I'm sorry."

"What we do not have, perhaps ultimately we do not miss." He looked at his watch. "We must be going."

"Where are we going?" Jenny was imagining beautiful food by candlelight and a chance to find out more about this strange mercurial young man.

"The Joffrey!" Dimitri's face lit up. "They are having a Kurt Jooss festival. We see *The Big City*, something about old Vienna, *The Green Table*, and the Spanish thing."

"That's wonderful, Dimitri." She smiled over her disappointment. There went the candlelight and the love scene. Still, like many classical dancers, Jenny was fascinated by the innovative, athletic work of the Joffrey Ballet. She got her coat, and his, and they left. "I won't be too late, Privy," said Jenny, kissing her at the door. "Tomorrow's a working day."

"Have fun, children." Privy beamed at them. There had been little enough fun in Jenny's young life. Maybe this nice Russian could do that for her. How young they looked, thought Privy, those two slender children going off into the night. Young and somehow vulnerable, even Dimitri in his comical cowboy hat looked like a child playing at dressing up. Yet this was the boy who was making headlines, breaking hearts, gaining fame. And at whose expense? Privy shivered, although the room was warm. Let it, she prayed silently, not be at the expense of Jennifer Hale.

"In the Kirov," said Dimitri in the taxi, "their idea of modern is to give new costumes for *Swan Lake*. A Joffrey could never exist in Russia. Nor de Lis either."

"That's why you defected?"

"That is what people tell me is reason. And it is, surely, a part of the reason. Yet at the moment I did not think of reasons. I flew."

"That took courage."

"When Nureyev came over, that was courage. Now the path is marked: Rudi, Makarova, poor Gaia Muldovska. . . ."

"Why 'poor'?"

"Dead, poor woman. A few months ago. Motor smash."

"I'm sorry. She was a genius."

"In Ireland." The cab passed a red neon sign, and Dimitri's face took on a sudden diabolical glow. He grinned the ur-chin's grin. "When the bird flies from his cage, Jenny, that is not courage. Is what he must do." The cab pulled up to the City Center and Jenny got out to confront her new fame.

Jenny could feel the eyes on her, could hear the whispers, notice the ripple that followed them as they moved through the too-small, too-crowded lobby. It was a new feeling, and not welcome. Instinctively, as if for protection, she reached for Dimitri's hand. It was one thing when people stared at you onstage. They were supposed to. This was another feeling altogether. She felt naked, guilty of some crime she hadn't committed, felt somehow threatened. The eyes and the whis-pers might have been friendly, but Jenny didn't want to find out. "Dimitri," she hissed, "is something wrong with my skirt? They're staring!"

He laughed loudly and squeezed her hand. "Your skirt is fine. It is your reputation—the Bridge review—that they stare at."

"It's creepy. It never happened before."

"You were never famous before." They were inside now. The crowd was less compacted. "Now," he went on, "if I take your hand, they will say Jenny and Dimitri are lovers. If I go walking a little dog on a leash, it will be said that the dog and I are lovers. I have luncheon with de Lis, then de Lis and I are lovers! It is a small price to pay, in truth. America, it seems to me, wants so much to be in love, they create lov-ers out of almost anything. Is charming. Better than hate." They walked into the big theater.

The Joffrey version of Kurt Jooss' *The Green Table* was famous, and Jenny had already seen it twice. But the rest of the program was new: an entire evening devoted to the Ger-man expressionist choreographer. Kurt Jooss was seminal; his mime-ballets had influenced many better-known choreogra-phers in Europe and America. Yet the actual ballets were mostly lost now. It had been a work of archaeology as much as love for the Joffrey to revive them.

As always, the supple young Joffrey dancers were superb. The ballets themselves were charged with electricity: bold, ironic, incisive and every bit as fresh as if they had been conceived yesterday, instead of forty years earlier. First on the program was *The Big City,* blue-collar Berlin in the 1930s, etched in acid and danced to perfection. The applause was long and loud, and after the last curtain call the principal male dancer made a sweeping gesture toward the orchestra section of the theater. A spotlight followed. Up stood a smiling, round-faced, white-haired man who looked like a slightly cynical cherub: Kurt Jooss himself! Jenny hadn't known he was alive. It was Jooss' birthday. The audience roared its congratulations. *How wonderful,* Jenny thought, *to have done all this marvelous work, and so long ago, and still to be alive to enjoy it. The man must be in his seventies.* Something about dancers seemed to make them long-lived. De Lis, after all, was seventy-something. Madame was . . . God only knew how old. Maybe the pain paid off in the end. They walked out to the lobby for some fresh air.

This, Jenny thought, was a connoisseur audience. Probably half the people in it were dancers; they stood out from the more earthbound mortals as if they were wearing uniforms. And in a way, Jenny knew, they did wear a uniform, the cloak of massive self-discipline, thin as rails, straight as young saplings, supple as wheat in a windstorm, charged with nervous energy that made them seem to be in motion even when they were standing still. That was what they got for the years of training, the low pay, the desperate competition, the fleeting chance at fleeting fame. They got this special look, good posture, aching muscles and nothing in the bank.

Jenny never analyzed her life as a dancer; it was simply what she did, and there were no alternatives at all. If it had been her fate to stay forever in the corps de ballet, she would have done it gladly. She danced and danced the best she could; this was all Jenny Hale knew or ever wanted to know, her world, her universe, her fate. If it was a narrow world, if there were books she'd never read and paintings she'd never see and pleasures she'd never taste, it mattered not one bit.

Dimitri touched her arm. "Behold Nadia." Nadia Beshanskaia swept past them, regal in black mink to the floor. Jenny gasped. She had never seen the famous ballerina except behind footlights and theatrical makeup. Nadia was, no doubt, beautiful. But it was a cold beauty. Her face was a ceremonial mask carved in ivory; the eyes were hard. Nadia was famous for her lovers and her tantrums, a scene maker in the great tradition. No one knew her age, but she must be nearing fifty. And she could still dance, and draw crowds, any-where she wanted, anytime she wanted. Nadia was currently favoring the International Ballet Theater with her presence. The backstage gossip was spiced with something rare in dancers: genuine dislike. It wouldn't take much acting, thought Jenny, for that one to play the black swan. And, indeed, the evil temptress of *Swan Lake* was one of Nadia's best roles. "Be careful, Dimitri"—Jenny giggled—"or she will eat you alive."

This brought on the imp's grin. "First," he said softly, but with a wicked edge, "she will have to catch me, and I can move pretty damn fast once upon a time."

"I'm sure you can," she said, laughing, as the lights dimmed.

The dancing continued as splendidly as it had begun; each ballet was different, individual, contrasting in tone and in form, yet somehow they all balanced into one impressive eve-ning. There was the *Pavane for a Dead Infanta*, never before seen in America, formal, tense, the plight of a free spirit trapped in the gloomy ritual of a sixteenth-century Spanish court. Then came a lighthearted comical ballet, *A Waltz in Old Vienna*, with the inimitable Gary Chryst outmiming Chaplin as the effete dance master. The last ballet of the eve-ning was the classic, haunting *Green Table*, a devastating comment on the hypocrisy of politics and the horror of war.

Jenny and Dimitri stayed for all the many curtain calls, clapping with all the fervor of true balletomanes—which they were. Then he led her out of the theater and around the cor-ner to Broadway, heading uptown. Dimitri took her hand au-tomatically, the guide. Jenny wondered, and feared, and hoped all at the same time. Everywhere Dimitri led her, no matter how close or familiar, would be a foreign country, ter-ritory unexplored, exciting surely, dangerous maybe. The night had its own cold sparkle, bright, expectant. He walked east on Fifty-seventh Street and said, "I am ready to eat a horse."

Dancers' favorite though it is, Jenny had never been to the Russian Tea Room. It was crowded, noisy, but the head-waiter knew Dimitri and conjured up a table for two halfway down the long, garishly decorated room. Jenny looked at the menu. "Isn't it awfully expensive?" She was so used to living on pennies per day that spending eight or nine dollars for an entrée shocked her. That was a week's worth of lunches for Jenny.

"For Giselle," Dimitri said, bowing and doffing the cowboy hat, "ultimately nothing is too expensive." Jenny had heard the rumors that de Lis must be paying Dimitri a fortune. That, in any case, was the rumor. And while Jenny wasn't given to rumormongering, instinct told her the young Russian had to be pulling down a heavy price. Jenny herself had only lately been elevated to the dizzy heights of thirteen thousand dollars a year. The kids in the corps got less. It was all you could do to eat and pay the rent. Now, she supposed, she'd earn more. But she didn't know how much more. She just hadn't thought about that part of her good fortune. Jenny looked around the big room. The people all looked rich and theatrical. The room itself was theatrical, decorated in an odd mixture of styles and trimmed here and there with what seemed to be leftover Christmas ornaments. There was a great bustling, and cheer, and the air was filled with unidentifiable but delicious cooking smells.

The menu had translations on the back, but even so, it was a mystery to Jenny. Dimitri ordered pirozhki, which turned out to be delicious flaky pastries filled with spicy meat and onions, and vodka to go with it. "But I never really drink anything but wine, Dimitri."

"Nor me. But is a *mortal sin*," he said, scowling with mock ferocity, "to eat pirozhki without it." The vodka came in tall thimbles and Dimitri showed her how to drink it: in one fell swoop. *"Na zdorovie!"* he exclaimed, lifting his glass. *"Naazdor-vy!"* The vodka burned as it went down, but Jenny managed not to gag on it. It burned after it went down, too. But joke or no joke, she wasn't going to commit mortal sins on her first date with Dimitri Lubov.

"Tell me what it means, *Naazd....*"

"Na zdorovie. To your health. It is the national toast." He looked at the wine list. "Criminals. They have no Russian wines."

"I never knew there were Russian wines."

"Sometimes I dream of Fetjaska. Is white, dry . . . like Chablis. There are others, mostly sweet. Russians have a very big sweet tooth ultimately." He ordered a Pouilly-Fuissé. Dimitri had a comical way of using "ultimately." "Ultimately," he would say, "we cross the street." Or "De Lis finds that out, ultimately he wets his pants." Jenny found this quaint, funny, charming. And Jenny wasn't signing on as Dimitri's grammar coach. She liked him just the way he was.

The pastries disappeared as if by magic and were replaced by *kotlety po-kyiv-skomu*, the famous chicken Kiev, breasts of chicken pounded thin, stuffed with herb butter, breaded and deep-fried. When Jenny cut into her cutlet, a squirt of butter came gushing out. "Is it supposed to do that?"

"Is the sign of a good chef, to make it spit."

"Do you get homesick, Dimitri?" She sipped her wine and thought: *Underneath all the charm, all the talent, he's only twenty-four, and he's left a world behind him.*

"Not for the home. My house was . . . not a house, was something I try to forget." His eyes seemed to take on a deeper shade of blue just then, but maybe it was a trick of the restaurant's lighting. "But I am missing my mother, my sister, old friends."

"You have just one sister?"

"Also a brother, but he has died when I am little."

"I'm sorry. How did he die?"

"He died," said Dimitri, pouring more wine into Jenny's glass and into his own, "of no money. Where we lived was far from the town. The town—Saratov—is ultimately not very big either. I am six, perhaps. Vlad, who is my brother, has something go wrong in his belly. Bleeds. There is no way—no horse, no taxicab, no phone, no ambulance—to get to hospital. There is a handbarrow, which my mother begs from a farmer. In the barrow we put straw. On the straw is Vlad, very pale, sometimes screaming. My mother and I push this barrow. The road is dirt, rocks, mud. The town is perhaps ten kilometers away. Before we are getting there, it is night. Nothing to eat but a little bread. We get to the hospital. They make my mother fill out papers. She cannot write. I fill out the papers. Only then do they look at Vlad. He is dead." Jenny said nothing for a moment, just looked at him. Unconsciously her hand moved across the table and found his hand. There was a sudden sharp noise. He had broken the stem of his wineglass.

"I think," said Jenny, "that's the worst thing I ever heard."

"Is why my sister is a doctor now. Is why I am here."

"To be away from Russia?"

"To never again be so helpless. To never be without a horse." Dimitri lifted the stemless wineglass and sipped the white Burgundy. A drop of blood found its way down the inside of his wrist and onto the pink tablecloth.

"Dimitri, you're bleeding!"

"Is nothing. Ultimately Russians are very temperamental, *nyet?*" He smiled over whatever was churning inside him, drained the glass and wiped off the palm of his hand on a clean handkerchief. It was a very small cut. Wedges of lemon had come with the chicken. Dimitri squeezed a few drops of lemon juice on the cut, winced, wiped it off. The bleeding stopped. "Let us," he said, signaling for the waiter to bring another glass, "talk of happy things."

"Give me your hand." She took his hand, palm up, and kissed the cut. "We have a saying, Privy always used it on me when I was little, that you kiss it and make it well."

"Nice saying. Nice woman, Miss Privet."

"My best friend. My mother, really."

"You have no mother?"

"No. I have no mother." Jenny wasn't going to go into that, not now, not tonight. She'd stirred up the waters enough as it was.

The food was delicious, and Jenny was starved. But as she ate, and talked, and smiled, she thought of a different, very young Dimitri pushing his dying brother down a lonely unpaved road. How easy it had been, growing up in the big apartment on Fifth Avenue, even with the problems, even with Daddy's drinking! They'd never been cold, never without food, never without hope. Jenny hardly thought about money, having it or not having it. Suddenly, and for the first time, she realized the terrible power of poverty, how hard it might drive someone born poor. Someone like Dimitri. It was not a good thought for this night, this restaurant. She sipped the wine and smiled. "When you were little, did you have a nickname?"

"My mother calls me always Dima." He pronounced it Deeema.

Jenny said it, softly. "Dima." Then, again, louder. "Dima!" May I call you that?"

Dimitri looked across the table at her, at those enormous gray eyes in the thin pale face, and saw her desire to please him, to be friendly, to erase the memory he hadn't meant to release for public consumption, the hut in Saratov, the death of Vlad, the hunger and fear. No, this was not what he'd planned. It was deeper, uncharted, perhaps dangerous. Perhaps better. Already the question had come; the boyhood pet name had been dragged from its mothballs. Could she call him Dima? She could call him anything she liked. "I would be proud if you did." And for no special reason but to break the uninvited tension, they both found themselves laughing. "And what," he asked, "do you suppose de Lis will do with us now?"

"He is," Jenny said, giggling, "just slightly more mysterious than the Delphic oracle. I'd be terrified to ask. I don't think he knows himself; things just sort of happen. Some days you're a star; others, you're in exile. He took me right out of the school and made me a soloist, zap, just like that. I still don't know why. People say I'm sleeping with him, but I'm not. I hardly know the man."

"But he knows you. Be sure of that: de Lis knows a dancer when he sees one. And in you he sees one of the best."

Jenny actually blushed. "I've had help, Dima. From him. From you. I can't imagine a better partner." Jenny looked down at the empty plate that had held her dessert. Was she talking too much? Would he think this was just silly flattery? She said no more but waited.

Dima watched her, and thought: *Here is a girl who has traded her girlhood for a compulsion to dance, who never went to the parties other American girls go to, who never learned to flirt, never learned the tricks.* Jenny, he suddenly realized, was something no one had any right to expect in New York, in America, in 1975. Jenny Hale was truly innocent, a combination of bashful child and supremely disciplined dancer, of gentle instincts and magic. He was shocked. It was like looking on the beach to find pretty pebbles and discovering a rare pearl. "It is," he said softly, "just the beginning of our partnership." Then he signaled for the check.

Jenny took one last look around the restaurant, a slightly panicked look, as though she were going to be led out into the street and shot. Death, she thought darkly, might be easier than what was probably going to happen now. He would, Jenny felt with grim fatalism, ask her up for a drink, ask her to make love, any girl's dream. Then why did it scare her? *Because he is Dimitri Lubov, the well-known lover, and you are a silly twit, and you bored him at dinner and you'll doubtless bore him in bed!* They said very little in the cab.

At his apartment Dimitri lit a fire, poured some wine, and

they sat on the fat leather couch, watching the flames. "In Russia," he said, "is a story that dancing comes from fire. In old times we were ultimately like Druids, and the young men—hunters—gather around the fire at night and dance, and there is a contest, a test of strength, who can dance highest over the flames. It is thus the Russians always love to dance, long before ballet. And to leap. When I am about to do some grand jeté, to leap high as I can, is those old flames I am thinking about."

"That's a beautiful story. Above the flames. When you jump like that, you really do look like you're flying." She looked at him. His arm was around her, lightly. It tightened. He kissed her, gently, thoughtfully, thoroughly.

"With you," he whispered, "I am flying."

Very soon after that they were out of their clothes and together on the big bed. Dima was gentle and bold, as strong and responsive and considerate as ever he had been onstage, and Jenny gave herself to his passion with a new wild passion of her own which came not from experience but from instinct, and was better for it. Their lovemaking soared beyond giving and taking into new country where sense played upon sense to orchestrate unforgettable new harmonies of love. Jenny felt the quick incandescent beauty of the instant, of love creating love, of love that was its own justification, love fueled by love, a bright and private universe of love, theirs to explore forever. His voice when he whispered seemed to come from far away. "Beautiful." Jenny could feel him the length of her as she nestled in the crook of his arm, his skin like warm ivory, muscles firm even while relaxing in the soft afterglow of love.

"Dima?"

"Yes?"

"There was a word you were saying, something *shka*."

"*Deushka*. Is Russian for darling."

"It was wonderful."

"And for me." He moved a little. She moved with him. Soon, Jenny knew, she'd have to leave; Privy would worry. His hand was moving now, gently stroking her shoulder, now teasing her breast. He said it again. *"Deushka."* It was starting all over, the love. It was beautiful and perfect, and as Jenny turned and reached out for him, she knew with a sudden and bottomless terror that nothing this lovely could ever, possibly, last.

The Fourth Murder

Paris, 1975

The only regret Yuri Ivanov had about his defection was that he hadn't done it sooner.

Yuri sat at his desk in the oddly shaped but spacious flat tucked up under the eaves of a seventeenth-century stone town house on the Île St. Louis in Paris. Through the narrow slit of a window he could catch a glimpse of the back of Notre Dame, just over the little footbridge on the neighboring Île de la Cité. Exile had been good to Yuri Ivanov. His novels were selling in the millions, even to the movies, and the royalties poured in. He had a life he liked in this beautiful city, a mistress he quite possibly loved and money in the bank. Thérèse, whose milkmaid freshness belied a deeply sensual nature, was, alas, in Orléans with her family this week. Still, it gave him a chance to revise the third chapter of his new novel, *Tanya's Revenge*, which showed every sign of becoming even more of a best-seller than *Tanya Awakens*.

He looked at the clock, a small bronze temple enameled in mat black with gilt decorations, early Empire and very fine. It was nearly two o'clock. The movie producer wasn't due until five. Yuri regretted even that interruption, but his agent had advised him to see this Reynard fellow. Just for a chat. United Artists was under contract to film *Tanya's Awakening* on location in Finland in the spring, and while Yuri was not involved in the scriptwriting, his contract did give him script approval. And apparently there was some snag. Yuri smiled and put a fresh sheet of paper into his new electric typewriter. For one hundred and twenty thousand dollars, he would be pleased to talk about snags, to Reynard or anybody else.

The work took him. In Tanya, he had created a character the world could not get enough of. Already he imagined extending the series to a third, even a fourth novel. Yuri Ivanov forgot the time, forgot his appointment, forgot everything but

Tanya herself, alive on the page. Maybe it wasn't such a bad thing for Thérèse to disappear every once in a while.

The doorbell rang its soft chimes.

Victor Reynard presented himself with a smile and an apology for the intrusion. *Very smooth,* thought Ivanov, *for Hollywood.* Of course, like everything else in this world, Hollywood was changing, too. Victor Reynard looked to Ivanov more like a doctor or a professor than a big-shot film producer. The visitor was tall, taller than Ivanov, with steel-gray hair and tortoise-rimmed eyeglasses and a dark navy suit that had been cut by someone who knew his business.

Yuri offered tea, but Reynard demurred. *How considerate,* thought the writer. *He knows I have no servants.* They talked. Reynard was well versed on *Tanya's Awakening.* Ivanov was flattered just enough to be relaxed more than he usually relaxed with strangers.

"May I smoke?" Ivanov hated tobacco smoke but smiled and nodded yes; the fellow would be gone in a few moments anyway. Reynard produced a cigarette case, extracted a long cigarette with filter and placed it between his lips. Then he reached into his jacket pocket for the lighter. The lighter was a cylinder of chased gold with a curious design. It looked old. "You might," said Reynard, "want to look at this more closely. It is said to have belonged to Catherine herself."

Reynard held the gold cylinder close for Ivanov's inspection. When it was a few inches from the writer's nose, Reynard's fingers pressed on the base of the cylinder. There was a small hissing noise, and an almost invisible cloud of mist shot out under Yuri Ivanov's nose. The novelist sniffed, suspecting some vulgar Hollywood joke. He sniffed only once. There was a deep, convulsive shudder, and Ivanov staggered to his desk chair, clutching at his throat and gasping for air. Then he leaned forward, threw his arms out violently across the desk as if to ward off flames, shuddered again and died.

The gray-haired visitor stood still for a moment, returned the unsmoked cigarette to its case, put the gold cylinder back in his pocket, felt Ivanov's pulse and left, wiping the antique doorknob with a silk pocket handkerchief as he opened the door.

Yuri Ivanov showed all the symptoms of a massive coronary occlusion. Tanya never got her revenge.

CHAPTER
✧◉ 6 ◉✧

The Rolls-Royce was the color of heavy cream. It had been specially built, in 1928, for a member of the Hungarian nobility. Diana Leighton found the car in ruins, at an estate auction, and she knew in an instant it would be the perfect rolling advertisement for Diana Leighton, Ltd. She bought the Rolls cheaply, had it gutted on the inside and stripped to the bare metal outside. And even after the expensive restoration, the twenty-two coats of cream lacquer, the new engine and transmission, the honey-colored glove leather interior, the stereophonic radio and tape deck, the little brassbound bar, even with all this the Rolls cost only a little more than a new Cadillac limousine, and Cadillacs were, to Diana, less than a dime a dozen.

She looked at the car now as it sat gleaming in the soft twilight of East Forty-ninth Street. The car spoke to her. She responded to the disdainful sweep of its clamshell fenders, the cool authority of its Greek-temple grille, the arrogant thrust of the hood, the surprising delicacy of its small, perfect passenger compartment. As deductible business expenses went, the Rolls wasn't bad, not bad at all. Diana's driver, a war-like-looking but entirely tame Sikh with a big black mustache and an imposing white turban, stood waiting as Diana and Jeremy Holt stepped into the car. "Lincoln Center, please, Krishna," said Diana happily. "We're going to the ballet." But Diana hoped they were going very much farther than that.

Jenny stood for a moment in the chill November afternoon, looking up at the windows of her father's apartment. She felt in the pocket of her blue jeans to see if the key was still there. It was still there. Her fingers rubbed the key again and again, as if by rubbing it she could summon a genie that would solve her problem. No genie appeared. Jenny turned and walked up Fifth Avenue to catch her crosstown bus. The key was to Dima's apartment. He had asked her, last night, to move in with him.

And how was she going to explain that to Privy? Learning to love Dima had taken Jenny's life from the stark simplicity of an existence totally dedicated to dancing to something dangerous and complicated, something in which nothing could be taken for granted. And Privy, Jenny realized with a sickening jolt, was a part of her life that she'd always taken for granted. Privy was simply there, ready to give comfort, to solve problems, to shield Jenny from dangers that Jenny would never know existed. Jenny was the center of Privy's life, and the thought of what might happen when she suddenly removed that center was more frightening than any problem Jenny had faced so far in her new affair with Dima. Yet she knew, standing there on the cold sidewalk, that she would have to face it, and soon, and alone. Jenny shivered and walked up the empty avenue to the bus stop.

The two weeks that Jenny had spent with Dima could seem like a minute or a lifetime. It was delicious, and scary, and always, every day, a new adventure. Jenny learned Dima as she might learn a completely new language with a grammar all its own. She discovered the shyness behind the bravado, the strangely dignified nineteenth-century man who often wore an urchin's grin, the taker-of-risks who loved to dance beyond the limits of caution, who felt quite at home on the razor edge of danger, the rough-hewn peasant boy whose classical education made Jenny's own small store of learning seem like nothing. Dimitri was a born iconoclast, a provocateur whose mischief-making mind was happiest when poking holes in the Establishment. It was easy to see why he'd driven the ponderous Soviet ballet bureaucracy mad.

Once, only half in fun, seeing her utter commitment to ballet, he had said, "Ultimately, Jenny, will come a day when you can no longer dance. It will come for all of us. And what then?"

"I'll die." Life without dancing was literally unimaginable. Jenny knew that Dima was trying to shake her out of a rut, but when she thought how much of her was invested in ballet, it was like being told she had some incurable disease. She looked up at Dima, who stood on a chair hanging a framed poster in his apartment. "I'll die," she repeated.

"*Nyet.* Teach? Maybe. Make dances? Better. Be rich and retire? Boring. But not to die. Is like the pot you watch does not boil. To think of dying is not to die. Is to cop out."

"Dima, I'm not yet twenty years old. Fonteyn's still dancing at fifty-six. Surely I've got a little time."

"Aha!" He jumped down from the ladder and kissed her, laughing. "And there is no such thing as ultimately injuring one's self?" He would do this, half-teasingly, half-seriously, just to provoke her.

"What do you suggest? That I learn a useful trade? Basket weaving, maybe?" She tried to keep it light, but the odds were against her.

"Who am I to suggest, *deushka?* I ask only that you think about it. One plans picnics, it rains, what then? That's all."

"I just don't know, Dima. I don't know what then."

He put down the hammer and looked in her eyes. He reached out and touched her under the chin, holding two fingers there as if she were some rare sculpture he was considering buying. These discussions had a way of ending in bed. "No," he said, softly, "and no more do I, Jenny. I am Dima, I make jokes, I am naughty. Many times, in Kirov School, am I punished for this. Always, when I am told an answer, I ask a question. Is vice."

"Is just fine. If more people asked more questions, there might be more answers. But not from me." She took his hand and squeezed it.

"You," said Dima with the urchin's grin instantly on his face, "are yourself an answer, Jennifer Hale, ballerina *extraordinaire.* You are answer to prayer of one poor Russian kid."

"What did he pray for?"

"What do all boys pray for? For love!"

And that became another of their conversations that ended in bed. Jenny accepted Dimitri's love as an extraordinary stroke of luck. She never quite believed she deserved it.

Dima realized this instinctively; it was part of her appeal, in this ballet world of towering egos and dense competition, that a girl of unquestioned talent should value herself so little. Slowly, gently, he tried to give her more self-confidence. Confidence to assert herself with de Lis. Confidence to leave the apartment on Fifth Avenue. Confidence to see herself as he saw her, as he wanted the world to see her. Dancing, Dima knew, in motion to music, Jenny's body had great authority. The rhythms were all there, the line was at the same time sharply etched and liquid, and she was turning into a very expressive actress. But Jenny inhabited a world so special, so private, that there were times when even Dimitri felt like an unwelcome ambassador there.

"Deushka," he said one night, walking back to his apartment after a performance of *Giselle,* "what do you feel, exactly, when the house goes crazy like tonight, when they throw flowers, make us take bow upon bow?"

"Flattered. Anyway, most of it's for you." Applause frightened Jenny. And as her popularity grew, it frightened her more and more. She would stand, and smile, and make her reverences perfectly, the way Madame had drilled her to do, but the smile was as mechanical as the graceful knee bend of the reverence, as artificial as the perfect, painful turnout of her feet. She was afraid of those roaring, clapping thousands of people. They wanted something from her that she did not know how to give them, something beyond dancing. Sometimes Jenny felt that they were going to rush up on stage and tear her to shreds.

Dima was holding her hand. He squeezed it, a signal that woke her out of a reverie. "You mystify me, Giselle," he said, "to dance so exquisitely, and care so little for the rewards."

"Maybe I feel I don't deserve them."

"Never think that, Jenny. You give them—we all give them—far more than they can ever give us back. They give us their affection, perhaps, and a little of their money—which most of them can well afford. But we, we give them our lives, our souls. Is ultimately a very unbalanced rate of exchange." They walked in silence for a moment.

"You like it, don't you? The applause, the rewards?"

"You bet!" He laughed. "Every night Dima goes to the theater as to a fountain, and very thirsty I am. For me applause is like opening so many presents." He stopped, reached out and touched her cold cheek. "When Dima was small boy, were not many presents for Dima. So it happens now, magically, why should I not love it? I make love to my audience, and they know it. Is this they respond to, ultimately, not is my toes pointed right—for many times is not right—but the fact that I love them and am not ashamed."

"I guess," said Jenny quietly, "that I'd probably be happy dancing in an empty room, if you were there, or de Lis, or Privy."

For a moment he just held her hand and kept walking. Dima knew that what she said was too true; Jenny really didn't care a damn about the response or the fame or the power that might follow. It was this very self-containment that gave her dancing its special magic. When Jenny danced, she moved through a world of her own devising, a world to whose gates only she had the key; the audience might follow her or not. The fact that they did follow, and in a loyal mob whose numbers increased with every performance, impressed Jenny not at all. It was her power and her weakness; de Lis was well aware of Jenny's innocence, her lack of vanity, her deep concentration, and he took full advantage.

Dima knew that if Jenny were ever going to be her own woman, she would have to awake from this strange and beautiful trance that was her career as a dancer. Dima wanted that awakening, and he feared it at the same time; Jenny had been sheltered all her life in an almost medieval seclusion, first by Privy, then by de Lis, and finally by her own total commitment to ballet. Dima thought this and smiled, for he wanted to protect her, too. But Dima's protection would take the form of helping her grow, to discover for herself the enormous possibilities he knew, instinctively, were there. He would do that, Dima suddenly realized, no matter where it led. He'd do it gently, with love, maybe with fear. But he'd do it, and damn de Lis! Finally he spoke. "Jenny, Jenny, what will we do with you?"

"Love me. Dance with me."

"I do that now, *deushka*, and hope always to do it. But what I am thinking is that ultimately we must get you a little transfusion from the Beshanskaia."

"Does her mink come with it?"

"Is possible. The fair Nadia looks after Nadia. Zip, zap, your liver is being served to you with onions on a plate."

"You don't want me like that."

"Just a tiny bit. Ten percent. Just enough so you realize what you are, *deushka*, just to make you think before you jump every time de Lis pulls your string."

"But I owe everything to de Lis. He gave me scholarships when we couldn't pay; he took me out of school and made me a soloist instantly; he even gave me you." Jenny felt herself trembling, even though it wasn't that cold. Dima had teased her about de Lis before, and it always made her feel nervous, disloyal even to listen to such subversive talk. She tried not to think about de Lis too much because deep inside Jenny knew that what Dima said was true. Alexander de Lis did manipulate them all. He did pull the strings, and if you wanted a career in his company, you damn well did jump when the string was pulled.

Once again Dima stopped walking, even though they were almost home now. He stopped on the sidewalk, right there on Broadway, put both arms around her in a great Russian bear hug and kissed her forehead. "And what do you give him, my Jenny? The de Lises of this world do not exist without their dancers. In that, they are like—what do you call the drinkers of blood, very scary?"

"Vampires."

"Vampires, then, feeding and feeding and feeding upon us."

"He helps us, Dima, helps me anyway."

"Yet also he hurts you."

"How? How could de Lis hurt me?" Jenny answered mechanically, afraid of what Dima might say next.

"By keeping you forever a child, my darling, waiting for his permission to cross the road. Then, one day, you will cross it and safely, and discover the view from the other side, and discover also that de Lis is not God. He must be very frightened of that moment."

"De Lis, frightened?" She laughed, but it was a brittle laugh.

"He is only a man. Men have fears."

"I admit he likes to run our lives for us. But he means no harm."

"Is not what he means, Jenny. Is what he does. The serpent that bites you does not personally dislike you. He is serpent, he bites, is his nature. One must avoid the serpents of this world, for ultimately they bite."

"I depend on de Lis."

"So does a junkie depend on his pusher. Is not necessarily a good thing."

"What do you want me to do?"

"Only think. Think about de Lis, what he is really doing."

"He is making dances, a dance company; it's his life. And mine." Suddenly Jenny felt as though someone were threatening to take that life away from her, and this terrified her profoundly; it was the only life she had.

"De Lis makes beautiful dances, as you say. But he does something else. He enslaves, makes dancers into something he owns, controls. I am Russian, Jenny. I know about enslavement. You do not find this a little frightening?"

"I find," said Jenny half under her breath, talking to herself as much as to Dima, "that the idea of not having de Lis behind me is even more frightening." Once when she was little, Privy had taken her to see a movie. With the movie had been playing a *Tom and Jerry* cartoon. Jenny never forgot how the cat had run off the edge of a tall building, his feet rotating like a helicopter's blade, never falling until he happened to look down and realized that there was nothing solid underneath him. Jenny felt like that every time she contemplated life without de Lis. De Lis was the framework of her life in dancing; his judgment, his dream, his criticism or praise had become as much a part of her as the air she breathed.

She stood in Dimitri's arms, very close to him on the cold sidewalk, oblivious of people passing by, chilled more by her fears than the December night, glad of his arms around her, afraid that if those arms weren't there she might fall down. "Take me home," she whispered. And he did. But even as they climbed the warm stairs to their warmer bed, Jenny knew that the problem was unsolved, that the question she dared not answer would be asked again and again. Dima did not get to be Dima by being anything but very persistent. She would have to plan; she'd have to think about it. But not, please not, tonight.

Jesus, Mary and Joseph! Dave Loughlin looked at the fat blue manila folder as though it were filled with angry rattlers. The folder had grown bigger these last two weeks, but Dave had grown no wiser. And now they—whoever "they" were—had got to Yuri Ivanov! Gregor Berisov, Peter Chablesky, Gaia Muldovska and now this. All defectors, all dead, all in less than a year. And so neatly done that the very lack of evidence was a kind of evidence itself: an apparent suicide (Berisov), a car smash (Muldovska) and two heart attacks (Chablesky and Ivanov). Undetectable heart attacks were hardly the latest thing in political assassination; the KGB had been doing it for years, to name just one instance. Fixing a

car was child's play. And the suicide, so called? Could have
been anything. Dave knew the Ivanov death cinched it. There
was a pattern. When he found the pattern, he'd have a shot
at the patternmakers. But the blue file, for all its CIA thor-
oughness, told him nothing. To all appearances, the four defectors had never known each other. But for Chablesky, they
had no special secrets that might be worth killing for. And if
the KGB had wanted Chablesky shut up, they would have
done it sooner; Chablesky had been out and debriefed and
working in public for years.

The local police had been very cooperative. Suspiciously
cooperative? Gaia's wrecked MG had been hauled up the
two-hundred-foot cliff and examined in detail: too late. What
hadn't exploded had rusted away in the salt air and the sea.
And the three others had had secondary autopsies which revealed nothing. It was the nothings piling up on nothings that
confirmed Dave's suspicions. Every death was clean as a
whistle. And the tune playing on that whistle was a dance of
death. Dave felt the frustration building in him. It mounted
like a torrent of water pressing against a thin dam, and all of
Dave Loughlin's instincts told him that if he didn't make
some progress very soon, that dam would burst, and who
knew what hell might break loose then?

He stood up and closed the folder and locked it away.
Dave Loughlin wanted a drink. He wanted something else,
too. He wanted a plan, a clue, a pattern behind the pattern.
He wanted his luck back from whatever sad dark place it had
seeped away to these last thirty years. Dave wanted all these
things. But in the meantime, a drink would do.

Alexander de Lis allowed himself to frown. He sat, alone
for once, in his big glass-walled office at the top of the New
York State Theater. He looked around the room, which usually pleased him, knowing too well why nothing, here or anywhere, would be likely to please him today. De Lis had heard
the reports and laughed; some of the dancers called this the
throne room, a place where favors were sought and sometimes granted, a place where a dancer's career could be made
or broken on de Lis' whim of steel, a scary, mysterious place.
To de Lis himself, the room was a sanctuary, a place to escape from the turbulence of the Civic Ballet. If he had
created that turbulence, so be it; all the more reason he
needed respite!

But today he must face a problem that could not be solved by silence. He had just come from a morning class. There, unobserved, in a corner, he had spent ten valuable minutes watching Dimitri and Jenny rehearsing the *Bayadère* pas de deux. How they danced! His instinct for pairing them had been so true there was danger in it. De Lis knew the danger too well. Half romantic, half cynic and all dancer, he knew just how Dimitri must feel in this, his first taste of glory in Western ballet. He knew the offers that would be raining around the boy's golden head like flowers at the curtain call. And he knew, too, about the love affair, which was by now common gossip in the company and beyond. He sighed.

It had been a calculated risk, bringing Dimitri Lubov into his carefully constructed "starless" company. De Lis knew that Dima was and would remain a star. His gamble was that the boy would choose to remain with the Civic. But now De Lis saw a pair of stars growing to such magnitude that their partnership was beginning to take on a life of its own, glittering, magnetic and powerful. For when audiences demanded Hale-Lubov nights, the delicate balance of the Civic repertory style of dancing was thrown off; already there were grumblings among his other principal dancers.

De Lis knew he stood a good chance of losing Dimitri, for Dimitri was not under long-term contract and was most definitely not a team player of the type that fitted best into the Civic style. But now there was a chance of losing Jenny, too—his own Jenny! Jenny, who had been nurtured in the Civic school and the Civic company from childhood. Jenny, his own creation! De Lis felt a tightness at the back of his muscular neck: tension. He stood up, paced the big room, sat down, stood up again. They were getting away from him! Helplessness was not a familiar feeling to Alex de Lis, and he resented its intrusion. To be so punished for doing his job too well!

The memory of last week burned hot and ugly in his mind. Just last week, only a little more than a month after that first triumphant *Giselle*, Jenny and Dimitri had been scheduled to dance *Giselle* again. But Jenny had twisted a foot in rehearsal and couldn't go on. He'd substituted Eleanora Mason—a superb ballerina, though no longer young—and when this was announced just before the curtain rose, there was an audible sigh of disappointment. He, de Lis, had been there to hear

BALLET!
[117]

that sigh, and he heard it still. In his mind it became a mocking sound, and a sound of mourning for lost dreams.

Jenny and Dimitri! There could be one of ballet's legendary teamings! There could be another Fonteyn-Nureyev or,
better yet, another Antoinette Sibley-Anthony Dowell, the
jeunesse dorée of the Royal Ballet, who had grown up together, whose partnership was legendary already, and them
still young. Jenny and Dimitri could achieve that kind of
glory. The thought that they would very likely not achieve it
for him was almost more than de Lis could bear. He felt the
impending loss like a physical pain. He knew, with seventy-
two years of practiced shrewdness and a keen dancer's instinct, that Dimitri Lubov would be impossible to hold. And
Jenny? His Jenny? Jenny, whom he had created, promoted,
made famous? There must be a way to keep her, at the very
least. He would find that way, and soon.

Alexander de Lis had not sustained his romantic dream of
a perfect ballet company for fifty years without salting his
dreams with an ample dose of cynicism. If he were Jenny
Hale, and had a Lubov on the string, and Lubov left the
Civic, de Lis knew just what he'd do. He sighed and put back
the paper. Not only that, if you could believe the well-es-
tablished de Lis espionage system, they were actually in love.
That was the maddening thing about dancers; they were always falling in love. For the moment, conveniently, he forgot
the five ballerinas who had become Mrs. Alexander de Lis.

Alex de Lis' intelligence network was based on the fanatical loyalty of many well-placed people who had been with him
for years. No bulge of overweight or bump of hidden preg-
nancy escaped the gimlet eye of the Princess Descharovna.
Stagehands saw everything and talked to de Lis as he wandered among the sets. Freddie Momontov, the confidant of
the whole corps de ballet, was a de Lis confidant, too. De Lis,
after all, made the lives of these people possible. They, in turn,
tried in every way they could to make his life easier.

So it happened that very little went on backstage that
failed to reach the alert ears of Alex de Lis. He was nothing
of a voyeur and the opposite of a gossip. But the more Alex
de Lis knew about his people, the better he could run the
Civic. When he learned, as he soon did, that Jenny was sleeping with Dimitri, the whole balance of that equation changed
dramatically.

Often, and to his credit, de Lis had helped people in the

company when they didn't even know he knew about their problem. Many a discreet loan had been arranged to a young dancer with family problems, and many a schedule had been readjusted so someone could take a day or two off and work out some problem on his own. All this paternalism increased the godlike aspect of de Lis' rule in the Civic Ballet. He was, beyond doubt, all-powerful. And he seemed omniscient. He had a talent, shared with the gods of mythology, for turning up in the unlikeliest places and doing the unlikeliest things.

He might appear from nowhere and take over a rehearsal himself. He cared, and showed his care, about the tiniest details, from the angle of the star ballerina's tiara to the length of the false eyelashes of the newest member of the corps de ballet. He was a volcano of well-meaning advice on everything from diet (yogurt, fish, granola and red wine) to pets (cats, and have two of them) to sex (enjoy it, but don't get pregnant) to holidays (stay out of the sun, and by no means go ice-skating because it develops the wrong muscles). It was a very special atmosphere in the Civic Ballet, and it took a special kind of dancer to fit in with it. The work was very hard, the pay minimal, the supervision intense.

Aesthetically the rewards could be enormous. De Lis created ballet after ballet for his dancers alone, and when he re-created a classic, it was likely to be the definitive production. Well-known dancers from legendary ballet companies around the world quit outright or finagled leaves of absence just to dance with de Lis. Yet at the same time he lost dancers. Some wanted more fame, some more money, some more independence.

Alexander de Lis knew that he was in danger of losing Dima Lubov, and maybe Jenny Hale, too. He knew that the Civic Ballet would go on without them, that new dancers would come along, maybe even better ones.

Then why was he getting his first headache of the year? And more important, what was he going to do about it?

He got up from his leather lounge chair and walked to the window. The great plaza was nearly empty at noon, the huge round fountain turned low. A dirty newspaper tossed and danced across the pavement, got caught up in a small whirlwind next to the fountain's black stone base and hung there for a moment, hovering in the breeze, flapping with a curiously graceful motion. Then it flew up and spread out exactly like a butterfly spreading its wings, flapping like wings, up and up, over the Philharmonic's gaunt facade, up into the gray-blue sky over Broadway, and out of sight.

The flying paper reminded de Lis of something; the motion was wild and at the same time enticing, evocative, curiously sensual, as though the scrap of paper were trying to escape from him and to seduce him at the same time. And in an instant he knew: there was a dance in it!

De Lis stood at the window for a moment longer, then stepped back. His arms rose from his side as he stepped back, rose slowly over his head, then came down again in a flapping motion, rose once more, slid back now as they flapped, a kind of swimming—that was it!—half flying, half swimming, fighting the current, and what should the feet be doing? His body answered. Now, moving faster, de Lis circled the room backward, reaching one leg far behind him then spinning on demi-pointe, then the next leg, another spin, and always with the exaggerated flapping motion, not at all a bird's movement but something wilder, more expressive, something that belonged to the earth and the sky at the same time.

As he moved, to his own rhythms, melodies raced through his head; what, what? It should be wild and tender. Liszt? Possibly. It would come. But there was a dance in it. So far only a fragment of a dance. But such a fragment; it was truly new. And not a solo. A pas de deux. He saw Jenny, trapped, flapping, all in pale gray. Tattered pale gray, like the paper. And Lubov, bold, thrusting, stalking her. Catching her? He wasn't sure. But there was a dance in it, maybe a good one. Then he stopped, sweating, breathing hard. And de Lis smiled at the irony of it. Of course, there was a dance in it. And for whom? He sat down heavily. He wasn't as young as he used to be. Once again, involuntarily, he thought about Jenny.

How very tacky, thought Diana Leighton in the moment before the great curtain rose. The curtain had become frayed, and there were holes in it, quite big, some of them, starting about halfway from the middle level and running up, tears and holes and frayed patches that looked as though the curtain had got caught in some grinding mechanism high above the proscenium arch. Yet the bottom of the ugly gold-on-gold curtain looked practically new. Diana wondered how the holes got there and why nobody had done anything about them. Then the ballet began, and she forgot the curtain, forgot Jeremy Holt sitting patiently beside her, forgot everything

but the beautiful blond young man spinning and leaping before her.

The ballet was *Le Jeune Homme et la Mort*. Here was
Dimitri, a starving poet, at odds with himself in a Paris garret, barefoot, blue-jeaned, bare-chested, acting out some un-
specified inner turmoil while soaring and plunging desperately
around the garret like a trapped bird. It was the avant-garde
of the mid-1940s, dated now, but nevertheless a sensational
bravura role that taxed the athletic ability of the male dancer
to the limit.

Diana watched him with the practiced eye of a balletomane, with the hungry eye of a woman looking for love.
That, she thought, *is some magnificent animal.* Onstage Dima
paced the length of the room, stalking his psyche through
uncharted jungles. Now he was a panther, prowling. Now an
eagle, soaring. He leaped, up, over a chair, landed and sprang
up again, onto a table now, trapped, dangerous, wild. The
young man and death. Enter Death. "Of course," Diana whispered to Jeremy, "Death is a woman." Death was danced by
Eleanora Mason, and in her interpretation Death was a
seductive older woman, tempting, scornful, leading the young
man on, challenging him and finally, melodramatically, making him hers.

Dima and Eleanora began their pas de deux, a dance of
temptation and death, a true danse macabre. It was a tormented, leaping, writhing dance that managed to convey several
kinds of longing: for love, for beauty, for the ultimate release
of death. Was the beautiful woman his lover, temptress or
Death itself? The ballet takes us into the darkest corners of a
troubled mind, raises questions that are left to our imagina-
tions for answering. The beautiful stranger left; the poet was
inconsolable. Suddenly, on impulse, he hanged himself from a
beam in the garret. The woman reappeared then, formally
gowned, wearing the mask of her true calling: the messenger
of Death. Slowly, ritualistically, she removed her mask—a
skull—gave it to her poet and led him off across the moonlit
rooftops, Death leading Death.

Jenny sat in the audience, tense as a watch spring. She
knew the ballet, had seen Dima rehearsing, and still the
image of him stretched taut by the brutal rope, his wild angel's head grotesquely angled, shocked her deeply. He had
been so alive ten seconds before. Knowing it was silly, she
shuddered, hugging herself tight as if from a sudden chill.

Such was the power of his acting, such was the velocity of his dancing that death filled the huge theater like a sudden ice storm. It seemed like a threat or a warning. Loyal as she was, for a moment Jenny wished she hadn't come.

Dima Lubov caught the essential wildness of the role. He made the sad, violent, introspective poet explode into something electric and cornered and dangerous, a human bomb programmed to explode, and soon. He created more tension with his body than there was in the role or the music. These were not the silky, fluid movements of a classical dancer. Dima flung himself around that stage, taking chances. He was part gymnast, part eagle, all poet. But it was tormented poetry.

As he leaped and writhed and vaulted tables and chairs, Dima thought of a bird he'd once seen, trapped inside a little church in the south of France. The bird must have flown in the open door just before the service, and now the door was shut, and the bird, hysterical. Fluttering, its small heart pounding, the bird racketed from one side of the narrow nave to the other, now pausing a moment in doubt, only to fly again with renewed desperation until, at last, exhausted, it made one final thrust at freedom and crashed suicidally into a cold stone statue. Dima had got up from the pew he was sharing with Felice, picked up the little bird and held it in its last convulsions. There was nothing to be done; the brittle neck was broken from the force of impact.

This was what Dima saw in the role of the young man: the free spirit trapped, the churning velocity of creation finding no outlet, the doubt and fear and final desperation. So effectively did he convey these feelings that the tired symbolism of the ballet suddenly took on new force. *The Young Man and Death* would have a renaissance now, thanks to Dima; the role of the poet would become a leaping, soaring, crashing metaphor for free spirits everywhere trapped in existential nets of their own devising.

The curtain fell, tacky or not, and the force of the applause alone might have torn more holes in it. Dima stepped out, glistening with sweat, side by side with Eleanora Mason, and bowed his formal bow. They took four calls together, two each individually; then Dima took two more. They knew his nickname now. One of the gossip columns had printed the fact that Jenny called him Dima.

So now the "Bravos!" were mixed with people simply calling his name: "Dima! Dima!" Every time he bowed and walked off the theater rang with his name until he came back, and back again. But there were three other ballets to be danced this night, and the time came when Dima did not answer the call of his name.

As Dima stood there, bowing, sweating, his heart still thumping from the tremendous exertion of the dance, barefoot and looking about seventeen in his blue jeans, Diana Leighton's hand reached out instinctively and found the hand of Jeremy Holt. Suddenly she wanted to go home, now, and make love. And not with Jeremy. But for the moment Jeremy would have to do.

Jenny wasn't dancing that night. She watched *Le Jeune Homme* from de Lis' house seats, fifth row center in the orchestra. She danced with Dimitri so much these days that it was an odd experience to watch him from out front. He was, she thought, very well worth watching. Only a trained dancer could know what chances he took in that role. But the excitement carried over to the audience. Jenny could feel it around her, vibrating, charging the air.

As the curtain came down and Dima took his bows, Jenny turned in her seat and looked at the huge auditorium. There must be thousands of them. At first she was proud, and then a little frightened. They were so hungry. They all wanted a piece of Dimitri Lubov. Jenny looked up at Dima, knowing what it cost him to keep the urchin's grin packed away out of sight. His bows were the perfection of formality, and only the slightest, most gracious echo of a smile crossed his lips. Fair enough. The grin would be for later. For her. Jenny smiled and clapped louder. It was for her! She didn't deserve it, she still didn't understand what he saw in her, but there it was, a glorious gift, Dima's love wrapped up in Dima's body. Jenny Hale could not imagine anything better.

Nor could Diana Leighton, as the cream-colored Rolls-Royce whispered its way back to her apricot silk bedroom at Forty-ninth Street.

For the first time since she could remember, Jenny Hale dreaded the thought of facing Privy. Yet it had to be done. Dima understood how she felt, how hard it was going to be to tell Privy that he wanted her to move in and that she was going to do it. This, Jenny knew, might be the straw that broke the camel's back. Privy had a widowed sister in Eng-

land; Privy might just pull up stakes and go back to England
to live with her sister.

For years now Jenny had lived her life day by day, and the
routine had been regular, if hard, and absolutely predictable:
class, class and more class. Now that she was performing,
now that there was Dima Lubov, Jenny found herself forced
to make plans, but almost paralyzed when the time actually
came to act on them. Her only plan had been to get through
the day and then tomorrow.

Jenny thought back on all the years Privy had been the
center of her life. Only because of Privy had she been able to
keep on dancing. Only because of Privy had she been in-
sulated from her father's accelerating decline into alcoholism.
Only because of Miss Jessica Privet had Jenny known something like a mother's love, known that someone else cared
about her more than anything in the world. Privy, who had
stretched the dollars until they were almost enough, Privy,
who had schemed and made do and made light of it all, who
had taught Jenny manners and courage and to rely on herself, who had comforted Jenny through her short sad affair
with Machito Ramirez, who had never asked for a thing but
Jenny's love—Privy deserved much better than to have Jenny
walk out on her. Yet that was what Jenny intended to do.
Today.

For a week the key to Dima's apartment had been burning
a hole in Jenny's pocket and in her conscience. For a moment she had considered asking Dima to move in with her—
and Privy. But that would be impossible. Dima's pride would
never permit it, and it wouldn't seem right in any case. In
some vague way Jenny imagined a future in which they all
lived happily together in a big brownstone town house, with
Privy as housekeeper forever. The fact that brownstone town
houses cost a fortune didn't deter Jenny. With Dima, everything was possible, even that. But the brownstone was in the
future. And Jenny had promised Dima she'd tell Privy today,
this very morning. She lay in the narrow white bed and
pulled the covers up over her head. The problem would not
go away. It had to be faced. She looked at the old green-
faced alarm clock. Time to get up. Privy would be making
breakfast.

Privy loved surprises. All through Jenny's childhood it had
been one of her chief delights to surprise the girl, sometimes
with a special expedition to the zoo or the circus, a new

dress, a movie. When times grew bad for Clifford Hale, a Privy surprise might take the form of simply having meat on the table or a special dessert. Privy planned the surprises for Jenny, but really they were for her pleasure, too, pleasure reflected, perhaps, but altogether real. Now Privy looked up from her tea and smiled as Jenny came into the big old kitchen. She had a surprise up her sleeve, and Jenny was going to love it. The girl looked as though she could use a treat, pale as she was, and nervous. Privy, direct as ever, sailed right into it. "If," she said, "you had a choice of any color scheme in the world to redo the apartment, what would it be?" Jenny looked at her and noticed a small pile of decorating magazines on the counter.

"Have we come into some money?" It had been so long since there had been extra cash even for necessities that Jenny couldn't remember when.

"I have consulted the Privy Purse," said Privy, referring to a joke of Jenny's childhood when, in a history lesson about Elizabethan England, a ten-year-old Jenny had first heard about the privy purse of England and assumed it was somehow connected with Miss Privet, "and it seems to me, now you're earning more, my pet, it might be possible to dip into the Purse a little. Not much, mind you. But enough to repaint a bit, perhaps do a spot of reupholstering. I was thinking of that, when your nice Dimitri was here. Your father would like it, too."

Then let him pay for it, thought Jenny, knowing how unlikely that was. Jenny forced herself to smile, but it was a smile built on pain. "You always think of the right thing, Privy. But I don't want you to pay. God knows how much you've done on your own as it is."

"If I didn't like it, my pet, I wouldn't do it."

"Privy, were you ever in love?"

"Yes, darling, very long ago. In the olden days, as you used to call them." Jenny took a deep breath.

"Dima wants me to move in with him. I told him I would."

"I see." Privy looked at the girl and made herself smile. "I realize, darling, that that sort of thing is done these days. But are you very sure?"

"I want to try. It's just possible I may be in love. But there isn't anything to measure it against, Privy, so no, no, I'm not sure. But it isn't far. On Seventy-fourth Street—just across the park!"

Privy looked at her. Only across the park! Only across the world. Of course, they wanted to leave the nest. Of course, it was her duty to make that easier, to help make it right, if there was a way to make it right. Privy had seen the change in Jenny these last few weeks, the glow, the new poise, the radiance. For a time Privy thought it might be the sudden success. But her first glimpse of Jenny and Dimitri together had altered that. Over the years Privy had seen dancing consuming Jenny, absorbing her almost to the exclusion of everything else. But there had always been time in Jenny's life for Privy, and that had been enough.

Privy looked at the girl and thought of Gerald Lanier. The Reverend Gerald, whose little gray church on Seventy-eighth Street reminded her of England, Gerald Lanier, on whose account Privy had done volunteer work two afternoons a week for years now, Gerald, who was perhaps her only other friend besides Jenny. Gerald Lanier always managed to bring a twinkle of humor and a welcoming human warmth to any problem, however serious. What would Gerald do, faced with this strange, disturbed, disturbing new Jenny?

Stalling for time, Privy lifted her teacup. Her glasses steamed; she blinked, wondering if Jenny saw the war she was waging with herself, the effort it took not to break down. Privy's father had been a military man; she knew all about stiff upper lips. Somehow the thought of Reverend Gerald helped. It wasn't the end, after all; what was so tragic about a young girl in love? Young girls were supposed to be in love! How many times had Privy prayed for the girl's happiness? How many times had she prayed that—somehow—they could be together always? Well, enough of that selfishness! What kind of woman was she anyhow? It was shocking. Let the girl have her moment, leave the nest; she, Jessica Privet, would be a tower of strength for the girl. The sure way to lose Jenny's love forever would be to take an ugly moral stand on the matter. Privy knew that whatever Gerald Lanier might do or say in a case like this, he'd never be unkind, never be abrupt, never do any of the terrible, unforgettable things that fear and prejudice and prudery so often breed.

Jenny ran on, fueled by nervousness, talking more and more quickly, as much to convince herself as Privy. "And I'll still see you all the time, truly, Privy, and you can come visit us, we're practically helpless, neither of us can cook. . . ."

Privy stirred one-half of a teaspoon of sugar into her tea, looked up and smiled. "My darling," she said quietly, managing a smile, "when love comes to us, we must take it any way we can. I only want you to be happy, my Jenny, and if Dimitri is what makes you happy, well, then he is making me happy, too. Don't ever think—or let him think—that he is taking you away, dearest. Of course, we'll still be close— maybe closer! And I don't have to tell you that the door is always open here, darling, for you and for your Dimitri."

Relief came rushing through Jenny's brain like a fever. "You're not angry?"

Privy laughed. "What heart is so hard it can be angry at love? I think love is the most beautiful thing there is, Jenny, except possibly the sight of you dancing. Now then. What color for the drawing room?" For a few minutes they played at color schemes. For a few minutes it was the way it always had been and could never be again: just the two of them, hoping, planning, dreaming. Together. Then Jenny noticed the time and ran off, kissing Privy good-bye just like any other morning.

She rode the elevator all the way down to the lobby before she realized she'd forgotten her dance bag with its vital supply of clean leotards and towels and makeup. Jenny rode back up and let herself in. The dance bag would be in her bedroom. She walked down the long hallway, opened the white door and stopped, shocked.

There sat Privy on the edge of her bed, bent over, sobbing, her face buried in her hands. In all these years Jenny had never seen Privy cry. But cry she did, and cried and cried, and didn't notice that Jenny was there. The girl sat down next to her and took the older woman in her arms and soon was crying herself. "Oh, Privy. I feel so awful to do this to you."

There was a sniffle, a snort. Then Privy sat upright and shook her head a little, as if waking from a bad dream. "Fiddlesticks! Will you look at us? You'd think we were the victims of some great disaster, instead of people who should be happy, rejoicing. I'm sorry, child, but you just took Privy by surprise, was all. The weepers, we used to call 'em when I was a girl, millions of years ago, the weepers. Well, we've had our weepers now, haven't we? And it's up and into the new day or Mr. de Lis will have you scrubbing the stage instead of dancing on it. And don't forget your lunch!"

Jenny got up, relieved. Here was the old Privy again, all love and energy. For the second time that morning Jenny kissed her and ran off for the crosstown bus. It was a bright, crisp day, warm for early December, a day to make anyone feel better, just being alive in it. Dima would be waiting after class. And Dima's apartment would be waiting, too, and in it Dima's bed. Her apartment? Her bed? Jenny had never known a feeling of ownership, of sharing, not of a thing or a place or a person. Could she ever feel really at home, living in Dima's apartment? Wouldn't she always be his guest, there on sufferance, be careful not to spill the tea? Would it last? Could she really trust this strange, mercurial boy-man-legend she'd known fewer than three months? Would she bore him? Was he as fickle as all the rumors claimed, the rumors she refused to listen to, but somehow heard anyway? In Privy's tears Jenny saw a reflection of what it would cost her to move in with Dima. It was a big investment, maybe bigger than she could afford. She sighed in the golden morning. Nothing came easy.

Nadia Beshanskaia was frightened. Her vanity, struggling in a dead-heat race with ambition as the strongest emotion in her mind and heart, only fueled the fear. There was a litany Nadia had taught herself these last few years, a kind of mantra that helped keep the fear at bay. *You are beautiful*, said the litany, *many men have loved you, still love you . . .* but at this point, on the bad days, on days like today, an insolent little voice would interrupt. It would say, *You're not as beautiful as you were, Nadia, and tomorrow you will be just that much less beautiful until, one day, it will all be gone, your famous beauty.*

But Nadia could fight the insolent voice, as she had fought many a battle in her time. *You are*, she would tell herself, knowing it to be the truth, *the prima ballerina of the International Ballet Theater. The critics love you; audiences weep for you, scream for you, shower you with flowers.* And the voice would creep in, whining but unrefutable, and it would say, *True, but will you still be able to do the famous thirty-two fouettés in* Swan Lake *if they ask you to dance it this season? You're not getting any younger, Nadia, and the story about being thirty-eight is wearing a bit thin. You know per-*

*fectly well you'll be forty-eight in January. And you know
your elevation isn't what it was; you know what the turns
cost you now, what extra agony it is to be en pointe for any
length of time.* Nadia's mantra would grow a little desperate
then; it would have to scrape the bottom of the barrel for
new assurances. *Remember the Kovarsky emerald, Nadia;
remember the furs and the villa in Antibes, the money in
Switzerland.*

But Nadia drew little warmth from her famous jewels or
anything material. Her energy, her very life itself could flour-
ish only under the cruel hot glare of a ballet theater's spotlights, a strange flower of darkness drawing sustenance from
the admiration of crowds, from star billing and the power her
fame bought her in choosing partners and specially equipped
dressing rooms and the highest performance fees. Nadia's
deepest fear was of losing this power, this privilege, for
without the visible trappings of fame she might have no existence at all. For Nadia, now, the darkness across the footlights was a terrifying abyss filled with nameless dangers.

Once that dark space had seemed no more than a happy
mirror reflecting her growing glory. She danced on nerve
alone now, on willpower and gut courage and the hard-won
treasure of dancer's tricks learned in thirty years on most of
the world's great stages. Nadia was spending her capital as a
dancer now. With every performance she had a little less to
give, had to rely that much more on easy charm, on tricks and
gestures. She chose her roles with enormous care; she wouldn't
dance her famous *Giselle* this season because the second act
was too demanding and the strain might show. Nadia chose
her partners with similar caution; they mustn't be too young,
too flashy. Yet if the rumors were true, and Dimitri Lubov
did join the International Ballet, what would she do? It only
befitted her position to take him as a partner. Nadia dreaded
the day she'd have to make that choice.

She lounged against the barre in the big white rehearsal
hall of the International, smoking. That had increased lately,
too, cutting her wind but soothing her over-tense nerves. It
was a private rehearsal, the kind Nadia liked best. Being surrounded by a huge corps de ballet filled with eager youngsters, and some of them talented, made her nervous. Her
partner came in, her hand-picked partner, smiling as usual,
eating an apple: Bayard Jordan. Nadia smiled back. Jordie
was a fool, but a useful fool. Sometimes Nadia teased him,

but always she used him. In many ways Jordie was the ideal partner: beautiful to look at, good-natured to the point—Nadia thought—of imbecility and a marvelous, unfailingly accurate dancer whose only intention was to make his partner look good.

Bayard Jordan was perfectly cast as all those faintly dim princes in the fairy-tale ballets she did so well. He never tried to steal a scene or hog a pas de deux. Nadia knew, and gloried in the knowledge, that she was in no danger of unexpected fireworks from Bayard Jordan onstage or off. He preferred boys, so there was no sexual threat. And even though she often treated him as a lackey, sometimes patronized him and put him down, the quiet young man from New Orleans seemed to like Nadia, to want to be near her, to do her bidding.

She spoke through a blue cloud of cigarette smoke. "Tell me, Jordie, what, exactly do you think of this little Lubov?"

Jordan was used to her style now, and he let the implied threat roll off him like raindrops; if Nadia wanted Lubov for a partner, she'd probably get him, and there wasn't much he could do about it. Bayard Jordan smiled. "Fabulous. No doubt about it. Best since Nureyev, maybe better because he's more of an actor. I haven't met him, but he sure can dance, you bet."

Bayard Jordan had large brown eyes and a gentle manner laced with irony. He knew what Nadia was up to, knew the fears that drove her because to some extent all dancers share those fears. The perfect feline, Nadia must have her cat-and-mouse game, unravel the yarn, do anything to upset the balance of a situation. If he, Bayard, happened to be the only mouse at hand, then it was his turn.

In Bayard the International Ballet had an invaluable resource and knew it. He knew it, too. He was the kind of principal dancer who is indispensable to a great company: very skilled, very professional, easygoing and relatively undemanding. You could always count on him. At the age of twenty-eight he had been known as "good old Bayard Jordan," and it was meant kindly.

If a choreographer needed a leading male to fill in at the last minute, Jordie would be there, rehearsed and smiling. He was never party to the intrigues and jealousies that often rocked the company; he could even get along with the terrible-tempered Nadia. He worked hard, danced well and left his private life at home.

Jordie knew now, as he stood there with Nadia, that he'd never be in the Nureyev-Bruhn-Lubov superstar category of dancer. That kind of talent was a cosmic accident, like being struck by lightning, and there was no point in losing sleep over the fact that it hadn't happened to him. He counted his blessings, and they were plenty: a good career in a first-class company, the affection of critics and the glory of partnering some of the world's best ballerinas—Nadia included. He was, and always would be, firmly lodged among the best of the second-rank male dancers. Ninety percent of the kids in the corps de ballet would never even get that far. So he smiled at Nadia even as he wondered what new devilment her neuroses might be cooking up now.

If Jordie has a fault, thought Nadia as she puffed deeply on the last of her Gauloises, *it is that I can never get a rise out of him.* She was used to stronger reactions to her provocations. She threw the butt on the floor in cheerful defiance of company rules and ground it out with a vicious thrust of her pointe shoe. The rehearsal began.

Jennifer Hale may have been the only girl in history to have lived all her life on Fifth Avenue in New York without ever having set foot in Bloomingdale's.

She knew now, as she stepped on the big escalator, that it was a mistake not to have brought Privy. But something had stopped her from calling Privy, maybe pride, maybe a lingering fear that, if given an inch of entry into Jenny's strange new life, she might take a mile. And even while that thought flickered across her mind, Jenny rejected it as untrue and unworthy. Nevertheless, some nagging desire to assert her new independence made her set out, alone, to furnish Dima's almost-empty kitchen.

The glass-sided escalator rose up and up through the huge glittering store. Jenny wore her usual Monday-off costume, which was exactly the same as her everyday go-to-work costume: blue jeans, boots, a cheap turtleneck and her old Navy-surplus pea jacket, knit navy cap and dark glasses. She felt, as she looked around her, like someone who should have been sent around to the delivery entrance.

Who, she wondered, were all these stupendously self-assured-looking people?

It was three o'clock on a Monday afternoon in early December. Mondays were the Civic's one day off, the company's one chance to shop. The Bloomingdale Christmas decorations were up already, and the store was filled with amazing people, some of the most elegant, chic people Jenny had ever seen. Gloria Bruce would have felt right at home here. There were women in mink who must have spent the entire morning at beauty parlors. There were sleek young men with bodies like snakes, no hips, no shoulders, in suits that fitted like skin and faces that always seemed just on the verge of sneering. Where did they come from? Where did they go? By the time she reached the kitchen department Jenny had decided there was a whole secret race of rich people in New York who did nothing whatsoever but dress up to go shopping at Bloomingdale's.

She walked into the kitchen department and instantly wished for Privy. Half an acre of glittering pots and pans and espresso makers and fondue pots and woks and duck presses stretched out before her, flanked by a picket fence of candles and racks of electrical devices whose uses she couldn't even guess. It was a frightening display for a girl whose cooking skills stopped, abruptly, at making toast.

There was a beautiful bright-red wok, with a sign that said, "This is the Year of the Wok." Thirty-seven-fifty. It was too close to next year, and suppose next year was the year of something else? At Bloomingdale's, Jenny had a hunch, no doubt it would be. Dima already had a teakettle. At least that was a start. She saw cookie sheets. She'd make cookies! Jenny remembered Privy's Christmas cookies and gingerbread men. Definitely a cookie sheet. A stewpot then. Stews were cheap and good for you. Dima liked red. She got a fat red stewpot. A salad bowl. They both loved salads. Knives. They needed a knife, several knives. A thing to grate cheese. Spoons to stir things, wooden spoons. An egg beater. A big frying pan. Jenny tried to remember what was in the kitchen at home, Privy's kitchen, where Privy's good cooking came from. Why had she been afraid to ask Privy? Privy would have loved shopping with her.

There was a pay phone in the corner. She dialed the familiar number. Even as the phone clicked and whirred, Jenny felt fear rising in her throat. The phone rang. No answer. *She's done it. She's left for England. Without even saying good-bye.* No. Privy would never do that. She was probably doing her church work with Reverend Lanier. Jenny realized, as she stood holding the phone in numb amazement, that she had very little idea how Privy spent her afternoons. The idea that Privy might have some life of her own simply hadn't ever occurred to her.

Well, wherever Privy might be, you could bet it wasn't in Bloomingdale's. Why hadn't she made a list? Any moron could make a list. She didn't even own a cookbook, for God's sake. Jenny asked a saleslady; the cookbooks were on another floor. She'd get one later. She wandered the area, her panic growing as the frightening possibilities multiplied. So many things to buy. So many chances to go wrong. "Excuse me, miss," Jenny said to another saleslady, "but what do you use to roast things in?"

The woman looked at her sternly, then decided this was not a put-on. She smiled. "A roasting pan, dearie. They're over here."

The lady took Jenny to the roasting pans. Jenny explained what she was doing, furnishing a kitchen for a friend. The lady looked at what Jenny had picked out so far. "Fine, fine, but you don't need this." She put back a funny-looking knife that had attracted Jenny. "And, if I may suggest a smaller pot, like this, with a cover, for rice or casseroles." They took a small pot. The lady was helpful. Jenny hadn't thought about potholders. Or a colander. Or a vegetable peeler. Jenny had never peeled a vegetable. Finally, they were through. "Cash or charge, dearie?"

"I hoped I could pay by check."

The nice saleslady looked a little dubious; she thought the girl was too young to have her own checking account. "That shouldn't be a problem. You have a driver's license? American Express?"

"Sorry. I don't drive. But here's my Social Security card. And you can call the bank if you like."

The lady looked at the card, then at Jenny. Jenny felt scared again. They didn't trust her. She must look like a thief. The bill was over a hundred dollars. Why was the lady looking at her so strangely? "You are Jennifer Hale?"

"Yes." Jenny answered in a small voice, feeling the way she had felt one time long ago when Gloria Bruce had been stopped by customs for bringing in illegal perfume. Gloria hadn't been able to charm her way out of that one. Jenny wondered if she'd be able to get all that stuff out of Bloomingdale's, where they obviously regarded girls without American Express cards as highly dubious characters.

"The dancer?" The previously nice saleslady had even more suspicion in her voice now. Obviously this tiny slip of a girl could not be Jenny Hale. She had seen Jenny Hale dance *Giselle*, seen her with her own two eyes. Jenny Hale was beautiful. Confident. Jenny Hale cast a spell. Jenny Hale was supposed to be the lover of that gorgeous Russian boy.

"Yes." Jenny's voice was almost a whisper now. She hadn't been this frightened since her confrontation with Privy. The woman just looked at her. Finally, Jenny took off her glasses. "Look," she said, "if there's anything wrong, you can call the people I work for." She fished in her wallet for the little blue card that admitted her into the stage door of the New York State Theater. The woman took the card, still dubious, saw that it was real and smiled a smile as wide as the grand tier.

"You must forgive me, child. You look so different onstage. My name's Geraldine Flynn, and I'm one of your biggest fans. You just sign that check, love, and then I'll ask you to sign an autograph! My, my. Jennifer Hale! Right here in Bloomingdale's." Geraldine Flynn was Jenny's slave from that moment on. She got stock boys to come for the pots and pans, to wrap them and ship them right then and there, and personally led Jenny up to the bookstore, where she suggested Volume I of Julia Child's *Mastering the Art of French Cooking*. Jenny signed the autograph and took the book home with her. The kitchen things would be delivered in a few days.

Geraldine Flynn told Jenny she went two or three times a week to the ballet, always in the third or fourth balcony, sometimes even standing. A true fan, and of Dima's, too, needless to say. Jenny made a note to send the nice woman complimentary tickets the next time she got some. Geraldine Flynn made almost as big an impression on Jenny as Jenny did on Miss Flynn. It was Jenny's first encounter with the power of fame, the first small door swept suddenly open by her talent. They should have accepted a check from anyone, so long as anyone had proper identification. But how nice it was to have things made a bit easier for you, and especially when it came as a surprise.

Jenny walked east on Fifty-ninth Street toward the park and suddenly decided to drop in on Privy. It had been a lovely afternoon so far; that would make it even better. And

Dima had been summoned to a meeting by his agent; she couldn't see him until suppertime anyway.

Sheldon Sylvester wore the unmistakable shimmer of show-business prosperity. His suits seemed to be spun of silk and moonbeams; they fitted a shade too well and gleamed in the dim light with a strange, phosphorescent authority of their own. Sheldon Sylvester's teeth were radiantly white, and his skin was burnished with a Palm Springs suntan of practically cordovan dimensions. Above this monument to jet planes and unguents and clever income-tax accountants, Sylvester's hair added a crowning glitter, receding from his high, sleek forehead in thick waves that seemed to be carved from stainless steel. Even his fingernails shone with the dull gleam of regular manicuring and perpetual lacquer. Dimitri regarded his agent with a grin; how handy to have such a man, who could be found so readily in the dark! But Sheldon Sylvester was the best dancer's agent in the business; Nureyev used him, and half the other big names in ballet and movies and Broadway. And when Sheldon Sylvester arranged a meeting, you went.

This meeting had been set up at Judith Winchester's request, in her suite of offices high above Madison Avenue, on top of the *Scope* building. Judith had invited them for three. Dimitri and his agent had met for luncheon first.

"I have met the lady," said Dima over his trout at Lutece, "only one time. She asks me to supper. Highly boring."

"There's nothing boring, Dima, about her money." Sheldon Sylvester was far beyond flattering his clients; it was a form of flattery that he considered a client important enough to take on. Dima wondered if he could persuade the man to help Jenny.

"She asked me to come to the International."

"What did you say?"

"That ultimately I think about it."

"What do you think, Dima?"

"In all the world are six companies to dance with. Two are no longer available to me. You will not catch Dima any more with the Kirov, nor Bolshoi either. And the Danes? Ultimately not. The Royals? Is possible, as a guest, who knows? And they have not asked me yet this year. I am thinking is likely they have all the Russians they need in Rudi. And so perhaps there are not six companies for Dima. Perhaps there are only two. If I leave de Lis, zip, zap! Good-bye, de Lis—forever. Is not a forgiving man. So, Shelly, ultimately is *one* company. If I leave de Lis."

Sylvester knew this perfectly well, but he wanted to be sure Dima understood it, too. The boy was being modest; he could pick up a fortune in guest shots any time he put his mind to it. The Canadians, for instance, were always amenable to that kind of thing. And the Paris Opéra Ballet would be *enchanté*. But what Sylvester wanted, more than simply the maximum fees of the moment, was a happy future for his dancers. His dancers knew this, and this was why they respected the man and his judgment.

"And so," Dima continued, "should Madame Winchester want Dima, Shelly must make it a contract wearing iron, OK?" Sylvester laughed.

"We call that an ironclad contract. Well, Dima, she hasn't made me a specific offer yet. Frankly it's a bit unusual for us to be invited like this together. Usually the offer would come to me, first, and if it looks good, we talk, you and me. One thing I can say is, no matter what she offers you this afternoon, no commitments, right?" He waved vaguely, and a waiter appeared.

"Right."

"Coffee, Dima?"

"Tea, please." Dima looked around the sunlit room. He had never been in New York's most famous French restaurant before, yet they knew him. The headwaiter had called him Mr. Lubov. The food had been wonderful, the Montrachet, superb. It was a style you could get used to, especially if you had spent the first twelve years of your life in a leaky hut on the windswept banks of the Volga. Dima smiled. He had once heard another dancer say, perhaps from jealousy, that Sheldon Sylvester wore a veneer over his veneer. *Nyet.* Dima was used to sizing up people quickly, and he had long since proved to himself a talent for it.

Sheldon Sylvester might look a bit like a gangster, but everything he said made perfect sense. And when Shelly said something would happen in a certain way, ultimately it did, just as had been predicted. This was perfectly fine by Dima Lubov. It was clear that the Winchester woman would be making some offer, an offer she would feel to be irresistible. Whatever it was, it would depend on Jenny. Dima had made several cautious attempts to budge Jenny from her almost fanatical loyalty to Alex de Lis. So far she simply refused to talk about it. He'd have to change that. If he could change it. And that was a very big "if."

"Shelly," he said, sipping the perfectly brewed tea, "have you seen me dance with Jenny?"

"Nope. But I can read reviews, Dima, and from where I sit it looks really special. You want me to take her on?"

"Would you?"

"I would if you want me to. Hell, she's the hottest kid dancing in America right now—except for you."

"Jenny has no agent. I talk to her tonight."

"From what I hear, you won't even have to pick up the phone, eh, Dima?" A flicker of lechery rode across Shelly's grin and stopped, suddenly, when he saw Dima's face.

Dima had his own way of lowering the iron curtain. Inside the boy, behind the dazzling dancer, there lived a very private Dimitri with ideas of gallantry that had been fixed hundreds of years ago. His face froze; his eyes turned hard. He simply looked at his agent, and in that moment Shelly became an unwelcome, uninvited trespasser in Dimitri's private life. Finally, quietly, he spoke. "I would be pleased, Shelly, if you would handle her business." It was a command.

"Dima, look, don't get me wrong, I mean—"

"Is OK, Shelly. Jenny and I are good friends. I talk to her. Ultimately you hear from Jenny, work things out between you. I would be hoping, should I go to the International, would be possible for Jenny to come also."

"We'll have to take things as they come, Dima," said Shelly as the relief flowed through his veins. "But they ought to be delighted." The check came, and Shelly signed it. Quarter to three. The two men walked out of New York's fanciest French restaurant, oblivious of the regiments of eyes that followed them.

It was the first time in years, Privy thought, that she'd heard Jenny babbling on like this. They sat in the big old kitchen just as they always had, drinking tea and chatting. Privy heard about the adventure at Bloomingdale's, the trials and errors of Jenny's first attempts at cooking, a hundred small pieces of her life that added up to happiness. Privy beamed. It was the conversation every happy new bride has with her mother, and if Jenny wasn't married and Privy wasn't her mother, it mattered not one bit. Happiness mattered, and Jenny fairly glowed with it. Only in dancing had Privy seen the like of this radiance come over the girl.

There had been times when it occurred to Miss Privet that Jenny's joy in dancing might be the only true joy she'd ever know. Then Machito had come along, Jenny's first boyfriend, first lover. And while in all fairness Privy knew the boy meant no harm, it was plain he did no good. Machito Ramirez would be casual all his life, a bee among the flowers, and it was Jenny's fate not to know how to be lighthearted about something that meant as much as falling in love. So Machito moved on and eventually left de Lis. There were, Jenny said, no hard feelings. This was because Jenny herself made huge efforts to simulate a casual attitude whenever she saw Machito. He accepted that with the same shallow good humor as he had accepted her affection and her virginity: one more tribute to the Crown Prince of Spanish Harlem, the first Puerto Rican kid to make it as a principal dancer with de Lis. There had been a time, Privy reflected, sipping the good China tea, when she had felt the Machito incident might have turned Jenny off boys for a good long while.

Privy looked at Jenny Hale and smiled. Dima Lubov was doing something right! Jenny asked, would Privy come to supper next Monday? "Wild horses," said Miss Privet, "could not keep me away." Jenny left her then, happy that she'd acted on impulse to drop in. And once again, down on Fifth Avenue, Jenny looked up at the apartment's windows. But there was no guilt this time, and no fear. Everything was going to be all right.

Judith Winchester's office had been designed, and by experts, for one purpose only: to intimidate visitors. After passing three receptionists, each with her own office, and checking with each of the three, who in turn checked with each other, the visitor was escorted into the antechamber of greatness. Here, in a foyer that might have measured thirty feet long by half that distance in width, sat the ambassador's nephew in solitary splendor, defended only by his Savile Row suit and the very famous name on the bronze nameplate in front of him.

He rose for Sheldon Sylvester and Dima and smiled a middle-level smile. The top-level smile was reserved for reigning monarchs and the presidents or dictators of significant NATO powers. "Mr. Lubov, Mr. Sylvester." The young man

said these names in a manner that proclaimed the names were
now official, their owners could keep them. "Mrs. Winchester
will see you in"—there was a dramatic pause as the young man
looked at the thin gold wafer on his wrist—"in seven minutes."
The private secretary cleared his throat. "Please, be seated."

In seven minutes, precisely, a small bell chimed twice. The
secretary stood up again. "If you please." He led them to a
massive pair of doors so beautifully integrated into the old
chestnut paneling of the foyer that neither Dima nor Shelly
had noticed it. The secretary opened these doors and announced, as if to royalty, "Mr. Lubov and Mr. Sylvester."

"Dimitri! Mr. Sylvester!" Judith rose from the immense
slab of polished steel that served her as a desk and came to
meet them as if their visit were a charming surprise. "How
nice of you to come. Would you like coffee, tea, a drink?"
They declined. "I caught your *Jeune Homme,* Dimitri. You
absolutely brought it to life. Brilliant!"

"You are"—Dima smiled—"very kind." He couldn't take
his eyes off the view that stretched on three sides of the huge
room: the park and Connecticut to the north, the East River
and Long Island to the east, the Hudson and New Jersey to
the west. Why, Dima asked himself, did she not get the south,
too, while she was at it? Some people, he reflected, were truly
insatiable.

"Let's," said Judith with a cheerleader's bright, unthinking
hope riding uneasily on her razor-edged sixty-year-old face,
"make ourselves comfy." She used words like "comfy" and
"swell," odd misplaced bits and pieces of Midwestern slang
from her girlhood, in a constant struggle to seem human. In a
way there was something endearing about this, although not
in the way Judith Winchester intended. You responded for a
note of gallantry in her dogged tries at warmth and humanity; they were so obviously doomed to failure.

Sheldon Sylvester looked at Judith across the slab of polished steel that reminded him of nothing more than a giant's
version of an embalming table he had once seen in the Los
Angeles morgue. *The crocodile,* thought Shelly, *is coy this afternoon.* And Sheldon Sylvester felt the tiny hairs rising on
the back of his well-tanned neck and a new shot of adrenaline rushing through his veins. He looked at Dima, whose
Tatar-god face had gone masklike. Dima and his lady friend
were going to need all the protection they could get, if they
wound up in the clutches of this specimen.

"Dima," she began, "may I call you Dima?"

"Please. Is my name." He smiled, but a chill ran through him. He was used to the nickname's being public property by now. Still, it was what Jenny called him, and it grated his nerves to hear it on Judith Winchester's cold lips.

Dimitri looked at this strange, disconcerting woman. Nothing in his experience had prepared him for a Judith Winchester. He was used to women—and some men—looking at him with unsatisfied hunger, eager to share in his fame or his energy or his love. But this woman wanted him for mysterious reasons of her own: not for love, surely, and surely, too, she had all the fame she needed. The uncertainty disturbed Dima. He didn't know where he was with her or how much leverage he might exert. And what could she give him? Money, perhaps, and plenty of it. Money was so new to Dima that he refused to believe it was real. The de Lis contract would soon be up, and he knew what company dancers—even principals—were paid by the Civic. He'd be lucky to pull in thirty thousand a year, him, Lubov! So Judith could give him money. Maybe that was enough. He took refuge in silence, and simply looked at her, and waited for her next words. Let her tell him what she wanted of him. And for him.

"I just don't know what to do," she began.

Right on, thought Shelly Sylvester. *And the Pope doesn't know where St. Peter's is.*

"I've plied Dima with champagne, praises, unlimited offers . . . I appeal to you, Mr. Sylvester. What will induce him to leave de Lis and dance with us?"

"You'd have to ask Dima. As far as I know, Mrs. Winchester, he's perfectly happy with de Lis."

"Please," she said, reaching across the desk to pat his hand, "call me Judith. I want us to be very good friends." She actually giggled.

Shelly wondered from what 1930s debutante party she had dredged up that one. "My friends call me Shelly."

"Well, Shelly, and Dima, at this point in my tired old life, I have just one ambition. And that is to make the International Ballet Theater unrivaled. Unrivaled. In the world. We're getting close. We have Nadia, of course, and Ramirez . . . but I don't have to tell you who we have. Dima would be the final glory. And I do not use that word unadvisedly. For, Dima, you are glorious. And—I know too well—not susceptible to flattery. Therefore, Mr. Gregory Holden, who can't be with us this afternoon, has authorized me to make you a very special offer." Judith paused for effect.

Greg Holden, as Dima and Shelly knew, was the young millionaire who had three years ago sold out Holden Aircraft and taken over the management of the International Ballet for a dollar a year. Holden had been at Judith's dinner party after Dima's *Giselle*. But he hadn't said much to Dima, nor Dima to him.

Judith continued. "We will pay you five thousand dollars per performance, with a guarantee of a minimum of two performances every week during the season. Should you be injured, the guarantee continues. Now I don't have to tell you, that is the absolute top rate. Not even Rudi gets more. It means a cool two hundred thousand a year, just as a base. Not counting guest spots, which, of course, you'll be free to do out of season. I think it's fair to say, gentlemen, that such an offer has never been made in all the history of ballet."

Her voice had changed now. The little girl had drifted out of it, and someone much older and tougher had come in. There was an edge to her voice now, almost a rasping quality. It had become a voice that could cut stone, fell trees, win wars. It was a frightening voice.

As if she realized that, Judith changed her tone. "Naturally, Dima"—she smiled—"to an artist like you money is certainly secondary. What you will find with us, is something de Lis can never promise you. True stardom. You *are* a star, Dima; it would be criminal stupidity not to acknowledge that fact. Hear them screaming your name: Dima! Dima! That's the kind of response that made Frank Sinatra. To have it as a ballet dancer—extraordinary. Only Rudi has ever gotten that kind of applause. No. More than applause. Adulation. And it's just beginning. You're only twenty-four. By thirty, Dima, if you come with us, you'll be twice a millionaire. More famous than even Rudi Nureyev. A household word." Again Judith paused. She smiled at Dima and blinked her eyes. The coy little girl was coming back again. "You know de Lis will never do that for you, Dima; it is his stated policy not to. But beyond fame and beyond money, there is one thing more that we can offer you."

Judith Winchester stood up suddenly and walked the length of the enormous room. "Come with me," she said, with the air of a little girl who knows a secret and can be persuaded to tell it.

The far end of Judith's office contained the big double doors, which were centered between two immense eight-panel eighteenth-century Chinese Coromandel screens. The carved, lacquered panels had been taken off their hinges and set into the wall on sliding tracks. They slid back on noiseless ball bearings, but only Judith and her secretaries knew what was behind them. One panel hid a small but completely equipped bar. Another, a tiny kitchen. Some panels simply concealed filing cabinets. And then there were two panels that hid something more special.

Judith stood before these panels and waited until Dima and Shelly Sylvester were very close. She slid back both panels and revealed a complete scale model of the stage at the New York State Theater, three-dimensional and complete even to the pattern of the gold curtain.

There were, Dima noticed with a grin, no holes in Judith Winchester's version of the curtain. She pressed a hidden button. The curtain rose, in perfect simulation of the real thing. A gong sounded with startling effect. The first eerie strains of an unfamiliar piece of music flowed out of stereo speakers.

The curtain rose to reveal a stylized, very beautiful stage setting. It was a fantasy of an Egyptian temple, stark, dramatic, awesome. The music continued, very modern, but somehow with an echo of the East.

"I can," Judith Winchester murmured, "offer you this!" She smiled as the two men stared in fascination at the little theater, the setting, the music. "It is a full-length ballet based on Shakespeare's *Antony and Cleopatra*. It will be Antony Tudor's first ballet in years. Commissioned by us. For you, Dima. And the first of many."

It took a lot to awe Dima Lubov. Now he was awed. He looked at the little stage, and at Judith, and then at Shelly. He remembered what Shelly had said at lunch. Don't agree to anything on the spot. Again Dima looked at this strange, obsessed woman. "You overwhelm me." It was perfectly true.

Judith led them back to her desk but did not sit down. "The contract has been drawn up, Dima," she said. "I know you'll want to think about this, and you, Shelly, will want to see the contract at your leisure. Here are two copies. I realize Dima's agreement with de Lis has some time to run . . . six weeks, is it not?"

"Six weeks." Dima's voice was subdued. He was trying to imagine Jenny's reaction to this offer.

"Today is Monday. If you can let me know within two weeks, gentlemen, then we can proceed with our plans."

Dima wanted to mention Jenny, but somehow he sensed Shelly wouldn't like that, not now, not when the International was so patently laying the world at their feet. They could negotiate about Jenny later. Shelly and Greg Holden. Or Shelly and this woman. Dima took one last look at the huge office, at the Chinese wall with its tiny theater, and at the woman who controlled it all.

She was right, of course, in thinking that what he wanted most, in the bottom of his dancer's heart, was to have ballets specially made for him alone. This was why he had left the frozen choreography of the Kirov. It was this, far more than any amount of money or any degree of fame, that spoke to the inner Dimitri. He could see that temple, full-scale. The music haunted him already. He, Dima, strode onto that stage, glittering in the armor of Imperial Rome. He imagined a warrior's dance, the dance of a conqueror. And then he blinked, and jerked his head a bit, and grinned. She was saying something else.

"I won't say good-bye, then, Dima, because I just *know* we'll be talking again soon, don't you?" The cheerleader had replaced the rasp in her voice. Dima took her hand, slowly, still half in his dream of the Egyptian ballet.

"Yes," he said softly, "ultimately we talk."

Sam Purcell rolled the bronze cannon across the smooth mahogany of his desktop. *Pow! Take that, Senator John Arthur Odell.* In his mind's eye, Sam blasted the Colorado senator who was making such a damn stink with his damn Odell Bill. Another damn good-doer who was bound and determined he'd keep the world safe from the CIA. If the Odell Bill went through, there might not be a CIA. There sure as hell wouldn't be a Sam Purcell, or a big mahogany desk or the office it sat in, with its silk drapes and its Persian rugs and leather armchairs.

Senator Odell was in love with détente, this year's buzzword around Washington. Détente! Naturally, they'd have to pick a French word for it. Couldn't call it by its rightful name, snake-livered cowardice. Ass-kissing servitude. Cocksucking obsequiousness. Détente! He'd show them détente.

There they sat, these highly educated powermongers who'd never seen a real Russian killer Commie eyeball to eyeball, who'd never *smelled* one of the unwashed brutes or heard the barracks laughter or picked up after one of their little multiple rapes in their friendly, comradely progress across East Germany in pursuit of the dregs of Hitler's armies.

Sam Purcell had spent thirty years building his hatred for everything Soviet into a pure and perfect thing. He knew. He knew in his heart and his bones what they were up to, what they wanted and how they'd get it. And détente was playing into their slimy, unwashed hands just as surely as handing them the fucking keys to the whole country, the whole free world.

Free world. That was a laugh. No sooner had men like Sam Purcell made sure it would be free than the Odells came right along to undo all the good so many Americans had bled and died for. Oh, they were soft, the Odells of the world. They were men of peace, self-described, men of goodwill. He'd like to see that goodwill rotting in the dungeons of the KGB. Digging shit ditches in the frozen earth of Siberia.

The cannon moved across the desk again. Sam loved the cannon. It was an eighteenth-century founder's model, and it actually worked, although he'd never dared shoot it off for fear the intricately worked bronze might shatter. The dealer in London had told him it was reputed to have belonged to Nelson himself. Now there was a man Sam could admire. No one ever talked détente to Nelson! No one ever accused Nelson of being too much a hawk. Oh, Sam knew they thought he was too much of a hawk. He'd never made any bones about it. In the 1950s he'd flown pretty high on his reputation as a hawk. It was all easier then. People knew the difference between keeping the peace and giving in. Now everything was changing, and not for the better. People didn't seem to care anymore. They didn't seem to know what a menace was building behind that iron curtain, growing stronger and more subtle every day. Détente! If Ivan himself had written the script, it couldn't have come out better.

Sam rolled the cannon back to its usual resting place and unlocked the drawer that contained his "in" box. He smiled, doing it. That had been one of his own pet ideas, the locked-drawer in box. That and the blind lunch counters. You couldn't be too careful, then or now. Unconsciously Sam looked around the big office as he pulled out the box. You never knew.

With the quick expertise honed by years of practice outwitting the CIA bureaucracy, Sam flipped through the contents of his in box. Half of it could be delegated, two items required his attention this morning and three others should be dealt with soon. Then there was the transcription of the coded message from Dave Loughlin. It contained, as usual, not much that Sam didn't know better already.

The death of Yuri Ivanov convinced Dave that there was, indeed, a pattern. What the pattern might be he had no idea. He was continuing low-level surveillance of known Soviet agents in the New York area; nothing to report so far. He was waiting for a break. *Aren't we all?* thought Sam Purcell, thinking of the Odell Bill. Unnecessarily, he reread Dave's message. There was much to be said for the plodders of this world he reflected, moving Dave's report back to the growing stack of "to-be-filed" materials; the plodders of the world were predictable. That was one thing he liked about Dave Loughlin, had always liked about the man. Predictable. Absolutely predictable.

CHAPTER
❦ 7 ❧

Jenny looked at the onion with grave suspicion. It was obviously a sneaky onion, an onion of no character, ready and waiting for the first chance to make a fool of her, hoping to make her cry.

In her right hand she held the shiny new knife from Bloomingdale's. Julia Child's book lay open on the counter, but Jenny got little comfort from its precise instructions on how to reduce the onion to tiny, regular cubes. It was all a question of showing the onion who was boss, she told herself. You must not let the onion get the upper hand. It could sense fear, just like certain dogs. And, to make matters worse, she'd forgotten to get a cutting board. Julia was very specific about that. So, as dancers learn to do early on, Jenny improvised. She used doubled paper towels.

The onion just lay there, playing dead. Thinking of ways to outwit her. Yet if she were going to make the sauce for the chicken breasts, the onion had to be dealt with. Jenny winced and grasped the onion with her left hand. Down came the knife. Off went the onion's head! Then its bottom. Then she cut it in half, vertically, just as the book told her to, then peeled it, laid the two split halves on their flat side, made several deep vertical cuts almost to the back of the onion half, then cut again, in thin slices at right angles to the first cuts. And there it was. Just like the diagram. The onion fell apart in neat little cubes. It had only been a little more frightening than her first *Giselle*.

The sauce Mornay was simmering happily on the gas burner when Dima came flying in with a bunch of apricot-colored tea roses and news of Judith's offer. It hit her like a thrown brick; here was the thing she'd dreaded most, a turn of events that had to force her to make a sudden choice. She saw his

joy and wanted to share it, but only her dancer's training let
her fake a smile.

She kissed him and turned the heat down under the sauce.
Soon they were having tea by the fire. On the most ordinary
day of his life Dima Lubov was irrepressible. This evening he
was flying, and Jenny knew the reasons were good even as
she forced herself to smile the congratulations. Of course,
he'd want to take the offer. He'd be a moron not to, all that
money, the new ballet. And of course, he'd want her to go
with him. And that made her worst fears come rushing at her
like the locomotives in those old melodramas, with guess who
tied to the track. He couldn't sit still. Dima was like a schoolboy in a very strict school who had just been told that every
other day from now on would be Christmas.

"For the money alone it would be worth it, Jenny! In a
few years we'll be rich."

You, Dima, she thought. *You'll be rich. It isn't a question
of "we" just yet.*

He was on his feet just then, and suddenly launched himself in one of the famous Lubov elevations, high in the air
with no visible preparations, his booted feet beating the air
like hummingbird's wings. Dima hovered there for an instant,
grinning the urchin grin, and landed at her side. His face
went serious then; he took her hand in both of his; the sky-
blue eyes went darker. "You will be coming." It could have
been a question, but he made it an accomplished fact.

"Oh, Dima." Why did she have such trouble knowing what
to say or how to say it? Some people were always ready with
a snappy comeback. Not Jenny Hale. One of the critics had
written about her "eloquent feet." *Try to play a love scene
with your feet sometime,* she thought, giggling, reading that.
But it was a fact, Jenny knew, that all her eloquence was in
her body, in motion. She often couldn't think of ordinary
things to say. When it came to the big moments, she was
completely at a loss. Maybe, she thought ruefully, that was
why she had so few big moments. "Dima, you must think I'm
stupid, or something, even to hesitate—"

"No, *deushka.* Not stupid." Dima could sense the struggle
in her. In Russian he knew the right words to say. In this
strange new language it was not so easy; he must go slowly
not to offend her, not to press too hard. There was no doubt
in Dima's mind that he would accept the International offer
sooner or later. And in a dancer's life, in the short bright tra-

jectory of even the most brilliant career, that "sooner" is far more urgent than other people's "sooners." Every day that Dima failed to realize his potential as a dancer was a day lost forever. For dancers there is no repenting at leisure, no over-painting of the false stroke, no editing beyond what you do with your body in the instant. Dima felt this terrible urgency more deeply than most dancers because he felt his years in the Kirov had been to some extent wasted. He had to work harder, dance harder, just to catch up.

The dancing with Alex de Lis was all a dancer could ask, with one glaring exception. With de Lis a dancer had no leverage. With a nonstar repertory system, all casting was subject to the master's whim. The favorite of the moment had all the plum parts on a silver tray without asking. But the favor of Alex de Lis was a moving searchlight, and the one sure thing about his Civic Ballet was that whoever was in favor this week, this month, this season was almost sure to be out of favor very soon.

To Dima this was a risk he simply could not afford as a dancer or as a man. He knew his own fiery temperament too well to imagine himself as anything but the star he could be—would be—with the International.

And as he sat there in the firelight, thinking how much he loved Jenny, he also thought how very different she was, inside, from him. Jenny, he knew, really didn't care about the star part of dancing. Once she had told him she could be happy dancing in an empty room. He looked at her now as she fought with herself, and a dark premonition flashed across his heart, what he called a "Russian thought." The thought was that Jenny would be dancing in a room empty of him. Her dedication had something almost religious about it, and in Jenny's religion Alex de Lis was the Pope, if not God Himself. And whatever sacrifices the god demanded, his servants were more than happy to make for him. Jenny's eyes seemed to grow larger in her small face. Her hand pressed his hand. And Dima wondered if he was going to be the next sacrifice to the god of dance, Alexander de Lis.

"Before I danced with you," she said quietly, "I thought it was silly—unprofessional—to care that much who I danced with. I thought a good ballerina ought to be able to dance with any good dancer and make it right for the audience. Now I don't know anymore. You changed all that."

"Should be changed. Is big difference. I am," he said, moving closer to her on the big leather sofa, "not knowing all the words. Dima is—do you know *muzhik?*"

"No."

"*Muzhik* is peasant. Country boy. Not smooth."

"You're smooth enough for me, Dima-Muzhik."

"Not knowing slick words. I want Jenny onstage. I want Jenny offstage. To dance, my Giselle, with you is not happening every day to every dancer." He kissed her cheek. "When ultimately Dima goes to the International, is right Jenny goes with him."

"How do you know they'd even want me?"

"Shelly makes them want you. I forget. Tomorrow call Shelly." He didn't have to say who Shelly was. Jenny knew, as every dancer knew, and the thought that an agent as prominent and influential as Sheldon Sylvester might take her on was as much a revelation as any Simon Bridge review or starring role.

Jenny looked at him and snuggled closer. In a minute they'd be making love. Which would be a lot better than trying to worm her way out of this one. Except that she wasn't sure she wanted to worm her way out. After all, why not go to the International? It sure as hell hadn't done Machito any harm, nor Bayard Jordan either. Of course, they'd got the old silent treatment from de Lis; their names were never mentioned, which was ironic since half the season they'd be dancing on the same nights within a few hundred yards of each other, one company in the new Met, the other in the New York State Theater. Why, Jenny wondered, did she have to make up her mind right now, just when everything else was going so well for her? If only there could be a way not to have to make up her mind, to face de Lis.

De Lis! The very thought of that scene gave her the shivers. To tell the man who had given her everything she was leaving for some silly reason like money? She knew exactly how he'd react. De Lis actively denied the existence of money. Money was something that no artist should even be concerned with. The board of directors talked about nothing but money. De Lis talked about nothing but dance. Somehow, by unseen compromises on both sides, they managed to run the company. But money was not a reason she could offer de Lis as an excuse for leaving. Love? A five-times-married man should know about love. Then she smiled. Five times married. And five times divorced.

Jenny didn't want to think about it anymore. Thinking about it made her nervous. She reached up with her long swan's neck and ran her tongue around the inside of Dima's ear. "Show me," she whispered as though the dark room was crowded with strangers, "how *muzhiks* make love." *But please, please, don't ask me to leave de Lis. Not right now. Not tonight.*

The Fifth Murder
Paris, 1975

He registered under the name Pierre St. Jacques, and indeed his Swiss passport bore witness to that name, and his likeness, and his residence in Lausanne. But the dapper little man had five other passports in five other names, all perfect, undetectable, as well they should have been since they were real, having been expertly revised at the KGB department of documentation in Moscow.

One of the passports was German, one Dutch, one Finnish and one American. He liked the Swiss one best because it made him feel richer, more mysterious. And the little man liked to feel mysterious.

He had been born on a back alley in Kiev and fought and killed and maneuvered his way through the dark underside of the Soviet bureaucracy all through the worst days of Stalin until the war ended and he found himself a minor but notably effective assassin for the KGB. The dapper little man was, of course, not as young as he used to be. But age had brought a certain polish the new boys lacked.

His languages, to name one example, had improved to the point where he could be convincing as any of the nationalities on his several passports. Only in America did he sometimes have to assume the guise of a recent citizen; the true cornfed Yankee accent eluded him. Still and all, the man who checked into Room 38 at the tremendously chic little Le Hôtel at number 13, Rue des Beaux-Arts on the left bank of the Seine in Paris, could look back on a full and satisfying career. He had eliminated more than sixty enemies of the Soviet. In all cases but two, his attentions to the subject had gone undetected. And even in the two deaths where foul play had been suspected, no finger of accusation had ever been pointed at him or at his masters.

Pierre St. Jacques looked around the elegant little room with satisfaction. What a charming concept, to panel the walls in bottle-green silk velvet and do all the furniture in the identical material. He ran his hand over the sensuous texture of the tailored velvet bedcover. Real silk, beyond any doubt. The color scheme effectively concealed the fact that the room was really small for a grand luxe class hotel. Still, he loved the little place and always stayed there when he was Pierre St. Jacques. He loved the private town house look of the hotel, with its big open stairwell and curving staircase, its tiny elevator, the lovely back garden, whose fountain was made from an enormous, real seashell, and the series of fifteenth-century caves in the cellar where one could get a glass of wine at night. It was all splendid, unexpected on the Left Bank, and perfectly done. The attitude of the management suited the special needs of Pierre St. Jacques, too. The place was run carefully, but with a kind of offhand discretion that reflected the more informal life-style of the new rich—and their lovers. For, Pierre St. Jacques was convinced, more lovers saw these silken walls than married couples. And more power to them!

Yes, it was perfect, even down to the tiny refrigerator with its splits of champagne and individual cans of fruit juice. He smiled as he surveyed the little jewel box of a room. How fitting it was that the servants of the world's greatest Communist power should be so rewarded! It had been a long time since anyone had questioned his expense account. The results were too good for niggling. The man called Pierre St. Jacques was on assignment now, but no one at headquarters would ever know what an easy hit it was going to be. So Pierre St. Jacques, so called, was treating himself to a little holiday. Tonight the opera. Later on a quiet supper someplace delightful. Then, who knew? He smiled again, at the pleasures and possibilities of the night.

The little man had showered and shaved and was knotting an Hermès cravat in a St. Laurent shirt when the knock came on the door.

"Who is that?" he asked in unaccented French. The reply

was indistinct. St. Jacques moved closer to the door and repeated his question.

"Alexander Nevsky." The little KGB agent shuddered involuntarily. Only three people in the world had any right to know this week's code word, and all of them were in Moscow. Or had been yesterday. His mind raced. Where had he slipped? What new crisis had arisen for them to send someone in person? Had there been some new purge in the Kremlin? It took him half a minute to master the shudder. Then he opened the door.

"You move slowly, comrade," said the tall gray-haired man in flawless Russian that was, nevertheless, not a native's Russian. St. Jacques looked at the stranger's face, a calm, bookish face, healthy but intelligent, the eyes a bluish shade of gray. No. St. Jacques had never seen the man before. The stranger smiled. Beneath the smile a gun appeared, a compact mat-black .32 caliber Beretta fitted with silencer. St. Jacques knew the gun well. It was exactly like the one he was fond of using, the gun that lay even now in the little refrigerator of the bedroom. The KGB man backed into the little bedroom. The sweat was trickling down his neck. He thought of the crisp shirt, the opera tickets. He still didn't know what the stranger wanted. He might be under arrest. The gun was a bad sign. But it might be a trick, a means of seizing the upper hand by catching him, St. Jacques, he of the nearly perfect record, off guard for once. Maybe someone had suggested he was slipping. Maybe someone was jealous. There were so many possibilities.

"What," asked the man called St. Jacques, "do you want?"

"You have been, Igor Smolensky, a very naughty boy." Smolensky trembled. Even in the KGB very few people knew the name he had been born with. "And," the stranger continued, "you are repentant—are you not?—as the years creep up on you. Suddenly you wonder about your eternal soul. And you think, perhaps, that if you confess your crimes, there may be some hope of salvation for you. Is that not true?"

Smolensky-St. Jacques-Rivolta-Leinsdorf-Beaulieu-Burke-Tarczynski said nothing. Having been born without a conscience, he had never been bothered by it. So they were after some sort of confession! A typical Stalinist trick. They all were still obsessed by confessions, even now, so many years later. It mattered not how false, or how preposterous; all they

wanted was a signed piece of paper. So that was the reason
for sending a bigwig in person. That was the reason for the
gun. Smolensky had no doubt that this was, indeed, a bigwig.
But if it was a question of confessing, then maybe there was
hope. He'd sign anything. They'd bring him back to Moscow,
for trial perhaps. If he cooperated, there was a chance. There
had to be. His face was sheeted with sweat now. His hands
felt clammy. Still, he said nothing.

"You will sit at the escritoire. Your hands will remain on
top of the escritoire." The stranger reached into his suit-
jacket pocket. Out came a neatly folded sheaf of notepaper.
Smolensky's eyes flicked to the paper, then away. He knew
that paper well. It was status paper, made of the finest rag
linen, used only in the uppermost echelons of the KGB. This
man must be influential indeed. Whoever he was. Whatever
he wanted.

Smolensky sat down and placed his hands side by side,
palms down on the desktop. He took some pride in the fact
that they were not trembling anymore. "What," he asked
again, "do you want?" He cleared his throat. "I have done
nothing that was not for the good of the Soviet."

"There are so many opinions on that it would take weeks
to explore them," said the stranger smoothly, "and—alas—I
must catch a plane and have no time for such games. You
will take the hotel pen and write, starting with today's date in
the upper-right-hand corner. You will write in Russian, precisely as I dictate. Start now!" The stranger handed a sheet of
the KGB paper to Igor Smolensky. Smolensky sighed and began to write. *"I, Pierre St. Jacques,"* began the stranger,
*"born Igor Smolensky in Kiev, Russia, on the eleventh of Au-
gust, 1929, can no longer continue in the hateful assignment
which has occupied me all this year. While since 1943 I
have been in the employment of the KGB in various capaci-
ties, and while this work has often forced me to eliminate enemies of the Soviet, never did I doubt the necessity of the
work. I have done my job well, and the world is better for it.
Still, as my work has taken me all through the free world,
there have been moments when I question whether it is
strictly necessary to be so severe in punishing the enemies of
the state. Political enemies? Perhaps. But to track down and
destroy innocent artists out of pure revenge, this is too much.
Last winter I was ordered to eliminate the poet Gregor Berisov, in Geneva. Thinking he had been perhaps a counter-*

agent, I did it. Then orders came to destroy Peter Chablesky, the physicist. Again, I complied without questioning. But when it was given me to kill Gaia Muldovska, a harmless woman whose music has given much pleasure to the world, I began for the first time to question the orders from my leaders. Still, I did it, fixing her automobile so that she had a fatal accident. Next on my list was Yuri Ivanov. To destroy such an artist curdled my very soul. Oh, I know the idea behind these punishments. To frighten young people who think of defecting! If defectors are tracked down like rabbits and killed, there will be no incentive to defect. I have searched my soul and find I can no longer be the instrument of such a senseless and ignoble policy. Yet there is no turning back for me. There is no place for me to hide, any more than there is any place for those artists whose names are on the list. It is my hope, then, that by this, my final action, those poor victims of Soviet revenge whose names remain on my list will be warned and, perhaps, may be able to save themselves. Therefore, take care! Take care, Sergei Rosoff, Nikolai Poussine, Lydia Malikovna and Dimitri Lubov. In this, my final statement, I, who was meant to kill you, bless you. Too late have I, who hoped to help build a better world, discovered that in fact I have only helped breed monsters. May God forgive Igor Smolensky"

The shot rang out exactly at the moment the pen stopped writing. While dictating, the stranger had taken a handkerchief from his pocket and wiped the gun very carefully, then held the gun with the fine linen handkerchief. Imperceptibly the gun barrel inched closer and closer to Smolensky's forehead. As the KGB assassin wrote the final "y" in "Smolensky," the gun went off. Quickly, while the dapper little man was still twitching, the stranger pressed the gun into his right hand. Rigor mortis would keep it there. The stranger stayed a few moments more in the little green-silk-velvet chamber, making very sure there was no evidence of his visit. He smiled. In an hour, from a public phone, anonymous calls would be made to the police and to three newspapers. Igor Smolensky would tell the world more, dead, than he ever had in life.

————————◆————————

There were days when Greg Holden wished he were a test pilot again, with nothing more complicated to do than trying to rip the wings off some experimental jet fighter plane in a power dive at twice the speed of sound. Greg's love of flying had taken him from the Air Force to testing jets to a vice-presidency of Lockridge Aircraft at thirty. Lockridge in time became Holden-Lockridge and then just plain Holden Aircraft. Those had been golden times for Greg. He'd married the right girl, Phillys, and Phillys had given him twelve beautiful years and two beautiful kids.

Greg had been growing restless as the top executive of Holden Aircraft when Phillys and both his sons had disappeared in a small charter plane flying from Antigua to their new house at St. Lucia. There had been a sudden storm of West Indian violence; it was a prop plane flying low. They'd never even found the wreckage. Greg had never forgiven himself for not being there. He'd been escorting three Pentagon types around the plant, hoping to win the contract for the newest jet bomber. Greg would feel for the rest of his life that if he had been with Phillys and the kids, he could have flown around the storm, or over it, or somehow pulled them out. Part of him went numb that day, five years ago, and part of him was numb still. He lost all appetite for work.

Within a year Greg had sold out of Holden for a handsome cash settlement and a lifetime consultant's fee that effectively removed his money problems forever. He was forty years old and rich, smart, healthy and good-looking in a rugged, up-from-grease-monkey style. And he had no idea what to do with the rest of his life. Phillys had always loved the ballet, and as soon as he sold their house in the suburbs and moved into a rented penthouse on Central Park West in Manhattan, Greg went about setting up a Phillys Holden Memorial Scholarship at the School of the International Ballet Theater, her favorite company. It was in the course of doing this that Greg became aware of the company's need for some sound, full-time managerial talent among all the artists, patrons and part-time directors. He had never been a fan, at least not the way Phillys was, but the challenges of running something as diverse and exotic as a ballet company fascinated his fastidious mechanic's brain.

Soon he was spending afternoon upon afternoon in the seedy International Ballet offices, checking books, suggesting schemes for financing, talking to charitable foundations, making himself useful in a hundred ways until, within a year, he found himself addicted to both the company and its product. Like many late-blooming balletomanes, Greg developed an almost fanatical passion for his new interest. His position was made formal, and for one dollar a year Greg Holden signed on as the managing director of the International Ballet Theater.

He took over in a time of turmoil. The chief patroness had just died, leaving the bulk of her estate to three hospitals. The company was, as always, in the red. It had no permanent theater. Union costs backstage were soaring. Temperaments flared. Only after three years as director did Greg begin to realize that this was the normal state of affairs in any big ballet company, three-alarm crises around the clock. Somehow the company kept itself together, attracted top dancers, continued to please the critics. It was exactly like that old rule of physics which proves it is totally impossible for a bumblebee to fly. The damn things fly because they want to fly, not because some physics book said they couldn't or shouldn't. And so it was with the International Ballet.

But today had been tough even by ballet standards. Nadia entered in a fine White Russian snit to announce in her best Lady Macbeth manner that she could not for one instant longer put up with her present dressing room; a new one must be created for her immediately, or she would find herself unable to dance. Greg had long since learned that the only way to deal with Nadia was pure flattery. Since the company did not own the theater, it was really impossible to make any alterations. And Nadia, as International Ballet's unquestioned prima ballerina, had already the best of the dressing rooms. As well she knew.

Greg looked at the raging ballerina, the flaring nostrils, the whip of scorn in her husky voice, the outraged eyebrows arching into infinity with the injustice of it all. The stupid broad, he figured, was on a fishing expedition. Nadia made scenes as regularly as clockwork, and since these scenes had to be appeased somehow, it was rare that she did not emerge with some new privilege, even if it wasn't what she had come for. Greg found Nadia vain, spoiled and not very intelligent. But onstage she somehow transformed herself into something lyrical and pure. Her most famous role was the Swan Queen in *Swan Lake*. And, Greg thought, very like a swan she was;

the beauty was best observed from a distance because up close, she snarled and snapped.

"Yes, Nadia, my dear," he said wearily, turning his mind on automatic pilot, "of course, Nadia. Certainly, Nadia. Naturally, Nadia." *And fuck you,* Nadia, he thought, idly wishing he were power-diving at thirty thousand feet, and she beside him and his finger on the handy little button that controlled the ejection seat.

Eventually she seemed appeased and left, sweeping out triumphantly in case there was anyone waiting outside Greg's small office to see. As long as there was a Nadia, there would be a Nadia problem. She was as predictable and unsettling as ants at a picnic. But Nadia Beshanskaia was not a major worry, only a noisy one. What really concerned Greg Holden this gray December afternoon was Judith Winchester and her encroaching influence on the company.

Judith Winchester was about the last thing Greg needed, he thought, remembering how she'd descended on the International Ballet like a hawk from the blue, swift and rapacious and very determined. Judith's patronage seemed a godsend at first, but only at first.

Greg soon recognized in Judith a type he'd often met in business and never really understood: driven, obsessive, compulsively seeking power for the sake of power itself, not what that power could accomplish. Judith Winchester was a singularly uncultured woman. Her interest in ballet as art was minimal. Judith obviously got her kicks from the accumulation of power, from manipulating people, and Greg was realist enough to sense that he would be high on the list of people she'd probably want to manipulate right out onto the sidewalk. He leaned back in his old shabby desk chair, looked around the small, dingy office and wondered why he cared. *Don't kid yourself that it's because of Phillys,* he told himself, *not completely, not after all this time.* Yes, his wife would have loved what he was doing in her memory.

But Greg would never have stuck it out through all the Nadia scenes and Winchester schemes and the hundred other crises ballet companies face every week if there hadn't been some weird fascination in it. His precise mind had only to see a mess before it began instinctively straightening out the confusion, making order from chaos. And Internationl Ballet, when Greg had come to it, had been chaotic from wall to wall. In two years he'd made some sense of it, working six-day weeks like the youngest kid in the corps, pleading for state and federal and private funds, stretching budgets past the breaking point, working up projections and presentations and all the other businesslike things that were unseen but absolutely vital to this essentially unbusinesslike operation.

And along came Judith. For the first few months after her appearance, Greg had scarcely noticed; if anything, he had been pleased. The Winchester influence and the Winchester money could be a lifesaver for a company that was perpetually in debt, even in a sold-out season. Then, at first subtly and then not so subtly, Judith's influence began to make itself felt in the day-to-day workings of the company. Some of her suggestions were small and easy to meet. She liked the color green, the costumes for a new ballet were based on shades of green. It seemed little to ask; after all, she had paid for the costumes. She came up with schemes for raising money: dinners, luncheons, in a few months a special gala. The schemes worked.

The entire resources of Winchester Publishing were suddenly at the disposal of the International. World-famous photographers were suddenly taking better pictures of the company's stars and productions than had ever been taken. Coverage in the Winchester publications increased, subtly, of course, not to show favoritism. Coverage of all ballet increased by executive decree, and Greg didn't have to waste much time guessing who was behind all that.

Her latest—and boldest—ploy was engineering Dimitri Lubov's switch from the Civic to the International. Again, on the surface of it, the move was brilliant, bound to reflect well on the International both artistically and at the box office. But from where Greg sat, it was disturbing. It was another building block of power for a sinister edifice he had come to think of as Fortress Winchester. Exactly how Judith intended to use that power, Greg had no idea. But his every gut instinct told him it would not be for the good of the International Ballet Theater.

And for the first time he could remember, Greg Holden was without a plan of action.

Jenny took the elevator up to the big rehearsal hall on the fifth level of the New York State Theater, thanking God for the exhausting routine that filled all her days and most of her nights. Sometimes she felt that only the velocity of this

routine kept her from falling apart. Morning class, afternoon
class, rehearsals, fittings, warm-ups, performance—there was
scarcely a moment to think, and for the first time in her
career Jenny was aware of a blessing hidden in the ache and
sweat of it. Maybe it was better not to think. She could drift
with the routine and put off the inevitable moment when she
must make up her mind about leaving the Civic with Dima
or staying with the company she loved and possibly losing the
man she loved.

Love was too new to Jenny to give her any perspective.
Dima was proud; Dima's temper had a short fuse; Dima
wanted to take the whole world and dance away with it and
take Jenny with him. Jenny loved his dream, wanted to share
it and felt herself torn into pieces every time she thought
about how de Lis would react.

Dima might represent love to her, but de Lis was a god.
Distant, mysterious, all-powerful and, literally, a creator.
Jenny felt to her toes that de Lis had created her out of nothing, even as God was supposed to have created Adam out of
clay.

In a way, to love Dima at all was disloyal to de Lis. To
leave the Civic would be the ultimate betrayal. Jenny understood de Lis' vision of a clockwork ballet company, with
hundreds of intricate parts working in perfect harmony, a
glorious impossible invention to which only he, only de Lis,
held the key.

Alexander de Lis might tolerate her being in love. But to
turn her back on his company, Jenny knew, would be considered treachery of the blackest kind. And yet the doubts
crept in, fed by Dima's gentle persuasion and by Dima's very
strong need of her, onstage and off. Would it be so impossible, dancing with Dima on some other stage, in someone
else's choreography? Jenny's head told her it would be very
possible indeed. Her heart was too deep in panic to answer at
all.

And so, for the moment, as she lived her future hour by
hour and loved Dima on borrowed time, Jenny's answer was
not to answer at all.

She walked into the rehearsal hall precisely on time. Being
on time precluded having to talk to anyone, having to answer
any more questions from Dima. Everything about the big
room was familiar, reassuring, from the sharp gymnasium
smell of sweat and rosin to the comforting touch of the

wooden barre, shiny with its patina of sweat, darkened and rubbed smooth as ivory from the touch of a thousand dancers' hands holding it for support while they faced the terrible judgment of the mirror that filled the wall and dominated their dreams of perfection in dancing.

Freddie Momontov led the drill, starting as almost all classes started with the half knee bends of demi-plié, then deeper plié, arms making parentheses in the air, port de bras, moving on to the precise little foot-against-leg beats called petits battements, on and on and on.

There would be an hour of barre work, maybe more, then an hour or more of center-floor work, unsupported, sometimes solo, sometimes pas de deux, all of them working like Trojans, gulping in great thirsty gulps of air, sweating like stokers at the furnace of hell itself. The strength must be built up and sustained and built again with a sadistic delicacy of application that always strained but never overstressed the violin-string tendons, the slender resilient muscles, the backs that arched like wheat in the wind, the slender, steel-spring calves, vulnerable ankles, precarious toes.

They looked more like refugees of some nameless central European disaster than gods and swans and sylphides and enchanted princesses; rags and motley were the order of the day in rehearsal. Iris Dowling had once asked if there would be a prize for the silliest costume. They all wore knitted woolen leg warmers over tights. This made their slender legs look comically swollen, but the leg warmers were vital. They kept the ever-flowing sweat from chilling muscles that couldn't stand a chill. On top, the dancers wore a tattered rainbow of sweat shirts and T-shirts, leotard tops for the girls, God-knows-what for the boys. Dima favored his floppy red Beethoven sweat shirt, and he had several of these, as well as one with the Mona Lisa, one with Bach, one with William Shakespeare. Jenny's old leotards were all simple black, a hangover from her days of poverty when one mended leotard might be all she had, washed and dried overnight, worn day after day until it literally fell apart. There was a bit more money in her paycheck now, but still the leotards were black, habit turning into trademark.

The rehearsal piano pounded on, emphasizing the beat, fueling the drill that was in many respects almost military in its force and precision. They worked at rehearsal tempo and worked hard. But always something was saved for the performance. And only at the performance would the wraps come off and the beautiful, soaring creatures emerge from this drab workaday cocoon into the magic, perfect, seemingly effortless glow of the performance itself.

Some of them practiced the smile. A dancer's smile is as necessary and as mechanically produced as the placement of a foot or the height of a leap; the smile is what makes it all seem easy, the performance tossed off as a charming little gift for the audience. The dancer's smile could paint over pain and fear and all the tensions of competition. It could mask a whispered warning, a hissed instruction to an underrehearsed partner, a gibe, a joke, a word of love. It was part of the basic equipment, like toe shoes and sweat and optimism.

The dancer's smile was a learned thing. To express emotions beyond the smile would forever elude many of the dancers in this big room. To act, to express love or fear or hate, to make these things felt on top of a technically perfect performance, this was the ideal. Like most ideals, it almost never happened. This was the special magic that Dimitri Lubov had in him, that Jenny Hale was learning fast. They were actors, too, and the acting was the rocket fuel for their dancing. It gave the dancing a reason for being, and it made the dancing that much more memorable. They all took classes in mime, but mime itself was mechanical. "Look, he is coming!" "Alas, she is dead!" "Help! I have forgotten my sword!" Simple emotions like these could be mimed, and it was necessary to learn to mime fluently for the classical ballets like *Giselle* and *Swan Lake*. But mime carries its own limitations. A famous choreographer had said, "It is impossible to indicate, through dance, that one dancer is another dancer's mother-in-law." Any acting ability that a dancer could bring to a role was a priceless asset.

Dima Lubov had taught Jenny many things about acting. He was a born mimic and could imitate any eccentric mannerism the minute he saw it. It was not unusual for Dima to be walking down the sidewalk perfectly normally, with that slightly Donald Duck dancer's walk that comes from working all day with feet turned out at right angles, and then suddenly go into a limping, lurching aged beggar's pathetic stagger, or an old fat lady's shuffle, or the skipping, bouncing progress of a manic eight-year-old boy. Dima would follow interesting people down side streets, taking mental notes, unself-con-

sciously becoming that person right down to the jut of an elbow, the bend of a back, the tilt of a jaw.

Jenny found this at first embarrassing, then funny, then
fascinating. Before long, in a quieter way, she herself was doing similar things. Dima could have her roaring with laughter
with his imitation of Alex de Lis being ferocious, or of Iris
Dowling flirting, or some comical stranger doing anything.
Dima could be a dog or a horse or a bird. He was a superb
goat.

Jenny looked at him now, across the rehearsal room, and
smiled at the memory. The smile turned into a frown as she
thought about the decision that was coming at her with the
sure, unstoppable progress of an avalanche. She looked in the
mirror. The angle of her wrist was off again. Damn! You had
to concentrate every single minute. Thank God.

The Washington *Post* broke the story of Smolensky's
suicide. Front page, upper-right-hand corner, headline type-
face one degree less dramatic than what the paper usually
reserved for world wars, major disasters, and presidential
elections. The headline read: SOVIET KILLER SUICIDE IN PARIS:
KGB AGENT CONFESSES DEFECTOR MURDERS. The story gave
the background of Smolensky's career with KGB—what was
known of it—plus a brief history of the KGB itself, citing
other killings and allegations of killings, playing up the irony
of such a plot running side by side with the current Soviet
play for détente. The only thing that was left out of the
Post's account was the names on the list that concluded Smolensky's suicide note. Sam Purcell had ordered that stopped,
the better to protect the intended victims.

The impact of the story was immediate and dramatic. Every major newspaper picked it up. There were headlines
around the world, loud and indignant denials from Moscow—which was exactly the reaction the free world had cyni-
cally come to expect from guilty parties in any government.
The memories burned bright of Dwight Eisenhower's denial
of the U-2 flights, of Nixon's antics vis-à-vis Watergate and
some of the Vietnam horrors and of other scandals in other
times and places.

The logic of the KGB plot was stark and complete in its
horror, a perfect reflection of paranoiac revenge, Soviet-style.
Of course, life was cheap. Of course there was a brain drain,
a national scandal, defection after defection. And of course,

this was exactly the kind of reaction a world marinated in the horrors of the Soviet secret police under Stalin had come to expect. The free world was shocked and sympathetic and completely ready to believe the confession at its face value.

Dima Lubov would have believed the story, too, but he never heard it. His English wasn't fluent enough yet to let him read papers. And Jenny, like most dancers, had been too busy all her life to get into the habit of reading newspapers or anything else.

In counterintelligence agencies from Tokyo to the Kremlin to Washington, D.C., a flurry of hastily summoned meetings intensified the alarm and did nothing to clear up the mystery. Only Sam Purcell and Dave Loughlin were prepared. Only they had seen the pattern forming. And now, as Dave met his boss' cold, intelligent eyes across the elegant old butler's that served as a coffee-table tray in Sam's office, Dave couldn't help smiling. The pure delight of "I told you so" launched that smile, and while Dave never had to say those words, the Old Man's congratulations said them for him.

"Do you buy that confession?" Dave was half inclined to.

"Not for a minute, Dave. Not on the surface of it, and not underneath it. Too damn pat. What I do buy, though, is that it is a deliberate plot, just as you thought."

"By Ivan?"

"Suppose," said Sam, taking off his gold-rimmed glasses and polishing them on a fine voile handkerchief, "that two rival branches within the KGB are having some kind of a death struggle. Happens all the time. Don't forget the Beria business. Suppose that Branch A, counterdefection squad, has for some reason pissed off Branch B. Branch A cooked up your plot. Branch B wants to discredit them and doesn't much care how or why. So B sets up A, and *voilà*, one dead agent with one too-perfect suicide note."

"That's a lot more likely than having to imagine a thug like Smolensky would suddenly go all queasy and repentant."

"It's a possibility—which I am having checked out." Sam smiled as a man can only smile who owns sure means of having something like that checked out under the very noses of the KGB.

"What bugs me," said Dave uneasily, "is what the hell we do to protect those other guys on the list—supposing Ivan keeps right on knocking 'em off?"

"I am perfectly sure, David, that whoever hatched this scheme will do just that. Not immediately, of course, but sooner or later. We must try to save any of those people who come under our jurisdiction, of course, and we must cooperate with any other agencies in other countries who might need our help. Lubov, for example, is the only one residing in the States right now."

"Poussine's in Japan. Rosoff was last heard of in Greece, but I'm not sure. I'm having him checked out. I'll take care of Lubov personally, if that's OK with you."

"It is very OK, Dave." Sam smiled. "We must treat this with cosmic delicacy, old sport, I don't have to tell you."

But, thought Dave with a trace of the old resentment, *he is telling me all the same.*

"Of course."

"Since we aren't sure precisely who's behind this, we don't want to tip our hand. Go very cautiously, Dave. Don't do anything dramatic."

"I'll have Lubov watched, get his patterns. And I'll coordinate with Japan and Greece—if Greece is cooperating these days."

"Greece will cooperate. Very willingly."

"I'd better be off then." Dave stood up, tall, feeling better than he had in years. His hunch had paid off. The Old Man was proud of him again, had gone so far as to say so. But, best of all, Dave was back in the saddle again, right where the action was, right where he could earn his paycheck again, where, maybe, he could get himself off the shelf, stop drifting, put some meaning back into his life just one more time. It was a good feeling. It was almost like the old days. The two men shook hands, and again Sam smiled.

"You haven't lost the touch, David, old sport. I wasn't really sure about your damfool inclinations when first you wandered in here, but right you were—and glad I am."

"Thanks, Sam." Dave never was one for the flowery speeches, but he knew Sam understood how he felt. Damnall! Sam Purcell understood just about everything. That was why he was who he was—and where he was. Dave closed the big walnut door and started down the long, shiny, green-tiled corridor. For once he walked right past the blind lunch counter without shuddering. It was going to be a good day. It was going to be the first of a lot of good days.

The cream-colored Rolls floated silently into a parking space in front of the Ballet Shop on the west side of Broadway near Lincoln Center. Soon Diana Leighton, sleek in her workday costume of a French-blue poplin jumpsuit and hot-pink scarf, was prowling the well-stocked bookshelves of the little gallery-bookshop. In two weeks she was going to meet Dimitri Lubov, and Diana had every intention of being more than superficially well informed about ballet when that day came.

Arranging to meet him had been child's play for Diana. Just a few discreet questions from her had produced more information than she needed; the ballet world is small and incestuous and loves to gossip, and Diana's balletomane pals had been happy to fill her in. In one afternoon, from four different sources, Diana had heard several versions of the Dima-Jenny Hale romance, the fat offer from the International Ballet Theater and speculations that Dima would be sure to take the offer. She already knew about Dima's stormy affair with Felice de la Tour-Fontaine, of his reputation as an insatiable ladies' man, of the likelihood that Jenny Hale would ever leave de Lis, even though Dima might ask her to.

The key to Dimitri Lubov, Diana quickly decided, was Judith Winchester. Diana, who knew everybody, knew Judith. It had been Diana whose educated eye conceived the new Winchester offices in the *Scope* building. She had found the priceless Coromandel screens in London, and, with her usual carte blanche arrangement, had got them at an excellent price: only fifty-two thousand dollars for the pair. Judith had been delighted. Judith was delighted, too, to have lunch with Diana: "just us girls." For Judith Winchester recognized in Diana Leighton qualities that she prized in herself: brains, talent and determination. They had tea and salade Niçoise at a small table in Judith's office. Diana talked of her new interest in ballet, was shown the miniature theater, heard about the Lubov offer.

"What's he like, Judith?"

"I wish I knew." Judith laughed with a girlish trill. "He's a mask. Very polite, a little distant, but when you think what he is dancing, you know there has to be a lot more to him than that. But he isn't giving it away, that's for sure."

"He's the best male dancer I've ever seen."

"Would you like to meet him?" Judith looked at her guest with the guileless eyes of a sixteen-year-old. Breathed there a woman who would not jump at a chance to meet the legendary Dima? Judith sensed that Diana was fishing for just such an invitation. And as it happened, this fell in perfectly with Judith's plans. For the romance of Jenny and Dima Lubov did not suit Judith Winchester at all. She had gotten where she was by a simple and highly effective policy of divide-and-conquer. She kept her publishing empire in a continual state of upheaval and reaped the benefits of being the one individual who could put all the pieces back together again when—and if—she chose to do so.

Judith knew that if Dima and Jenny arrived as a team, they would be that much harder to manipulate than either of them could ever be individually. So anything Judith could do, subtly or directly, to break up that little affair could work only to Judith's interest.

She looked at Diana Leighton with frank speculation. There was no sexual jealousy in this; the girl was young enough to be her daughter, if she had had a daughter. What Judith saw in Diana was a delicious, hopefully irresistible bit of bait to dangle before Dimitri Lubov. Not, God knew, that he had any shortage of women. But it might just work. Surely, it was worth a try.

"I'd adore it, Judith. How?"

"Ha!" Judith laughed the arch little laugh of a 1930s movie drawing-room comedienne. "It'll cost you. Two weeks from Thursday I'm giving a small dinner dance for the Friends. Dima's agreed to come. So, my dear, out with your checkbook. Five hundred, and you're automatically a Friend of the International Ballet Theater. Deductible, naturally. And after all, it is a good cause." Diana was writing before Judith finished talking. She smiled and handed over the check.

"I can hardly believe it," said Diana. "I saw him for the first time only last week, in *Jeune Homme*. Fabulous."

"You bet he is. It'll be a feather in our cap at the International if we can snare him."

"Your offer sounds irresistible, Judith."

"Let's hope so. They're funny creatures, though. Really, one never knows. Goodness!" She looked at her watch in mock alarm. "Darling, forgive me, this has been such fun, but the Vice President is dropping by at two, and I haven't had my briefing yet." Diana smiled, knowing there was only one Vice President as far as Judith Winchester was concerned, and it wasn't of the corner candy store. They stood, and Judith allowed herself to be kissed, the New York social kiss, a glancing caress on the cheek.

"Two weeks from Thursday then. And thanks, Judith."

"My pleasure, darling. Thank you for the contribution." It had been as simple as that. Diana spent an hour in the Ballet Shop, choosing carefully. With the advice of a helpful young man who worked there, she ended up with a heavy armful of books and a wallet lighter by more than fifty dollars. She had technical manuals, histories, biographies, Edwin Denby's collected criticism, a child's introduction to ballet, and three picture books.

If Dima Lubov liked to talk about dancing, Diana intended to be well versed. It was a strange feeling, wandering about the little square shop, hatching her plan to meet Dima Lubov. In the center of the room was a counter selling postcards and publicity pictures of famous dancers. Dima's image was prominent among them: a dramatic Dima, bare-chested and sexy in *Jeune Homme*, romantic Dima as Albrecht, regal Dima as the Prince in *Swan Lake* and two close-up facial studies, one stark and formal, the other featuring the urchin's grin. Diana looked at these many different Dimas and wondered which one she'd get—if she got any at all. And she wondered, too, where this sudden impulse would lead her and why exactly she was extending herself so far to meet this wild and enigmatic boy.

There were other pictures: Nureyev, Nagy, several ballerinas, fake-antique portraits in sepia of Nijinsky and Pavlova. Looking at them, Diana realized that she wasn't really interested in the dance. She was interested in Dima Lubov and would have been interested if he happened to be a tree surgeon. This made her laugh, and she was laughing still as she paid the bill and walked out of the shop to the purring Rolls. Whatever Dima was and wherever this infatuation might lead her, she'd know the answer soon enough. In the meantime, there was homework to be done.

Privy was no help at all. Jenny had dragged her problem across Central Park, had a long session with her friend and mentor, and for the first time ever Privy let her down. And this scared Jenny even more than she was scared already, if that were possible. "It's a decision, my pet, that no one can possibly make but you." As always, they were drinking tea.

"It would be easy, my pet, to advise you to be cautious, to do the conventional thing. I can't judge, Jenny. Maybe Dima's right. Maybe de Lis is standing in your way."

Jenny's big eyes grew bigger with surprise that Privy could sit there so calmly and even consider the possibility. "I just don't know how to face him."

"De Lis?" Privy had always liked and respected Alexander de Lis.

"There's no way of counting what I owe him. If I leave de Lis, I'm being disloyal to him, to the company. If I don't leave, I'm being disloyal to Dima." She managed a rueful smile, but inside, Jenny felt anything but cheerful.

"How about being loyal to Jennifer Hale?"

"I just don't know what that means, Privy. Maybe I don't know who Jennifer Hale is, if ever I did. I feel like part of de Lis when he's coaching me, and the rest of the time I feel like part of Dima Lubov."

The older woman looked kindly at the girl. *And did you ever*, Privy wondered, *feel part of me?* But Privy wasn't going to add to the girl's confusion. "Dima would be upset if you stayed?"

"To put it mildly. And, Privy, he's right. It is special when we dance together."

"You couldn't be in different companies and still do that?"

"Not really. Only once or twice a year, maybe, for galas, or something like that."

"Yet, even as it is, you don't always dance with Dima."

"Of course not. No pair ever does. Yet, when we dance together, each of us dances better. I feel it. The critics see it."

"A kind of magic. I see it, too, Jenny."

"It's awful. I've got to decide this week." Jenny put down her teacup. She closed her eyes. The bottom was falling out of her world, and she had no idea at all what to do about it.

The kitchen door opened. Privy looked up, alarmed. They thought they were alone in the old apartment.

"Am I interrupting something?" Clifford Hale stood in the doorway, immaculately dressed for evening, smiling, looking sober for the first time in years. Jenny jumped up and kissed her father, trying to remember when it was that she'd seen him last. Months, surely, before that famous *Giselle*. He'd been consulting on a job in Brazil, the only kind of work he got these days, and little enough of that.

"Daddy!"

"Jenny, Jenny, my Jenny Pavlova. You made it, didn't you?"

"It's been going quite well, Daddy." His voice was strange at first, quieter than she remembered it. But as he spoke, Jenny realized why there was a difference. This was Clifford Hale's sober voice talking, a voice they hadn't heard in a very long time.

"And there's a young man in the picture, the Russian boy?"

"Dima. I hope you'll come and meet him, Daddy."

"To give a father's blessing?" He smiled, and there was a hint of bitterness in the smile. "I've pretty well abdicated my right to play the heavy father, haven't I?" He stood, holding the back of a kitchen chair as if for support. He looked a little thinner than Jenny remembered, and older. *What a very handsome man he had been*, she thought, as he stood there looking at them hesitantly. "I'm afraid I've caused some bad times for both of you ladies. And I can only thank God that Miss Privet had the guts to put up with me and that Jenny didn't end up—"

"I'm fine, Daddy." He seemed to be gathering his strength to make some kind of announcement. Jenny wondered what and feared as she wondered.

"It seems I have some kind of guardian angel. From time to time the old angel gets lost for a while in the wine cellar, but sooner or later back she comes, halo askew, heart of gold. I've got some good news, ladies. The University of Colorado wants me to teach architecture. They'll house me and feed me and give me a pretty good salary. We'll be able to hang onto the apartment. I'd been afraid we'd have to let it go. Of course, it means I'll be in Boulder nine months of the year. But it's a healthy climate out there. I used to ski once. Might just take it up again. It's a second chance, girls. What do you think?"

"Daddy, it's wonderful!" Jenny jumped up and kissed him again. So that's where the sobriety came from. She was grateful to the University of Colorado for that alone. And he'd be a wonderful teacher. He was charming, and funny; he knew everyone in architecture; maybe there were still a few places where his reputation held up. "You must do it."

"Oh, never fear. I'll do it. And I'll do it sober. I leave right after Christmas, to start the January term fresh."

"Congratulations, Mr. Hale." Through all the long years

and through all his vaulting ups and dramatic downs, Miss
Privet had preserved this formality between them; he was Mr.
Hale, she was Miss Privet. They poured him some tea, and
Jenny lingered, suddenly full of plans. They all must have
supper together; he must meet Dima; he must come to the
ballet. It did Jenny good to see him, to see his face animated
with hope instead of brandy, to see him growing younger as
he talked, described Boulder—which sounded beautiful—and
created seminars and study plans before their eyes. Finally,
Jenny left, in a shower of kisses and promises, happy that for
one member of the Hale family, at least, something was going well.

Dave Loughlin sat in the blue Chevy Nova from the motor
pool. He had two magazines and a *Daily News,* but they
were props; he hadn't really read them. The blue Chevy was
parked across the street from Dimitri Lubov's front door. It
was eight in the morning and December-cold. The engine was
running, and smoothly for once; the radio was off, the heater
on. Dave had never seen Lubov in the flesh. He had the authority, now, to have the boy tailed day and night, but he
wasn't sure that was necessary. A complete, two-man, three-
shift, round-the-clock surveillance job was expensive. More
than a thousand a week. Plus expenses. Dave wanted to form
his own idea about the Russian kid's life-style before he authorized such a tail. Quickly he ran through his very small
stock of information about the boy. Twenty-four and already
famous. Defected in Amsterdam, about two years ago. Li-
aison with a fancy Frenchwoman. Great success with the
Civic Ballet. Known to be temperamental, very fond of
girls—this came as a surprise to Dave, who had grown up
thinking male dancers were all pansies—presently in
residence with the Hale girl, Jenny Hale, also of the Civic,
only daughter of Clifford Hale. That meant double handling
with kid gloves. It also meant double danger. If they were always together, then they'd both be in danger. Whoever was
doing the killing was totally professional, absolutely ruthless.
Killing the girl along with the boy would mean nothing to
him—them—whoever it was.

Whoever it was was cold, clever and totally professional.
You're supposed to be professional, too, Dave told himself.
That didn't stop him from shuddering in the warmth of the
rented car. He sat there, shifting his weight in the compact

front seat, wondering exactly how he'd set about knocking off
the dancer if someone put that problem to him.

The front door opened, and a girl came out, closely followed by a blond young man. They looked like teenagers.
The girl could have been fifteen, and skinny at that, pale with
huge eyes and a small head and a sweep of shoulder-length
chestnut hair. Blue jeans and an old Navy-surplus pea jacket.
She could have been heading for a Girl Scout meeting. The
boy looked almost as young, skinny, too, and surprisingly
short, also in blue jeans and a cowboy's leather-lined-with-
sheepskin coat, a mop of straw-colored hair flying every
which way from underneath a comical-looking bright-red and
green plaid Scotsman's tam. Jenny Hale and Dimitri Lubov.
They walked down Seventy-fourth Street, holding hands, joking, schoolkids.

It was hard for Dave Loughlin to take them seriously as
stars of the ballet, let alone as potential murder victims. He
eased the Chevy out of its parking space and slowly followed
them to the corner of Broadway. There, they turned left,
walking, no doubt, to Lincoln Center nine blocks away. Now
the boy was clowning, running ahead of the girl, pretending
some kind of grotesque limp, a hunched back, an old man's
stagger. The girl stopped, broke up, ran to catch up with
young Lubov, still laughing. He caught her as she ran,
whirled her around and around in what—Dave assumed—
was a kind of parody of a ballet step. They laughed and they
laughed. Dave smiled, just looking at them. Healthy young
athletes, not a thought in their heads, not a care in the world
and, if you could believe the ballet reviews, all the world before them. They had eyes only for each other on this crystal
December morning. Dave knew instinctively that he didn't
need to be as cautious with the tailing as he had been. *Love,*
he reflected, *might not be blind, but it sure gives you a good
case of tunnel vision.* And if they made tailing them so very
easy, what a setup they'd be for the killers.

The blue Chevy moved slowly down Broadway as Jenny
and Dima made their laughing way toward Lincoln Center.
Loughlin saw them cross the big empty plaza and vanish into
the New York State Theater. There they'd be all day and
maybe into the night if they were performing tonight. And
they'd probably be pretty safe in class, in rehearsal, Dave figured. There was a security system, he knew that, but not its
details. Simply to keep fans and groupies from disrupting

classes. In performance, in that huge cavernous, five-balcon-
ied auditorium, in the dark, among more than two thousand
people, that would be another story. If a sharpshooter wanted
to pick off a dancer, it would be a snap. A lightweight,
break-down rifle with a telescopic sight, a climactic moment
in the score, a dancer frozen in attitude, a classic setup.
Dave gave Jenny and Dimitri ten minutes and then strolled
into the box office to check performances. He had never been
inside the great theater before. Well, so what? His job had
taken him to stranger places than a ballet company. Or had
it? Here, Dave sensed, was a world with its own rules, its
own rituals, foreign as Mars. Suddenly, not for the first time
this day, Dave felt lost, bewildered. It was a very intimidating
way to feel.

Every time Jenny opened the door to Dima's apartment
she half expected it wouldn't be there, that the stagehands
might have sneaked in and taken it all away, and with it this
little month of happiness. More than a month, she thought, as
the door opened and she stood still for a moment, quietly
smiling to see it was all there.

In the short time she had been living with Dimitri, Jenny
had made more discoveries about herself than she could
count or remember. For the first time in her twenty years
Jenny began to have a sense of herself as an individual, not
just a dutiful pupil of de Lis, not just a machine for making
dances. Hers was a slow awakening, and a late one, and she
took it slowly. Day by day and night by night Dima showed
her the unlimited possibilities of simply being Jenny.

For all her girlhood Jenny Hale had been whatever Privy
or Alexander de Lis had wanted her to be. This was the
secret of her immense dedication, her ability to *become* the
role she danced, completely and absolutely. It was easier for
Jenny Hale to become another character in dancing because
there was so little of herself to put aside. Jenny could be the
village charmer of *Giselle,* but in real life the girl could no
more flirt than swim the ocean, not if her life depended on it.
Jenny Hale had never rebelled, never questioned too much,
never asked the reason why. For Jenny, dance itself was reason enough for her whole life, and all the energy she had
went into dancing better and better. Only Dima changed her
outlook.

With Dima, at first, Jenny was ready to be anything she

imagined he wanted her to be. Slowly it dawned on her that what he wanted her to be was Jenny Hale. This frightened her because at any minute Dima might discover her terrible secret. He might learn how very little there was of Jenny Hale. Forced to think about herself, Jenny was horrified. *I can take,* she reflected, *the five positions of ballet and make them into something people seem to want to look at. Beyond this, I hardly exist.* This harsh judgment was near the truth. Slowly Jenny realized she had pawned her girlhood for toe shoes and sweat and fame; the books she hadn't read, the trips she hadn't taken, the parties she hadn't gone to, the pictures she hadn't looked at were all gone forever.

Dima's mind, like his body, was a soaring impetuous thing. The Kirov Ballet School gave its pupils a sound and rounded classical education. Dima could read and write in French and in Russian, and he read widely. His English got better every day. Dima knew the subtleties of good food and fine wine. He was mad for modern painting and sculpture because there was none in Russia, and their precious Mondays off were often spent at the Guggenheim and the Modern Museum and the Whitney.

"Look, *deushka.* Is *alive!*" Dima pointed at Picasso's iron found-object sculpture of a goat in the Modern Museum's garden. Jenny saw the goat and the humor in it. Suddenly Dima was next to the goat and crouching, elbows akimbo, hands beside his ears, fingers pointing to make horns. And there were two Picasso goats, one living.

Jenny had never thought about clothes. She hadn't needed them, or wanted them, or been able to afford them. Dima Lubov had a wild and amusing sense of color and style, and he liked nothing better than dressing himself in exotic getups, the more shocking the better. He made Jenny see the fun in it, the fact that there could be more to clothing than merely keeping out the weather. Dima seemed to know by instinct where the interesting new boutiques were. Sometimes they went shopping togther. Dima was not extravagant, but he was absolutely indifferent to money. If he wanted something, he wanted it, and that was that, regardless of price. Certain cheap things were precious to him, and there were expensive things he used like rags.

For Jenny, who had long been in the habit of spending not a penny more than absolute necessity demanded, this was shocking. But it was also great fun, and liberating.

He liked her in pink, and before long pink offerings would appear at unexpected times, unannounced except by Dima's urchin grin. He gave her pinks the rainbow had long forgotten, a cyclamen's ghost of a silk blouse, a sari in the seething pink of India, a pale, pale blushing nightgown. Day by day he was creating her and helping her create herself. It seemed to Jenny that there had always been a choreographer in her life; if it was to be Dimitri Lubov, so much the better. It was fun, and she loved him, but the moment always came when she asked herself, shivering in the cold rush of her new awareness of Jenny Hale the person, when, oh, when would she be able to truly think and act on her own, free from fear, no longer the prisoner of doubt?

In the meantime, they danced, and were applauded, and spent their spare time discovering the city, and each other, and the possibilities of love.

Because she never felt herself deserving of his love, Jenny was always uneasy with it. She treated love gently, tentatively, like the wild thing it was, fearing always that it might take fright and run away. Jenny herself was quiet, steady and introverted. But Dima was a walking explosion. He gave off sparks, electricity, fire, and Jenny was perfectly content to bask in this radiance from a little distance, flattered that the show was for her, unable to convince herself it could last.

His temper terrified her. She had heard of Dima's volcanic rages long before she saw one, amplified by company gossip. Ninety-nine percent of the time Dima was like a lively puppy: frolicking, happy, gentle, meaning and doing no harm. Rarely and briefly dark moods would come on him, "Russian moods" he called them later on, laughing. Then he'd sink into deep, unreachable silences. These moods came seldom and went quickly. The fits of temper came seldom, too, but they were violent and interruptive as a rock thrown through glass. Dima, Jenny knew, was wonderfully considerate and gentle in helping less gifted dancers; he'd spend hours coaching a frightened kid from the corps. But he once made an unforgettable scene attacking a rehearsal pianist who kept slowing down a quick tempo, literally hauling the poor man off the piano stool and playing the piece himself, beautifully.

Incompetence on any level made him furious, and he had no inhibitions whatever about expressing his fury. Once in a fancy restaurant Dima sent his soup back to be reheated. It returned, with suspicious speed, cooler than ever. In one graceful motion he rose, scooped up the soup bowl, drenched the cringing waiter with a limp puree of watercress and marched out of the astonished room with Jenny quivering at his side, fearful of instant arrest. The temper had never been aimed at Jenny. She was sure she would die on the spot if the day ever came when it was.

She thought of Dima's deadline, and just thinking of it was like a knife in her heart.

The two weeks were almost up now, the time when Dima had promised Judith Winchester his decision. He didn't press Jenny, but she could feel the pressure building in him all the same. And the more she felt this, the more panic-stricken Jenny became. She smiled over the panic as dancers must. But there it was, gnawing away somewhere inside her, uninvited, deadly, impossible to tame or send away.

Dave Loughlin looked at the peeling paint on his office ceiling and thought about Sam Purcell. Sam had never been inside the offices of Delage Feather and Trimming Company on West Thirty-first Street, and Dave was just as glad. The place was a mess. Dave sighed. He'd have to fix it up a little. New paint anyway.

Delage Feather and Trimming was one of six New York branch offices of the CIA, each with its own special function. There was, naturally, competition, but Dave Loughlin had long since refused to compete. He did what he was asked to do with care and efficiency, and if he wasn't winning any prizes, who was to care? Certainly not Dave. Not until this thing had materialized in his bourbon-blunted imagination.

He could never put his finger on the exact moment when he'd stopped caring, when the job had become just a job and all the fun had gone out of it. But for years Dave Loughlin had been a time server and hadn't known what to do about it. There was nothing terribly wrong with his life, at least nothing he could point to and wince, but there was nothing very wonderful about it either. The patriotism that made him volunteer for OSS in 1943 as one of the greenest kids ever to leave Staten Island, his hero worship of General Bill Donovan and Sam Purcell, his thirst for the job, looking forward to every new day like an unwrapped present—all these feelings had faded in time to be replaced by . . . nothing. If Dave Loughlin had seen an alternative, he probably would have taken it. But there he was, and there, still on Staten Island, were Effie and the kids and the dog and the mortgage. So Dave took the ferry every morning to the Delage Feather and Trimming Company and let himself get out of shape and drank a little too much and didn't care.

Somehow these killings had made him care again. He didn't know why. Thirty years in the CIA had desensitized Dave's stock of outrage to a point where he was surprised it existed at all. He had the blue folder from Records Integration on his desk. Fatter but still meaningless. Dave looked at it with building impatience. Somewhere in those five deaths lay the means of saving the Lubov kid's life. Dave had no more idea what that might be than he had a quick cure for cancer. He was about to open the folder one more time when the phone rang.

"Daaavey, old pal, old buddy, I just blew into town, and I'm looking for action!" Dave looked at the phone in disbelief. It had been nearly thirty years since he'd heard that voice, but he could never forget it.

After Sam Purcell had been invalided home, Dave was attached to another unit, advancing with the Eisenhower thrust through Belgium and into Germany. The year 1945 found him in Berlin, literally sifting through the ruins, trying to make some sense out of the wreckage of the Reich. The Russians were friends, then, in the first careless rush of cameraderie fueled by victory. Ivan Sokolovny was Dave's opposite number in Soviet Intelligence, a year or two older but just as green, just as brave, just as puppy-eager to get the job done and make a better world for everyone. And hadn't it seemed simple then? Ivan had learned most of his English from 1930s gangster movies and laughed about it with everybody else, but the Cagney malapropisms on Ivan's tongue were only the bubbling surface of a sharp mind and a quick humor.

Work threw them together, and soon they became something like friends. As rising enlisted men in very special intelligence operations, they had ways and means of avoiding the crushing military bureaucracy. Jeeps could be requisitioned, supplies ordered, schedules manipulated. What it boiled down to was a year of outrageous drinking and wenching and general merrymaking in the ravaged city. There was no dramatic incident, no heroic actions; they were young and idealistic, they had just won a war and they were going to save the world. In the meantime, there was steam to be let off and skirts to be chased and SS wine cellars to be emptied.

After a year of this Dave was sent back to the States. He never saw Ivan Sokolovny again although, for a time, through CIA channels, Dave glimpsed his old friend's progress—steadily upward in the ranks of the Byzantine KGB. Ivan had survived Stalin and Beria and the fall of Khrushchev. After a time Dave lost interest and stopped looking at the KGB summaries that made the rounds of senior officers in the CIA from time to time. And now, by what plot or miracle, here was Ivan on the other end of his own telephone!

"Ivan?" Dave still couldn't believe it.

"In the flesh, old pal. Wanna know how I got your number?" Dave very definitely did want to know that. He looked at the phone cord as though it might be a black snake all set to strike out at him. Was he compromised already? Was his line tapped? They had periodical checks, of course. But the damn thing might be monitored from within. It wouldn't surprise Dave Loughlin one bit to find Sam Purcell doing something like that. No one left Russia without a reason. If Ivan Sokolovny was in town and had this number, the reason had to have something to do with David Loughlin. Dave would have traded his left leg to know what.

"Look, Ivan, it's great to hear from you. I'm in a meeting right now." Dave looked at his empty office and wondered if the lie was as obvious to Ivan as it seemed to him.

"Up to your ears in feathers and trimmings, I have no doubts."

"Could we meet for a drink?" *In about a hundred years,* Dave thought. *Just get off this damn line and now.*

"Twenty-three skiddoo. I'm staying at the Soviet Legation, old pal, old chum, but your feathered friends might not think it too nifty-dandy to find you calling there. How's about the small bar in the Carlyle—the one with the pictures—at six?"

"The Bemelmans Bar. Right. See you then, pal." Ivan always had a distinctly un-Communistic taste for the best of everything. The Carlyle would be just his style. Dave wondered at Ivan's familiarity with the city. How many times had he been here before and not called Dave Loughlin? It would be interesting to find out.

"Hunky-dory. Six it is then." Ivan's laughter stopped with a click. Dave hung up. Ivan Sokolovny! Funny, the way everyone in the CIA always referred to Soviets, collectively and individually, as Ivan. Every time that happened. Dave found himself thinking of his old friend, wondering if the all-inclusive "Ivan" of CIA jargon actually did include old Sokolovny. "Ivan," someone would say, "just drove thirty-seven tanks into downtown Budapest." Or, "Ivan wants to play footsie with Madame Nhu." On and on it went, a litany, always Ivan. From what he remembered of Ivan Sokolovny's progress in the KGB, Dave knew full well he'd had a finger in many of the world's messiest pies, lo these thirty years. It was very hard for Dave to imagine his old friend doing some of the things he surely must have done merely to survive within the uncharted minefield of the KGB.

It was a constant amazement to Jenny Hale that hands as strong as the hands of Waldo Ninimaya could also be supernaturally soft, unexpectedly gentle. The blind Japanese masseur came to them every day now, came to Dima, really, Dima paid, but did them both on the long parson's table bought for just this purpose. Waldo came at eight in the morning and gave them both fifteen minutes, Jenny first, while Dima made them all tea.

"Waldo," said Jenny softly, still not really awake, half-hypnotized by the supple rhythms of his wide, insistent hands on the tense muscles of her lower back, "tell me about the International Ballet. Is it a happy company?" Dima, in the small nook that served as a kitchen, angled his head to hear the reply.

"Well," said Waldo in his curiously formal and high-pitched voice, "how does one measure that? Waldo hears much scandal, which Waldo does not repeat. . . ." He had the habit of referring to himself in the third person, as though he were stationed on some platform in space, observing the whole charade from a seemly distance. *And*, thought Jenny, *being blind, perhaps he does have that cool distance.* "But," Waldo continued, "one thing is very sure about that company. It changes. Everything changes. So, should a thing be true today, it shall be highly unlikely to also be true tomorrow."

He talked with a kind of courtly formality, never missing a beat of the massage. He worked on Jenny's legs now, soothing, pulling, kneading. "Waldo does Nadia. Nadia is a highly—let us say—volatile individual. Waldo also does Jor-

dan. Jordan is in himself happy. But Waldo has no conclusions to make about the International. It is a collection of
hghly individual individuals, perhaps more than a de Lis type
of situation. The individuals bring with them whatever they
bring, as must we all."

Terrific, Waldo, thought Jenny. *The inscrutable East strikes
again.*

Part of Waldo's fame was based on just that: his absolute
integrity in keeping his client's secrets. Waldo Ninimaya
knew things that, if publicized, could have turned the ballet
world upside down. He was a genius masseur. But he was
also priest, psychiatrist, oracle and adviser-to-the-lovelorn of
the ballet aristocracy. Waldo had an aura. Wherever he went
in the turbulent backstage world, he brought with him a permanent floating island of calmness and discretion. Fifteen
minutes with Waldo, out of a dancer's frenzied day, was the
equivalent of a month in the Bahamas.

But Waldo's aura did nothing to reassure Jenny Hale this
gray December morning. Change was exactly what Jenny
didn't need. The appeal of Alexander de Lis' imperial regime
was its very structure, the fact that individuality was not a
cult, that stars were banned from the firmament, that all decisions were made by fiat, irreversible and, to Jenny Hale,
strangely reassuring simply because of the enormous weight
they carried, the weight of all the dictatorial authority of
Alexander de Lis.

She pressed her cheek into the towel that covered the hard
white Formica surface of the massage table. But there was no
place to hide. She was going to have to tell Dima she couldn't
leave de Lis, not just yet. And she was going to have to do it
today. But not now. Please, not now!

Diana Leighton plucked another leaf from the artichaut
Béarnaise and regarded her luncheon companion with impartial admiration. If more Frenchwomen looked like Felice de
la Tour-Fontaine, thought Diana, Paris might regain the tarnished crown of its lost chic. Felice was the definition of chic.
Forty-two, and looking it, and looking wonderful. Felice's
body was slim and disciplined, and if her face had lines here
and there, they were interesting lines and not disguised by
paint or coquetry. Her eyes were large and gray and intelligent. Only the mouth hinted at her well-known sensuality.
She was an honest hedonist, with style and humor and a fine

Gallic determination to ride high on the merry-go-round
while there was still a spin or two left in the silly, charming
plaything, before the Visigoths succeeded entirely in their international conspiracy to turn the world to plastic. And, Diana knew, if she played her cards right, Felice could be very
helpful in teaching her what made Dimitri Lubov tick.

How lucky that Diana had to be in Paris this week, that
Felice was in town, that Felice even remembered her. They'd
only met twice. Yes, the Countess de la Tour-Fontaine would
be delighted to have luncheon with Mlle. Leighton.

"Only an American," said Felice, laughing, "would fly
three thousand miles in pursuit of velvet." *Or in pursuit of
me,* Felice thought, wondering why this pretty girl had sought
her out.

"But a very special velvet. You must know it, Felice, the
wine-colored silk velvet the Venetians wove in the seventeenth century."

"With the khaki backing? But it is lovely. Especially when
a bit worn." *She did not,* thought Felice, *come all this way to
discuss antique fabrics.* Felice didn't mind playing games, but
she liked to know the rules. They talked, discussed the restaurant, the food, the scandal that was on every front page, the
suicide and confession of Smolensky, the KGB killer. Once
that subject came up, it seemed almost natural that their conversation should turn to defectors in general and to Dima in
particular. Diana hoped it sounded casual. In fact, she was
steering the talk like a ship in a storm. Anything she could
learn about Dima Lubov was going to help, and Diana sensed
she needed help.

"Someone," Diana began guilelessly, "told me you were
friends."

"They lied. We were lovers." Felice was far beyond caring
about scandal, and as a result, scandal hardly ever touched
her. She was unshockable, and it was impossible to embarrass
her, so the shockers and scandalizers tried to sell their rancid
wares elsewhere. Felice made her own rules about life and
lived by them with more integrity than do most people who
must borrow their little rules from dead philosophies and dying codes of honor.

Felice cut through the incestuous, self-absorbed upper crust
of *le tout Paris* like a laser through meringue. They could
take her or leave her; she cared not one whit. The result,
naturally, was that the Countess de la Tour-Fontaine was in-

dispensable at any fashionable party or weekend. Felice
merely laughed and went her own way. If the world was a
joke, the very least she could do was write her own punch
lines. "We were lovers," she went on, smiling in what might
almost have been a motherly fashion because now, at least,
the visit made sense. The girl wanted Dima. Well, let her
have him. Felice, God knew, was through with the boy.
". . . for nearly two long years. I helped arrange his defection,
but that's a bit of a long story."

The waiter appeared with a bone-white pot of filtre.

"I think," said Diana for the second time this week, "that
he's the most amazing dancer I've ever seen."

"And do you know him?"

"We meet for the first time in a week." *Help me,* thought
Diana as she stirred the dark bitter coffee.

"What you must remember about Dima Lubov," said Felice with a small frown, "is that he is a wild creature. He can
be very charming, as a panther's kitten is charming. He can
be tender, as an eagle is tender who watches over a nest. But
fires burn inside Dima that simply don't exist in other men.
He can become furious, suddenly and for no reason at all.
He is truly passionate, in every sense of that word, not only
in bed. Dima cares almost desperately about whatever he
cares about for the moment. In many ways, like all artists, he
is a child, a puppy. But then the puppy turns into a roaring
lion before your eyes and—beware!" There was a small
metallic noise as Felice put the spoon down on her saucer.

"He is," said Diana quietly, "well on the way to being very
famous." She looked across the table and compared herself to
the Countess de la Tour-Fontaine. *How did you do it, Felice?
What's the trick of it? You're nearly twenty years older than
Dimitri, and handsome as you are, you're far from beautiful.*
Diana hadn't the nerve to ask that question, and so she determined to listen harder than she'd ever listened before. There
had to be a clue somewhere in what Felice was saying.

"Destined from the first. He is magical. Only Rudi is anything like." *Of course,* thought Diana with a small rueful
smile, *Nureyev would be Rudi to Felice. And when I grow
up, maybe he'll be Rudi to me, too.*

"You don't mind," asked Diana, suddenly shifting gears
from tact into boldness, "that I'm interested?"

"My dear, it would be a phenomenon of nature—and not

an especially endearing one—if you were not. Do the flowers not open when the sun appears? Dima can't help being what he is—a human magnet if you will—and we most certainly cannot help being what we are. The trick is to get some good out of it."

"To harness the sun?"

"To build castles of moonbeams, Diana. No one, as I learned to my sorrow, will harness that one. Not a woman, not a government, no one."

"Why are you telling me all this?"

"Isn't that what you hoped for? You seem a pleasant girl. He is not my enemy. He could do worse."

Yes, thought Diana, *and is there not an unspoken hint that he has already done better?*

Felice went on. "We had our time together, most of it very good. Two orbits, one might say, that moved together for a time through the darkness." She made a small waving gesture with one hand, including all the restaurant, all France, all the universe.

"Little girls follow him on the streets."

"Here, too. Whoever loves Dimitri Lubov is in for a lively time. But, my dear"—Felice smiled infectiously and reached across the table to touch Diana's hand—"to light the fire we first must strike the match. And what a fire it can be! I wish you well of him, Diana."

Diana smiled back, but under the smile she thought of the fire in Felice's image of Dima. Would his be a fire to warm her, comfort her, excite her? Or the kind that consumes what it touches, that burns and destroys?

Diana signed the check. The luncheon had been just what she hoped, yet curiously unsatisfying. Whatever this interest in Dima Lubov might bring her, it wouldn't be boredom. That, at the very least, was sure.

Felice thanked her, kissed her lightly on the cheek and vanished in the direction of Dior with a sweep of her understated tweed cape and an airy *"Bonne chance!"*

Good luck, indeed, thought Diana, grinning. *Thanks, Felice, old pal. I need all the luck I can get.* She hailed a cab and started to scour the antique shops of the Left Bank in search of old velvet and new ideas for Diana Leighton, Ltd. About Diana Leighton the woman, she had all the ideas she could possibly use.

For once Sam Purcell smiled as he read the Washington
Post. Détente was having its ass whipped in a manner that
sent waves of delight through the deputy director from his
steel-gray hair to his bespoke calfskin loafers. Growls of protest against the Odell Bill were building on the floor of
Congress every day. The Smolensky incident was polarizing
all the conservatives who had kept their silence before, out of
fear or out of fashion, afraid to be lone hawks in a sky filled
with simpering doves. The Smolensky confession, whatever
else it might be or mean, had effectively put a stick in the
spokes of détente, enough to slow it or stop it for a good
long time. Maybe now they'd remember who had told them
so, who had warned them all these years, in hot wars and
cold wars, what Ivan was really up to. Coat it with marsh-
mallow all you like, it was still rat poison. Sam Purcell smiled
and rang for more tea. It wasn't every day he got to see a
dream come true.

They danced *Giselle* again that night. The magic happened
right on schedule, as it always seemed to happen now, when
Jenny and Dima danced. Was there a special poignancy in
the way he looked at her in the love scene? Was there a fury
more intense when he danced for his life in Act II? Dima's
energy level was always very high, and highest during and after performance. It seemed to Jenny that tonight he was adding something extra even to that.

Tonight Dima projected a quality very like desperation in
his dancing. The fact that this fitted the role of Albrecht was
secondary to the startling abandon in Dima Lubov. The audience felt it, too, in great jolts of emotion, to which they responded in great waves of applause. It was hard for Jenny to
gauge the level of applause these days; there was always so
much of it. He was dancing magnificently, and instinctively
she increased her own efforts to match his. Then why did it
frighten her? Why did she dread the final curtain coming
down, the moments after when they'd be together, when she'd
have to face his silent pleas or meet them with answers, actions, decisions, all the things Jenny knew she couldn't do.
There was a message in Dima's dancing tonight, the message
was for Jenny Hale alone, and what it said was: "This is it,
you've stalled long enough, it's now or never."

His wildness shocked her. He was like some great polished
racing car without any brakes, speeding for a finish line she

couldn't even see or yet imagine. They danced the final pas de deux, his arms like straps of steel around her, fusing his mad ardor with her apprehension in one burning hymn to hopeless love. The audience had never seen dancing like this, nor had Jenny. It scared her to her toes; it made her shiver; it threatened to consume her completely.

From the wings, unseen, Alex de Lis watched Jenny's face as the final curtain fell. What he saw was terror, confusion, the seeds of panic. De Lis turned, frowning, and walked away from some of the most ecstatic applause ever heard in Lincoln Center. Something must be done about Jenny, and soon, and by de Lis personally. All at once the frown turned into the beginning of a smile. Instinct, out of whatever far cranny of the huge backstage jungle where it usually lurked in silence, flew down to help Alex de Lis one more time. Suddenly he knew exactly what to do and when to do it.

There were seven curtain calls, and the house was still full, the applause still cresting, when Jenny ran into the wings and all the way to her dressing room and never looked back. She had to pull herself together, to be alone for a few minutes, to steel herself for the coming scene with Dima. She ran into the dressing room and closed the door and locked it.

Dima stood onstage for a moment in the sudden darkness behind the enormous curtain, looked at the back of his lover as she vanished into the wings, started after her, stopped, shrugged, grinned and slowly walked back to his own dressing room. He knew his Jenny. She was as timid and flighty as some small, shy creature of the woods that feels the snare tightening. Dima Lubov had poached enough rabbits in his time to know that look, to imagine an emotion he had never felt, to be sympathetic. This was why he hadn't yet forced the issue, made a scene, turned the full force of his charm or his persuasiveness on the girl. He couldn't bully her into something she might regret.

Whatever happened, Dima had decided, must come from Jenny herself, whatever it cost him, whatever it did to her. Dima Lubov would not play God. Leave that to Alex de Lis. Still, even as the thought of de Lis passed through Dima's seething brain, something clicked into place. He'd have to face de Lis. Soon. Why not now?

Jenny closed the door and stood panting for a moment, leaning against the cold steel of the fireproof door as though all the wolves in Russia were howling at her heels. She clicked the lock and reached for a towel, sweat running in rivers through Giselle's pale Act II makeup. It was then that she saw the small white rectangle of expensive cardboard that would change her life.

"Alexander de Lis," said the card in elegant, spidery black engraving. On the back, in handwriting nearly as fine, were these words: "Dear Jenny, could you stop by my office after the performance? Thank you. de Lis." She stood there looking at the card until she noticed it was trembling as her hand trembled in apprehension of what he might want.

A formal summons from de Lis! It was unheard of. He dropped in, appeared as if by magic from behind a stage flat or had his secretary post a little notice on the big dancer's callboard where all their many appointments were announced: "J. HALE TO DESCHAROVNA." "LUBOV TO CORSAIRE REHEARSAL, 3PM." "J. HALE TO MR. DE LIS." That had happened from time to time. But a personal summons from on high? Never. Jenny dabbed at her face, not even noticing that the blue eye shadow ended up on the side of her nose, grabbed for her old cotton-flannel bathrobe and headed for the elevator.

It was dark on the executive floor high up in the New York State Theater. Jenny stepped from the big elevator into a carpeted foyer lit only by the red fire-exit light by the fire stairs. She knew de Lis' office, down there, at the end of the long corridor, there, where the one light shone in the darkness and hush.

Dimiy, as she made her way down the hallway that might have been the last mile in some old prison movie, Jenny Hale heard the waves of soft thunder vibrating up from the auditorium. They were still clapping, still hoping the dancers would make one last bow. Maybe Dima was taking a few extra calls on his own! She grinned at that thought, knowing how unlikely it was. How silly he must think her, running off like that! One more thing to face, one more irrational piece of behavior to smooth over—how? Dima didn't have to put up with lunatics. Plenty of girls would be only too happy to fill Jenny's place in his life, in his bed, in his heart. She was trembling still as she approached the half-open door of Alexander de Lis' big office.

De Lis stood at the huge window, his back to the door, staring out onto the central plaza of Lincoln Center as though he had built it with his own two hands. The crowd

poured out from under his feet, a river of contented balletomanes, their breaths white in the frosty night, their hands
still tingling from the fond violence of applause. He sighed,
softly, and in the black rectangle of the window saw the pale
reflection of Jenny Hale behind him as she hesitated at his
door. The ghostly reflection lifted its thin hand to knock.

"Come in, my dear," said de Lis, smiling when the hand in
the reflection jumped back from the door as if burned.
"Come in." De Lis's smile got broader. They all believed, or
half believed, that he had magical powers, eyes in the back of
his head, winged feet. Well, let them. This would only con-
firm it.

He turned, holding the smile with his perfect actor's timing. "You look a little tired, Jenny." Keep it benevolent; put
her off guard with this subtle suggestion that she might not be
quite at the top of her form. Knock them down a little, so
it'll feel that much better when you pick them up again.
Alexander de Lis had been manipulating temperamental artists, dancers and musicians and painters and costume design-
ers, for years. He did it so well that the mechanics of
manipulation came naturally to him now. He did it without
thinking or even without much calculation anymore. Bending
people to his will was as natural to de Lis as flying is to birds,
a tool of the trade. "You danced well, tonight, my dear."
From de Lis, this was extravagant praise.

He looked at her, knowing that this might be the night
she'd walk out on him, knowing that for all he'd invested in
the girl the twin temptations of Dimitri and the International
Ballet might simply prove too strong. De Lis had gambled before and lost before, and while he felt it every time, the other
dancers he had lost weren't Jenny Hale. There was only one
Jenny. Perhaps there would be only one Jenny in this whole
generation of dancers. He looked at her like the most calcu-
lating of seducers, and wondered what magic might work to
keep her, and paused while he waited for her answer.

"Thank you." Had he dragged her up here just to say that?

"We appreciate you, Jenny. No one knows better than I
that it is terribly hard to be a dancer. At the risk of seeming
foolish, I want to give you a small present." He smiled a mischievous smile, and suddenly Jenny saw a hint of Dima
Lubov in the old man, saw a flash of what the famous five
wives of Alexander de Lis must have responded to. Here was
a man who genuinely loved women, loved them in the flesh

and in motion and as an ideal of delicacy and cool fire. De Lis went to a cabinet and opened a drawer and pulled out a long blue cardboard box. Suddenly Jenny knew what the gift would be. She gasped.

The scarves of Alex de Lis were only one of many legends about him. Every once in a long while, for a rare and favored ballerina, de Lis would exercise his famous sense of color and style. This would be embodied in the gift of one lone silk crepe de Chine scarf in a special color, and that color would instantly become the signature color for the ballerina, a mark of favor from the master, a shade that any other dancer in the company would flaunt at her peril.

Each of his five wives, ballerinas all, had in her turn been given a de Lis scarf. The scarves went to certain other ballerinas, too, and while rumor had it that the famous scarves were trophies of de Lis' bedroom, Jenny knew that wasn't necessarily the case. Eleanora, for example, had one in a special shade of green, and she had been a card-carrying lesbian for years. Of the seven principal ballerinas now dancing in the Civic Ballet, only two had this mark of favor.

"You can perhaps guess what this is," he said, savoring the moment, appreciating to the smallest quiver of the girl's nostrils what impact the simple gesture would have. For twenty-seven dollars and fifty cents Alex de Lis had put his seal, irrevocably, on her legend in the company.

Silently, with hands that were still not quite in control, she took the box and opened it. The scarf lay there, gleaming softly in the low light, unaware of its magic. It was a rosy shade of peach, a kind of pink really, not unlike a skirt Dima had given her only last week. Jenny picked up the scarf and held it in both her hands as though it were alive and fragile.

"It suits you, Jenny, even better than I hoped."

"I can't. . . ." Jenny started to thank him, and the words hung trapped somewhere deep inside her. "I can't. . . ." Two times she tried to say the simple words of thanks before all the floods of emotion Jenny had been storing up for her confrontation with Dima broke through and the words were replaced with sobs. She had never cried like this before. The sobbing built in her, choked her, made her gasp, quivering, clutching the peach-colored silk as if by letting go, she might fall a thousand feet onto knives.

Instinctively de Lis moved closer, took her in his arms, held her, tried to let even a little of his power make contact with this trembling bundle of fear and nerves and genius. "You must try to be happy, little Jenny. You deserve all the happiness in the world." He held her closer, and the sobbing went on and worsened, for the words de Lis had spoken burned the raw place in her soul like acid. And still, de Lis held her, silent now, wondering where this scene would end, thinking as he stood there of a thousand ways to try to help, to turn this unexpected explosion to his favor, thinking, too, as if some other, disembodied Alexander de Lis were observing the sad tableau from outside the window, . . . *and she is probably getting her damned blue makeup on my shirt.*

The words were gathering in de Lis' throat when the cold fury of Dimitri's voice cut across the room with the brutal sting of a cracked whip. "If he buys you with scarves, *deushka,* he is getting a rare bargain!" Jenny looked up at him, startled out of her tears. *God in heaven,* she thought. *He thinks this is a love scene.* Of course. De Lis, with that reputation. The scarf, trailing all the lurid legends of two generations of vicious backstage gossip. De Lis, with his arms around her! Startled, Jenny stepped back, swallowed the sob that was still in her throat, dropped her hands that were still clutching at the scarf. "Dima. . . ." She never got farther than that.

"Do not," Dimitri continued, standing formally in the doorway in Albrecht's Act II finery, the shirt soaked through with sweat now and a big towel carelessly wrapped around his pulsing throat, "do not let me interrupt this charming scene. I came, Mr. de Lis, to tell you that this afternoon I have signed the contract of the International Ballet."

Jenny had seen only flashes of Dima's famous temper, the flickering summer lightning that barely hinted at the icy rage he flung at her now, and at de Lis, at the world and the sky and the stars themselves.

He didn't rant or scream, and the veneer of calm served only to compress his anger, to concentrate it and focus it, to make it more painful for him, more shocking to them. Dima looked at de Lis as he said it and then at Jenny. His look was something she would never forget. Dima looked at her as though she had suddenly been transformed into a loathsome insect crawling across the polished parquet of his life. "I could wait no longer, Jenny, for something that was ultimately never going to happen." He bowed slightly, from the waist, a perfect eighteenth-century courtier's bow, Kirov-style, and a thin, bitter smile formed on his lips. Then he turned and vanished in the darkness outside de Lis' office.

"Dima!" It started as a shout and ended as a sob. Jenny started for the door, and suddenly felt the iron clasp of Alexander de Lis' strong dancer's hand on her wrist.

"No, Jenny," he said with quiet authority. "He is mad enough to kill. And I have no idea why."

She looked up at the man who had invented her, wanting to believe him, to believe in anything, to have a center in her life again. Down the hallway the elevator door closed with a quiet click that rang in Jenny's ears like an ax cutting flesh. Still de Lis held onto her hand. The sobbing stopped. She was far beyond tears now, as the elevator descended taking half her life with it.

"Nor do I," she replied quietly, thinking that what she had always feared was coming true, that happiness was never meant to last, that the world offstage was choreographed by a sadistic madman. "Thank you very much for the scarf, Mr. de Lis," she said, looking up at him, blinking the tears away. "I do appreciate it. And everything you've done for me." She even managed a smile now, the training had been that good. *And even this,* she thought, as the smile struggled to form itself on her ravaged face, slipped, came back, stayed, *is by grace of Alex de Lis. So be it.* Still smiling out of fear of what might happen if she stopped, Jenny turned and walked out of the office. The last de Lis saw of her that night was a trailing wisp of peach crepe de Chine flickering against the darkness of the hall outside.

De Lis watched her as she left and stood in silence watching the dark rectangle of the doorway after she passed through it. *She won't leave with him,* he thought, shaken, but feeling a small flush of accomplishment building somewhere inside, *at least not tonight, at least not for some time. And maybe, just maybe, not ever.* Then he heaved a long Russian sigh and crossed the room to switch off the light. He walked out of his office and down the empty hall, his balding head illuminated only by the satanic red exit lights that marked the elevator bank.

He pressed the button and heard the cable of the lift rumbling in the huge, nearly deserted theater. Somewhere down there Jenny would be changing, frantic, thinking her own thoughts. And Lubov. Lubov would be—where? And doing what? De Lis smiled a thin smile that held only the smallest triumph. He knew in his proud Russian soul that wherever Dimitri would be and whatever he would be doing, it would not involve Jenny. Such a small, sad victory, and at the expense of whose happiness? Well, nowhere was it written that dancers were entitled to happiness.

The big, richly carpeted elevator stopped, and the doors slid open. De Lis blinked at the sudden illumination and stepped in. He hoped no one else would get on the elevator before it reached the stage-exit level. Suddenly de Lis was very tired of the human race, including, possibly, himself. He closed his eyes as the elevator dropped smoothly nine floors to the ground level. He closed his eyes and tried not to think at all.

CHAPTER
❦ 8 ❧

In the bureaucratic jargon of the new CIA they called it tradecraft, and you can believe it had nothing to do with selling Aunt Martha's homemade jellies. Tradecraft was any of a hundred techniques for covering up an operation. The Delage Feather and Trimming Company was tradecraft. It traded in counterespionage and information gathering and sometimes in death. Whatever you called it, thought Dave Loughlin, it was high time to turn on the old tradecraft faucet, rusty these years and months.

Dave stood in the early darkness of six o'clock, checking out the side entrance of the Hotel Carlyle, the Seventy-sixth Street side. A doorman, so complacent-looking he might have been carved in stone, stood tall and gleaming in his comic-opera uniform and cap under the infrared heat reflectors that glowed with costly warmth from the underside of the immaculate marquee. A huge black Mercedes-Benz 600L limousine floated up to the entrance and disgorged a young woman in floor-length white mink. It was not your typical Holiday Inn, this Carlyle, all class and Continental understatement, tea in the lobby that resembled one of the smaller drawing rooms in Buckingham Palace, Jack Kennedy's New York address during his presidency, playground of kings. Ivan Sokolovny had come up in the world.

The hotel filled the corner at Madison Avenue and Seventy-sixth. The logical way into the elegant little Bemelmans Bar was to use its own entrance on Madison. Tradecraft suggested a more circuitous route, through the Seventy-sixth Street entrance, past the discreet little registration desk, turn left, through Small Drawing room Number One—too chic ever to be called a lobby—turn right, through Drawing Room Number Two and up the three stairs into the bar itself. That was how tradecraft might attempt to throw a setup off balance.

And Dave Loughlin knew it could be a setup, maybe a hit, maybe a compromise. A small but well-remembered tremor started its cold journey up his spine. Fear. How long had it been since Dave had involved himself in something big enough or risky enough to generate fear? And fear of what? Of Ivan? Of the very possible assumption that KGB had a mole planted at Langley, that they knew what he suspected, that they wanted his little investigation nipped in the bud? Dave rubbed his chilly hands together and walked past the unsmiling doorman, uncomfortably aware of how unlike a typical Carlyle guest he must look.

Dave was halfway through Small Drawing Room Number One when he felt a sharp pressure at the base of his spine, the unmistakable thrust of a gun barrel. *Very good, David,* he told himself with more irony than fear. *You really walked right into this one. Maybe in your next incarnation you could find work as a bowling pin.* He said nothing, kept walking, looked neither left nor right. The thing at his back was not imaginary. It kept right on walking with him. And immediately behind the gun barrel were the bulk and the warmth of a large physical presence, hanging with him, meaning business. Dave wondered what showed on his face, wondered whether these fancy types sipping tea and chatting knew they were right in the midst of a KGB hitman and his victim.

Then the voice came, traveling down the distance of thirty years: *"All right, youse guys, putcherhandsup, this is a raid! We got the joint surrounded! One false move, and you've had it!"* Ivan Sokolovny came dancing comically around beside him, giggling. Dave was still in shock when he found himself hugging more than two hundred and fifty pounds of laughing KGB agent. "Davey, old fart, so you thought you'd sneak up on your buddy-pal?"

"You're looking good, Ivan, for a lousy Commie fink." Dave slapped his old companion on the back and wondered if the gun had been a gun, and if the grin were real, and what he was doing in a place like this with a man like the irrepressible Ivan. Ivan who had learned his English from old movies. Ivan who would always be Ivan, KGB killer or not, boyishly amused by his own cleverness, a grinning porpoise in the dark sea of espionage and death. What lay behind the grin these days, Dave could only guess.

They went into the bar together and found a dark corner banquette. All the corners were dark, and Dave thanked God for it. Less chance of being seen. The tables were fairly wide-spaced, too. Less chance of being heard. And a cocktail pianist was playing cocktail piano. As he looked around at the very discreet clientele, Dave had to admit this might not be such a bad place for a rendezvous after all. Tradecraft, it would seem, was not unknown in the KGB. Dave ordered sour mash bourbon on the rocks, Ivan, a glass of Chablis.

For twenty minutes or so they drank their drinks, ordered more drinks and danced upon the thin surface of the truth, while filling in all the gaps of two careers that totaled sixty years' worth of sworn-oath secrecy.

Dave learned that Ivan had married early, split fast and now enjoyed the privileges of an upper-level bureaucrat: travel, girls, a small dacha on the seacoast of Dalmatia, a little sailboat and caviar at cost. "Newport it's not, but Ivan's not complaining." Dave smiled. His old friend was the picture of decadent capitalism. The suits—made in Rome, he learned—the girls, the boat—Ivan Sokolovny, spear-bearer for the armies of Communism, lived a far richer and more voluptuous life than Dave had ever dreamed of.

They kept the conversation going, and by the time the second drink had had a chance to soak into his consciousness and warm him up a little Dave was somehow convinced that, whatever Ivan might be up to, it wasn't a hit. He suggested they grab a bite to eat. Ivan agreed, flashing his solid-gold Rolex. "For you, old buddy-roo, Ivan has all the time in the whole damned world." And Ivan paid the check from a banana-sized roll of freshly minted ten-dollar bills.

They went in a cab to a small Mafia clam house on the Lower East Side where the pasta was fresh and the waiters were discreet. They ate linguine with clam sauce washed down with two bottles of Soave. The waiter came and took away their empty plates. Ivan cleared his throat in a way that sounded like a rumble of distant thunder, a warning, maybe a portent. Dave looked at him over the rim of his wineglass. "OK, kiddo, here it comes. Ready or not."

Ivan wasn't smiling now. "Don't tell me what you've been thinking, old pal, because, whatever it is, Ivan is here to tell you the truth is stranger yet than anything you might have dreamed up at the Delage Feather and Trimming Company."

He giggled, as ever, at the name. "The truth is, Davey, old pal, that we didn't do it."

"Do what?"

"Cross the fucking street on the red light." Ivan sipped his wine and looked at Dave accusingly. It was the look of a parent whose child has been naughty one time too many. "Look, chum. Here we sit, two dilapidated whores trying to convince each other we're virgins, right? Well, I will make a unilateral treaty with you, Davey, right here and now. The name of the treaty is the No Shit Treaty, OK? Right?"

"I wish to Christ I knew what you're getting at."

"Actually, David, I was just glancing through the Manhattan phone book and the name Delage caught my fancy. Thought a feather or two might tickle my imagination, so to speak. We didn't do it, Davey. We didn't kill those guys." He buttered some bread, put it in his mouth and went right on talking. "I'm not going to tell you how we know you're heading up the investigation. But here's installment number two on the treaty information; guess who's heading it up for our side?"

"You have to be kidding." But as he said it, Dave knew Ivan wouldn't be kidding. Not now. Not about this. It all made a kind of crazy sense that fitted in with the fundamental craziness of the whole situation. Of course, Ivan would be heading it. Of course, Ivan might be trying to set him up in some convoluted Russian way. Of course, he ought to be dripping fear into the linguine. Then why wasn't he? Dave began laughing and kept on laughing, a big Irish laugh that could be heard across the restaurant and, for all he cared, down in Langley, Virginia. "Remember," Dave gasped, "remember 1945, two drunk soldiers who were going to save the world?"

"Berlin," said Ivan, looking gravely at his friend, "is not what it used to be." *And neither are you, and neither are you*, he thought, remembering the old Dave, Dave who had seemed to a much younger and very provincial Ivan like all the dreams of a new golden land rolled up into one laughing, easygoing and completely invincible presence. "You betcha I remember." Ivan's quick grin came, flickered, vanished. "We didn't make such a good job of it, did we, old sport?" *I probably outrank him*, thought Ivan. *It's a sure thing I live better. Back then I thought he'd own the world.*

Dave shifted in his seat. "I guess we didn't." *No use going*

*sentimental. Ivan! Ivan, the scrawny, eager kid, earnest, reli-
able, good for a laugh when he relaxed a little and in some
offbeat rustic way a magnet for the girls. Berlin wasn't what
it was. Nothing was what it was. Not Ivan, surely, who
looked like the chairman of the board. Not Dave. Not the
world.* "Look," Dave continued, "suppose someone sees us together?"

"I'll deny everything. We are only friends."

"It could mean trouble—especially for you."

"Not on your ass, old fart. It is a simple case of entrap-
ment. I am recruiting you or—have it your way—you are recruiting me. Could anything be more patriotic? I should think
it's exactly the kind of activity for the president of the Delage
Feather and Trimming Company."

Dave reflected on that. Ivan was right. Ivan usually had
been right. And Ivan had never, never lied to him, at least
not in the old days. Dave looked across the table. There,
framed in the fat of thirty years' worth of Communist-
financed self-indulgence, were the same clear brown eyes, with
the same twinkle in them. Two old whores? Two old whores.
And what did Dave Loughlin look like to Ivan? Dave decided
not to think about that right now. "We thought," said Dave
quietly, committing himself as he spoke, "that maybe it was
one KGB faction versus another."

"Shrewd guess. Wrong-o." Ivan waved to the waiter and
ordered Courvoisier Napoleon cognac, doubles. "For a moment we thought the same thing. Not true. Davey, without
trying to play little sad tunes upon your sensitive heartstrings,
let me tell you that your old buddy has not been raising Afri-
can violets these thirty years."

The cognac came, and Ivan reached out for his glass reflexively, never taking his eyes away from Dave's eyes. The glass
floated out of the darkness and up to Ivan's lips, and before
he drank he lifted it in a silent toast. Then he drank half the
contents straight off like vodka. He put the glass down and
continued. "I have seen times so bad that death looked like a
friend. I have seen Beria come and go, and many is the time
I almost went myself. The price of my little dacha was not
cheap, Davey. And the security for its mortgage is here,
across the table from you. If I do not find out what is at the
bottom of this, chum, it is my ass."

"That bad?" Something clicked inside Dave's head, and it
wasn't the mere fact of downshifting into the third level of

drunkenness. All at once and for no special reason other than deep-gut instinct, Dave knew Ivan was telling the literal truth. This sudden knowledge was so clear and strong Dave knew he'd bet his life on it. He also knew he might have to bet his life on it. And he was glad. It had been too long since he'd cared enough about a thing—anything—to bet his life.

Once more Ivan reached out for his glass, drained it, signaled for the waiter, ordered refills for both of them. "If you boys could see what's going on right this minute behind those steel gates at Lubyanka Square," Ivan said softly, savoring the cognac, "you would giggle and hoot. Talk about old whores! It is hyster-i-cal, Davey. The righteous indignation! The scurrying! The hot denials!" Ivan grinned. "But the fact is, for just this one time, the old whore is innocent. Whoever did it, it isn't us."

"I'll tell you something," said Dave Loughlin as he put down his empty glass and picked up the new one. "I believe you." There was a pause. Ivan looked at him.

"Thank you, old buddy-roo."

"I'm not sure where that leads us, Ivan. Right now my main concern is trying to protect Dimitri Lubov."

"But you don't know from what?"

"The 'what' is death. I don't know from whom."

"Well," said Ivan, rubbing his hands together as though they were cold, "perhaps we have eliminated one suspect."

"Leaving us with only all the rest of the civilized and uncivilized world to worry about?"

"My list is much like your list, beyond doubt. Starts in Peking. Moves daintily to Tokyo. Iran. Cairo. Possibly Lebanon. Conceivably Rome. One of the so-called emerging nations? It is possible. And last but most assuredly not least, the good old US of A."

"What makes you say that?" Dave's reply was hot. This was one prospect he hadn't considered.

"Elementary, my dear Davey. Consider the effect of these murders, in the light of that faked confession. It is to discredit the Soviet. Now to whose interest would that be?"

Dave shook his head, vainly hoping to clear it. This was something to ponder, and in depth, but not now. The cognac told him not to try. Dave was more than a little drunk now. He swirled the amber cognac in its big crystal balloon glass as though the patterns might tell him what he wanted to know. "You may have a point there. But, Ivan, face it, your home team is not exactly well loved around the world. Damn near anyone might have it in for you enough to hatch something like this."

"True, true, true. But think about it."

"I've done nothing else for about three months. I cast my little net, and every time it comes up empty."

"Well, kiddo, now we have two fishermen." Ivan's laugh came all the way from 1945. "It might even be fun, Davey, old fart. It's going to be like the old days." Dave looked across the table at this fat, convincing stranger whom, for reasons he would never be able to explain or justify, he now trusted absolutely. "Let's hope so, Ivan. Let's fucking well hope so." So there it was—one question answered. And a million tougher questions left to solve. Alone. Well, almost alone. Already Dave knew, and hated living with the knowledge, that whatever this was, it wasn't like the old days. Not at all.

People turned and looked after the skinny figure running up Broadway. But Jenny didn't look left or right or backward, especially not backward, because all the fears she'd ever had were running after her, maybe gaining. Finally, she got to Dima's brownstone. She felt like a burglar, someone uninvited, as she fitted her key—the magic key!—into the lock. For the last time. She climbed the three flights of stairs, breathing hard, still feeling the demons behind her.

And there was the apartment door. It might have been the Great Wall of China.

Jenny had no idea what she would have said or done if Dima had been in the apartment when she got there. But he wasn't there. She stood just inside the front door, looking at the big, familiar living room; it was empty, cold, etched in lamplight, underfurnished still, a stage set whose actors had long gone home. Then she switched on the light. Numbly, automatically, she packed her few clothes in the worn Vuitton suitcase Gloria Bruce had somehow left behind. There wasn't much to pack: a few memories, a few dreams, a package of unbearable pain that was already starting to unravel. The rest of her life.

Jenny's mind had gone into a kind of benevolent shock. She couldn't bear to think that what was left behind in these high-ceilinged rooms was the only dream of love she'd ever known. Jenny finished her hasty packing and stood once more just inside the front door. Slowly, as if performing some

ancient ritual, she detached Dima's key from her worn
key case and placed it where he'd be sure to find it, on the
massage table. Then she closed the door and walked out into
the cold December night.

The creative director of the International Ballet Theater
was not at all like Alexander de Lis. Boris Mogador was more
executive than artist, more personnel manager than choreographer, one of the rare jolly Russians. Where de Lis retained
absolute control of nearly every aspect of the Civic, Boris
was happy to delegate responsibilities; he interpreted his job as
keeping the ship on course in stormy seas. He looked across
the desk at Greg Holden and grinned ruefully; the seas were
getting stormier by the minute. They were having a working
lunch in Greg's office. It was almost the only kind of lunch
they ever had these days. "Who," asked Boris, "in his right
mind, could resist an offer like that?"

"I know he doesn't mean to make trouble. . . ." Greg was
faced with the sudden and melodramatic arrival of Dimitri
Lubov in the midst of a ballet company already fraught with
temperament troubles.

"So far," Boris reminded him, "the boy's been a lamb. He
could, you know, make all kinds of demands."

"There are stories of his temper."

"He's an artist." Boris was, naturally, on the side of the
artist.

"OK. But how do we tell our guys they're going to be
bumped from some of their favorite roles, Boris? That'll fall
on you. We'll get walkouts. Even the girls may resent it."

"Maybe not. He is a huge asset. He can help. He can even
help other male dancers. He likes to coach; he wants to
choreograph; he wants to work with us. And he is probably
tired of the great classical roles. We can switch around: put
Dima in the modern things, give our guys a change to play
the dumb princes."

"Maybe you're right. I still smell trouble." From Greg's
point of view the arrival of Dima Lubov was a very mixed
blessing. It would mean headlines; it would sell seats. But
even a sold-out house didn't break even. And although for
the moment both Dima's salary and the cost of the new ballet
were being underwritten by Judith Winchester, Greg knew
that Judith could withdraw her patronage at any minute,
leaving them stuck with a very expensive contract and no

way to make good on it without getting the International even more deeply into hock than it was already. This was one source of Judith's growing power on the board of directors. If Greg had thought for a minute that Judith really had the best artistic interests of the International at heart, he wouldn't have minded at all. But Greg had met compulsive, obsessive types like Judith before. He could sense that Judith Winchester was on some weird kind of power trip, and it worried him. It worried him a lot.

Exactly what it was, and where it might lead, Greg had no idea. But it scared him because there seemed to be no real logic in it. Judith and her meddling were like some errant force of nature accidentally loosed on the unsuspecting International. For the moment the only way Greg could think of to deal with her threat was to keep a low profile, to wait and watch and be ready. Ready for what?

"Luckily," said Boris, "she didn't specify roles for the boy, other than the new ballet. She guaranteed him two performances per week throughout the season. That still gives our own guys a chance. There are four other nights in the week after all. And if we do mixed programs, we can spread the good parts around. He shouldn't mind that."

"You want him, don't you, Boris?"

"Damn right. The boy is *luminous,* for heaven's sake. There is no one like Lubov, not even Rudi."

"Why do you say that?"

"Rudi is always Rudi. Lubov becomes what he dances and in some mysterious way improves the role—and everyone else's performance—while he does it. I don't say that to knock Rudi, mind you. There is also no one like Rudi. But they are two completely different animals."

"Well," said Greg, putting down a paper cup half filled with cooling coffee, "want him or not, here he comes."

"Just in time for the China tour. Double your headlines, double your fun."

Whatever you might say about Boris Mogador, Greg thought with a smile, he met each new challenge with a sense of humor. The China tour was Judith's idea, too, and had been arranged through her influence. The International—for once truly living up to its name—was to be the first American ballet company to tour the People's Republic. They'd be away for a month, with two weeks in Tokyo and two in Peking. The logistics were terrifying; merely getting the sets and

costumes halfway around the world was epochal in itself.
The thought of dealing with Japanese- and Chinese-speaking
stagehands, and what the electrical facilities might be in Peking boggled Greg's mind. Still and all, through the Winchester
connections, somehow, the U.S. State Department was under-
writing the entire tour. It wouldn't cost the International a
penny, and its share of the receipts would be clear profit. So
there was no arguing, and no arguing about the prestige the
tour would bring to the International in particular and to
American ballet in general.

Still and all, Greg felt he was being manipulated, and the
whole company with him. If Winchester wanted them pir-
ouetting with penguins on the Antarctic ice floes, she would no
doubt be able to arrange it, no questions asked. It scared
Greg Holden, and Greg Holden was not a man to whom fear
came naturally.

Jenny Hale pulled the pillow over her face and repeated,
"I won't go!"

"You bloody well will." Privy set down the tray with tea
and toast.

Jenny lay in her narrow white bed at home, the sheets
tangled from a restless night, the pillow damp with fresh
tears.

"My love," Privy went on, more gently now, "you'll never
forgive yourself if you don't. After Mr. de Lis has given you
this honor."—Privy looked at the rumpled silk scarf, carelessly thrown across the back of a chair, and made a mental
note to iron it before Jenny went off to her morning's
classes—"it just wouldn't be right to let him down. Or let
yourself down."

"Privy, Privy, he'll be there."

"Which is all the more reason why you must go. Whatever
has passed between you in private, Jenny, simply cannot affect you professionally. You ought to know better than I—it
isn't necessary to be in love with the men you dance with."

"I'll die, Privy. How can I face him?"

Privy sat on the edge of the bed and took Jenny's pale
hand.

"My darling," she said quietly, "you will get up from this
bed and put on that scarf, and you will walk into that class
like a queen, and smiling. And although this may come as a
surprise to you, Jenny Hale, you will find that the floor of the

practice hall is still a floor, that the mirrors are still made of glass, the piano still slightly out of tune, the day still has twenty-four hours in it and night follows day."

"He hates me." Jenny's brain was a turbulent mixture of her own guilt at having disappointed Dima and rage at his reaction last night.

"I doubt that. The boy has a temper. He's proud. Think, Jenny. Dimitri has a lot to be proud of. I can't tell you how to deal with Dimitri or even if you should deal with him. But I can and will tell you this. You can—and must—deal with yourself. This is an incident, Jenny; it's like stubbing your toe or being caught in the rain. It won't go on forever. Few things do."

"I'll leave the country. I could get work in England." Jenny meant it, and the thought made her feel worse, that she could even think it.

"And bring your sorrows with you? They haven't invented an airplane that fast, darling, that will let you outrun troubles like these."

"But I'm sick. I'm not well."

"Fiddlesticks! You're healthy as a horse. Come on, Jenny, this isn't like you. To let me down, or de Lis, or yourself, most important of all. 'This above all. . . .' "

"I know, Privy, 'to thine own self be true.' " *Oh,* she thought, *to be that age again, when it was that simple, when questions had answers.*

" 'And it must follow, as the night the day. . . .' " Privy would play this game or any game, but her patience was running thin.

" 'Thou canst not then be false to any man!' Dima was plenty false to me, Privy. He as much as accused me of—"

"No, my love. Mistaken, perhaps; angry, to be sure; mixed up, possibly. But take my word for it, wherever it may end between the two of you, that boy does not have it in him to be false. If anything, he may be too direct."

Jenny pulled the pillow from her face and looked at Miss Privet. "You're right, of course. But then you're always right. I just wish it made me feel better." Jenny's voice was a little stronger; there was less of a whine in it. Privy took this small cue and ran with it.

"Shall I tell you time heals all wounds? It's God's own truth, my Jenny; clichés don't get to be clichés for nothing."

The response was a stifled giggle. "And you've felt sorry for yourself long enough, my pet."

"Susan di Lallo," said Jenny, "says 'Time wounds all heels.' I never thought it was funny until now." There was a small, lingering smile, after the little pun, the first hope of the morning.

Privy pressed on. "Up with you, then! You'll be late." Privy herself stood up and smiled as Jenny got out of bed. The infant was taking its first fumbling steps. Soon it might learn to walk and then to run. Privy turned and walked out of the room so that Jenny wouldn't see the tears forming in her eyes, tears for Jenny and for all young lovers whose hearts played in the minefield. As Privy left the room she picked up the peach silk scarf. It would never do for her Jenny to make an important entrance wearing a wrinkled trophy.

In an otherwise empty rehearsal hall at the International Ballet Theater Machito Ramirez ran across the room en chasse and spun up into the air in yet another grand jeté en tournant, more to work off steam than from necessity, for Machito was already famous for the big, dramatic leaping turns that left him suspended in air like a swimmer in the sea, his long, supple legs flung out behind him with the careless-seeming grace of a prince tossing alms to the poor. Again and again he ran and jumped and turned, in silence, to the rhythms of his own counting. The sweat poured off him, soaking the orange cotton turtleneck, turning the black nylon tights clammy with moisture, and still he ran, and still he jumped.

Machito often rehearsed alone like this, early or late, without the distraction of a class or Boris, good-hearted, boring Boris, correcting him. So Jenny's latest lover was coming! Run, leap, turn! Run, leap, turn! And how many miles of grands pirouettes had he spun, what tall buildings had he leaped, if all his grands jetés had been piled one upon the other? The road from 117th Street was paved in pirouettes and jetés and anguish, but Machito had traveled it, fast and young and smiling, the first Puerto Rican kid ever to make it big in the toughest ballet competition in the world. The road had led to de Lis' classes, and one short season with the Civic itself, in featured roles at age eighteen, with critical raves and one short detour through the bed of Jenny Hale, then an offer from the International, better roles, more money, the first hot flush of fame coming at him before the age of twenty-one, all that and the promise of much more. For young as he was, Machito was the unquestioned male star of the International. Had been. Until the news of Dima Lubov's coming. And why did it have to happen just now, and why to him? Run, leap, turn. Run, leap, turn!

Finally, gasping, Machito stopped. Exhausted. The way he wanted to be, too tired, he hoped, to think. Machito's was a fundamentally cheerful nature. He didn't think too much or worry. There were always new steps to be learned, new girls to fuck, new headlines to make. But now he thought, and now he worried. He hadn't even met Dima Lubov or seen him dance. He'd heard the gossip, the Dima-and-Jenny gossip, the Judith-wants-Dima gossip, the Nadia-dumps-Jordan gossip, and most of it passed off him like rain down a duck's back.

Then the rumors all came true. Next week Dima Lubov started dancing with the International. How many of Machito's hard-earned roles would be given, de facto, to the dazzling newcomer? Would Dima bring Jenny with him? Machito grinned at that thought; he wouldn't mind seeing more of Jenny. They hadn't parted in anger. In fact, they hadn't really parted at all, just drifted and drifted until there was nothing left. Well, thought Machito, who hated no one and surely not Dima Lubov, che sarà sarà. He reached for a towel and got up from the dusty old floor. Only time would tell. He wondered, as he walked back to his dressing room, if the offer from Stuttgart still held?

Diana Leighton never thought of herself as a clotheshorse. She liked what she wore to be simply cut and made of good fabric and, naturally, becoming, but Diana had no time for the endless fitting and fussing that went hand in hand with the best-dressed list. Yet this evening, as Diana opened the eighteenth-century French boiserie panels that had been installed along one wall of her bedroom to make a closet door that didn't look like a closet door, she wondered what to wear for her first meeting with Dima Lubov. For tonight was Judith's dinner-dance for the Friends of the International Ballet. It would be a fancy crowd, she could be sure of that. And most of the women would be older than Diana Leighton. She'd know many of them, some would even be clients. It would be the kind of group in which Diana had felt perfectly at home from childhood. Then why did she feel little hollow places where her self-confidence usually was? No jewels, that was for sure.

This was the kind of group where the ladies would make quick, almost furtive visits to the safety-deposit vaults in the late afternoon or send their drivers for the heavy-artillery jewels. Not Diana, she reasoned; a self-made boy like Dimitri might be put off by that kind of excess. Should she take a cab instead of the Rolls? Diana grinned. Things should only get so far that she'd be offering him a ride home! She'd cross that bridge when she came to it.

Meanwhile, what in the name of heaven could she wear? There was plenty to choose from. The back face of the closet door panel was a floor-length mirror. She looked at her reflection, fresh from the bath, the long tawny-blond hair just washed, figure slim and firm, not bad. So she was thirty to Dima's twenty-four. That was a step in the right direction down from Felice's forty-what. Now. The gown. Something unexpected, to match the unexpected lack of jewelry.

A gleam from the far end of the closet caught her eye, dull gold against a faded lacquer red. Of course! The sultan's robe she'd found in Isfahan last year! It was simply cut from old silk velvet, fitted around the chest, tapering to a full sweep of skirt, with sleeves that started narrow and tapered out in proportion, just edged with rich but simple embroidery in thread of solid gold interspersed with tiny pearls. The embroidery made its own simple necklace around the shallow circle of the neck. And a row of fifty-three gold buttons running straight down the front was the only other ornamentation. It was from the seventeenth century, but in nearly perfect condition. Rich, simple and slightly barbaric. Perfect-o! You could be very damn sure, if you cared about such things, that there would be no duplicates of that number in the room. Diana reached for the ancient robe and held it against her reflection in the mirror. Definitely. If you were going to bait the trap, she thought, feeling slightly wicked, you might as well bait it with the genuine article.

Dimitri frowned, stretched, flung back the sheets and hurled himself out of the unwelcome spaciousness of his empty bed. He crossed the room to the kitchen to make tea, looking at the front door as he passed it, half expecting Jenny to walk back into his life as suddenly as she'd left it. Yesterday's anger had faded overnight; his dark moods were always passing events, not to be dwelt on. Jenny must know that by now. And it must be Jenny who came to him.

Dima stayed longer than usual in the shower, basking in the stinging heat of it, thinking how it would be, what she'd say to apologize, how he'd be gracious, forgive her, take her hand, how they'd kiss and make love. This must happen today, no later. Then he could take Jenny to the boring party of Mrs. Winchester that Shelly insisted he attend. Diplomacy had never been Dimitri's strong suit, but even he could see the sense in coddling the old bitch for a while at least. Yes! He'd be gracious and forgiving when Jenny came to him. He'd overcome the Russian pride, show her that his dark moods had a bright side, too. They'd meet in class, if not before. They were even scheduled for a rehearsal together this afternoon. And the night after tomorrow they were performing together. His last week in the Civic! Crafty old de Lis had him dancing nearly every night.

Dima thought of de Lis with his Jenny and felt the anger building. He knew there was probably nothing in it, on her part at least. But the thought of her with someone else was grating. And with de Lis, you never knew. He was famous, in gossip anyhow, for trying it on with practically all the straight girls in the company. But Jenny? Not his Jenny! Dima dressed, gulped his morning tea and raced out the door. He wanted to give himself plenty of time for the big reconciliation scene with Jenny.

Sam Purcell's tanned and perfectly manicured hand reached across the waxed mahogany of his desktop for the little mahogany call box with its four ivory buttons. He pressed the nearest of the buttons once.

"Yes, Mr. Purcell?" Ellie's voice had the cool efficiency of someone in a hospital operating room.

"I'd like to hear the last two weeks' worth of tapes from the Delage Feather Company, please, Ellie."

"Right away, sir."

All the local stations were monitored, for their own security and for Sam's private information. Most of the operatives knew this and used pay phones for their more intimate messages. But from the ones who didn't know or didn't care, Sam had, over the years, extracted a gold mine of information that gave him extra leverage in waging the interior political wars that had been typical of the CIA lately. Dave Loughlin was one of the operatives who didn't know about the monitoring, not for sure anyway. The years had taught Sam to recognize, and almost instantly, a voice that knew it was being monitored. Ellie appeared with four cassettes. Sam smiled, thanked her, opened one of his desk drawers and pulled out a small Sony tape player. He clicked the first cassette into the elegant little machine and settled back in the big leather wing chair to listen.

The big square in front of the New York State Theater was empty this gray morning. Jenny crossed the plaza with all the grim resignation of a soldier going into combat. At the side of the square, scurrying along the sidewalk, peering into the big wire-mesh trash cans for unimaginable treasures, was one of the area's shopping-bag ladies, a tiny, hunched figure wearing three overcoats and a black shawl, wild-eyed, muttering a litany of curses from toothless lips, lacking only a broomstick to embody the classic ideal of a witch. Jenny looked at the pathetic creature and shuddered. *And that's how I'll end up,* she thought, only half-humorously, *bonkers and raving, because he never came back to me.* Jenny's first instinct, after Privy had psyched her out of bed, was to pick up the phone or hop into a cab and have it out with Dima, to tell him what really happened with de Lis, to apologize, throw plates, make love, do anything. But she couldn't make a move. Her fear of rejection was stronger than any other emotion, stronger even than the sadness itself.

Time and time again the terrible scene in de Lis' office replayed itself in the cold theater of her mind. Trained from childhood in stagecraft, Jenny knew perfectly well what it must have looked like to Dima, her in de Lis' arms, the scarf, de Lis with his lecherous reputation. For the first time in her life Jenny found herself wishing someone were gay. If de Lis were homosexual, there could have been no doubt. Or could there? It wasn't sexual jealousy in any case, she felt that. Dima knew her better than that. No, it was far more complicated than sex. It was, she began to realize, a question of pride and possession, of her belonging to Dima Lubov in some wild Russian way. *And it's true,* she thought. *I do belong to Dima. I always will.* And the more she thought about it, the more she hurt. But no matter how it hurt, Jenny

couldn't face the possibility of Dima's rejecting her again.
Anything would be better than that.

And in the meantime, well, she would get through her life
minute by minute. *"You will walk in there like a queen, and
smiling,"* Privy had said. Slink in like a rat, and cringing, was
more like it. The scarf, newly ironed and wrapped in tissue,
lay like a silent time bomb in the new brown paper bag that
held Jenny's yogurt-and-apple lunch. But she would put it on,
that scarf, and her new leotard, too, and she would walk into
that rehearsal room like a queen. *The Swan Queen, too,* she
told herself, sternly, as if speaking to a troublesome stranger.
*Or better yet, the black swan, all sexy and mysterious, and let
them think what they will. Let them think I am sleeping with
de Lis, if they want to. They probably say that anyway. And
a girl could do worse.*

Swan Lake was one of the few classic ballets not yet in the
Civic repertoire, but it was rumored that de Lis was contem-
plating a new production for next year. Jenny knew, sure as
sunrise, that he'd let her dance the Swan Queen, the famous
dual role of the good swan and the evil black swan, to the
haunting Tchaikovsky score. Jenny had seen *Swan Lake*
whenever she could, seen the well-known International Ballet
version six times, usually with Nadia Beshanskaia in the lead,
and she wanted to dance the role as much as she had ever
wanted anything. Except Dima.

How would the black swan deal with the scorn of Dima
Lubov? Slowly, as she went to her dressing room and
changed into rehearsal clothes, Jenny Hale became the black
swan. The role possessed her like a drug. Her back stiffened,
there was a new regal arch to her brow and ice was forming
in her soul. *I am,* she instructed this new and invulnerable
Jenny, *a femme fatale, a wicked princess, luring men to their
destruction.* Jenny looked at herself in the mirror as she tied
the de Lis scarf around her waist like a sash, where it would
float spectacularly when she pirouetted. And she smiled. The
black swan smiled back. All right. So it was only a role.
If it got her through the next few hours, if it let her face
Dima and still keep some of her self-respect or whatever tiny
shreds might be left of it, that would be more than enough.
And damn it, she would have some self-respect. She played
roles well, everyone said so, said so in print even. Maybe it
was time to do a bit of playing roles offstage, too. God knew,
being plain little Jenny was getting her zero and zip.

Jenny paused in front of the mirror, examining the effect of her scarf. Then, for the first time in her life, she put on a touch of makeup for rehearsal. That's what the black swan would have done, and scent, too, and let's see what the mad Russian makes of that.

Judith Winchester hated entertaining. There was nothing domestic about her at all; she entertained because entertaining was a political weapon in her world. Entertaining bred power, and power was what fueled the dark engine that drove Judith Winchester all the days of her life. Power was the ability to make people do what she, Judith, wanted them to do, to make things happen, to change the course of events.

It wasn't the result of these maneuverings that interested Judith, but rather the complicated and often cruel methods she used to set them in motion. It was the individual steps of the dance that fascinated Judith, not the overall pattern. Her enthusiasms were short-lived, but while they lived, nothing else mattered. When Judith Winchester decided to take control of the International Ballet Company, to be its guiding creative force, its principal patron and most influential director, there was literally nothing she would not do to achieve it.

Now, as she inspected the empty suite she had reserved at the Hotel Pierre for her dinner-dance, Judith smiled. The smile had no warmth in it; it was the compliment one shrewd professional pays to others. Judith Winchester always demanded the best of the best and didn't mind paying for it. The Pierre, as ever, had outdone itself. One hundred and fifty of New York's most influential men and women would soon be in this room, basking in one another's company, excited with the prospect of meeting Judith's own captive lion, the exotic Dimitri Lubov, radiant in the nimbus of money and power and position. Judith looked at the several rooms, with their flowers and cocktail bars, and the ballroom, where soon the orchestra would be playing, and she smiled. But as she smiled, she saw the flames again, and she was a young girl and her father was casually lighting a match to the manuscript that held all her dreams of a career in journalism. The flames burned higher. Judith smiled. The flames burned inside her, too, had never quite been extinguished all these forty-five years. The flames burned especially brightly this evening, always a good sign.

She smiled a little girl's smile, the smile of a playful cobra.

It was going to be a successful evening. Judith's underground in the ballet world had already brought news of Dima's split with Jenny Hale. And so much the better. The Leighton girl would be just the thing to take his mind off that. And the China trip would separate them by half the world, deepen the breach. Dima didn't know about the China tour as yet. He'd learn. Yes, thought Judith, Diana Leighton was going to serve her purpose most admirably. Starting, with any luck at all, right in this room and right this evening.

The big elevator was empty as Jenny rode up from her stage-level dressing room to the big rehearsal hall on the fifth level of the theater. Only soloists and principal dancers had dressing rooms on the stage level. The kids in the corps de ballet shared the happy bedlam of communal dressing rooms on the rehearsal-hall level, filled with gossip and laughter and the controlled hysteria of overtrained young bodies getting ready for the start of a race that wasn't really over when the curtain fell.

Jenny was a few minutes late; the class had already begun and seventy-three dancers were working at the barre, warming up with the customary pliés to a ragtime tune from the rehearsal piano. Jenny nodded to Freddie Momontov, the dance master, and got back the surly frown that was his usual greeting to latecomers. Situation normal. Freddie's Russian-bear exterior hid a heart of melted butter, he loved dancing and dancers and was a father figure to many of the youngsters in the Civic, as formidable in his way as de Lis but far more approachable.

Jenny's nod was gracious; after all, she was the Swan Queen, and these were her subjects, noblesse oblige, but one false move on their part, and she'd have their heads. From the corner of her eye Jenny could see the unmistakable figure of Dima Lubov halfway down the barre, lost in concentration, wearing the inevitable comic sweat shirt, a bright yellow one this time, with Snoopy on it in black, a shirt Jenny had given him. Was that a good sign? Was he wearing it deliberately? Would the sight of the de Lis scarf set him off again? Across the room Freddie Momontov looked at Jenny, registered both her untypical lateness and the scarf, whose symbolism was well known to him. There was something different about the girl this morning. Maybe the de Lis scarves did

have the magic powers gossip attributed to them. Maybe
Jenny Hale was growing up at last.

Jenny held onto the barre as though her life depended on it
and let the familiar narcotic of hard work transform her
from a frightened twenty-year-old girl to a supple machine
whose product was pure line, grace and magic. The warm-up
progressed—plié, battement tender, battement dégagé—rond
de jambe, a soldier drill old as the court of Versailles and new
as continuous self-improvement could make it. Jenny lost herself in the criticism of the image in the enormous mirror. She
had long forgotten any sense of the mirror as a physical object, as a silvered glass barrier. The girl in the mirror was
more real to Jenny Hale than the sweating, fearful, perfec-
tionist creature whose damp hands grasped the fat wooden
barre, whose arms and legs and sword-steel spine forever
sought an ever more elusive ideal of beauty.

For dance can never be fixed in time or space; this is its
magic and its curse, and all the great masterpieces in dance
are illusions of the instant, never to be repeated again, never
to hang upon a museum wall, never to be cast in bronze.
Even the greatest of critics, describing the greatest of dancers,
can only say, "if you have been there!" It is this sure
knowledge of the fundamental impermanence of dancing that
consumes dancers with a frenzy to dance, and dance constantly, and now, right now, not next year or the year after
that, because next year may be too late, because their brief
radiant trajectory may be peaking and even tomorrow may
be too late.

Jenny Hale at twenty did not consider herself young; she
was already a veteran of twelve years at the barre, of constant
practice all year round, and if she were still dancing at forty,
it would be a miracle. The time was now, with Dima or without him; the urgency was to dance, and dance at the peak of
her form, and keep improving, storing up technique and
strength and inspiration against that inevitable day when she
would have to ration these things out in little teaspoons to an
audience perpetually in search of the new young talents, the
Jennys and the Dima Lubovs of tomorrow.

The Black Swan Queen looked at her reflection in the mirror and was not pleased. The angle of her wrist kept going
off in port de bras. Again she swept her arm up in a graceful
arc. Better this time, nearly right, almost acceptable. It wasn't
a failing anyone would notice in the third balcony. But Jenny

noticed, and de Lis would notice, and the rage within her demanded, with all the urgency of an order from the Swan Queen herself, that the tiny failing be corrected. Up came the arm again. Better still. Almost there. Jenny relaxed a little. The class went on. But there would always be an "almost there" for Jenny and for every dancer who knew the difference between adequate and superb and was willing to try and bridge that gap. And this afternoon she was rehearsing *Corsaire* with Dima! If, that is, she didn't die of sheer embarrassment first.

The Sixth Murder

Tokyo, 1975

Nikolai Poussine was the second-ranking chess grand master in Russia, and most people felt it was only a question of time before he defeated Spassky. They might never know, now, because Poussine had defected in 1969 while playing in a tournament in London. His defection sent shock waves all through the USSR, where chess is an art form second only to dancing and consumption of vodka. Now Poussine had settled in Tokyo, where a publisher of chess manuals had offered him a lucrative contract to edit a series of how-to books for a worldwide market.

Japanese culture fascinated the forty-year-old Poussine. His mathematical mind responded to the precision and delicacy of the way the Japanese designed their lives, from the spare elegant sweep of a great pagoda down to the smallest perfection of a carved radish floating in a soup bowl. It was pleasantly exotic to Poussine, whose life in Russia, even with the privileges of a great chess star, had been simple and restricted. He sat now in his tiny garden, in the chill of a gray December afternoon, enjoying the carefully spaced boulders and two tiny bonsai pines in his miniature Zen garden, all raked sand and philosophy. Soon the American reporter would be here, his servingwoman would prepare tea and almond cookies and the interview would be upon him.

He disliked interviews, for he was anything but verbal and anything but fluent in English. But it had been arranged through his publisher, who considered—perhaps rightly—that all such publicity helped sales. And sales, Poussine remembered with a little smile, were doing very well indeed. It wouldn't be all that bad. Provided the reporter was patient. The servant appeared. My goodness. He hadn't even heard the chime. Deaf as a cod, he was getting. Well, still and all, life wasn't treating him so badly. He must think of getting a hearing aid, though. Deaf as a cod.

Nikolai Poussine walked into his living room, which was as Japanese as he could make it while still retaining comfortable armchairs and man-sized tables. Still, the Oriental touches pleased the Russian. There was an old altar low on the floor, seventeenth century, the dealer had told him, and on it a gilt and polychromed wooden figure of a temple guardian from the Kamakura period in the thirteenth century, fierce but also somehow benevolent, and guarding, Poussine was quite sure, the serenity of his household.

The servant appeared with the reporter in tow, bowed and disappeared for tea. The reporter was the kind Poussine liked best: quiet, dignified and older, not one of your flashy, brassy youngsters. The reporter was tall and quite elegant-looking, really, gray-haired and with professorial steel-rimmed eyeglasses and well-cut tweeds in the British manner. Chess reporting must do well by him, thought Poussine, who had only lately come to think of categorizing people by the salaries they might command. Or perhaps the stranger had money of his own, not unlikely by the look of him. The reporter said his name, and they shook hands and sat down. Poussine didn't quite get the name; no matter, they'd have a record of it at the office, it wouldn't be polite to ask again and what did it matter in any case? But my goodness! Deaf as a cod he was getting.

The stranger said something. The man must be mumbling. Poussine leaned forward to hear better. There was a roaring in his ear, a numbness.

Nikolai Poussine slumped forward and fell out of his chair, instantly dead. The .22 caliber bullet from the reporter's tiny revolver had entered neatly in his ear. The gray-haired stranger was gone when the maid returned with the tea. The Kamakura temple guardian loomed fiercely, benevolently over the body of his owner, bearing a message from the gods, but six hundred years too late.

◆

Dimitri Lubov was only twenty-four, but a thousand years of proud Tatar blood rode in his veins, and there it mingled with another kind of pride, the pride of a self-made man who knows and values the strength of his own swift achievement. It was Dima's good luck to be born with talent. But it was Dima's raw guts and energy that turned that talent into something approaching genius at full gallop. Dima rode his luck bareback with a wild careless grace, and luck carried him higher and farther than he ever dared dream. From a hovel in Saratov to the pinnacle of fame in fewer than twelve years! Along the way he had learned to wear many masks, masks of art and manners, masks of pride. The man behind these masks had moved so fast he hardly knew himself. There would be time, one day, to explore the real Dima. But for the moment it was far more urgent to dance, to love, to reclaim Jenny.

Dima wished for a mask as he stood at the end of the great rehearsal hall, waiting for the *Corsaire* rehearsal to begin, as he watched Jenny come toward him across the smooth floor of battleship-gray linoleum, Jenny walking proud as any queen, the de Lis scarf flagrant at her waist, her expression calm, poised, a new Jenny altogether or, just possibly, his Jenny in a mask of her own devising. As he watched this new Jenny, the mask Dima had wished for built itself on his pale blond face; it would be a Kirov eighteenth-century courtier's mask, a mask of reserve and grace mixed with a touch of irony. She was playing then! Well, he could play, too! It would be a performance then, this rehearsal. They would see who'd win at that game. It was not a game Dima wanted to play or even win. But for once his pride took him in a direction he hadn't intended. He looked at Jenny and smiled a cold stage smile and bowed a little bow. She, by all the gods of old Russia, must come to him!

For the first time in years Jessica Privet could walk into the apartment without wincing. The Privy Purse had done its work well, and fresh paint brightened the entire place. There were new draperies in the living room, and a small, worn-but-good Persian carpet filled the space in front of the fireplace. On the walls, bright framed posters took the place of the auctioned Matisse and Picasso and Léger. It was a major improvement, supervised by Clifford Hale himself before he left for Boulder. And Jenny was even back home to enjoy it all. Why, she asked herself, was she feeling like the bottom of the well? What would the intrepid Gerald Lanier say about such a down-in-the-dumps point of view? It all came back to Jenny. It always had, probably always would.

The change that came over Jenny after she walked out on Dima did not please Miss Privet one bit, glad as she was to have the girl back home.

Growing up was one thing. Growing hard was something else. Privy had noticed a tough little shell forming and hardening on the gentle surface of her Jenny's character. Of course, it was a defense. God knew, the girl had few enough defenses. Maybe she could use defenses. Still and all, Privy didn't like what was happening. And she tried to think of ways to bring Jenny and Dima back together. But in Jenny's present frame of mind it wouldn't do even to mention such an idea.

Jenny was suddenly all pride and independence, and the day after she'd first worn the controversial de Lis scarf she'd asked Privy to run over to Bonwit's and buy six more, so she'd have a fresh one every day. That had been three days ago. Jenny had rehearsed with Dima, performed with him twice to continuing rave notices, and now, next week, Dima was leaving the company. Privy had no idea where it might end. But she did know things would have to change.

Jenny might fool herself that she was being brave, being tough, being strong. But Privy could see the self-generated acid eating at the girl, turning her bitter. It wasn't healthy. Privy looked around the living room. She had so looked forward to Christmas this year! For the first time in a long time they'd really have something to celebrate. But Jenny minus Dima was no cause for rejoicing. and Privy with this strange new Jenny on her hands felt about as Christmasy as the Fourth of July. Miss Privet sighed and went into the kitchen to make herself a cup of tea.

At the end of the week the small smile on Jenny's face reflected a major triumph in her career as an actress. She was actually doing it! On the haughty wings of the role of the

black swan, she had really made it halfway across the rehearsal hall toward Dima without breaking down in tears,
without begging his forgiveness for—what?

Almost in a trance now, she kept on walking. That gentle
fluttering at her waist was the peach-colored silk scarf of
Alexander de Lis. There was magic in it, like something in a
medieval legend; the scarf gave her courage when she needed
it most. Miles and miles Jenny walked across that floor; it
seemed to take years, the distance seemed to recede, she'd
never get there. Dima stood tall in his silly yellow sweat shirt,
his arms at his side, waiting. As she got closer and closer,
moving with the black swan's predatory glide, smiling the
black swan's distant, wicked smile, Jenny could see a change
come over Dima. His face had been blank, questioning. Now
he began smiling too, a smile that was dangerously close to a
sneer, a courtly, mocking smile, a smile with knives in it. Was
this the man who meant more to her than anyone ever had,
more than she'd ever dreamed anyone ever could? Was this
the Dima whose life, and house, and bed she'd shared for six
magical weeks? It most definitely was not! This was a
stranger, cold and threatening, armed and lurking behind an
impregnable fortress of good manners. This was the ultimate
rudeness!

Jenny walked up to Dimitri Lubov and, from the depth of
resources she didn't know she owned, summoned one last
burst of dramatic skill. Keeping it low, keeping it casual, she
spoke first. "Hi, Dima." It cost her as much as signing her
own death warrant.

"Let us begin," he said, tossing the ball back into her
court, "with the second pas de deux."

Dave Loughlin didn't even try to repress the shudder that
went through him as he read the paper. They'd gotten to
Nikolai Poussine! Shot dead in his own living room. The
method was changing, it seemed, growing less subtle. All the
other murders, except for the faked suicide, had been made
to look accidental or suicidal and were even now undetectable. The game had suddenly changed, and Dave wondered
why. He also wondered what he and Ivan were going to do
about Dimitri Lubov. One thing was sure. It was time to stop
the pussyfooting around. It was time, and now, to go at this
new menace with everything they had.

Lubov could be guarded; maybe he could even be persuaded to accept protective custody. That was one thing the CIA had plenty of experience in; many were the remote Canadian ranches and Brazilian haciendas and New Zealand fishing villages where a friend of the CIA could relax in security while this or that situation cooled down. But the first thing was to make sure the boy was guarded, and around the clock, and wherever he went. Even before he clipped *The New York Times* article on the murder of Poussine, Dave reached for the telephone. Lubov must be protected.

Black-tie dinners, thought Greg Holden, ought to be outlawed. Once again, the managing director of the International Ballet Theater struggled with black silk tie that seemed to have a will of its own, a fighting will that had perversely decided its ends would never, under any circumstances, come out even. Greg pulled and tugged and prodded and cursed. Tied and retied the wretched thing. Finally, the fight went out of the tie. Or, rather, it changed its tactics. It lay there against his cream silk shirt, sulking, limp and looking more or less like a proper bow tie, but waiting, Greg knew all too well, for its chance to creep out of shape when he wasn't looking, to take him by surprise when, hours too late, he'd catch a glimpse of himself in some mirror and discover the tie had won its filthy game after all.

Tying the tie was just one reason Greg hated formal parties. He hated them all, even the best ones, and especially he hated the idea of tonight's bash, with Judith Winchester parading young Lubov like the spoils of war before all the board of directors and rich patrons of the International. For a moment Greg felt sorry for Dimitri, pawn that the kid was in a game whose rules were invented by Judith minute by minute. Then he remembered what problems the kid was going to cause him, and Boris Mogador, and how the morale of the International was going to need plenty of shoring up that wasn't going to be coming from Judith Winchester.

Greg took one last disgusted look at his tie in the mirror, trying to stare it down and losing, then slipped on his dinner jacket and walked out of his penthouse apartment. A time was coming, and maybe tonight, when he'd have a showdown with Judith, for his own sake, for the sake of the company. Greg dreaded that confrontation because he wasn't at all sure he'd win.

Dave Loughlin looked at the six men before he spoke and hoped that his own sense of futility didn't show. They were a mixed lot. Two wore the work clothes and carried the tool kits of stagehands and gaffers, one was a freaked-out hippie, one a cabdriver, one a Black Muslim, one a distinguished-looking plump businessman. They formed a crack surveillance team, rung in from all six Manhattan CIA groups to cover Dimitri Lubov day and night, in and out of the theater, everywhere he went.

These men were the best in the business, maybe the best in the world, and still, Dave felt it was hopeless. He had called in the heavy-artillery surveillance boys more to assuage his own conscience than because he really thought they could stand between Lubov and the death that was surely stalking him. Still, they had to try, to do the best they could for as long as they could. If only there were one little clue! The killers could apparently strike anywhere in the world, subtly and without warning, setting themselves up in the most harmless-seeming manner.

As a piece of tradecraft the string of remorseless killings was a textbook lesson. As a menace it was profoundly frightening. As a professional challenge it looked impossible to beat.

Loughlin briefed the surveillance teams, set up the usual codes and check-in times, feeling hollow as he went through the exercise. Still, it had to be done. There was nothing else to do. Not even Ivan, of the jolly laugh and devious mind, had come up with a plan.

Tonight Dave had another meeting with Ivan, at the Carlyle bar again. Sure, he'd go. But Dave Loughlin felt futile about Ivan, these days, too. He thanked the surveillance teams and ushered them out of the Delage Feather and Trimming Company. Then he sat down and thought hard about Dimitri Lubov's chances of surviving the next few months. They seemed right up there with the chance of a snowball in hell.

The floor-length sable, thought Diana Leighton, was over-kill, Russian or not. That left her with two other evening coats to choose from, a dull-gold lamé and a plain black velvet. She chose the velvet. Simplicity was all. Judith's invitation had said seven-thirty. Diana calculated her arrival for eight-fifteen, and it was almost exactly that time when the cream-colored Rolls-Royce swam out of the river of traffic on Fifth

Avenue and up to the door of the Hotel Pierre. The doorman helped her out as though Rollses were an everyday thing for him, which they probably were; the most sophisticated people in the world, Diana thought, were doormen and hairdressers. They saw it all. She swept regally through the marble and gilt lobby and into the elevator to meet the man she had been dreaming about for nearly two months.

"He builds a wall around himself, Privy." Jenny sat at home, in the kitchen with Miss Privet, eating an apple and pretending to read a magazine.

"And you, my pet, aren't you doing the same thing?" *Tread lightly,* Privy told herself, *this is the first time the girl has really opened up about Dima.*

"He insulted me. He practically accused me of sleeping with de Lis. And I know what he wants, Privy, he wants me—*me!*—to come back on bended knee, asking his forgiveness. Well, I'm not going to. Just because I didn't jump through his hoop at exactly the minute he wanted me to, honestly, he is arrogant." And even as she said it and even knowing it was true, Jenny could hear her words ringing false. All she was doing was fighting off the emptiness now, keeping the wolves at bay, whistling in the dark. She knew it, and Privy knew it, and neither of them was going to call the truth the truth. If Dima was arrogant, if Jenny were stubborn, if the bold wings of the black swan could take her only so far, what good would talking about it do?

"No one," said Privy quietly, "ever said love was logical."

"You think I'm wrong, don't you? You think I should humiliate myself. Dima's fickle, you know, Privy; he might not even want me back by now. He's got girls beating down his door day and night."

"That must be terribly noisy for him. I like your Dimitri, my dear. But it isn't for me to suggest what your heart must do."

"Tomorrow's his last day with the Civic. And the International's going on that Far East tour. It may be months before I even see him again."

"Sometimes a little rest is good for everybody, isn't it? When things get overwrought?"

"Speaking of rest," said Jenny, standing up and kissing Privy on the cheek, "it's been a long day. Good night, dear."

"Good night, my darling." It had all been very low-key, al-

most casual. But as Jenny walked down the hall to her bedroom, she made up her mind to do something—anything—to
reach Dima before he walked out of her life completely.

Good, thought Diana as she entered the ballroom, *he isn't
here yet*. She had already made up her mind that most of the
women there would zero in on Dimitri Lubov like so many
heat-seeking missiles. She, Diana Leighton, would be cool,
only distantly interested. That, plus the fact that she would
almost certainly be the youngest woman there, ought to at-
tract him. If she were guessing right. If he were attractable.
Diana entered smiling, kissed Judith, spotted a few friends
and several clients.

It was, she realized, definitely an A group. This was the
top of the top, the serious old money and the even more serious new power, legendary robber-baron names mixing with
Washington movers and doers and a discreet sprinkling of
media heavyweights. This was the level of power and privilege that was beyond publicity, serious and discreet, people so
secure in their fame that for them the limelight was merely
an unwelcome glare. Here were none of the giddy jet set,
none of the empty hedonists who fluttered around the world
like gilded moths, existing only in the bright shallow flickering light of their names and deeds and dressmakers reflected
in the gossip columns. No, thought Diana, this was definitely
the top of the top drawer. She spotted an old friend of her
father's, a gaunt witty old man through whose pipelines
flowed thirty-seven point nine percent of all the natural gas in
Oklahoma. She crossed the room to chat, accepting, en route,
a glass of chilled white Burgundy from a passing footman.

The big drawing room where Judith served drinks was
nearly full now, and the murmur of well-bred voices was
punctuated with the occasional tinkle of a glass and the
bright counterpoint of laughter. Then the character of the
noise changed, suddenly, and a discreet but excited buzz
arose from the entrance. Diana stood pointedly with her back
to the door, deep in quiet conversation with her father's
friend, not looking at the source of the excitement, which she
knew perfectly well could only be one man. She sipped Judith's expensive wine and smiled at something her companion
said. *Don't count the minutes, damn it,* she told herself under
the smile; *the time will come*. Diana knew she could trust
Judith Winchester to see to that. In some way, for some

unknown reason, Diana sensed that she fitted in to some larger scheme of Judith's. Judith, one could be sure, always had a scheme of some sort cooking. Well, so be it; it was an ill scheme, she decided, smiling, that blew no good.

And before long it happened; there came a touch on her arm, and Judith herself had materialized with Dima Lubov in tow. "Diana, darling," said Judith in her best schoolgirl-enthusiastic voice, "you simply must meet our new star." At the word "star" Dima visibly winced.

Diana laughed and took his hand. "It's a pleasure, Mr. Lubov," she said, "and welcome aboard." Dima smiled and bowed and was swept on for more introductions. So there it was. The rest would be up to her. "Tell me," said Diana, fixing the old gentleman with her most intensive stare, "about the shah."

Dima looked at the room through a mist of good manners and suppressed rage. *The old Romans,* he thought, *used to do this, to lead their captives through the streets in chains.* Still, he allowed himself to be led; he bowed and smiled and met them all. Not a one did he recognize except Greg Holden, whom he recalled from that dinner party of Judith's long ago. He should have asked Shelly. He should have brought Jenny, although she'd hate a room filled with rich strangers almost as much as he did. Then he remembered, for he had allowed himself to forget just a little, that there was no question of asking Jenny. *Two hundred thousand dollars a year,* he kept reminding himself. *So you have to give a few extra performances like this, nondancing appearances, the hardest performance of all. Cheap at the price.*

Dima registered the lovely blond girl in passing, made a mental note automatically, for she was the only woman in the room who held even the possibility of love. And Dima Lubov's radar was highly sensitized when it came to seeking out that possibility, marking the chance and making the move. It was an instinct, something felt, not thought out. And the instinct started working when he was introduced to Diana Leighton.

It was a very tame Dimitri who followed as Judith circled the big room with her prize, moving like the wind through a ripe wheatfield, enjoying the ripples she made even as she made them. Yes! It was all working, and just as she'd hoped. Even the famous Lubov temperament was being kept in check tonight, as well it should be. And Diana looked lovely.

As well she should. All the board of the International Ballet was here, responding to the greatest single coup in the ballet's history. And she, Judith, had scored that coup.

If ever they'd doubted her intentions or the range of her capabilities, they would doubt no more. She saw Greg Holden in a corner, deep in conversation with one of the other board members. Too independent by far was Greg Holden, and far too removed from her reach. He couldn't be bought; he couldn't be frightened; he couldn't be wooed by the thought of more power or position because he had these things already. Without a doubt, Greg Holden was someone to keep an eye on. But that would be another day. Tonight Judith would simply enjoy the moment of triumph. The first, she was very sure, of many. She gave a signal, and supper was announced.

It did not surprise Diana that she was seated at a table several tables away from Judith and Dimitri. That would have been too much to expect and, when you thought about it, maybe too obvious.

There were fifteen tables of ten, set handsomely with pink tablecloths and red roses and tall silver candlesticks. A string quartet played chamber music. The food was superb, the conversation interesting, the mood elegant. Then why was she bored?

All through the five courses Diana kept the conversation sparkling, laughed and nodded and made herself the very picture of charm and wit and beauty. And with every forkful she wished she were with Dima Lubov. The time would come. She hoped—no, prayed—for it. She felt it in her bones. And why did it seem to matter so? What about her life was so empty that she had to pick up vagrant Russian dancers? Was she turning into a cradle robber? She thought of Dima and laughed out loud. He was many things, but scarcely a child. The man on her right responded to the sudden laugh with a questioning look; he hadn't been saying anything funny.

"I'm sorry," she said, touching his hand with a spontaneous warmth that made his wife frown across the roses at them, "but I was thinking of something Judith said earlier on. . . ." Diana saved the situation by telling a mildly salacious story about the secretary of state, an Arabian princess, and a representative of the People's Republic of China. There

was general laughter. She must watch herself. This was
getting out of hand.

At last the dessert appeared, apriot mousse with cremè an-
glaise, and Dom Pérignon 1959 to wash it down. Judith was
outdoing herself for the good of the International Ballet. Everyone was most impressed. Everyone, that is, but Dima, and
Greg Holden, and Diana Leighton.

The dancing began. Dimitri danced the first dance with
Judith; that was expected. *She dances,* Diana thought, *remarkably well when you consider her age and her personality.* But
a stick could dance with Lubov and look graceful.

The man next to Diana said something. She replied. He
said something else. She was about to reply to that when
there was a stirring behind her chair, more sensed than felt,
and a low unfamiliar voice asked, "Excuse me, but could I
persuade you to dance?" Dimitri Lubov stood by her chair,
smiling the smile of a da Vinci angel. *Could you persuade a
bird to fly?*

Her answer was a smile, a murmured excuse to her partner
at the table. Then she was with Lubov and moving toward
the dance floor and thinking; *thank God I wore low-heeled
shoes.* Onstage he looked like something carved from marble
for a Greek temple, but in real life he was almost exactly her
height, five-six. Good. At least they matched in one thing.

The music struck up, a Strauss waltz, and suddenly they
were moving across the floor. Diana had always enjoyed ballroom dancing, but this was more than dancing. It was somewhere between gliding and skiing and making love. "For you
to dance at a dance like this," she said, laughing, "is like Escoffier making hamburgers."

"But," Dima replied with mock ferocity, "Escoffier did
make hamburgers! Beautiful ones, with Brie inside, and
mushroom sauce. I have eaten." Diana could well guess who
had introduced him to that particular recipe.

"You are enjoying?" Dimitri did a rather formal waltz, a
classical Kirov waltz, holding her almost at arm's length,
twirling and twirling, reversing and reversing, and always
looking directly into her eyes. It was, in fact, a trick to prevent dizziness. But it convinced Diana Leighton that she
would be perfectly willing to waltz right off the edge of the
earth with him, and now, tonight!

"I am enjoying this part of it very much, Mr. Lubov."

"Please, Dima."

"Dima. But earlier on I was beginning to feel a bit sorry for you."

"Sorry?" The look changed; the smile stiffened; the gray-blue eyes went a shade deeper into the spectrum of blue. Dima Lubov was not used to beautiful women—or anyone else—feeling sorry for him. It was not a welcome sensation.

"I wanted to cut your leash." She grinned impishly. The only way to make an impression was to startle him, to do and say the unexpected. Too many women would be throwing themselves at this beautiful young man in every conventional way available. "I've seen you dance, Dima. You should be free. For a moment there, it seemed as though you were being—oh, a captive trained bear, you know, performing for your supper."

"Ultimately," he said, laughing, the mood changing on the instant, "Dima *is* performing for his supper. For many suppers."

"But you know what I mean."

"Yes," he said, suddenly a street urchin again, "I know. And you are correct. The tiger's head stuffed upon the wall, is it not? Poor tiger!"

"I rather doubt," said Diana as the rhythms of the waltz spun them to a climax, "that she'll go that far. You're more valuable on the hoof."

Dima laughed and took her hand as the music stopped. He put his face close to her ear and whispered, "Do you suppose is too early to leave this place?"

"I think," said Diana, not even trying to hide the delight in her voice, "that it's a perfect time to leave, Dima. But not together, or Judith will be furious at me for stealing her tiger. I'll meet you in the lobby in ten minutes."

"Grrrrr!" His reply was a tiger's purr and a grin and a wink. He turned in place and was gone.

Diana moved slowly, thoughtfully back to her table to get her purse. It was a chance, no doubt about that. But it felt right. And Diana Leighton had never minded taking chances. She wasn't coy or a flirt, never had been. Diana knew line and verse what would happen now; it was a question only of where—his place or hers. The real question, though, was could she turn this lucky accident into something more than a one-night stand? At the table Diana turned to check out the dance floor. Judith was batting her eyelashes at the president of a major television network. That would hold her for a while. A note in the morning would do for thanks. She slipped out of the big room to get her robe. The elevator was waiting. And as it plunged her noiselessly toward a night charged with possibilities, Diana couldn't help wondering just how long the ride would be and where it would end.

Greg Holden sat back in his chair and idly stirred his coffee. Judith had placed him as far from her table as possible, and maybe that was just as well. Maybe it lessened the chance of the tension that was building between them turning into something more dramatic than just tension. Greg's mind was on automatic pilot, making small talk with the kindly, but mindless, wife of one of the directors of the ballet. He asked her permission to light a cigar. The woman's words reached him as if from a distance. "It's absolutely too thrilling for words, isn't it?" she chirped, talking about Lubov's arrival in their midst.

Greg surveyed the dance floor through a blue curl of expired Havana. Lubov and the blond girl whirled past, and the other dancers all suddenly looked handicapped. Some dancer. Some girl. He must find out her name. The lady kept on chirping, blissfully ignorant of the fact that she had lost her audience to a reverie of romantic speculation. "I'm just absolutely beside myself," the lady cried, "aren't you?"

"Absolutely," said Greg Holden. "There's no doubt about it."

It was eleven-thirty. Jenny Hale sat on the edge of her bed, flipped idly through the magazine, got up, looked in the mirror, made a face at herself, paced the tiny room and then, impulsively, went out to the phone and dialed Dima's number. It rang and rang, and no one answered. The apartment was dark and quiet. Privy had gone to bed.

Suddenly something clicked into gear inside Jenny's mind. She went back to her room, got a purse and some money, picked up her keys, pulled on an old fuzzy sweater and her warm Navy-surplus pea jacket and a heavy knit wool seaman's cap and walked out of the apartment. She'd do what Dima wanted. She'd go to him, say whatever came into her head, it didn't matter; she'd just make everything all right again, however she had to go about it, whatever she had to say or do. It wasn't going to be easy, but anything—anything—would be better than this, than the enormous hollow

space she felt in her life since she'd walked out on Dima
Lubov. Smiling spontaneously for the first time in weeks, she
walked out into the cold December night.

She found a cab right away, a lucky omen, and so what if
it was an extravagance? Love was finding a way. She had the
cab stop at the corner of West Seventy-fourth Street and Central Park West. Jenny didn't want to come screeching back
into Dima's life like the Fire Department to the rescue. She
wanted to stroll back, almost casually. *I was just passing by,
Dima, and it occurred to me to ring your bell.* Sure. What
would the black swan do at a time like this? Well, for beginners, the black swan wouldn't let herself get painted into a
corner like this one. The gentleman in question would come
to her. But in any case, the black swan had been packed
away for the moment. The black swan had led Jenny astray
just as surely as she led Siegfried astray in *Swan Lake*. West
Seventy-fourth Street was empty. The half block from the
corner to Dima's apartment was one of the longest walks
Jenny Hale ever took. She climbed the brownstone steps and
rang the familiar buzzer.

The buzzer echoed off the emptiness inside her. Not there.
She rang again, just in case, and once more for luck.

The outer door opened behind Jenny then, and she turned,
smiling, sure it was Dima. The smile froze. An enormous
black man stood there, towering over her, menacing. She
stepped back, sure he was a rapist. The stranger smiled,
nodded, took out his house key and went in.

For a moment Jenny stood there, shaken, not knowing
what to do. She'd go down to the corner and have a cup of
coffee and come back, try again. After she had come all this
way, it seemed foolish not to wait a few minutes. She left the
foyer and walked down the steps and across the street. A yellow taxicab waited, doubleparked, its fat driver deeply en-
grossed in the *Daily News*. Jenny hesitated in the shadows,
looked back at the house and up at Dima's windows. They
were dark. She stood there for a few minutes until the cold
got to her. And it was cold, even for the first week in December. She shivered and thought twice about that cup of coffee
and wondered if there was a way to leave Dima a note.

Then, as she stood there in the darkness, a pale, glittering
motorcar came down the street, silent as memory, a low polished extravagance of cream lacquer and bright nickel with a
grille like the Parthenon and immense twin headlamps the

size of apple baskets, driven by a bearded, turbaned warrior out of some Persian myth. It was Diana Leighton's Rolls-Royce, and it glided up to Dima's front door as Jenny stood there in dread and fascination. The driver got out and opened the passenger's door. The lights in the small jewel box of a passenger compartment flicked on, and Jenny got a glimpse of quilted honey leather, polished walnut, a bud vase with spray of tiny white orchids.

And Dima! And a lovely blond girl Jenny had never seen before!

They got out and started up the steps. The girl turned to the driver and said, "I think that will be all, Krishna." The words were softly spoken, but they carried on the crisp, cold air, and they were sharp enough to cleave Jenny's heart in two. She didn't wait to see the light go on. Jenny shrank deeper into the shadows as Dima and his girl climbed laughing up the stairs. Then she turned and ran like a thief for the corner, for a cab, for her life.

The driver of the double-parked yellow cab put down his paper and picked up the microphone. "Twelve-oh-three A.M. Subject and unidentified blond arrive at subject's apartment in cream Rolls-Royce with chauffeur, license NY two eleven DLX. Unidentified visitor rang subject's bell at eleven-fifty-five P.M., saw subject arrive with girl, ran toward Central Park West. Visitor young, probably female, dressed in Navy pea jacket, sailor-type knit hat pulled down over face, blue jeans, boots. Slender, possibly teenaged groupie. Knew Lubov's buzzer without looking. Seemed upset when subject arrived. Over."

"We have got," said Ivan with a frown, "to head them off at the pass."

"Thanks for the helpful advice." Dave Loughlin was into his third bourbon, and they weren't helping. The two oddly matched men had been sitting in the Bemelmans Bar for two hours, talking in low voices, reaching no new conclusions whatsoever. Dave had mentioned the surveillance. Ivan's only comment was that it probably couldn't hurt. This was so precisely what Dave himself felt that it was pointless even to discuss it.

"Hungry?" Come love, come death, come war, come

peace, Ivan Sokolovny would find time to give his belly the tender loving care it was accustomed to.

"Sure."

Ivan signaled for the check and paid from the fat roll of tens that seemed to Dave's eyes to be magically self-renewing. He'd been seeing Ivan on and off for two weeks now, and Ivan always insisted on paying and always paid with the same fat roll of tens. "Remember, old pal, old buddy, I am recruiting you. Can't let my old chums back at Lubyanka Square think Ivan isn't pulling his oar these days."

If that was the way Ivan wanted it, Dave wasn't going to complain. It saved Dave the trouble of having to explain Ivan to Sam Purcell. Dave hadn't mentioned the appearance of his old comrade. Which was a little out of line, maybe, but what the hell? This was his project; he'd handle it the way he wanted. But every day he failed to report Ivan's presence it got progressively harder to do it, more awkward, more likely that maybe he, Dave Loughlin, really did have something to hide. Maybe Ivan really was trying to recruit him. That would be beautiful. That would just take the fucking cake. That would be exactly like Ivan. Old pal. Old buddy. Dave knocked back the last inch of warming bourbon in the Carlyle's crystal glass. Stay in this business long enough and you'd get to be suspicious of your dead grandmother and her dog.

They left, grabbed a cab, headed for a Chinese restaurant Ivan knew.

"Hunam, old sot," said Ivan with an anticipatory grin. "The best of the best."

As Dave might have known, this was no run-of-the-mill chop-suey house. Large, subtly lighted, quiet and filled with happy-looking diners. The headwaiter knew Ivan and led them to a small table isolated in a niche in the lower level of the restaurant, in a handsome room papered with dull gold patterned with Chinese birds and branches. Ivan ordered in fluent Chinese. Soon they were tasting amazingly delicate balls of shrimp mousse coated in sesame seeds and quickly deep-fried until they were crunchy on the outside, light and smooth inside. Dave had never tasted anything like them and said so.

"Stick with me, kiddo, and you'll be wearing diamonds."

"If we don't get a break on the Lubov operation, we'll both be wearing egg on our faces."

Ivan speared the last shrimp ball in triumph just as the waiter appeared with their entrées: spicy shreds of lamb with scallions and tree ears for Ivan, chicken with almonds for Dave, and crunchy dry-fried string beans for both of them. They were drinking a white California Pinot Chardonnay.

"Tell me, pardner," said Ivan slipping from his gangster-movie fantasy metaphors to his Wild-West jargon, "if it would be possible to check on the comings and goings of certain individuals employed by your . . . firm."

"It might be. Why?"

"I only know," said Ivan with the look of a benign panda, "what I read in the papers. But let us suppose—and this is just what your late lamented Mr. Nixon would call a game plan, you understand, pure hypothesis—but just let us imagine, buddy mine, that there was a person-or-persons in your firm who felt a certain distaste for the Union of Soviet Socialist Republics."

"It's just possible someone could feel that way."

"Now take that one step further, Davey, baby, and assume that such a person-or-persons also felt threatened by the recently blossoming détente between our two great and pure nations. And that certain legislation now pending in your Congress might put the heat on a little hotter so to speak, in a manner that would make our purely hypothetical person-or-persons feel that he-or-they might not have a job in a few months, thus adding fuel to the fire of his-or-their smoldering dislike of my side. And then suppose. . . ."

"That our hypothetical pals cooked this up? That's pretty wild, Ivan."

"It is wild, David. But somebody cooked it up. And did it. Think, Davey! Think how beautifully it's all been done! Think what a clue that is, in itself. We are dealing with the very top of the top of professionals. Think, David, *tovarich*, not only of the skill with which each of these killings have been brought off, but the scope of the whole operation. Here is a person, Mr. Hypothetical, let's call him, who can appear anywhere in the world, undetected, as if by magic. Do you know what it costs to fly to Tokyo these days? It is not something one does lightly. Not like hopping a cab."

"If Mr. Hypothetical works for my guys, it would be easy. We own at least six airlines that I know about. And probably any number of shipping firms and so forth. So how would we trace him? He'd be using faked passports beyond any doubt."

"From home, old fart. Find someone who was known to be out of town at the crucial times and we narrow the field."

"I'm not sure I buy it."

Dave toyed with his fork. Ivan was nimbly using chopsticks. For a moment the only sound at their table was the muted wooden click of the chopsticks as they flew from Ivan's plate to his mouth in an oddly delicate dance in homage to greed. Like many heavy men, Ivan could be strangely graceful in his movements. He wielded the chopsticks like a symphony conductor's baton, fast and with rhythmic precision.

Dave was stalling, not from doubt, but because Ivan's proposition made so much common sense that it scared him. He'd known from the first that this was the work of a top professional, so very top that only three or four nations in the world might conceivably be involved. The key word was "professional." Dave had ruled out fanatics from the beginning. If this was a fanatic—and, in a sense, it had to be; it was that crazy a thing to do—it was a very highly trained fanatic. A cool, intelligent fanatic. Someone who could sit and wait and choose his moment, cloaked in the perfect disguise of the professional agent's day-by-day necessity for absolute secrecy in all his movements. If Mr. Hypothetical were in the CIA, he might be tracking Dave Loughlin this very moment! It was a can of worms inside a can of worms, and the can opener was not in sight.

Dave shuddered and reached for his wine. The agency was in enough hot water as is, right this minute. Watergate had opened wounds so slow to heal that all kinds of other infections had festered around the original hurt. If what Ivan suggested were true, it would tear the CIA limb from limb. And, Dave thought, hating the thought as it formed in his bewildered, bourbon-soaked head, if this were true and it wrecked the CIA, it might just be that the CIA deserved it.

"Every cloud," said Ivan merrily, signaling for more wine, "has a silver lining."

"Fuck you."

"No, truly. Young Lubov will be safe in China. Mr. Hypothetical will not find it easy to go there at least."

"You're right. We'll have to arrange something for Japan."

"I'm sure you can do that, pardner."

"Yeah." Dave sipped the wine as if it might solve his problems. The waiter took their plates away and asked if they wanted dessert.

"Fortune cookies!" Ivan was excited as a five-year-old. They came. Ivan opened his first. "Watch your ass, old buddy; it says 'the night is made for love.' "

Dave laughed and reached for his cookie. "Are you ready for this? 'Ignore previous fortunes!' " Dave put that one in his wallet and ate the cookie. It was funny enough. But why did it make him think of Sam Purcell?

CHAPTER
❦ 9 ❧

Dancing was a drug for Jenny now. Always a hard worker with a gift for deep concentration, now she pushed herself to the limit, beyond the limit, because sometimes in the sweat of class and rehearsal and performance there would come blessed narcotic moments when she simply hadn't the time or the strength to think about Dima Lubov.

Jenny moved through her days and nights mechanically, conscious only of work and emptiness. She tried to fill in the emptiness with more work, better dancing. Thinking about her life was simply too painful, so Jenny let her body think for her; in class and onstage she became a perfect machine for dancing. De Lis fed her need with more and more roles.

Now Jenny was dancing three or four times a week. The critics kept up their praise, but Jenny was too preoccupied to notice. The audiences showered her with applause, flowers, curtain call after curtain call. She merely endured this. It was part of the job. Their enthusiasm had almost no meaning for her personally. She was unable to respond with anything like the same spontaneous affection the ballet audience poured out to her. Privy kept the scrapbook, but Jenny hardly looked in it.

But her success was marked in the company. De Lis raised her salary again and gave her a better dressing room. She bought a dozen white leotards and had them dyed the special de Lis shade of peach, her trademark now, along with a vaguely distracted gaze offstage and a new tension in the cords of Jenny's neck. All the surfaces of Jenny's life were much the way they had been before she met Dimitri, but something at the core was frozen, and Jenny had no idea at all what to do about it. Privy, she knew, worried, watched and waited—

for what? There was nothing Privy could whip up in the kitchen to cure a damaged heart.

In the meantime, gratefully, Jenny danced and danced and kept on dancing. She knew in her heart that de Lis was manipulating her, and she was grateful even for that, for not having to think, for being able to abandon even the pretense of running her own life. Where it would end she had no idea. But in the meantime, dancing was enough.

Dimitri, typically, soared into his new career with the International Ballet like a dolphin through surf: joyously, triumphantly. He had regrets about Jenny, but he wasn't going to show them to the world. That wasn't what the world paid to see. Meanwhile, there were new friends to make, new roles to learn, and there was Diana Leighton.

The International Ballet had no permanent theater of its own and had to mold its schedule to the convenience of other, luckier companies. Sometimes it used the Metropolitan Opera House, sometimes the New York State Theater, now and then the new Uris, from time to time the old City Center on Fifty-fifth Street. When Dima joined the company, they were in the midst of a run at the Uris, New York's first theater-in-a-skyscraper, on West Forty-eighth Street. Shelly Sylvester had some interesting conversations about Dima's billing, and very soon huge posters were to be seen on the street level of the Uris, blazing the name LUBOV into the minds of the few balletgoers who didn't know it already. Dima danced, joyously, and found a kind of joy with Diana.

Dima, at twenty-four, knew much of sex but little of love. Penned up all through his adolescence in the rigid, military-academy atmosphere of the Kirov School, his teenage adventures with girls had been confined to quick wild adventures on holidays and weekends. His first real affair—at twenty-two—had been Felice. Then Jenny. Now Diana Leighton. Diana was frankly a sensualist and, at thirty, as different from Jenny as Jenny had been from Felice. Diana had none of Jenny's vulnerability to hurt or her elfin, quicksilver innocence. Diana knew what she wanted and how to get it, and when Dima discovered how much she wanted him, he was very agreeable and, being Dima, was never at a loss to express that agreement with his body. Dima was used to living for the moment. Even with Jenny he had made no serious plans. If he had thought about marriage at all, it would have been in some distant, more leisurely future.

Now, with Diana, warmed by the shared pleasure of her bed and by the gilded ambience of her life, he found it easier every day to forget the pain of his breakup with Jenny. Partly by design and partly because it was her nature, Diana made everything easy; everything about her was positive, upbeat, eager. Diana had moods, but they never surfaced to interrupt a moment with her lover. Diana was direct, funny, beautiful and gifted with a talent for making the small arrangements of life seem effortless. She was also undemanding. If she resented the ballet groupies who followed Dima in public, if she had any jealousy over the fact that he spent his days rehearsing with dozens of lovely young girls who might be more than willing to deepen their acquaintance. Diana never let it show. Dima's feeling for Diana had none of the intensity he had shared with Jenny. If anyone had asked him that, he would have been the first to admit it. But no one did ask, and he basked in the glow of his new romance with the unquestioning pleasure of a child on Christmas morning.

Greg Holden was surprised and very pleased to discover how smoothly Lubov fitted into the International Ballet Theater. Dimitri had pride but no vanity. He had a puppy's eagerness to please, a sense of humor, great energy and an infectious charm that touched everybody from the toughest old stagehand to the youngest kid in the corps de ballet. Dimitri worked himself harder than anyone would dare to ask him to work. He was malleable in problems of casting and refused to throw his weight around; one Nadia in a company, Dima thought, was more than enough.

Greg had worried about the possibility of rivalry between Dimitri and the International's other spectacular young star, Machito Ramirez; it didn't happen. In fact, before long the two young men became friends.

Dima had felt tension building when he first met Machito; it was natural. After all, the young Puerto Rican had worked furiously to achieve his position in the company, and why wouldn't he want to protect that position from any interlopers, Russian or otherwise? But there was nothing of the backstage politician in Dima. He wasn't going to enter into any kind of maneuvering-for-position contest with Machito or anyone else, and Dima made this obvious from the start. He asked Machito to coach him in a role Dima had never danced: Antony Tudor's subtle modern fantasy *Shadowplay*. Flattered, Machito exerted himself. They danced the lead part on alternating nights, and both won raves for it. Soon they were working out together, trying bits of choreography on each other, laughing, inventing mad ways of eluding Nadia and in general erasing any fears Greg Holden might have had about an explosive rivalry.

Boris Mogador saw them practicing entrechats-six de volée one afternoon and began thinking of ways to cast them together, maybe as Romeo and Mercutio on alternate nights in the same production. Different types physically, Machito was taller than Dima by five inches and dark where Dima was blond. But they moved with the same soaring, defiant grace, the same fluid élan, the same careless disdain for all the laws of gravity.

At first these two young men who had grown up half a world apart were a little formal with each other. Slowly they discovered how very alike fate had made them. Both Dima and Machito had been slum kids, boys who had lived by their wits until some unplanned magic in their bodies answered a golden invitation from the gods of dance.

There was a period, early in their friendship, when they played a game of comparative poverty as sad and silly as any two Princeton boys comparing ancestors or yachts.

"I stole chickens from the supermarket," Machito said proudly.

In that moment Dima knew the tall dancer would be his friend. He laughed. "Aha! But you, at least, are having a supermarket to steal from, while Dima is out in the fields—and sometimes with no shoes—and chasing rabbits. Not, you understand, frozen supermarket rabbits. Running bunnies, Machito! Which at age six years I am running after, catching. Sometimes."

"I was arrested at ten."

"Where I lived, there were no gendarmes. Is a *luxury* to be arrested!" By this time they were both roaring with laughter. "Hey," said Dima, slapping the barre in mirth, "for two little criminals, we aren't doing so very bad, eh?"

"Not so bad. I think, maybe," said Machito, suddenly grave, "that we'll get along, Lubov."

"Dima. I hope so. No reason not to. Not"—and the urchin

grinned through the star dancer with sudden impish radiance—"when you are such a damn good chicken stealer."

The rapport was quick, and before very long the two young men were friends. Other than Felice, and Jenny, and perhaps Diana, Dima had never had a friend in the West. It was a new experience, and he intended to make the most of it.

Sam Purcell loved gadgets. It was largely due to Sam's growing influence that TSD had become such a thriving operation within the CIA. TSD was Technical Services Division, and Sam Purcell was its patron saint. It was TSD, in its earliest incarnation, that had developed the famous plastique bombs so beloved of the French underground during and after World War II. But TSD had gone far beyond explosives. Explosives belonged to the Gothic age of counterintelligence.

What interested TSD most these days was advanced electronics, listening devices of such elegance and sophistication that at last, for the first time, it was safe to say that literally nothing was sacred. It was such a device that Sam played with now, fondling it and aiming it and just admiring it, in his big office at CIA headquarters.

The device was encased in the aluminum tube that usually held an Upmann cigar. The flat cap of the tube was a sensor capable of picking up a whisper at fifty yards. The little device—as yet unnamed—had another trick. It could detect conversations going on indoors by picking up minute vibrations from window glass. And whatever it picked up, it recorded on a miniature tape cassette, also self-contained. The sound quality was excellent. This would free field operatives from lurking in cars and cellars with bulky batteries and full-sized recorders. Sam smiled. It would have many uses, this little cigar-tube sensor.

Alex de Lis watched *Giselle* as though he had never seen it before. Here was the same girl in the same production, yet not the same at all. Jenny was dancing better every night. Always skinny, the girl had lost weight lately, one pound less and she'd look like Buchenwald; he must speak to her about that, set her to ice-cream sodas for lunch instead of the inevitable dancer's yogurt. But how she'd matured these last few weeks! It was a pleasure to watch such development, a flower opening before his eyes, a flower, too—never forget—of his own planting and nurturing and pruning. There had been

several new Albrechts since Lubov left, all adequate, none
with Lubov's fire, but somehow Jenny Hale made up the
difference.

Even Simon Bridge had been impressed, rereviewing her
performance to comment on how quickly Jenny was fulfilling
the great promise shown in her debut just a few months ago.
Yes! His instinct had been right again: push her on; give her
always a little more than she could reasonably be expected to
do. When had ballet concerned itself with reasonableness in
any case? De Lis smiled. That the new intensity of Jenny's
dancing, her concentration, the loss of weight might reflect
some deep unhappiness concerned him not in the least.

Happiness, he often thought, turned people into contented
cows. Madame had told him long ago about the words of
little Jenny Hale, aged eight, auditioning for the school of the
Civic Ballet: "I want to be a dancer, Madame, because
dancers make people happy." Well, at any rate she was making de Lis happy, and the audience. No doubt about that,
none at all. The curtain fell on Act II with the usual thunder-
ing applause. De Lis joined in from his vantage point in the
wings. Let the Lubovs of the world come and go! The Civic
would continue, unruffled, and de Lis with it, and Jenny with
de Lis. So it had always been. So it would always be.

Dimitri looked at Diana as she walked toward him, naked
and radiant, across the ivory carpet in her silk-walled bedroom. Diana's body was a generous thing, rounder and more
voluptuous than ballerina's bodies could ever afford to be, a
body one might find in a Botticelli drawing, the kind of body
myths were made on. He looked at her in the gathering
warmth of his desire and knew it was a desire as basic and
timeless as breathing, beautiful as sunsets, warm as red em-
bers. It seemed to Dima in that moment that everything
about this woman had been designed and cultivated for his
pleasure, and for this he was grateful. And ready.

She came to him in the simple wonder of her luck. Diana
knew she had set up her meeting with Dimitri Lubov as coldly and precisely as any Mafia killing, on a whim, out of rest-
lessness. She had never dared dream it might last or turn to
something like love. "Love" was a word Diana used rarely
because she felt that overuse had cheapened it in her set.
"Don't you just *love* Percy?" some giddy Junior League guer-
rilla would shriek about someone Diana scarcely knew and

barely liked. Now she looked at Dima as he stood waiting
next to her bed, proud, golden, sex rising, a fountain of such
energy that might spring directly from the sun itself, this
tame-wild man-boy-beast out of the mists of some half-remembered Tatar legend. She reached for him, and he for her.
They entwined, and as Diana felt his hands hot on her flesh,
she thought of other hands, of the enormous theater filled
with hands clapping, reaching out for this human explosion
they screamed for: "Dima! Dima!" Her voice in the bedroom
mingled with the imagined voices in the theater, and then
she stopped thinking altogether.

Judith Winchester had a timetable for almost everything.
Her plan for being officially recognized as the most important
patron of the International Ballet had taken form gradually
over the months, but now she saw it clearly.

First, the introduction of Dimitri Lubov into the company
gave her a piece of physical evidence of her effectiveness.
This would be subtly but definitely emphasized by judicious
publicity in her magazines. Next would come the Oriental
tour, inspired by Judith, made possible by Judith's connections in the United States government and, of course, publicized again in her magazines. When the tour was over,
Judith would launch a major fund-raising campaign, whose
end result would be to obtain a theater for the exclusive use
of the International. To do this, Judith had been advised,
would cost about fifteen or twenty million dollars. So be it.
She'd start by contributing a million of her own; it was, after
all, deductible.

With the theater built or bought, Judith knew she'd be in a
position of unquestioned power. Maybe she'd get herself
made chairman of the board of directors. Certainly she'd
eliminate Gregory Holden.

She sat at her steel desk and looked at the calendar. She
wouldn't be able to join the tour in Tokyo, but it might just
be possible to make the Peking opening. Judith had been
twice to Peking already, but it might be worth the tiring
flight. She might be able to consolidate her position a little
more strongly.

Judith never questioned her need for absolute control of a
situation any more than a ravening shark questions his appe-
tites; it was her nature, and she tended the demands her
nature made as carefully as a good gardener pulls weeds.

Now she stood up and walked the length of her office and opened the Coromandel screen to reveal the little theater. She intended that the International Ballet Company would be every bit as much at her disposal as this expensively made toy. Toy? It had served its purpose. It had gotten her Dima Lubov! She switched on the music, raised the miniature curtain, threw her head back and laughed out loud.

The Spic and the Commie were drinking red wine in Dima's apartment. That's what Dima and Machito had taken to calling each other in the warmth of their new friendship; no one else would have dared to play with pejoratives around the proud Machito or the temperamental Lubov. Dima was packing. The day after tomorrow they were leaving for Tokyo. Machito sprawled on the big brown leather couch by the fire, laughing. "So, Commie, we'll get to find out if what they say about Japanese girls is true."

"Would you be betting, Spic?"

"What I really want," said Machito, "is to get a look at Kabuki."

"The music has a totally different vocabulary, Machito. Is not musical."

"Monkeys on a hot tin roof."

"Like that. Screeching and wailing and the sudden explosions. Ultimately is highly irritating, tough to move to." Dima picked a worn black leotard out of a drawer, started to pack it, realized it belonged to Jenny. He frowned and put it back in the drawer. She hadn't asked for it. She hadn't tried to communicate at all.

Somehow he felt ashamed, with the sad old leotard and the sad memory, here, while laughing with Machito. Dima had heard, just rumors, about Machito's brief affair with Jenny. But Machito himself had never mentioned it, knowing as he must that Dima and Jenny had shared this same apartment for nearly two months. Dima reached for his wineglass, sipped, smiled. One test of a friend, he thought, was just that kind of discretion. To be able to tell a friend anything at all. to have the judgment that shows you when not to tell.

Diana was out of town tonight. Tomorrow they'd have a farewell supper at her house, just the two of them, and Dima well knew what the dessert course would be. He couldn't pretend to feel for Diana what he had felt and, face it, Dima—still felt for Jenny Hale. But in the meantime, before

whatever final resolution happened between Dima and Jenny,
Diana made a lovely interlude. In a way it was like his affair
with Felice; he gave, Dima knew very well, just as good as he
got. There was nothing about it of seducing virgins or breaking hearts.

In the case of Jenny, well, that was something else. Dima
thought about her more and more even as he realized how
neatly his wounded pride had painted him into a corner. He
knew his Jenny. And even in the heat of the moment when
he'd found her, weeping, in the arms of Alex de Lis, Dimitri
had known there was nothing sexual about it. That
knowledge hadn't made his anger less hot or cooled his
outrage that Jenny couldn't bring herself to make a simple
decision like leaving that possessive old Svengali, de Lis. And
by every standard he'd ever lived by, Dima knew he was
right to stand his ground, to make Jenny come to him. That
his might be a hollow stand, that pride was a tragically poor
bargain when it could be quickly traded in for love, was only
slowly dawning on Dimitri Lubov. He hadn't seen Jenny at
all since those few awkward classes and performances after
their split. Oh, they'd been professional all right! The audience never knew. But not a word passed between them in
those last terrible days that went beyond functional good
manners: "Could you place your hand a little higher in the
lift, Dima?" His hands on her, burning, on what had been his
and might never be his again, his brain frozen with pride.

"Of course. Here?"

"There. Thank you."

That had been worse than throwing bricks, but neither of
them would give, certainly not Dima Lubov. And what had it
gained him, this small tarnished treasure, his pride? He would
think that over on this long and probably lonely trip. And
when he got back? Time and only time would tell. He closed
the suitcase and walked into the living room. "OK, Spic, how
about a bite to eat?"

"Right on, Commie. Soul food?"

"Ultimately, I take you to the Russian Tea Room, nyet?"

It was almost laughably easy. For the first time in all his
years Dave Loughlin thanked God for the creeping bureaucracy that had so enmeshed the CIA that nothing whatever
got done without accompanying convoys of meticulously detailed paperwork. Shitfuck, Dave well knew you couldn't get

a typewriter ribbon without three requests and four carbons. Then there were the ubiquitious and well-hated time sheets. No training school for insurance actuaries could have been more finicky in accounting for hours devoted to this or that project, trips taken, expense accounts, all that. Dave hardly took cabs anymore; it was that much of a pain in the ass to get reimbursed for them.

But there was a good side to all the paperwork; it existed. It was all on file, and Records Integration had it, and Dave Loughlin had total carte blanche for anything he needed. "Need to know" was the ancient byword that greased the wheels of secrecy.

It was never a question of were you cleared for such-and-such a level of secrecy classification, because almost everyone was, but did you need to know. Was it urgent for your particular project at this particular time? The concept made sense.

What happened in reality was that all the bureaucratic busy-bodies, the empire builders and the just plain curious developed a wild itching need to know everything. Copies proliferated. Classification slowly evolved from a tight and vital and fairly efficient precaution to an international joke. Congressmen were taking top secret documents home to their wives to read over cocktails. *The New York Times* was printing items no one knew it had.

And Dave Loughlin was getting the data he needed.

The request had been deceptively simple; he wanted all the monthly time sheets of everyone in headquarters at Langley who held the rank of GS13 or over. No explanation asked or given. Dave picked GS13—his own rank and the equivalent of a lieutenant colonel in the Army—simply because he figured it was unlikely that anyone with less rank could possibly have the skill and the freedom of movement to pull off something like the defector murders so smoothly. His secretary at Delage Feather and Trimming had an excellent head for figures and a top-secret clearance from the CIA. Rita would love the task of winnowing out the two hundred-odd folders.

Even though counterintelligence was by nature a traveling business, Dave felt it pretty unlikely that any one individual would have been out of the office at all five of the crucial dates. Of course, there was always the possibility it was someone not at headquarters. But if Ivan's crackpot theory had anything to it, chances were this was a very top-level job. And while Dave didn't really believe it himself, he was the first to admit that Ivan's was the only theory they had on them. He'd wait. He'd see.

The night Dimitri Lubov and the entire International Ballet Theater took off for Tokyo on a chartered Japan Airlines 747, Jenny danced the lead in *Coppélia*. The great comic role of Swanilda, de Lis thought, would be an effective contrast with the tragic Giselle. And, just possibly, the lighthearted role might rub off a little on Jenny. The girl was definitely overwrought these days.

Jenny studied the score, read what she could about past interpretations, rehearsed and rehearsed and rehearsed. "Coppélia," the score read, "or, The Girl with Enamel Eyes." *Well then, let my eyes be enamel,* she thought, *and maybe my heart, too.* Jenny tried not to think about Dima Lubov, but the small gossip-ridden world of ballet conspired against that, as did the big, publicity-oriented world outside the theater door.

Judith Winchester's five magazines lost no chance of publicizing Dimitri Lubov. Her sports magazine did a feature on Dima as a pure athlete. The money magazine discussed his amazing financial success and potential. The basic newsmagazine followed him one way or the other week by week. And the show-business magazine covered the entire ballet world, with special emphasis on the International Ballet. Dima was photographed in rehearsal, surrounded by high-fashion models, for Judith's fashion magazine. If he had grown so much as a petunia, Jenny was sure, Judith would have wormed him into her gardening magazine, too.

The newspapers were full of his romance with Diana Leighton, who was considered newsworthy herself. That was how Jenny found out who owned the cream-colored Rolls-Royce. And whatever she didn't read about, Iris Dowling was sure to tell her in person.

Jenny's reaction was work. She danced harder and better and with less regard for the hundred risks every dancer faces every minute onstage. Most dancers save themselves for a few high points in a ballet. Jenny was dancing all-out, all through every performance now. She burned white-hot in her energy and talent. She danced like someone obsessed because, really, she was obsessed. Jenny wanted the dance to consume her totally. And finally, it did.

It seemed all New York had come to see Jenny Hale's first

Coppélia. The theater was packed to the walls; the backstage rumor was that they were turning standees away.

But the excitement of it washed off Jenny like a mild rain as she forced her concentration to sink deeper and deeper into the cardboard, comical role of Swanilda. With her pert manner, Jenny thought, and her fickle boyfriend.

It seemed there was always a fickle boyfriend. Jenny liked the boy who was dancing the fickle Franz: Terry Shaw was a fine, bouncy, exhuberant young dancer, who in his private life preferred boys to girls. That suited Jenny just fine, too. Terry presented no threat, no danger. There was no chance of Jenny's being lured out of her cage again.

The ballet would be fun. She willed it to be fun. It was a challenge, naturally. That was why de Lis had assigned her the coveted part. The mechanical, jerking movements in the second act were one of ballet's trickier obstacle courses for ballerinas. And the great romantic adagio in the third act, the wedding dance, was a popular favorite.

I am, thought Jenny as she applied just a shade more rouge than might be necessary for a highly colored village temptress, *shrewder than Giselle. I am the ringleader of all the village girls. I get them up to all kinds of mischief. Then why is my boyfriend so stupid that he thinks he's in love with a mechanical toy?*

Which brought her back to reality and Diana Leighton. A toy Diana might well be, but not mechanical. In the badly choreographed world that began outside the theater door and terrified Jenny more every day, mechanical toys did not cruise the world in cream-colored antique Rolls-Royces. Nor did they win men like Dima Lubov for lovers. Dima, who was racing across the sky away from her right this minute, at six hundred miles an hour.

"Fifteen minutes to curtain, fifteen minutes to curtain." The stage manager's voice came crackling through Jenny's fear.

She stared at the reflection in her mirror. The libretto described the mechanical doll, Coppélia, as "the girl with enamel eyes," and Jenny, as Swanilda, mischievously impersonated her. "I am the girl with enamel eyes." It pleased her somehow, that image. Enamel eyes. Hard, cold, unable to cry. It was something to think about, something to strive for. "Five minutes to curtain."

Jenny had already warmed up for an hour, but she slipped

her leg warmers on over Swanilda's tights, pulled a crocheted shawl over the peasant girl's blouse, and walked out of her dressing room to warm up some more behind the flats.

Hers was the first entrance, the first dance. She quickly found the flat that was Swanilda's cottage, the door through which she must make that entrance. How like the first act of *Giselle* it was, though seen in a fun-house mirror. But Swanilda wasn't going to let an oaf like Franz drive her mad with love. Not that girl. Swanilda took matters into her own hands, and cleverly, too. *And when*, Jenny wondered, bending in demi-plié, *would Jenny Hale learn that simple lesson?*

The familiar rustling noises found their way from the excited audience back to the bustling world behind the scenery. The expected shrieks and moans emerged from the orchestra pit as horns and fiddles and brass wailed their protest at being put through their paces one more time. Terry Shaw— Franz—emerged from the shadows in his leg warmers to wish her *merde*. "*Merde!*" said Jenny brightly, a little too brightly, the way Swanilda might have said it. If there had been a Swanilda. If anything at all was real but pain.

The expected wave of applause greeted the arrival of the conductor. Silence. The familiar Delibes overture started up. The curtain went up. The dream began.

They loved their new Swanilda in the first act and loved her even more in the wonderful mechanical doll dance in Act II. And as Jenny went into the big romantic adagio with Terry in the third act, the wedding pas de deux, some of the tension seemed to flow out of her. There was a special joy in all the company now; they could feel the pleasure they'd given the audience come bouncing back in great waves of enthusiasm.

There are two big lifts for Swanilda in the wedding pas de deux. The first was a soaring joyous thing. On the second lift Jenny put her foot down wrong. The toe buckled under her; she fell forward, couldn't save herself, fell to the floor in a flash of pain and humiliation, and just lay there for a second, clutching the foot, before she struggled up, assisted by a frantic Terry Shaw.

There was a gasp from the audience. Somehow they could tell this was worse, far worse, than just a casual slip.

Bravely, without thinking, Jenny tried to move the foot, to go on dancing. The whole bottom of her leg flashed white-hot with pain now. She fainted with the pain, and only because

Terry already had his arms around her was she prevented from falling again. He scooped her up without another thought for the continuity of the ballet and carried her backstage. Then he went back and resumed the dance alone.

There were three doctors in the house and one was an orthopedic man. "I'm afraid, young lady," said the doctor, "that it's one of the metatarsals. At least one. We'd better get you to the hospital."

Alex de Lis and the doctor rushed Jenny to Lenox Hill, and de Lis called Privy from there.

Through all the pain and the confusion, Jenny had said almost nothing. Her mind was frozen with fear, and all she could hear inside her head was Dimitri's taunt, sometime in the dim and sad past *Ultimately, deushka, there comes a time when you can no longer dance. It comes for all of us, late or soon.* She looked up at de Lis through Swanilda's streaked makeup and said in a small voice, "I'm terribly sorry, Mr. de Lis."

"Jenny, little Jenny, don't even think about it. You were glorious tonight. These things happen. My goodness, child, Eddie Villella has eight breaks in just his right foot alone. One forgets how many in the other. And still, he dances, and superbly. All this means, Jenny, is that you will get a lovely little holiday, a month, six weeks, but not to worry about. You must promise me not to worry." De Lis held her hand as they processed the X-rays and put on the cast.

"Plaster," said the doctor, "it's less comfortable than a soft cast, but with Jennifer Hale one does not take chances."

"Chances of what, Doctor?" Jenny couldn't keep the fear out of her voice. She didn't even try.

"Oh, sometimes a bone—especially those damned metatarsals—can set a bit out of line. No problem. But for a dancer, well, we must make sure the architecture of your foot is perfect. And it will be."

"When will I be able to use it?"

"Between six weeks and two months. It depends. We'll have you in a walking cast in three weeks. Until then, of course, it will be crutches. And I advise complete rest for a few days. You look—forgive me—a little wrung out." He smiled a professional, fatherly smile. It didn't reassure Jenny one bit. She'd be surprised if she had a foot at all when they took off the damned cast.

"Thank you," said the small voice. The trained dancer's

smile flickered for a brief moment across her face. He gave
her a hypodermic for the pain, and the pain, to be sure, began slowly floating away.

Privy appeared, all brisk efficiency on top of her deep
concern.

"My darling! What happened? Mr. de Lis, were you there?"

"Just a common dancer's accident, Miss Privet, too common, I'm afraid. We've had three such breaks just this month.
Jennifer will be fine. And you should have seen her dance
tonight! Glorious! Well, ladies, I must be going. The hospital
will lend you crutches, I believe, Jenny. Call me in the morning. And"—he took her hand again and squeezed it—"you
were a delightful Swanilda, my dear. Absolutely delightful."

Alex de Lis knew perfectly well why dancers fall. They fall
because tension makes them careless. And what makes the
tension? Of all the many answers to that question, the answer
at the top of the list had to be Alexander de Lis himself. De
Lis knew the pressure he put on everyone in the Civic, lived
with that pressure every day and most nights. He must demand excellence. He must drill and nag and promote and
demote and star and unstar and create and juggle the budget
and worry about next year's deficit and balance the entire
Civic Ballet Company with the precision of a tightrope walker
working without a net.

Of course, it created tension. Of course, the pressures were
intolerable. But it also created a glorious ballet company. It
created magic, night after night, all through the season. You
stretched yourself to the breaking point and expected others
to extend themselves, too.

De Lis thought of Jenny, thought of her tormented face,
the anguish in those huge gray eyes, reflecting a pain that
must go far deeper than any injured foot.

De Lis needed Jenny. He needed her, and dancers like her,
with an urgency that was almost physical. He hated to confront this need. If Jenny were really injured! If the injury
gave Jenny too much time to think, too much time to need
Lubov. Too much time to make plans. All those possibilities
were the enemies of Alex de Lis, of the Civic Ballet, of what
de Lis lived for and dreamed of, and needed so desperately
he would probably be capable of killing for.

Star system or no star system, the public wanted Jenny
Hale, stood in line for Jenny Hale, would turn in tickets
when it was announced she wasn't dancing.

De Lis thought of Jenny, thought of the huge deficit that loomed over the company like some mythic curse. He made his good-byes and walked out into the night, knowing he'd have to think of ways to keep Jenny involved in the daily life of the company during her recovery. Losing Dimitri had been one thing, too bad but not unexpected. To lose Jenny for any reason would be much more than too bad. It would be a disaster.

CHAPTER
❦❧ 10 ❦❧

"On the darkest night," said Ivan Sokolovny, looking meaningfully across the restaurant table at Dave Loughlin, "the man who has one candle owns a thousand suns."

"In case you guys in the KGB haven't noticed," said Dave, grinning, "Comrade Khrushchev is no longer with us. Cryptic folk sayings are out. And this is too serious to kid about."

"Davey, old fart, you are losing your well-known sense of humor."

Ivan examined his old friend's face, still not used to the changes in it. *Ah,* he told himself, *but we all change. It is inevitable to change.* All the gods knew, he'd changed himself. But Dave Loughlin's changes, these thirty years, were sad ones.

Ivan well remembered the old days, that happy time when, in the flush of victory and youth and optimism everything was fresh and polished and attainable and even the ruins of Berlin, smoking and stinking, looked not so bad because those burned stones were going to be the foundation of something bright and better, something Dave Loughlin and Ivan were going to help build, together, and together with all the world.

The good old days! Could they ever have happened? Happen they had, and never to be forgotten, days when thin ice looked just as good as thick, when trust was more than a word in the dictionary, when hope was a fact of life. Reality, Ivan thought, had not been kind to David Loughlin.

Ivan sighed a bottomless Russian sigh and picked up his cognac. The dreams had been replaced by alcohol in Dave Loughlin's brain, the smooth, warming, numbing, releasing elixirs seeped into Dave's consciousness with the sad, irrefutable logic of despair. When, Ivan wondered, had he given up? For himself, Ivan had chosen a certain path, had weighed his pleasures against what it cost him to earn those pleasures, had made a bargain with the devils and himself and had been reasonably happy.

"Maybe," said Dave, his rough voice a little thicker now with the wine and the brandy, "I ought to find it funnier that one of my own guys could be behind all this. You'll just have to bear with me, Ivan. God, but I hope it isn't true."

"We should know——"

"By the end of the week. At least Rita will be finished processing all those papers by then. We'll have it narrowed down. An inkling."

"What is 'inkling'?"

"Clue. Hint."

"Should we get our Mr. Inkling, whoever he is, or a few of them, then what?" *Get him planning,* thought Ivan, *get the wheels moving again. Don't just let him sit there shredding himself to pieces.*

"We put a tail on Mr. Inkling. Easier than guarding Lubov, although, needless to say we'll keep right on doing that too."

"And if there is no Mr. Inkling?"

"We try the British. Although I'm not quite sure how we go about that."

"I could help there." Ivan's grin would have told another CIA man priceless things about Soviet penetration of British Intelligence. But Dave hardly noticed. Ivan had counted on that and hated himself for having the shrewdness and the reflexive guile to manipulate his old friend, like a puppet, almost without thinking. "But, in all modesty, old motherfucker, history has proved this Russian kid one good guesser."

"Time will tell," Dave muttered, "to coin a phrase."

"In this, Davey, we Russians have a built-in advantage. What we are dealing with is the work of a lovely, full-grown, baroque paranoid. And Russians know more about paranoia than anyone. It's our national flower, practically. The British—yes!—they have the techniques. The sophistication. After all, they just about invented counterintelligence. But— and this is one huge but, Davey—no paranoia. No motive. No impetus. A certain style of old-school-tie Briton might well get crazy on the subject, let us say, of recapturing the Empah. Or preventing nylon from supplanting tweed. Or cruelty to animals. Or membership into the club of gentlemen. But anti-Communism? That's an American virus, Davey. One that this country ought to be immune to by now, after your fascinating interlude with the good Senator Joe McCarthy. But like syphilis, the really evil sicknesses have a way of going underground, only to emerge again, when you least suspect them, more virulent than ever. Think, for just one example, of what happened with your prohibition of alcohol and of what happens now with your prohibition of other drugs. Some fine day America will learn. But it happens slowly, old fart, and at what cost to how many innocents?"

"I'll drink to that." Dave Loughlin waved for the waiter. This meal, he insisted, was on the CIA. It was time, Dave thought, that Sam Purcell bought him a drink or two, Sam with his Persian carpets and leather wing chairs and deputy directorship. The waiter brought another round of double cognacs, their third. Yes, no doubt about it. This was on good old Sam, and fuck the paperwork.

Judith Winchester read all the galleys of all her magazines every week. These final editorial meetings were famous; grown men trembled; Pulitzer Prize-winning reporters and photographers were reduced to quivering jellies in anticipation of nobody-knew-what caprice might come at them next from behind the huge steel desk on the top floor of the *Scope* building. This web of fear and surprise was created by Judith Winchester with all the care and affection that might go into the weaving of some delicate bit of lace.

She hired the best and paid the best salaries and her five magazines gave writers and photographers a worldwide showcase unequaled anywhere. That was why they came, and that was why so many of them stayed on, trading their ethics for fame, mortgaging their right to say "No" for the right to get rich. And for all her whims and cruelties, there was a lot to be said for the Winchester publications.

Once you had the cover by-line on *Scope*, the world of journalism had little more to offer. This was a trap, but a gilded trap, and some of the finest minds in journalism were caught in it.

Each magazine had its own hour of review on Thursdays. In these reviews the editor would present the entire next week's edition before the gimlet eye of Judith Winchester. Only the editor-in-chief was present at these sessions. And only when Judith was out of town did they go smoothly.

She seems to be in a good mood today, thought Edward

Dahl, the editor-in-chief of *Scope*, as he laid the red folder containing the next week's edition of his magazine on Judith's polished-steel desk. *I wonder who she's done in now.* And, involuntarily, he swallowed, hoping she wouldn't notice, because Eddie Dahl knew very well that the done-in person was just as likely to be him as anyone else on the premises. Judith smiled as she turned the pages. The only comments she made were murmured nods of approval. She might have been a high school girl reading her diary.

Scope had invented a section about people-in-the-news called—Judith's name—"Peoplescope." It featured short paragraphs on celebrities, often with pictures, a gossipy, middlebrow and enormously popular section that Dahl wanted made into a separate, spin-off magazine. "Peoplescope" usually filled the center spread of the magazine, except when that spread was preempted by some special news feature or by a special, half-again-the-regular-spread-rate advertisement. Judith flipped to the "Peoplescope" section, stopped, frowned. "Kill the Jenny Hale item, Eddie." She turned the page and the page after that.

"But, Mrs. Winchester, she's the—"

"Kill it, Eddie. I don't care if she set herself on fire in Cartier's window. Get it out of there."

"Yes, Mrs. Winchester." The stabbing pain came back to Eddie's gut. He reached into his jacket pocket. Damn and damn! He'd left the Gelusil on his desk. Someone had estimated that the consumption of the antiulcer stomach-coating wafers quadrupled on editorial-review days. It was plenty high the rest of the week, too.

Eddie stood there in silence as the pages flipped, as the cold gray eyes zigged and zagged from item to item. Slowly the frown faded on her hatchet face. Slowly the little-girl smile began to form. She got to the back of the magazine, to the book reviews. The page flipping stopped. She was actually reading something!

Judith's capacity for reading and writing was the subject of lively and irreverent debate among her staff. Little gems of her prose were treasured as rubies. Eddie's all-time favorite was a small note on her private notepaper that contained the word "THANX." Judith looked up at him from the book review as if he were some rare wild flower growing unexpectedly from the carpet. "What a lovely review of the ambassador's autobiography, Eddie. I just know he'll be thrilled!"

She closed the folder and handed it to him, still smiling; the session was over. His stomach was throbbing a little less. He managed a smile and thanked her and walked out of the enormous office without actually tripping.

Alone for the moment, Judith got up and walked to the huge window. She could see for miles. Somewhere down there lay Jenny Hale, seriously injured, possibly never to dance again. And somewhere in Japan was Dima Lubov. If he heard about Jenny's fall, it wasn't going to be courtesy of Judith Winchester, you could bet on that.

The miniature Westminster chime that replaced a buzzer on her phone chimed softly. She picked up the custom-built polished steel instrument. "Yes?"

The editor-in-chief of *Cash* was waiting, as well she knew, a loyal, longtime employee who had taken to having that one drink too many over lunch, who had begun to take the old-timer's familiarity of grousing a little too loudly about the vagaries of the Establishment, meaning her, meaning Judith. His replacement was already under contract, but the editor didn't know that yet. He'd be told, not by Judith, later this week. The door opened. She turned. "Come in, Harry," she said, taking in his haggard face, the eyes rimmed with red from tears or alcohol or maybe both. "How well you're looking!"

Jenny lay in bed with her eyes closed, even though it was nearly noon and she was wide awake. If she opened her eyes, she'd see the flowers. Even as it was, in the dark-red gloom behind her closed eyelids, she could smell them, the flowers, roses and carnations, flowers from de Lis, from the company—ha! they wished her dead, she knew it—flowers from Daddy, from Privy even, more flowers than Jenny had ever seen or even imagined outside a florist's. Even that nice Geraldine Flynn had sent flowers. Here it was, the third day since her fall, and Privy was sending the flowers right on to the children's ward at Lenox Hill Hospital, because they threatened to fill up the entire apartment; enough was enough.

"Gangster funeral!" was Privy's amused comment after the second day. Still, Privy was pleased; it was a measure of what her Jenny had achieved, and still so young. *And still*, thought Jessica Privet with a sigh, *so sad.*

Jenny lay there in a trance of her own making, straining every fiber in one huge effort not to think. She failed, and this seemed to be the final failure, the ultimate ignominy, crowning her shortcomings as a dancer and as a woman with a crown, not of thorns, but of some burning substance that threatened to slice her head in two. Of all the thousands of costly flowers, there was not one weed from Dima. Of course, Dima was in Japan. Of course, he hadn't bothered even to pick up a phone when he was in New York. Of course, he hated her. Of course, her life was over. Jenny frowned, gritted her teeth, clamped her eyes even tighter shut. If she could see herself, thought Privy, who poked her head in from time to time, she'd either laugh or cry. More likely cry.

Why, Jenny thought, *doesn't this bed up and fly all the way to Tokyo?* He'd care, if only he knew. It must be in the papers, on TV, in the magazines. But Dima hardly ever read English papers. Never watched TV except old Fred Astaire movies. *Then why doesn't this bed sink through the floor, right down through the crust of the earth into the fiery furnace?*

Privy saw the face making and made a face of her own, frowning. Then she decided to take matters into her own hands. "Jennifer Hale, you ought to be ashamed of yourself. Have you no character? There you lay, like a bump on a log, feeling sorry for yourself. With all the misery there is in the world, this is simply shocking."

It was a tone Jenny hadn't heard for years. Here was the Privy of her childhood, all fire and brimstone, ready to take on the whole world in a just cause. And, Jenny knew perfectly well, Privy was right. Privy was always right. Then why were elephants stampeding in her head, why was there a dust bowl in her heart?

Slowly, slowly, Jenny opened her eyes. There were the flowers, the two dozen white roses from de Lis, her father's mixed bouquet and Privy's small pink azalea. The only ones Jenny wanted near her bed. The only ones, to be honest, that would fit in the tiny bedroom without crowding. There was Privy, too, looking more concerned than she had on the night of the fall.

Jenny managed the feeblest of smiles. "I'm sorry, Privy. It is selfish. Do you think I ought to see a shrink? Because it really feels like the end of the world. Not just losing Dima. Everything. Nothing seems to mean anything anymore. I lie here and think: Why get up, ever? Why ever dance again? What's in it for me? Nice people—the kids in the corps— chip in to send me flowers and I wonder what they mean by it. It's like all the world is ganging up on me, Privy. I know in my head they aren't. In my heart, well, I'm not so sure. The bottom seems to drop out of everything."

"What you need," said Privy, sitting on the foot of Jenny's bed, "is a nice cup of tea and a walk in the fresh air." She saw the surprise on Jenny's face at the suggestion of a walk. "Yes! A walk! If you think of yourself as a cripple, well, by the old Harry, then you will be one. Now! I'll put on the tea, and you get yourself up and out of this bed of pain. You think too much about yourself, Jenny. That's bad for anyone. It's a glorious day, in case you've been too droopy to notice. There are things to be done, child! Why not take the next bunch of flowers up to the hospital yourself? It's not that far. You'd see tiny children who really have things to feel bad about, some of them incurable. Or if that's too much, why not go to rehearsal? They must need help teaching people your roles. The trick, child, is to be useful. To do something for someone else, for someone less fortunate. And don't look surprised, Jenny Hale. You may have a broken leg, and you may have a broken heart—or think you do—but you're young and famous and very pretty, and how many girls in the world do you think have ever been so talented they made an entire theater leap to its feet and clap its hands raw with applauding? Feel sorry for yourself? Fiddlesticks and double fiddlesticks, Jenny! That's the silliest thing I ever heard. Now. Up, up with you!" Privy turned, a plump English tornado that brooked no interference. When Privy was on the march, there were only two things to do: join the march or flee the battlefield.

Jenny stretched in the narrow bed, tried to wiggle her toes in the heavy cast and, without quite knowing why, smiled for the first time in three days. There was nothing for it; she'd have to get up and do whatever Privy had in mind.

Down came the covers. One leg over. Now the cast. Now the crutches. There! Up! It wasn't hard at all. And by God, if she didn't start moving about, she'd atrophy. It might take her forever to get back in shape.

Jenny reached out, held onto the top of her dresser and executed a demi-plié with her good leg. *She'd show Dima Lubov. She'd show them all! There was more to Jenny Hale than a lousy broken metatarsal could keep down.*

Now the shower. Maybe it would be fun to take the flowers to the hospital. Or visit anyway. And maybe, just maybe, she would drop by a rehearsal. Smiling. Wearing the de Lis scarf. Showing them she had the stuff. Being gracious to her replacements. Maybe even making a few friends. Clump, clump, on toward the bathroom. She sounded, thought this new Jennifer Hale, exactly like Blind Pew with his cane, tap-tap-tap. And she smiled.

Dima never thought he'd find a city more crowded or costly than New York, but here it was, Tokyo, Japan. In boots, blue jeans and cowboy hat, Dima strolled the Ginza with Machito at midnight and found it just as bright and bustling as Broadway, but with two pleasing differences. Difference one, it was immaculately clean. Difference two, for the first time in his twenty-four years, Dima found himself among people whose height was about the same as his five-six. Some of the kids were shooting taller, the new vitamin generation, beardless ivory stringbeans, but the diminutive scale of the majority gave Dima an eerie sense of being at home here. His athleticism and early fame had erased any tendencies to develop a Napoleon complex.

Most dancers were slightly built; the taller girls were always in a fix to find partners in proportion. Machito, at six-two, was a giant among dancers, a colossus in Japan. The two friends walked, laughing, down the gaudy street, each with a girl on his arm, for it seemed there were always girls here.

The American ambassador had given a big reception for the company after their sold-out opening night, and ever since, their lives had been a steady round of parties, girls, parties. The State Department put them up in style; Machito and Dima shared a suite in the Okura Hotel, two bedrooms and an adjoining sitting room, and in nearly two weeks neither of the two young stars had gone to bed alone. *And so what,* thought Dima, *it's offered, it gives pleasure, it hurts no one.* As with everything he did, when Dima set out to prove to himself he could get along very nicely, thank you, without Jenny or any woman in particular, he did it totally, enthusiastically and successfully.

The Japanese girls fascinated him. He was intrigued by the way they looked, delighted by the enormous differences that lurked beneath their superficial similarity, astonished by the eager sensuality that seemed to be the flip side of their delicacy and containment. They were like sexy little cats, he decided. There was a feline ease about them, a hint, even in the outmost reaches of abandonment in sex, that something was being withheld. You could never, thought Dima, quite own one of these girls. There would always be a sense of mystery, of territory unexplored, forbidden, locked shut. Yet for all that, they knew about making love, knew as if from the cradle more about deferring to a man's desires than most Western women would learn in five lifetimes. Dima was too much an actor himself not to sense the theater in it; this was a role they played, and to perfection, and who knew what lay beneath?

In the meantime, he thought, grinning the urchin's grin, who cared? Let them fill his bed, with their rituals of servitude, with their polished-silk skin and acrobatic tongues. Dima gave himself freely to the gaiety, the social whirl, the lovemaking. Everyone said, store it up, things will be different in China, they're ironclad prudes in China, they discourage even holding hands in China. Well and good; they'd see what they'd see. In the meantime, there was another week of Tokyo to revel in, and Dima had every intention of making the most of it.

They were instant celebrities in Japan. Classical ballet was still something of a novelty here; there was no permanent Tokyo company yet, and few international troupes could afford the huge expense of shipping sets and costumes—let alone dancers—halfway around the world. So, while the native audience was anything but sophisticated in ballet, they made up for it by their intelligent interest, their generous hospitality and the pleasures of their women. Only Nadia grumbled; she hated the food, the bed was too soft, there were no immediate suitors. But then Nadia always grumbled.

Dave Loughlin looked up at the cracked and peeling ceiling of his office. Damn and damn! He'd have to do something about that lousy paint. Sometime soon. Sometime when he didn't have a hangover so bad he could hardy remember his own name. Ivan had really socked it to him last night. Or had he socked it to Ivan? He couldn't remember much after that second cognac. But somehow Ivan had gotten him a room at the Statler Hilton, almost across the street from good old Delage. Trust trusty Ivan. Or could he? What had he said to Ivan, plastered as he must have been to judge by the volcanoes going off in his head? Shitfuck, what could Dave Loughlin tell Ivan that Ivan didn't know backward already? Ivan could probably have told him what color underpants Effie was wearing on the second Tuesday in February 1958, if it came to that.

Dave reached for the coffee. It was cold. He rang for Rita. Thank God for old Rita. She had the face of an underprivileged sea lion and the disposition of a barracuda in heat, but she got things done. In fact, if the truth were known, old Rita pretty much ran Delage Feather and Trimming all by herself. Dave wondered if Sam Purcell knew that. Most likely. Sam Purcell knew just about everything. Just like Ivan. He must fix them up sometime. Ha-ha.

Rita poked her pointed nose around the door and rasped, "Yes?"

"Could you get a dying man some more coffee, please, Rita?"

"Coming right up. By the way, Mr. Loughlin," she said with the flat disdain of one addressing the lowest of the low, "I'm just about finished with those files."

"That's fine, Rita, thanks. Coffee first, then files." Dave got up, grimacing, and walked twice around his desk. He was just about to sit down again when she reappeared with a thermos of coffee on a tray and four neat manila folders. He thanked her again, sat down, poured the coffee, drank half a cup and opened the first file. And the second. And the rest of them. There were, naturally, four names. Two he had never heard of. One he knew from somewhere. The fourth was Sam Purcell. Dave sat there for a minute, fighting a rush of sickness in his gut, a queasy feeling that had nothing to do with his hangover.

Diana put down the ivory-colored telephone and laughed out loud from pure delight. Dima was going to have a surprise visitor! From the moment she'd heard about the tour, Diana had considered joining him. Japan was no problem. The visas to China could probably be managed; her Uncle Alf was very good at that sort of thing. But in China, she knew, everything would be regulated. She'd probably be isolated from the ballet tour like any other visitor. So she had remained undecided. But the phone call had done it.

Mable Harrington, of the Harrington Aluminum Harringtons, had just got back from a Far East tour and wanted her beach house totally redone à *la Japonais*. Diana was just the girl to do it for her. Little did she know the extremes of pleasure and consideration her request would get or what quick priority!

Real Japanese cypress, said Mable Harrington, joined and fitted and tongued-and-grooved with never a nail, just like the ancient Shinto shrine at Ihse. "And screens, Diana! Lots of screens. And some of those cute iron teapots. Scrolls, Diana! Caligraphy, Diana! The real thing, Diana!"

"Yes, Mable. I know just what you mean, darling, and I know exactly where to get it. Where? Where else, Mabel? I'll go to the source, Mabel. Smelt a little more aluminum, Mable; you're going to need it. Shinto shrines don't come cheap, dear. Yes, Mabel, naturally, I'll leave this very week. I know, Mabel. The sky's the limit. It always is."

Diana reached for the phone again and dialed a number she knew by heart. In minutes her travel agent called back, confirming the flight, first class, needless to say, on Japan Airlines, leaving Thursday, the polar route, yes, she'd be there in eighteen hours. Thursday was the day after tomorrow. Diana packed a week's worth of lightweight silk knits into a soft-sided carry-on bag. If there was more to be worn, she'd buy it there. If she had time. The Okura! Dima's hotel.

Maybe she ought to simply move right in with him. No. The surprise would be more fun. The whole trip would be fun. She could hardly wait to see his face. She could hardly wait for the rest of him, either. Japan was very romantic at any time of year: right now, and with Dima, it might just be the place where a girl could finally admit to herself that she'd fallen well and truly in love.

Alex de Lis looked up and smiled a long, slow smile. That was his little Jenny! In she came to the rehearsal hall, head held high, moving with a curious grace on the awkward wooden crutches, wearing bluejeans cut to make room for the big cast, a dark turtleneck and—*brava!*—his scarf at her waist like a sash. De Lis stopped what he was doing and walked across the big room and kissed her. There was a ripple of applause from the kids who weren't actually practicing. Several dancers came flocking around her. Their concern had more warmth in it than Jenny had ever hoped for. She knew in her heart that some were jealous, some spiteful, that some just didn't care, they were so self-absorbed. Just like Jenny herself. But the concern was real. They knew what it meant to Jenny, to any dancer, to be injured. They'd been there. They dreaded even a small hurt, even a strained muscle or a sudden chill. A break was catastrophe. Iris ran up and kissed her and said: "Double *merde!* How long in the cast?"

"Two more weeks in this one, then a walking cast. About two months in all."

Jenny smiled, she was calm, gracious, with the wan courage of exiled royalty.

De Lis took her aside, clapped his hands, and a chair was brought.

She sat and watched the rehearsal. It was the moment Jenny had dreaded. Another girl learning her part! I will do it, she told herself, I won't let them see how much I care, I will sit here and smile if I turn to a pillar of salt doing it. They were teaching Iris Swanilda. Well, and why not? Iris was Swanilda born and bred. The saucy village flirt. Tart, more likely, thought Jenny with a sudden untypical smirk, followed by an even more untypical giggle. Privy had been right. If Jenny Hale had a dollar bill for every time Jessica Privet had been right, she could retire right this minute and never dance another step. She looked down at her plaster-shrouded foot. Even it was suddenly comical, a parody of the slender precise instrument buried inside. De Lis could make a dance on her: the Waltz of the Elephants.

The piano started up again. Iris was rehearsing the hardest part of *Coppélia,* the mechanical doll dance from Act II. And something was amiss. Iris, Jenny knew, would be perfect for the Swanilda of Act I. Better, maybe, in typecasting terms at least, than Jenny herself. Jenny was perhaps a bit ethereal for the part. Iris had more flesh on her. You could imagine Iris hauling buckets from the well, tumbling in the hay. It took, Jenny figured, more practice than she, Jenny Hale, recent virgin, had accumulated.

Jenny watched Iris, saw her with a new detachment and saw what was going wrong. The girl was throwing too much weight into the movements. She looked less like a clever mechanical doll than a science-fiction robot from a cheap horror movie. She was trying too hard. Jenny looked away, embarrassed, afraid that possibly her presence in the hall was doing this to Iris, that she was making the girl self-conscious. The music stopped; de Lis called a break for ten minutes and walked out of the hall.

Iris walked across the room, away from Jenny, picked up her dance bag and toweled off. Then she came to Jenny's chair and sat on the floor. "I fucked up."

That was Iris, Jenny thought, delicate as ever. "Listen," Jenny heard herself saying, "I thought de Lis was going to absolutely murder me, I made so many mistakes in that old second act."

Here was a breakthrough; it was the first time Jenny had called him anything but Mr. de Lis.

"I feel like a klutz. But then," said Iris, "I guess it's a klutzy part."

"Freddie Momontov," said Jenny, "taught me a trick about that. *'Underplay zee doll, dolling,'* says Freddie. And you know what? It worked. At least for me. When I tried it first, I really sort of threw myself into it, you know, klunk-klunk, Godzilla strikes again. But Freddie showed me this." Jenny shot out her arms like a crucifix, waited two beats, then slowly, slowly, with only the smallest jerking motions, turned her head, in three separate moves, toward Iris. The effect was uncanny. It really looked as though her head were moving on ungreased gears. Iris laughed. "See? A little goes a long way. You try it."

Iris tried it. Like all dancers, she was a fine mimic. In three tries she had it down pat. She smiled and kissed Jenny on the cheek, started to turn away, stopped, turned back. "Jenny, thanks. You didn't have to do that."

Jenny blushed, looked down at her cast, smiled. She could feel the tears starting. "Yes, I did. Hell, Iris. Freddie helped me. Why shouldn't I help you?"

"Got a couple of hours? Anyway, thanks. Really thanks." Embarrassed, Iris turned and went back to her dance bag just as de Lis returned. The music began again, and Iris went into the mechanical doll dance. The improvement was enormous.

When the rehearsal ended, de Lis came to Jenny. "What in the world," he asked, pointing a finger in mock accusation, "did you do to her? It is night and day, the difference. I obviously can't turn my back for so much as a minute, little Jenny, and you are, what do you say, unsurping me?" He laughed a conspiratorial laugh that made Jenny very glad she had worked up the courage to come to rehearsal today.

"I just told her what Freddie told me—underplay a little."

"Should you ever, little Jenny, want to stop dancing and take up coaching, you know where to come first."

"Thank you, Mr. de Lis. I'll never stop dancing."

"Margot has a saying which I think is from her Brazilian ancestors. 'Never,' says dear Margot, 'name the well from which you will not drink.' How long, do you think it is, Jennifer Hale, since this old man stopped dancing?"

"But you didn't stop!"

"In public I did. And let me tell you, I have only the smallest nostalgia for it. Even when I was onstage, it was not the applause that moved me. Forty years, Jenny. Twice your lifetime. That is how long I have not danced, yet lived and breathed dancing. Perhaps there is more of dancing in me now than ever there was when I performed. Do you not see how that can happen?"

"But to a genius."

"Genius be damned. Sweat, Jenny! Strain. Pain. Working and working at it and never for one single minute thinking: Aha! now here it is, I have done it, this is perfection, there is no more to be done. It is a curse, perhaps a disease; one should see a psychiatrist. No?"

"No! Never. Not you." She was half-serious, half-amused. But she saw what he meant. It wasn't all onstage, not by a long shot. Jenny looked at the cast, and imagined nameless horrors developing underneath the spotless white plaster, her foot deformed in some incurable way, a life without dancing. And in that instant, for the first time in her life, Jenny Hale knew that there could be such a thing. She felt this with an almost physical jolt, as if the floor had suddenly heaved beneath her.

"It was brave of you to come today, Jenny. Come tomorrow, also, if you can. You're on the payroll, don't forget. We must make you earn your keep, child. You have more than earned it today, with Iris."

"Thank you."

"We," said Alex de Lis with an imperial smile that took in Jenny, the entire ballet company, the theater itself and all the world of dance, "thank you."

He turned and walked briskly away from her. Jenny closed her eyes then, hoping to shut out the world altogether. But

when she closed her eyes, Jenny saw what she most feared
seeing. She saw Dima, saw Dima dancing, and his partner
was someone else.

Dave Loughlin had always lived his life by simple rules.
First, there was the church, then his country, then Effie and
the kids, a job he'd once believed in, a cause to fight for, and
kill for, if it came to that. And slowly over the years Dave's
faith in these things had worn away, eroded until all that was
left now was the pale memory of convictions that had once
burned bright but were now reduced to infinitely delicate
ashes, shifting in the slightest breeze. Dave started out knowing right from wrong, love from hate, bad from good. This
afternoon in January, wracked with hangover, sitting in the
dingy office looking at Sam Purcell's CIA time sheets, Dave
knew no anger or fear but a dull sense of loss. There was
enough humor in him to see the irony of it. Of course. It figured. In a world where attorney generals planned burglaries
and elected Presidents committed crimes in the Oval Office itself, it should surprise no one if a man whose trade was deception and death decided to enlarge his sphere of influence a
little. In, Dave was sure, what Sam believed to be a good
cause.

Dave had shut his ears to the scuttlebutt all during Sam's
steady rise in the CIA. Too ambitious, they'd said, too crafty
by half, mad with power, only wants to call the tune. Men
who had been passed over snarled their resentment in a tradition that went back to Alexander the Great and beyond.
What, Dave wondered, had the generals whose profiles hadn't
ended up on the ancient coins called old Alexander?

Dave sat with his cooling coffee and his building headache
and tried to imagine what he'd have to do now and what it
would cost him.

Of the four folders, Dave dismissed two out of hand. One
man was a crippled intelligence analyst who simply would
not be capable of the physical effort involved in the murders.
And another was a lawyer who lacked the necessary tradecraft. That left someone called Putney Lawrence and Sam
Purcell. Dave would check out Lawrence, but all his reawak-
ened instincts told Dave it had to be Sam. It was not a
thought that gave him any pleasure.

It was all perfect, very smoothly done. A flash of a grin
came and went on Dave's gray morning-after face. How Sam

must have laughed when his old sidekick came strolling into headquarters with his crazy theory! And how perfect it must have seemed to Sam, to let dull, loyal old Loughlin handle it. Mishandle it! Sam would no doubt see to that. No one in the CIA would so much as raise an eyebrow if old Dave Loughlin fucked up. Sooner or later, the whole case would just fade away. It would get too expensive after a while, too boring, sounding too much like paranoia. And Sam Purcell would gently, diplomatically, ease Dave out of it, just as he'd eased Dave out of plenty of other messes over the years. Good old loyal Purcell. How Dave had always relied on his one friend in high places. And how Sam relied on him now, on his plodding, on his rusty skills, on his mind dulled with bourbon. Sam must have taken one look at Dave and guessed that here was double insurance for his plan, the perfect way to cover his tracks inside and outside the CIA. As ever, Sam guessed right. But for Ivan's shrewd suspicions, Dave's investigation—which he'd been so proud of, which gave him such hope!—had been going just where Sam wanted it to go. Nowhere. Did Sam know about Ivan? Dave had never mentioned his old friend's arrival. The phone must be tapped, but Dave had been fairly careful about the phone, after that first call. He wasn't being tailed, that was sure. Or was it? Was anything sure in this upside-down-and-sideways world? Dave reached for the phone. Then he jerked his hand back as though the phone had suddenly turned into a coiled rattlesnake.

Ivan must be told. Sam might be setting him up even as Dave sat there. Where was Ivan right this minute? Their next appointment wasn't until tomorrow night. There was no point in calling the Soviet Consulate. That, beyond doubt, would be bugged.

Dave's mind raced at unaccustomed speeds. Ivan was well known at the Carlyle bar. Probably he went there even when he wasn't with Dave. Dave got up, grabbed his overcoat and headed for the door. He'd check out the bar. Ivan or no Ivan, Dave Loughlin could use a drink. Maybe two.

Greg Holden didn't really have to go to Tokyo. There was plenty to be done right here in New York. But Greg knew himself, and he knew when he needed a change. He'd been working six days a week for the International Ballet Theater for two years now, for a dollar a year and a lot of aggravation. Especially from Judith Winchester. The idea of a change of scene, of six thousand miles between him and that woman, was vastly appealing. And the International's Tokyo tour provided just the excuse. He wouldn't go for the whole three weeks, and he wouldn't tag along to China. Winchester herself was going to China. But a week in Tokyo, maybe a few days layover in Tahiti on the way back—why not? And if anybody complained—Greg knew no one would—they could take their damn ballet company and stuff it up Winchester's ass.

The day was bright as Greg's cab sped towards JFK International Airport. He hated long flights. Jet fighter pilot, test pilot, plane builder that he had been, long flights made him doubly restless. He always had the pilot's classic syndrome of flying the aircraft himself, feeling every bump and headwind, viewing every cloud with the grudging admiration of a veteran fighter sizing up a crafty new opponent. Still, first class on Japan Airlines guaranteed him probably the best service in the air. He might be able to relax this time. And you never knew, maybe there'd be someone interesting on board.

Sam Purcell sat in his dentist's waiting room, idly flipping through last week's issue of *Scope*. The "Arts" section had a color spread on the International Ballet's tour of the Far East. Among several photos, one stood out. Dimitri Lubov as Albrecht to Nadia Beshanskaia's Giselle. Dimitri was soaring in some spectacular Act II feat of gravity reversal, soaring and almost alive with pleasure, even on the printed page.

Sam looked at the picture and read the accompanying article with interest. For the first time in years he regretted his prominence in the CIA. There was a staff conference next week that he simply couldn't miss. Not if he wanted to keep himself in line for the directorship. And there was the International, in Tokyo, surrounded by unfamiliar people, in an unfamiliar setting. Particularly vulnerable, Sam thought, although performers were always vulnerable. And China was out of the question. CIA men simply did not flit in and out of the People's Republic, regardless of their mission. Well, so be it.

The ballet would return in March. In March there would be a spectacular gala. Sam thought about that. Maybe the gala would be more spectacular than Judith Winchester imagined. Sam turned the page and smiled the smile of a contented man.

To the world, she was thirty-nine. In an obscure little town hall in a shabby suburb of Paris was a certificate that would add seven more years to Nadia Beshanskaia's age, if anyone knew where to look for it. Nadia had gone to some lengths to assure that they would not look. And, God knew, thirty-nine was old enough for a ballerina!

She stood in her hotel room now, staring intently into the mirror that had always been her friend. The mirror had been a comfort to Nadia all these years.

The rehearsal mirrors, the huge sheets of silvered glass behind the barre, were filled with compliments for Mlle. Beshanskaia's purity of line, her supple flow of movement, her fetching smile. A flicker of that smile came darting onto her face now, came and quickly vanished like some small, timid, wild thing astonished at its own visibility. It was Vulnerable Maiden Smile Number One, always her favorite, so useful in *Giselle* and the other virginal roles of the classical ballet, the roles that were her speciality and had been for longer than the scripted ages of the Giselles and Juliets and Swanildas themselves.

But the smile, now, was merely an accessory, to be tried on and rejected like a new hat. For Nadia felt not at all like smiling. How sad that rage was so destructive to the contours of one's face! Nadia's face was approaching the stage where the tracks of anger on it were a luxury she could not afford. She settled, reluctantly, for a pout. Another compromise in a sea of compromises!

Nadia had maneuvered herself into partnership with Dima Lubov, and it was not working out at all as she had hoped. What Nadia had imagined was a re-creation of the famous teaming of Nureyev and Margot Fonteyn, in which the aging ballerina had been magically transformed into a new being, and her career extended almost indefinitely as a result. Margot was still dancing, and coining money too, at fifty-six! Unheard of! And here came Dima to do the same for Nadia!

But it wasn't working out that way. Yes, they danced together. Yes, she danced well with him; they suited each other as physical types; he was beyond question a superb partner. But even as her wish came true, Nadia had the dancer's intuition to see what was wrong with it.

At forty-six, Nadia was long past the peak of her energy. Oh, the beauty was still there, most of it anyway; from the fifteenth row she looked very much as she had always looked. The technique was there, too, every movement refined with time's own scalpel so an elegant distillation of poise and grace. But the fire, the sparks, the radiance were diminishing with every year. And this young Lubov was all fire, all sparks and radiance, a charismatic force onstage who might give Rudi himself cause for wondering. And the contrast of their partnership did not reflect well on Nadia. The names—in an advertisement, on a program—generated fire. But what fires were lit onstage were lit by Dima Lubov, and if Nadia chose to warm herself in the reflection of that flame, so be it.

It was this very question that was troubling Nadia now. Might it not be better, wiser, to play it safe with good old Bayard Jordan, solid, reliable and just a bit ordinary?

Still, she stood there, fascinated by the image of a world-famous ballerina in the glass. So this was the imcomparable Nadia! A swan princess come to life. Nadia of the sables and emeralds and lovers. Nadia, who could take a phrase of music and etch it unforgettably into the minds of entire theatersful of balletomanes. Nadia, whose whims were cast in stone. Nadia, who would be forty-seven on her next birthday, Nadia, who was afraid of age as some people are afraid of the dark.

She had tormented poor Jordie. "But, Jordie," she had said with Village Maiden Giggle Number Two, "aren't you just the tiniest bit jealous?"

And Bayard Jordan had looked at her with those big brown eyes she had always thought doglike, eyes that shone with a calm light from a source Nadia would never know, the eyes of a human being at ease with himself. "And should I be jealous of the sun, darlin', because it's brighter than my little candle? I *like* Dima, honey. He's going to do us a lot of good. Better to have him with us than agin us." The soft southern drawl was unanswerable. It was nearly impossible to get a rise out of Bayard Jordan. Nadia sometimes wondered why she tried.

The famous ballerina in the mirror risked a frown. There was no quick answer to this question. If Dima was not going to make another Margot of her, was Dima worth dancing with at all? Was the contrast too great already? How soon would the inevitable day come when a critic noticed, and had the bad taste to mention, her fading powers? She turned, wondering, and walked out of her hotel room. With the damned Tokyo traffic, she'd barely make it to the performance on time.

Greg knew he'd seen the blonde before. Where? He sat in the JAL boarding lounge at Kennedy reading the *Wall Street Journal* with the secret schoolboy delight of knowing he'd be away from all that for a week, ten days maybe. And wishing even now the damned flight was over.

There were more people than he'd expected in the lounge. The usual covey of soft-spoken Japanese businessmen, a gaggle of GIs, six older couples who looked like a group tour booking, several American businessmen, usually in pairs, and one blue-jeaned boy and girl of college age who might have been brother and sister, they looked that much alike, except for the fact that they'd spent the last fifteen minutes unselfconsciously kissing, hugging and holding hands. They looked like nice kids. Greg wished them well. It was good to think of people loving each other.

In the nearly five years since he'd lost his wife and kids, Greg had found no woman who meant a thing to him. To tell the truth, he hadn't looked very hard. After the first year, after he'd unloaded Holden Aircraft and moved into the city and got himself involved with the International Ballet, Greg had drifted into—and out of—four or five casual relationships. Signifying nothing.

There was a numb place in Greg Holden where his heart used to live and feel and respond. He tried not to think about it too much. In some instinctive act of faith Greg assumed that sooner or later he'd get over that numbness, that he'd find someone else. Not, surely, another Phillys, but, anyway, someone. And five years had taught Greg it wasn't going to happen sooner.

He folded the paper and looked at his watch and felt for his boarding pass. That was when the blonde came flowing into the lounge like a strain of music.

Now there was a girl! Greg Holden had seen all of the world he wanted to see, and he had a healthy appreciation of the world's women. Yet, say what you will, there was a certain type of American girl who had no competition anywhere. And the blonde was an outstanding specimen of that breed. Part of it was sheer radiant health, a sense of competence, a hint that she would know what to do on a racing sloop or a powder-glazed *piste* at twelve thousand feet in the Rockies. There was an easy confidence about the girl that suggested ability without aggressiveness, poise without snobbery, intelligence without pedantry. If she noticed him staring, she gave no sign.

He had seen her, damn it! He'd even met her. And not so long ago, either. Where the hell? Annoyed with himself, and unwilling to try the tired ploy of "haven't-we-met-someplace-before?" Greg turned his head, bent down and adjusted a strap on his carry-on bag.

Her voice came as a surprise to him. "Excuse me, but aren't you Greg Holden?"

He looked up, grinned and was on his feet in an instant.

"I sure am. And I was wondering where we'd met. In fact, I was trying to work up my courage to ask."

"And you were afraid I'd be offended? I'm Diana Leighton, and we met at that bash for the International Ballet about a month ago. I had to leave early. Judith just barely introduced us. Why should you remember?"

But he did remember. He remembered watching her dance with Dimitri Lubov, the look in Lubov's eye, how the two of them had suddenly vanished, Judith's barely veiled indignation at her prize lion's being swiped so suddenly from the main ring of the Winchester Flying Circus.

Yes, Greg remembered. And here was Diana Leighton boarding a jet for Tokyo. Not, he imagined, to pick herself a few cherry blossoms. Then he smiled, putting about twenty percent more into it than he really felt, because he was ashamed of the way his mind was working. *And so what if she was having an affair with Lubov? Go on this way, Holden, and you'll turn yourself into a card-carrying Curmudgeon. Let them have their fun. What made it OK for those blue-jeaned kids and not OK for Lubov and Diana? Face it, Gregory Bryan Holden, jealousy made it not OK. You wouldn't mind having this glorious blond number for your own, now would you? No. You wouldn't mind at all.*

"Of course. Stupid of me. Are you going to Tokyo, too?"

"Promise," she said with a grin, "that you won't spill the beans. It's a surprise for Dima Lubov."

"Your secret," said Greg Holden in his best false-avuncular manner, "is safe with me. I'm just out for a week myself.

Pretending it's business. But really, I just was getting restless for a change of scene."

"Tokyo," said Diana thoughtfully, "will be about as complete a change as this little world can offer."

"Maybe," said Greg with more wistfulness in his voice than he realized, "we can sit together. What's your ticket number?"

"B-two."

"There is a Santa Claus. I'm B-one!"

"I cannot tell a lie. That's because I saw your name on the passenger list."

"If anything," said Greg, looking at her with new interest, "can shape up this flight, it'll be you, Miss Leighton."

"Diana, please."

"Greg."

"Greg." The loudspeaker crackled and announced the boarding of JAL Flight 21 for Fairbanks and Tokyo.

There was no sign of Ivan Sokolovny in the Carlyle Bar. Six o'clock turned into seven, and Dave's three drinks turned into four. No Ivan and no answers. He paid the check and thought ruefully as he did that this, too, was coming out of some unaudited fund of Sam Purcell's. As had the means to knock off five defectors and the KGB man in Paris. As would the bullets for the gun that knocked off Dave himself, and Ivan too, if Sam caught on.

Dave went to a restaurant where Ivan had once taken him, Hunam, the Chinese one with the spicy food. No Ivan. He checked out three more places, and still, there was no Ivan. Then he had two cheeseburgers and three beers and took the Staten Island ferry back to Effie and the kids.

As the slow ferryboat pushed through the oily black harbor, Dave's thoughts turned darker and dirtier than the water, thoughts of Sam, questions about Ivan. If Ivan were still alive. . . .

Jessica Privet placed the steaming shepherd's pie on the hot tray and turned to Jenny in the full pride of creation. "This'll stick to your ribs, my pet. We've got to get some meat on you, Jenny Hale, for in no time you'll be back dancing and needing every ounce of strength you can get." Privy served two generous portions and sat down at the big round kitchen table. "Why, you're positively wasting away."

"This afternoon," said Jenny quietly, "I happened to be hobbling past that travel agent's office on Broadway, on my way to the bus. I went in. Guess what I asked them?"

"The flight to Japan."

"The flight to Tokyo. It costs nearly thirteen hundred dollars, Privy." Jenny played with her food. Dima wouldn't talk to her in New York. Was there any point in blowing thirteen hundred dollars she didn't have so he could repeat the performance in Tokyo? All logic argued against it. All instinct screamed, *"Do it!"*

"I think I could borrow that much, darling, if you really want to do it. But I'm not sure—"

"Oh, Privy! I'm not sure either! It was just a crazy idea. I'm not going to do it. No just because of the money, but because if I did go, if I did travel all that way and he still rejected me, I just don't know what I'd do then. Throw myself in the volcano, most likely." She tried to make it a joke, but the joke fell flat. It cut too close to the bone.

"They will be coming back in a month, won't they?"

"Exactly in a month. Just about the time the doctor says I can begin practicing again. I'll bet he doesn't even know I fell."

"I'm sure if he did, he'd be in touch, Jenny. He may be proud, my love, but he isn't cruel."

"The trouble is, Dima's a creature of impulse. Half the time—more than half the time—he doesn't think. He acts."

"Well, my dear, then we'll just have to see how he acts when he gets back, won't we?" Privy looked sharply at the girl. This was thin ice. Privy knew very well on what brittle foundations Jenny Hale's stability was built.

Privy thought of Sandra Hale, Jenny's mother, whom she'd never met, locked up all these years at the costly sanitorium in Connecticut. The trauma of childbirth had triggered that in the mother. One must be very, very careful of the daughter. It had been Miss Privet's private crusade, these twenty years, to do that. She would do it still, and as long as she could, and with every weapon in her small, poor arsenal.

"Eat, for the night is coming!" When all else failed, Privy ladled on the food.

"He'd laugh at me."

"I doubt that, Jenny."

"What'll I ever say to him when I do see him?"

Jenny had entered a new phase in her separation from

Dima and without realizing it. She now took it for granted that she would see Dima again, that he had not gone out of her life forever or vanished off the thin edge of the earth.

"Don't worry too much about that, child. It's really less a question of what you say than of what you feel."

Jenny made no reply but ate the delicious lamb-and-vegetable stew with its flaky crust. If all else failed, they could open a restaurant.

Unseen by Nadia, Dimitri watched her enter the big rehearsal hall. Late, as usual, trailing cigarette smoke and hauteur.

Nadia didn't realize it, thought Dima, but she was a type, rather a common type in the performing arts, a type Dima had met many times before, a type of whom Dima had long since learned to be wary. The fading star, unable to deal with the implacable progress of the clock. *Garbo,* thought Dima as he observed his partner insult a stagehand, snub a girl from the corps de ballet and toss a burning cigarette where burning cigarettes should not be tossed, *was right.* Yes, Garbo had been right, quitting forever at the top of her form, leaving an unblemished image of beauty and mystery and talent. That took a depth of guts and imagination and a quality of humanity that Nadia Beshanskaia would never know or understand.

Nadia had played her game and won for so long now that she was unable to detect the sea change as the odds slowly turned against her. She must stay on, fighting, exploiting her hard-won fame, clawing ever more desperately for the place in the limelight that had once been hers without asking. *What a drug it was, fame,* thought Dima. *How shallow we must be not to see all there is of life beyond these little stages!*

She saw him now and smiled. A charming smile, aimed like a missile. *Well,* thought Dima as he smiled back, out of good manners and sympathy more than affection, *you can say this for her: ultimately she is very, very pro.* That was true. Dima had endured far worse partners than a slightly shopworn Nadia. On her worst days, Nadia was a better dancer than ninety percent of all the ballerinas in the world.

But still and all, with growing unease, Dima knew there was no ballerina in the International Ballet who could be, for him, the equal of Jenny Hale. That was a cool professional judgment, not a romantic one.

When Dima danced Albrecht to Nadia's Giselle, and took Nadia in his arms, and tried to look enraptured, no amount of professionalism could stop him from thinking: *This vain and foolish woman is old enough to be my mother.* And although the performance looked beautiful from the orchestra and magical from the balconies, it simply wasn't the same. Nor would it ever be, try as he might.

He couldn't try for both of them. He couldn't make Nadia into something she had perhaps never been, even as a girl. He couldn't make her human. Nadia had all the vulnerability of a scalpel. Shyness, a tentative exploration of love, a broken heart—these were emotions as remote from Nadia's experience as fire is from ice. And to simulate them, she used a kind of acting that was somewhere between mime and satire. The hands fluttered daintily, but the eyes remained cold as steel.

No wonder that Nadia's best—and most famous—role was Odette/Odile, the white swan and the black swan in *Swan Lake*. As a bird, and a rather cruel and evil-tempered bird at that, she was perfectly cast. With a small sigh, Dima left his practice at the barre and went to Nadia. They were rehearsing Stravinsky's *Firebird*.

Dima walked up to her and bowed slightly, an eighteenth-century bow directly descended from the court of Louis XIV, a gesture in which he had been so thoroughly drilled at the Kirov School that he never forgot it, a reflexive homage to the ballerina of the moment, whoever she might be. Nadia loved it. "Ultimately, I think, Nadia, Japan is agreeing with you."

"It would agree with me more, if only I didn't know that next week we will be among those ghastly Chinese peasants. They will probably drive their bicycles right up on the stage."

"Let us hope not."

The music began, and he led her into the pas de deux from the first act. And for the second time this morning, Dimitri Lubov found himself lost in thoughts of Jenny. Jenny, dancing. Jenny's pale face with its immense tragic eyes. The warmth of Jenny next to him, just holding hands, maybe, walking down Broadway toward Lincoln Center. Jenny in bed, another Jenny altogether and equally memorable.

He had been rash about Jenny. His Russian mood had come on him so strongly that it had erased all their happiness in one dark swoop. And could he get it back, that happiness?

Would she have him? Was her pride, though more quiet, not the match of his? Was she not ultimately perhaps the stronger?

Dima danced as he always danced: superbly. The music became part of him, the music told his muscles what to do, Nadia responded with her best and her best was very good indeed. They danced so well in the half-empty rehearsal hall that stagehands stopped to look, heads turned from the barre. But Dima Lubov's mind was across an ocean and across a continent, chasing a dream that might be lost, and lost by his own doing.

He touched Nadia, lifted Nadia, smiled for Nadia and leaped for Nadia, so high it might be flying. And all his thoughts reached out for Jenny Hale.

The laughter broke like thunder: "Oh-ho-ho! Ho. Ho-ho! Heee-he. Ha-ha. Oh-oh-ho. Ha!" Ivan shook with the mirth of it; he trembled and all his three chins trembled; his glass shook so that he had to put it down with two hands for fear of spilling the white wine inside. "Ha-ha! So all this time he plays you like a fish. Not even like a wild fish, but a fish who was already caught and did not know. Oho, my friend, it is a strange and wonderful world we live in, is it not?"

It was late in the small Italian restaurant. Heads turned, and turned away. It was the kind of place where loud laughter and loud arguments were stock-in-trade.

"Are you finished?"

Dave could understand his friend's laughter, but he was far from being amused himself. All Dave Loughlin felt was tired. Very, very tired.

"Do not think, kiddo, that Ivan makes fun of you. Not that. But, pardner, there is a certain irony in it, am I not right?"

"You're right, Ivan, it's just as funny as can be. I'm just all tuckered out with laughing, forgive me." Dave picked up his glass and looked at it as though it had just arrived from Mars. He lowered his voice. "Six people are dead, one of them yours, and Lubov yet to come—or go. How funny is that, Ivan?"

"One grows most serious. Not funny, Dave, old fart. Not at all funny. Ivan is happy his hunch paid off. Ivan is only human after all. The sweetest words of all: 'I told you so.' But you, of course, are right, Davey, don't let me forget it.

The balance has changed now. And in one sense, it changes in our favor. We know who the bad guys are."

"And they know who we are."

"Including me? He knows about me?"

"Not from me, he doesn't, Ivan. But I'm not betting on anything anymore."

"You can bet upon Ivan. Ivan continues to wear white hat."

Sure, thought Dave, *most KGB agents do. And carry white knives and white poison and tell white lies to old pals.* "You feel better then? You know the story or some of it?"

"I know," said Ivan, "that we are dealing with the most dangerous type. Who has access to everything, every technology of intelligence and of death. Who has—what do you say?—slipped his mooring? Gone bonkers? In any case, irrational. But smart. He must, I am sure, be acting alone."

"Why do you say that?"

"It is too crazy otherwise. And the timing. If it were teamwork—like some of your other operations one could mention—it would either go much faster, much more smoothly, or explode and go nowhere."

"He probably is alone. He always was a loner. That's one reason he got where he is. Trusting no one."

"But he trusted you. You saved his life after all."

"I sure did."

"It means something, old chum."

"Don't mean dogshit to him, Ivan."

"To you, old buddy, it means a lot. It means, Davey, that you owe him nothing."

"You realize we're helpless unless we trap him? No one, and I mean no one at all, would believe a minute of this. I mean, he *is* the goddamned deputy director."

"And what was Dicky-tricky Nixon? Credibility has been getting quite a lot of exercise in these here United States lately, old fart. In case you hadn't noticed."

"Yeah. Still, they wouldn't. He is mad. And what he's done *sounds* mad. I didn't believe you for a moment when you suggested it."

"Madness is relative. Possibly one could say your Mr. Hypothetical Suspect is exceeding conventional limits of behavior by quite a margin. But mad? Think, Davey! From Suspect's point of view, it is all absolutely logical. Think what he wanted to achieve, what he has achieved. He wants to stop détente. Is détente not effectively stopped? At least for some time. He wants to shelve the Odell Bill because the Odell Bill is a threat to his very position, which, like all empire builders, is highly important to him. And is the Odell Bill not shelved? So what he has done has worked, Davey. It has worked perfectly—as far as it goes. If there is madness, the madness must be a question of where and when will he stop. We have already seen that he did not stop with the forged confession of our little fellow in Paris. Poussine, and in Japan yet, was killed. And killed in a manner less subtle than the others, in a manner that speaks of a certain desperation. He got away with it, nonetheless. But it is a sign—perhaps—that the desperation is building, that for some reason we can only guess he is so trapped in his own plan that he literally *cannot* stop, no matter how dangerous it might become. That, I admit, is madness."

"You've got it all figured out, haven't you?"

"I have had so much practice, Davey, in setting traps. You must forgive me for not being a virgin like yourself."

Dave Loughlin sipped his wine slowly. He didn't seem to need it as much tonight as usual. He tried to conjure up an image of Sam Purcell's face, but all he got was the props: the gold-rimmed glasses, the suntan, the neat steel-gray hair. Sam's was probably the last face seen by the poet Berisov, by Gaia Muldovska, by all the rest. He shuddered and put down his glass. Dave looked across the table at Ivan and knew that here was his last hope of trapping Purcell, of stopping the murder of Lubov. "I don't think," he said, "that we should finish our talk indoors." Then he waved for the check.

They must make a plan, and make it tonight, and hope against hope that they had some kind of a jump on Sam Purcell. If they didn't have that element of surprise, Dave knew all too well, neither of their lives was worth a wooden nickel.

CHAPTER
⚫❧ 11 ❧⚫

Diana Leighton looked across the console at her newfound traveling companion and was glad she'd taken the initiative. She didn't know much about Greg Holden. He wasn't a very public kind of person. In studying the International Ballet, Diana had heard the bare outlines of his story: the self-made fortune, the tragic plane crash that took his wife and children, the sudden, late-blooming interest in the ballet.

He seemed a decent man, his own man, with the right kind of face. Greg's was not a fashionable face, not a face out of any fancy mold. His thick brown hair, now flecked with gray, was a little shorter than the art directors of *Esquire* might have cut it. His nose had been broken at least once (twice, she later learned) and never quite restored to its original straightness. The mouth was wide and ready to smile, eyes set deep, deep brown in color, watchful eyes, eyes you could trust.

Diana could imagine him chopping pioneer trees with a hand-sharpened ax, fighting off Indians, swimming rivers. But managing a ballet company? It had been, Diana knew, his wife's passion. And Greg had set up a scholarship trust in her memory, and that had led, by indirection, into the actual management of the company, filling a void.

He was a man to take charge. A man, very likely, who could do Dima Lubov a lot of good. Not, God knew, that Dima needed anyone's help! Still and all, if you had to spend eighteen hours on an airplane, you could spend them with far less interesting people than Greg Holden of the International Ballet Theater. He was a nice man. If he wasn't Dima, that was nobody's fault, least of all Greg's. She turned a page in her paperback. Somehow she was finding it hard to concentrate.

Click!

Sam Purcell's finger pressed the cutoff button on the small tape player. The last week's tapes of the tapped phone at Delage Feather and Trimming Company told him nothing that he didn't know already. Namely, that Dave Loughlin ran a slow-moving, if tidy, operation up there. There were never going to be any fireworks from old Davey. Which was exactly what Sam wanted. Then why was he uneasy?

The investigation was going nowhere. Even Dave, grudgingly, his voice thick with yesterday's bourbon, admitted that in his twice-weekly phoned reports. These were always brief, always disguised as either weather or stock market reports. In these reports, their code for the defector killings was the Alfalfa Sale. "And how," Sam would ask, "is the Alfalfa Sale coming?"

"Slowly, very slowly. We seem to have trouble finding out just exactly what they want."

"They're a cagey lot, aren't they?"

"Very cagey. And very subtle. One of their salesmen had an accident in Tokyo last week, but even that didn't clear things up any."

"Yes, so I heard. Well, keep after them. It's only a question of time now."

"I hope so, chief."

It was a schoolboy's game, a leftover from the old days when every operation had a trick code name and every operative had several covers and disguises. It sprang from the British influence. The OSS had inevitably patterned itself on the only model it had access to, British Intelligence, an old-boy network if ever there was one, terribly fond, don't you know, of playing games. Sam kept up the old ways partly out of habit, partly from snobbery, from the old hand's delight at fluency in a language the new boys would never quite master, and partly because, from time to time, it really worked.

But Sam Purcell hadn't risen to the deputy directorship of the Central Intelligence Agency by playing schoolboy games. He might sip China tea from Dresden cups, but Sam ran on gut instinct and a sense of timing common to great actors and born killers.

The years and his own hard work had made Sam Purcell into a highly refined instrument for detection and reprisal, cruising the world of international politics as a hunting owl glides through the night sky, silent, alert, invisible until the strike.

Constant hard exercise of these deadly skills had long since pared away the moral encumbrances that held back other men. Sam traveled lightly, without the burden of conscience, scruple, pity or regret.

He stood up, paced the floor, pressed the button that opened the long sweep of curtains on the peaceful country-side below his windows. He rang for tea, tasted it, put the cup down, paced the floor again. This should be a moment of building triumph. The Odell Bill was dead and all but buried.

It would be years before the lily-livers could put some feeble attempt at détente back together again. And all be-cause of him! His plan! His action! His vision! In many ways, and for many years, Sam Purcell had helped change the course of history. The feeling wasn't new to him. But to achieve this, on his own initiative, this should be a moment of supreme triumph.

Oh, there were still two more defectors on the list—the list could be expanded, if it came to that. It had been an arbi-trary number to begin with, the victims chosen for a special vulnerability and innocence, for their value as objects of pub-lic outrage and sympathy. The job was really done even now. Sam would finish it because he hated unfinished business of any kind. Once a pattern had been chosen, it must be carried through to the utmost. But this was mere detail. To eliminate Lubov was the easiest of all. And the other, the final name on the list, the humanitarian diplomat Sergei Rosoff, that was just a question of time and convenience. His, Sam's con-venience. He did have to exercise great caution in moving about the world, simply because of his increasing prominence within the agency. That was the only reason why he wasn't in Japan right this minute, attending to Lubov.

Then what was this odd, nagging, uneasy feeling? It had something to do with Loughlin, with the Alfalfa Sale. There had been that one unlikely phone call to Delage Feather and Trimming, oh, a month ago, the oddly cheerful, forced heart-iness of a nearly accentless (meaning trained in whose lan-guage school?) voice playing at being an old pal, throwing the 1930s slang around like so much confetti at a blue-collar wedding. Sam had ordered a voiceprint on that one, but there was no record of the voice, no matching voiceprint anywhere in the CIA voice bank. Which could mean anything or nothing. They'd been taking voiceprints for less than ten years.

It could be the voice of an agent who was simply too cagey to get himself on tape. It could really be an old chum; not everybody with a Slavic undercurrent in his voice was necessarily an operative. It could be anything.

Sam looked at his desk calendar. Then he picked up the phone. "Charlotte, will you get a chopper on the pad in twenty minutes? I'm going to New York."

Greg Holden had nothing against laughter, but he knew too well how long it had been since he'd laughed so deeply or so long. And at stories told by a beautiful young woman. Diana might be fancy, but she sure as hell wasn't taken in by it. And while she only mentioned it in passing, it was obvious the girl was very good at her job. Come to think of it, he'd heard the name of her firm, always imagining it was some long-established, only-dowagers-need-apply kind of operation.

"Basically," she said, when asked, "what I do is take their mad whims and turn them into something that won't actually make your eyes cross when you look at it."

"You did Judith Winchester's office?" Greg hated Judith's office, but maybe that was reflection of the way he felt about Judith. To him it was cold and intimidating. That big steel desk looked more like something Dr. Frankenstein might have in his laboratory than a place for a woman—or anybody else—to do a day's work.

"I tried to salvage it, Greg. She had fallen afoul of one of the trendies. You know—this week everything's blue mirrors, next week everything's Biafran basketwork. Bullshit, needless to say. Well, this particular trendy—who shall be nameless because you'd know the name—saw Judith as all polished steel. Not," she said with a wicked grin, "necessarily an inappropriate image for that dame. But the result was like the inside of a meat freezer. Even Judith saw that it didn't work. So she called me in. I thought of those screens, and the rugs, and the plantings. She insisted on keeping that damn desk, over my dead body. My part of the deal was that she never mention my name in connection with it."

"The screens are beautiful." Greg was strangely relieved that she hadn't designed the desk. Only a true creep could have done that, and he was suddenly anxious not to think of Diana as a creep, whoever's girl she might be.

"I," said Jenny majestically, "am going to get fat and watch soap operas."

Privy looked at the girl and for a moment wished she would do just that. They were sitting in the living room watching their new toy, a small black-and-white television set. They'd never had television before. The curiously elegant little machine was perched incongruously on a second-class but nevertheless real eighteenth-century French bureau that Parke-Bernet hadn't considered worth auctioning. They were watching an afternoon game show with the glazed fascination of Martians.

After a few minutes Privy got up to make tea, leaving a giggling Jenny seated, her cast propped up on a stack of huge books. This was a new Jenny, these last few days, ever since the girl had taken to going back to class and rehearsal. Even sitting on the sidelines and ocasionally helping de Lis coaching was a big help, Privy knew, and she thanked God that the child seemed to be pulling out of her depression.

It might be a brave facade, but Privy felt it was more than that. Jenny was finally taking stock of her young life, asking questions, making plans. And they were, for the first time in months, plans that did not revolve around Dimitri.

Privy knew that lovable as she was, Jenny lived her life with blinders on, that she saw straight ahead only, that anything—anyone—in the world not immediately connected with Jenny as a dancer was simply invisible to the girl. This was concentration, not selfishness, but to other people it could look like selfishness. This was why Jenny had never taken the time to make friends. This was why other young dancers in the Civic were more than usually jealous of her sudden success. And it was why Dima meant so very much to Jenny, why the breakup was that much more devastating. Privy sensed how much de Lis depended on the girl, but Jenny herself was only slowly coming to realize this. De Lis, after all, must play the Inscrutable Deity of the Civic Ballet Company; he must never seem too accessible, too soft.

For the first time since her injury, Privy had seen a Jenny without the pain-killing, mind-numbing drug of dancing. For days the girl had been in shock, physically and emotionally, double shock, faced with the unthinkable, faced with the possibility of a life without Dima, of a life without dancing. And at last, the girl seemed to be coming out of it. She smiled sometimes now, without forcing it. She laughed. It was a very small foundation, Privy knew, to build a castle of hope on, but it was all she had. It was better than nothing.

Privy had taken great care never to mention Dimitri. Secretly, she screened the newspapers and magazines Jenny had suddenly taken to reading for mention of Lubov or the International. Jenny hardly ever mentioned Dima now. What she thought, or hoped, or dreamed, Privy could only guess. In the meantime, Privy would devote herself, as she had always devoted herself, to encouraging these small, hope-filled signs of a new and more confident Jenny. She came back into the room, smiling over the tea tray, and her smile was a silent prayer.

Dimitri stepped out of the shower and toweled himself dry. Adrenaline shot through him, generated for the performance, and his athelte's heart sent blood racing until the veins of his legs stood out against the muscles like snakes coiled on rock, ready to strike. He was in a foul mood and couldn't for the life of him have told anyone why. It was a Russian mood, a dark mood, the kind of mood he'd promised himself never to have anymore, not after what it had done to Jenny. He dressed mechanically, reevaluating his performance with the merciless appraisal of a master surgeon about to cut. There was a knock on the dressing-room door.

Machito, freshly dressed but still pink from the after-performance shower, poked his dark head in. "Hey, Commie, you look like you just lost your last revolution. Coming to the party?"

"Ultimately, Spic, I come." Dima's voice was uncharacteristically flat as he pulled on a burgundy turtleneck over his new Japanese suede jeans.

"Dr. Ramirez," said Machito, "say honorable Russian boy suffering from too much Oriental nookie." He threw a sweaty towel at his friend. Dima reached out effortlessly and caught it but didn't throw it back.

"Is no such thing as too much."

"I know. You're afraid of China. You want to be the only Commie on the block. You think they're gonna lock you up in some great big fortune cookie and put you on display in the Forbidden City. Is that it?"

"They should only try," said Dima with a little spark now,

"but they dare not. Even in Russia, is too dangerous, politically. They prefer to think Dima does not exist. Is official law now, I am nonperson. My picture is no more in the Kirov School; I am not in record books; prize I won at Valna not recorded either. They do everything but bury me." He got up and walked out of the dressing room with Machito.

"Nonperson. Hey, I like that! There have been times when I might imply you're a nondancer, but nonperson. It takes a Russky to think up something like that."

"Ultimately, Spic, they have had a lot of practice."

"You're not feeling too good, though, am I right?"

Machito was worried. In the three months he'd known Dima Lubov he'd never seen anything but the highest of high spirits. "You must be homesick."

"Ah, but where is my home, Spic? Is *there!*" Dima gestured at the stage without turning to look at it.

"But you'll be an American now, won't you? Take out citizenship? Settle down?"

"Yes, and weave an American flag to wave. Is not something one puts on and off like a shirt, citizenship. I am Russian peasant. To step upon an airplane does not change that. Alas." Then Dima called up the grin, and slapped his friend on the arm, and laughed. "But you are right, maybe for the first time in your wicked Spic life, Spic. Dima was in a Russian mood, black as night. Is an illness that comes and goes, and for it there is no medicine. We go now to the party, we laugh, we drink, there are girls, what-do-you-say, Oriental nookie?"

"You're a promising kid, for a Commie, Dima; you're learning fast." They walked out into the welcoming Tokyo night. Dimitri smiled, laughed, slapped his friend on the back. But he thought of Jenny Hale.

The absolutely standard Air Force helicopter sideslipped gently onto the United Nations pad. The CIA always used planes with military markings for these domestic flights; everyone had seen such planes before, and no one looked twice. Sam walked off, carrying his worn British raincoat over his arm. It was warm for January. He had a briefcase and a well-read copy of the Washington *Post*. As he climbed down from the little chopper, Sam turned to the pilot. "I'll be leaving here tomorrow at noon exactly."

"Yes, sir!" If the uniformed pilot knew who Sam was, he gave no indication. And that was just the way Sam liked it. Sam climbed the stairs and walked out to First Avenue, where he hailed an old Checker cab.

"Statler Hilton, please, Seventh Avenue and Thirty-Third Street." The shabby old hotel was almost across the street from Delage Feather and Trimming.

Sam's first impulse was to drop in on Dave Loughlin without warning. He could tell more from watching a man's face than from reading a week's worth of tape transcriptions or trailing reports. It would have been easy to have Davey tailed. But—you never knew—Davey might still have enough of the old Loughlin left in him to spot a tail, to elude a tail, to run scared, to get suspicious. An ordinary tail would never do. A tail by Sam himself might do quite a lot.

Sam weighed the balance as the cab made its sluggish way through the clotted arteries of New York's workaday side streets. Something made him wary of dropping in on Davey. He'd never done that, not in all these years. There would be no way to make such a visit seem casual.

It could, of course, take the form of a private reprimand. There was certainly enough to reprimand Dave Loughlin about, including his apparent lack of progress on this, his most important case in years. But no. It rang false somehow. If the years had taught Sam Purcell anything, they had taught him the value of caution. Let him become an invisible shadow for a day. Let Dave Loughlin show him if there was any real foundation for this strange unease. Let Dave lead him to the Slavic, laughing stranger. Let Dave spill whatever beans he had to spill.

Across the street from Delage Feather and Trimming was a small dingy coffeeshop. Luckily, thought Sam as he sat gingerly on the cracked vinyl-covered stool at the counter, he'd had both cholera and typhoid shots just last month before his trip to Japan. "Black coffee, please," he said, and opened the paper to shield his face as the vigil began.

It had been Uncle Alf, dear Uncle Alf, who had arranged for Diana to be given super-VIP treatment at the Okura Hotel. They'd sent a limousine for her and assigned a special management trainee to make sure she was absolutely comfortable.

But Uncle Alf might be shocked at the way Diana intended to use her privilege. A whispered request to the young manager was all it took: Miss Leighton was an old friend of Mr. Lubov, Miss Leighton wanted to surprise him with a champagne breakfast, yes, it could be done even as early as nine A.M., naturally, a key would be provided, would that be all? That would be more than enough, thought Diana as she dismissed the waiter with a five-dollar tip and let herself into the Lubov-Ramirez suite. The assistant manager had been careful to brief her on which bedroom was Dima's.

The suite was deeply carpeted, more Western than Japanese, but with a few nice Oriental touches: an old camphorwood chest of drawers with fantastic silver hardware, a large bronze vase with branches of blossming quince, a silk tapestry of some flying female deity with a smile and an escort of white doves. The tea wagon moved noiselessly under its burden of iced Dom Pérignon 1959, a pitcher of orange juice, almond cakes and a pot of coffee for two. Who had it been, Diana wondered, who taught her to open champagne properly, silently, with only the faintest hiss instead of a loud vulgar pop?

Whoever it was, she thanked him now as she paused outside the bedroom door and untwisted the protective wire from around the phallic cork, then held the cork firmly while she slowly, slowly twisted the bottle, taking great care not to disturb the wine, the guardian and miser of its bubbles. No cork was going to come between Diana Leighton and her greeting Dima. The cork slid out obediently, with a gentle hiss. From behind the bedroom door came a sigh in counterpoint, a voice Diana knew and cherished, Dima's voice. She opened the door, wishing she had rehearsed a speech.

The smile froze on Diana's expectant face, and she involuntarily stepped back and bumped the tea cart. But Dima didn't hear the soft collision, nor did he see her.

Dima lay on his back, sprawled on the big bed, golden against deep blue sheets, eyes closed, a smile of pleasure flickering on his lips. The Japanese girl, all soft ivory skin and a river of midnight hair, lay crosswise on the bed, one tapering hand massaging the taut muscles of Dima's belly, her head bobbing to an unheard rhythm as she orchestrated her own private variations on the timeless theme of oral sex.

Diana was nothing of a voyeur. She'd seen half of a pornographic film once. Now, as she stood there unseen while her lover and the nameless Japanese girl acted out their own road-company version of *Fanny Hill,* Diana found herself strangely fascinated. Her first emotion was rage, followed closely by cynical humor and then by a kind of detachment. The girl surely enjoyed her work. Diana felt a strange dislocation, as though she were watching a movie. Maybe it was jet lag, maybe some kind of emotional defense mechanism that stopped her from thinking, that temporarily numbed her outraged heart. To come so far. To plan such a nice surprise. To find this! To her own surprise, Diana felt a primitive wail building in her throat, and it was only by a serious effort that she stopped it there. Her cheeks flushed with wave upon wave of blind anger. Suddenly she understood why the violence of love so often leads to just plain violence. And the next thing Diana did was violent.

She reached out behind her for the chilled bottle of champagne. Slowly, deliberately, she lifted it from its silver bucket, carefully wiping the condensation with a towel. Then she put her thumb tightly over the bottle's mouth and shook it for all it was worth.

The world's most expensive champagne made a most effective squirt gun. Suddenly the air was filled with ice-cold Dom Pérignon, aimed with an athlete's skill at Dima's bare chest. He gasped, not from sex this time, and his eyes popped open and bugged wider at the sight of Diana and her weapon. For an instant Diana thought she saw a glimmer of fear, but it might have been pure astonishment. The Japanese girl kept up her good work below. *Very persistent,* Diana thought, *these Japanese.*

Then she spoke. "Such a waste," said Diana in a voice coldly plated with scorn, "of decent wine. Good-bye, Dima. It was fun."

"Diana!" He sat up on the bed, still encumbered by his playmate. "Is not *fair!* You do not understand!" But she was gone.

Diana liked to think of herself as a cool customer, as being in control, rational, organized. *Lots of luck,* she thought, *there goes Miss Cool.* It had been uncool to chase Dima in the first place. And what did she expect of a boy superstar of twenty-four, alone for weeks in a foreign country, bursting with sex, surrounded by girls? Nobody had to tell Diana how girls chased Lubov; she'd done some pretty enthusiastic chasing herself. Diana walked down the hall to the elevator. It seemed like miles. She hardly knew where she was. *You gambled, you lost, Diana Leighton, face it.*

And before the elevator door closed on her frozen smile, Diana realized that the operative word was *"boy."* That was where you had to pay the piper if you went chasing twenty-four-year-olds.

Dima Lubov might have the body of a Tatar god and the athleticism of a coursing cheetah and the sexuality of a satyr in springtime, but there was no escaping the fact that he was only twenty-four and a very sheltered, untamed, provincial twenty-four at that. Diana, at thirty, hardly felt she was robbing the cradle. But Diana had lived those thirty years in a silk cocoon of culture and privilege, of opportunities perceived and taken, of pleasure constantly refined, of choices progressively more selective.

What Diana responded to in Dima Lubov was visceral, instinctive, quick. Being with Dima had the sudden excitement of a perfect run down a deep-powder ski trail. Part of the thrill was that you knew, gut-deep, that it couldn't ever be repeated, not just like this time, and it wasn't going to last forever. The speed and the danger were an inseparable part of the pleasure. It was a thing you might long for, but not something you'd ever regret. That was what Diana told herself as the blessedly empty elevator rose toward her floor. It was comforting to think that. It was not very comforting to find yourself alone in a Tokyo elevator, uncontrollably crying.

The doorman of the Hotel Carlyle frowned. The gray-haired man was back again. He'd been coming and going across the street for nearly an hour now. The gray-haired man looked perfectly respectable, but you never knew. He'd walk, slowly, deliberately, as though, possibly, there were something the matter with his left leg. The doorman was an ex-cop. He knew a pattern when he saw one. The old guy would walk to the corner of Madison and Seventy-sixth, cross to the southwest side, wait there for ten or fifteen minutes, then walk slowly back. Obviously waiting for somebody. Well, that was none of the doorman's business. He, the doorman, was all snug and warm under the big infrared heat reflectors that lined the underside of the marquee. So maybe the old geezer's girlfriend had stood him up. Or boyfriend. Around this neck of the woods, you never knew. The doorman could tell some pretty weird stories if you asked him. Unfortunately nobody ever asked him.

There was a whirring noise, and two boisterous men came out into the cold January night. Laughing and giggling and slapping each other on the back. College reunion, maybe. One looked rich, and the other looked a little down at the heel. But they were happy enough. He got them a cab, and the rich one tipped him a dollar. Not bad. Some of these fancy old dowagers, all diamonds and looking down their noses at the likes of him, were good for about a quarter. On their best day. The doorman pocketed the bill and looked around. The man in gray was gone. And good riddance, too. You never knew what some of these creeps might be up to.

"He just loves to pull those strings. A born manipulator." Iris Dowling stirred her coffee and frowned. "Not, you understand, that I'm not grateful. But there are times when he bugs the hell out of me."

Iris and Jenny were having coffee after rehearsal. This was something new for Jenny. She had made a friend. The relationship was still a little stiff, a little uneasy. But it was growing. It was more than it had been a week ago, less than it would be in a month. Jenny had never had a girlfriend, and she suspected that Iris was too preoccupied with her various boyfriends to bother much with girls. It had started when Jenny helped coach Iris for the part of Swanilda. Now they sat in the window at O'Neal's Balloon, across the street from the New York State Theater, talking about de Lis. De Lis, sex and dancing. Sex, dancing and de Lis. It always came down to these three basic topics, and small sprinklings of gossip about other dance companies, new health-food fads and other logistical information.

Their conversation, like their bodies, had all the superfluities stripped away in the strain and heat of practice and performance. Iris was giving Jenny her patented, all-purpose, de Lis-as-Svengali number.

"Well, sure, Iris. But manipulating people is what choreographers do. I mean, he's got to manipulate us. It's his job, more or less." This was dangerous ground for Jenny, but Iris didn't know that. Dima had been there before and turned it into a minefield of conflicting doubts and loyalties.

"I, for one," said Iris with a giggle, "would be willing to settle for less."

"I never knew my mother. And my dad wasn't around a whole lot either. I have—we have—this really great woman, Miss Privet, who took care of me. Really was a mother. Still is, when you think about it. Well, what I'm trying to say—I think—is that maybe it isn't the worst thing in the world that somebody cares about you, about if you're happy, if the company's in good shape." Unconsciously, Jenny's left hand found its way down to the peach-colored scarf that was tied as a sash around her tiny waist.

"Jenny, Jenny, Jenny, you amaze me. Look. I think— hope—that I'm getting over being jealous of you. Don't think I wasn't. Pissed me off, de Lis picking you right out of the school and all that. Not that you aren't terrific; you are, I'm the first to say it. We all thought you were shacking up with him, or your daddy was giving him money, who knew? Anyway, I know you have reason to stick up for the old bastard. When it comes right down to it, so do I. But let me tell you something. He isn't what he wants us all to believe he is. He isn't the *only* man in the world who knows how to run a ballet company. You don't automatically die and go to hell if you leave the Civic. I mean, look at Dima. Flying high."

"I wish I were."

"Flying high?"

"Looking at Dima. We split, you know."

This was the first time Jenny had been able to bring herself to say those words to anyone but Privy. She formed the words, moved her throat, they came out, she didn't disappear through a trap door in the floor, didn't die right there from embarrassment.

Iris just smiled a motherly smile and put her hand over Jenny's hand and said, "He'll be back. I'll bet a ticket to the Joffrey. New York never saw anything like the two of you in *Giselle*. He'll be back. Take the word of a sophisticated lady."

Iris was the veteran of too many one-night stands to mention her evening with Dima, the night of Jenny's first *Giselle*, the night of de Lis' party. Iris knew, and hated herself for knowing, that it had been a convenience, that she had meant no more to Dima than the momentary outlet for an urge.

"You really think so?" Jenny was surprised and very pleased to hear these words of comfort from an impartial source. But she didn't dare hope they were true.

"Just you wait." Iris fumbled in her dance bag, found a

worn pocketbook and pulled out an equally worn bill. "It's on me, Swanilda."

"Only if you let me get it next time."

They all were always broke, always borrowing five bucks till payday, always on the edge. This was one of the strings that de Lis held: their purse strings. Even with her recent raises, Jenny Hale was earning less than what a moderately competent secretary might take home—this, for the brightest new star in the ballet firmament. Jenny never saw the irony of this or even thought about it very much. She was grateful for the chance to dance, to dance leading roles and in de Lis productions. Dancing was its own reward, and lucky for Jenny that she felt that way, because it would be the only reward forthcoming from Alexander de Lis. Jenny stood up, balancing gracefully with her cane, and giggled. "Thanks, Swanilda. We're both Swanilda, don't forget. And thanks for the moral support."

"Just remember," said Iris with a grin, "where you heard it first. And about de Lis, well, that particular argument has been going on as long as there's been a Civic. And it will, as long as there's a de Lis."

"There was a Broadway show once," said Jenny, "called *No Strings*. One of my stepmothers took me."

"You know," said Iris, suddenly grave, "what happens to good little puppets when the strings get cut. I guess what I want all of us to do is start growing some strings of our own. Like Dima."

"Like Dima. You can bet anything there are no strings on that one." *Especially*, she thought, *not binding him to me.*

"And don't think it doesn't drive de Lis bonkers."

"Think so?" Jenny managed a smile, *but where*, she wondered, *was Dima right this minute—where, and with whom?*

"I know so. I was around when Machito left for the International. De Lis ranted and fumed like you wouldn't believe. He resents that more than anything."

"I guess I never thought de Lis was capable of resenting something—someone." *Dima resents me. Resents the fact that I didn't jump when he pulled my strings. And there were strings.*

"Honey, you've seen his sweet side, the Russian Easter bunny side. There is another. Many others. Hell hath no fury like Alexander de Lis scorned."

"Makes him more human in a way." Jenny thought of Dima's rage that night, of his ice-cold fury. She shivered.

"Not if you're on the receiving end." They walked out into the early darkness. And all the way across Central Park, alone at the front of the bus, Jenny tried and failed to get the image out of her head of herself, in costume, slumped in a boneless heap on the stage floor, a puppet without strings. And laughter from the wings, the laugh of Alex de Lis.

They are either very arrogant, thought Sam Purcell, *or very careless, or maybe they really are old pals having a reunion.* In any event, Ivan Sokolovny and Dave Loughlin acted as though they hadn't a care in the world or any idea they were under surveillance.

It had taken years for Sam to learn how to make himself invisible. This was a question of coloration, of fading into shadows, of pace, of never moving suddenly, of always looking like a man on an errand. Only outside the Carlyle had Sam deviated from his usual approach, and that was from necessity. The hotel had two entrances, and they both had to be covered: the Madison Avenue side and the Seventy-Sixth Street side. Thank God Loughlin hadn't chosen the Plaza or one of the newer places with entrances into the subway. But once Sam had the trail, there was no seeing him and no stopping him.

And there they sat, like wooden ducks in a shooting gallery, smack in the window of the little Italian restaurant, chattering like magpies, perfectly positioned for a hit. But this was still the "search" part of Sam Purcell's mission; the "destroy" would come later, if it came at all.

The two men drank, ordered food and ate it, drank wine and more wine, laughed, ordered cognac, talked some more. And all the while Sam stood motionless and invisible in the shadows of an alley across the street, holding a slender aluminum cigar tube innocently in his gloved hand, the blunt end of the tube pointed casually at the steamy restaurant window.

When he saw the fat stranger motion for the check, Sam slipped out of the alley and around the corner and hailed a taxi. Enough was enough; the supersensitive listening device in the cigar tube should tell him as much as he needed to know about the relationship of his old sidekick to this jolly stranger. And watching the two men eat made Sam realize how hungry he was. Nothing but coffee since breakfast, and it was well after ten P.M.

Sam directed the cabby to the Beekman Tower Hotel, where for years he'd kept a room and a few changes of clothes, extra passports and hand baggage for sudden overseas trips. All courtesy of the unaudited slush fund. There was a splendid French restaurant in the Beekman Tower, La Petite Marmite. Sam prayed it'd still be open.

The cab sped up the FDR Drive on the eastern perimeter of Manhattan island. Sam gazed out across the purple night river to the enormous red Pepsi-Cola sign that touched the squalor of Long Island City with false gaiety. And he thought, with a thin smile, how few questions would be asked, how soon the ripples would smooth out if, one day soon, Davey Loughlin and his pal were to pay an unexpected, but permanent, visit to that cold river's bottom. For nothing and no one, certainly no one as clumsy as Loughlin, could be permitted to interfere with the successful completion of his plan.

Diana wondered how long it would take for the flowers to appear, and Dima's note, and the boy himself. For she knew that these things would happen, and quickly, and she was already beginning to form a shell of amused detachment that was, if not entirely genuine, functional. At least it would get her over the shock of having been so abruptly deprived of her expectations.

And what had those expectations been? To change a pattern that she saw closing in on her. To add a new dimension to a life that was running just a bit too smoothly, too true to form. To pleasure herself with a new and wilder sexual excitement. Somehow to cannibalize the magic that Dimitri Lubov generated as naturally as the sun generates flowers. Diana showered, changed her clothes, ordered another breakfast, sans champagne, and began making phone calls to her Tokyo connections in the decorating world. And all the time she did these things, Diana's fine, honest, ironic mind was appraising her own situation, her own motives, her own dreams. She found them shallow, lacking in quality, a little flashy, just a touch cheap. She found them, in other words, to contain many of the values she most despised in others. The breakfast came; she sipped the tea but could hardly eat the delicate little almond cakes.

There was a gentle but persistent knock at her door. Diana knew at once it was not the knock of a servant. The flowers were roses, pink and enormous, and there was no note. Dima had brought them himself.

"What," he asked, eyes blazing the deepest blue that Diana had ever seen them, "can I say?"

"How about hello?" She kissed him on the cheek, all casual and sisterly, and took the flowers. "They're lovely, Dima. Thank you. And I am the one who should apologize. I hope I didn't frighten your friend too much."

"Ultimately, is Dima who gets frightened. I am thinking, *double murder!*"

"You must realize, my dear," she said, returning with an ice bucket filled with roses, "that I am an art collector. I do not destroy things of beauty. How's the tour going?"

"Well. They have not much ballet here. Is novelty. Diana, we must talk." He sat on a fake Louis XVI settee, and his face was a mask of overstated misery, the nearly comical grief of a ten-year-old who had been caught robbing the cooking jar.

"Dima, I never imagined you were coming to Japan to join a monastery. And I didn't come here to chase you. A client assigned me to come, to pick up some Japanese art. Naturally, I assumed . . . I thought it might be fun . . . I assumed too much. But don't apologize for being what you are, Dima. It is what you are that attracted me to you."

"You speak," he said in a monotone, "in the past."

"I'm afraid it is past, our little fling. But it was a lovely fling, Dima. I'll remember it all my life, and I'll remember it happily. I thank you for it."

"You discard me then?"

"Not discard, Dima. Outgrow. You taught me a valuable lesson about myself. You taught me that there are certain games I'm not equipped—anymore—to play. I'm thirty years old, Dima. It's time to find a different pattern."

"Is meaningless, your age."

"Tell me that six years from now. I love the idea of living for the moment, Dima; it sounds like fun. But suddenly I find the moments all add up, and they add up to something I'm not sure I like."

"You find me cruel?"

He looked at Diana. He was thinking of Jenny Hale. Jenny, too, was not a girl who lived for the moment.

"Impetuous. Is the wind cruel? Not when it cools you on a warm day, not when it flies a kite or sets the flowers dancing. When it tears the roof off, then it may be cruel. But first it is the wind, Dima, and the wind makes its own rules. And who rides the wind must take their chances."

"So I am the wind?"

He rather liked the idea. But he was still thinking of Jenny. The roof torn off. The wind.

"You're many things, and many of them are wonderful. It's just that our time is over. If it hadn't ended here, this morning, it would have ended soon, someplace else. No regrets, Dima."

"Not to regret." He stood up, shook his head a little like a wet puppy shaking off drops of water. "You are . . . splendid girl." He was Dima the gallant actor now; he moved the few feet to where she stood, and seemed to grow taller with every step. He took her hand in both of his and kissed her lips.

"Good-bye, Dima."

"*Dasvidaniya.* Good-bye." He smiled for the first time. "But not good-bye."

"But not good-bye." She smiled too, and he was gone.

Diana turned and touched one of the pink roses, then walked to the window with its breathtaking view out across the moat and gardens of the Imperial Palace, to the palace itself. She expected the tears to come now, but there was nothing, nothing at all.

The young man from Technical Services was frankly terrified. He knew very well that Sam Purcell could have his hide nailed to the Washington Monument at high noon and nobody would even bat an eyelash. And from the way the Old Man was looking at him, that just might happen.

The young man knew about Sam. He knew that under Sam's thoughtful guidance, the Technical Services Department of the Central Intelligence Agency had blossomed into a university of death and deception, a dark place where undetectable poisons grew, where some of the most sophisticated electronics in the world were focused on the problem of invading the privacy of princes and prostitutes, of diplomats and dupes. The young man knew all this, and more, and he trembled.

The elegant little listening device in its aluminum cigar tube had failed.

"I used the thing exactly as instructed. One turn to the left to set it operating, right?"

"Right."

"I was no more than twenty-five yards away. Subject was behind a big plate-glass window in a half-empty restaurant. The device was level, held firmly, aimed directly at the window. Now, I have one little question: Why in God's name didn't it work?"

"I just don't know, sir. We'll have to tear it apart to find out. These things happen."

"These things better not happen to me, never again. Do you realize you've cost me two irreplacable days? That a critical operation might be blown for what your wretched little machine did not feel like picking up? That matters of national security might be in danger?"

"Yes, sir. I'm sorry, sir."

"It's a pleasure to hear it." Sam's voice got softer, more dangerous. The gray eyes glittered behind their gold-rimmed glasses. The young man felt exactly as though he was about to be flunked out of school. "You're sorry. Well, I'm sorry, too. And I have a small suggestion."

"Sir?" The sweat was forming on his upper lip now, on his forehead.

"My suggestion, young man, is that you get your ass back down to that laboratory and find out what went wrong with this little toy of yours, and if you value your future here in the agency, you just make very, very sure it doesn't fail me—or anyone else—again. Is that absolutely clear?"

"Yes, sir." The young man wished for the floor to open up underneath him, wished he'd evaporate, turn invisible, anything. A drop of sweat came trickling down his forehead. He was afraid to wipe it off. Sam reached for the aluminum cigar tube and picked it up with two fingers, as though it might bite him. He handed it to the young engineer.

"Good luck, Roberts."

"Yes, sir. Thank you, sir." Roberts turned and scurried out of Sam's big office.

Sam walked to the window and sat in the big leather wing chair. He leaned back and put his handmade Italian loafers on the low teak campaign chest that served as a coffee table. He closed his eyes. There were two possibilities.

He could have Loughlin trailed, officially, on the supposition that the fat stranger was recruiting him for a foreign intelligence network. Stranger things had happened, but Sam knew perfectly well that they'd never get to Davey, not old Davey, no matter how much of a drunk he became, no matter how shabby he looked. The other possibility was to wait it out a little, to lay low, to hold off on Sergei Rosoff or the Lubov boy, to watch Davey, to see him in person, summon him to headquarters for an in-depth briefing, perhaps to make another unannounced visit to New York when the lab got its act together.

And as it usually did with Sam Purcell, the more careful choice won out. To have Loughlin trailed was to risk a leak. To make more explanations than he felt like making. To chance alarming Davey himself. No, he'd wait. And watch. Sam looked at his watch, with its date-day calendar. The International Ballet would be back in fewer than three weeks now. That was plenty of time to have another crack at Dave Loughlin. The secret was not to do anything precipitous. It was, almost always, the cool hand that hit the mark. And Sam Purcell was determined to hit his mark.

Greg Holden was at the cashier's desk changing money when Diana appeared to do the same thing. All over again Greg felt the rush of appreciation he'd first encountered when Diana walked into the JAL lounge at Kennedy Airport. He smiled, hoping it didn't look as lecherous as it felt. "I don't suppose," he asked quietly, "that you'd be free for supper tonight or tomorrow night?"

She looked at him, startled, as if he'd just stepped down from a flying saucer wearing four heads and one red eye. Then the smile came, breaking like dawn and just as glorious. "Seldom," she murmured, "have I been freer."

There were days, and this was one of them, when Jenny Hale felt more like a seamstress than a dancer. There was always something needing a stitch in time, usually shoes. The classic pink satin toe shoes, with their fatally slippery toes and stiff reinforcements designed by the Spanish Inquisition, had to be darned on the toe surface before the first wearing, the ribbons had to be strengthened or adjusted to your own foot and the damned canvas casings in the toes had to be softened somehow so they wouldn't actually cut your toes when you went up en pointe.

Then there were costume adjustments and, it seemed, a

million other tiny emergencies backstage, all requiring needle
and thread. Every dancer, including most of the boys, kept a
sewing kit of some sort handy. For the girls, it was imper-
ative. Now Jenny sat in her dressing room at the New York
State Theater, getting ready for the big day. Four more days,
and the god-awful cast would be off! Four more days, and
she'd be a ballerina again; she'd have something to get out of
bed for in the morning; she'd be able to get back in shape.

In the meantime, she was getting everything ready. She'd
drawn six new pairs of toe shoes from wardrobe and was darn-
ing and restrapping every one of them. Plus repairing all the
old ones she hadn't had time to in those frantic days before
the accident. Before the fall! It sounded almost Biblical. And,
God knew, it had felt like hell. But the end was in sight now,
and to tell the truth, it hadn't been a totally bad experience.
Her friendship with Iris, tentative as that might be, had
grown out of it. So had a new confidence, a sense that her
life really wouldn't end if she had to stop dancing. Two
months! If anyone had told Jenny even a year ago that she
would survive two months of not dancing, Jenny would have
laughed in disbelief.

Of course, she wouldn't be performing right away. De Lis
had already told her it might be a question of several weeks
before she got back to performance condition. "You must figure," he had said gravely, "that for every day—beyond just
one or two—that you have been away from the barre, it will
take you at least two days to make it up."

What went unsaid was the speculation that terrified Jenny
Hale to her toes, the assumption that everything was all right,
that the injured foot worked as well as new. But she couldn't
think about that; it was too scary. It would work because
she'd make it work. And in the meantime, there were toe
shoes to be sewn, plans to be planned.

Planning a life without Dima might just take the rest of
her life, thought Jenny. If she were up to it.

Peking matched Dima Lubov's mood. It was grim, gray, a
city of immense spaces under gray skies, whose ant armies of
sexless workers streaming by on bicycles and on foot made
only the smallest dent in the impersonal, monolithic and
unhuman scale of the place.

That the workers were well fed and smiling, that in one
generation the vast country had lifted itself most spectacu-

larly out of starvation, impressed Dima not at all. What he
saw was the hordes of identically clad workers riding identical bicycles and smiling identical smiles as they flowed
through the city, diligent and colorless as drone bees or
worker ants.

Dima lived on movement, color, style. His life was a continuous explosion of these things, and to be thrown into a
country where color and style and creativity were repressed
as a matter of policy depressed him deeply. For three thousand years, he thought, China had given the world incompa-
rable painting, sculpture and design. And it had been done
away with almost overnight, all that glorious energy chan-
neled into the iron smelters of the Maoist dream. Dimitri was
still too close to the oppression of his native Russia to take
the People's Republic lightly, the way everyone else in the International Ballet seemed to take it: as an amusing diversion,
a lark.

Dima smiled and was gracious and did everything that was
expected of him. But the gloom he brought with him from
Tokyo didn't lift. He danced, and danced brilliantly, but—he
thought—for nothing. Nothing but the political ambitions of
Judith Winchester.

There was no real ballet audience in China; classical ballet
was considered frivolous, decadent, luxurious. They were
taken to performances of the People's Ballet, but it wasn't
ballet at all, only ritualized propaganda in which girls in
army uniforms brandished rifles and won battles stiffly and
smiled woodenly and depressed Dima even more. The acrobats were fun and amazingly skillful, juggling plates on the
tips of tall broomsticks, making and unmaking spectacular human pyramids and performing impossible feats of contortion.
Yet it seemed to Dima that there was no joy in it. The performers smiled their mechanical-monkey grins, and they all
looked precisely alike.

Somewhere in the hills, thought Dima with an involuntary
shudder, *is a factory where they turn out these acrobats and
dancers like so many dolls.* He began smiling as mechanically
as any Chinese acrobat. He began counting the days.

"Of course," said Dave Loughlin in a sad monotone, "we
still don't know for a fact that it is Mr. Suspect." Early in the
hunt, they'd started to call the killer Mr. Suspect. Now they

kept it up, partly from habit, partly from fear of listening devices.

"It is the easiest thing in the world, Davey, for me to have him tailed." Ivan's voice was anything but jocular now.

"God, no! Absolutely not! Are you kidding? He'd be on to you in five seconds, no matter how good your guys are. And there's no predicting what he'd do then. My bet is, our lives wouldn't be worth whaleshit."

"At the bottom of de ocean. What a good memory you have, old friend."

"The actual expression," said Loughlin with a harsh laugh, "is: 'You motherfuckers is lower than whaleshit at de bottom of de ocean.' It's very important to get both 'de's' in there."

"Master Sergeant Billie-Bob Spainhoward."

"Berlin HQ, 1945!"

"I wish," said Ivan with a sigh that could have dredged the Volga, "that it was still 1945."

"I saved his life, Ivan. I saved the fucker's life."

"Spainhoward?"

"Mr. Suspect."

"Ah. In a way, Davey, that's good."

"If I live to be a million years old, which gets less and less likely, I will never understand the so-called Russky mentality. Why good?"

"Good for your personal conscience, old fart. If you have such an animal. Good because you owe him nothing—no loyalty, no affection."

"I've always looked up to the man. He stood for something."

"He stands for something now, David. He stands for madness and murder."

"He was—is—so goddamned smart, Ivan. That's what I really can't figure. Smart-smart. Intellectual smart. Reads Spinoza for breakfast. Collects old-master etchings. Had a really nice wife, a really classy woman, you know, gentle. She died about five years ago."

"Children?"

"No kids. She couldn't have kids."

Ivan sat still, toying with his wineglass, thinking about the small pear tree that grew outside his little summerhouse on the Dalmatian coast. It was not a particularly beautiful tree, and the birds often got to its fruit before Ivan did, yet in springtime it put out delicate white blossoms, a few more each year. It made quite a little cloud, now. Ivan looked at Dave Loughlin and wondered if he'd ever see his pear tree again. Then he spoke. "Let's kill him."

"You're kidding."

"Negative. *Nyet.*"

"We'd still never be able to prove he did it. All those murders." Dave wasn't going to insult Ivan by pretending surprise, or even moral outrage. They had set themselves beyond morality, these two, right out there in the jungle, with Sam, where the rule was simple enough to be summed up in one word: *survive!* Just then an ambulance came screaming by, flashing its lights, burning rubber as it lurched around the corner. As if it were a signal, both men got up and fumbled for their coats. This conversation was best finished on the street.

High in the Beekman Tower Hotel two hours later a tall gray-haired man paced the thick carpet of a luxuriously furnished residential apartment. On the black-walnut sideboard a small tape cassette player whirred its way to silence as the sound of the ambulance wiped out the end of Dave Loughlin's conversation with Ivan.

The decision made itself then. Sam's only questions were how, and where, and precisely when. Dave must be eliminated, and the Russian, too. Perhaps it could be made to look like a shoot-out. But in any case, it had to happen, and very soon.

For the first time in her life, Jenny Hale began to make plans. She faced the fact of a life without Dimitri. She bought three schoolchild's ruled notebooks and made lists. Lists! The simple act of writing them down had made magic in it. By putting her lists on paper, she made her plans come true before her eyes as she sat in the freshly painted living room of the old apartment. It was late afternoon, the last day before her cast would come off for good. Jenny sat in the softest chair, a slightly sagging old club chair newly slipcovered by Privy in a brave white, yellow and green flowered chintz.

Jenny's broken foot in its walking cast was propped on a pillow on a makeshift footstool that consisted of two dictionaries and a big Bible. She wrote and smiled and wrote some more.

London! They'd go to London soon, maybe next Christmas. Privy would love that, you could get these quite cheap tours on the installment plan, they'd go! No doubt about it. And she'd buy a hat, a floppy, sexy, Greta Garbo felt number like the one Iris had, only not red. Some deep, mysterious color. She, Jennifer Hale, ballerina, would become a creature of mystery and romance. Men would swoon. And—ugh— she'd go to the dentist, the visit she'd been postponing for two years, half from fear and half from poverty. It wouldn't do for a glamorous lady of mystery to have a toothache. She'd buy some really beautiful gloves, *très chic* gloves like the ones Gloria Bruce used to lose by the dozens, and some for Privy, too. And she'd take cooking lessons. She, Jennifer Hale, ballerina and woman of mystery, would give small, fascinating little suppers after the theater, her emeralds flashing as she flamed the crepes.

The doorbell rang. "I'll get it, my love!" Privy, as always, was on the move, bustling about the apartment.

Jenny sat there in a kind of daze, looking at all the interesting things she'd written in a little book. They'd come true. She knew they would. It would all come true.

There was a footstep. Not Privy's footstep. Jenny looked up.

Dimitri Lubov stood in the doorway, his cowboy hat in one hand and a huge bunch of violets in the other.

How much time passed as he stood there, Jenny would never be able to guess. Their eyes locked. Jenny's throat went dry as dust. She started to form his name, opened her mouth to say it, but no sound came out.

There was no smile on Dima's face, the most mobile face Jenny had ever seen. That face, whose every plane and curve Jenny knew by heart, a face that could be angel, satyr, urchin, lover, warrior or scamp, Dima's face!

He looked at her as one who mourns at the final resting place of a dream. And then he spoke, a voice with no joy in it, the ghost of a voice visiting from some dark country far away. "In Japan," he said quietly, "someone asked was I homesick. The ballet stage, I said, is Dima's home. But ultimately I am wrong, Jenny. You are my home."

He put down the hat and walked across the room, knelt and kissed her hand. It was only then that she saw his tears.

"Dima, Dima. You're here." She kept repeating his name to make it real because Jenny had a terrible feeling that this wasn't happening, it was too good, too perfect, not the kind of thing that happened to her at all. He sat at her feet, still holding her hand, his eyes never moving from her eyes.

"Is possible," he asked in that same quiet voice, "that you forgive stupid Russian boy?"

"Dima, Dima. . . ." Her treacherous voice had left her incapable of saying anything but his name. So she bent down and answered with a kiss.

CHAPTER
~⊛(12)⊛~

Greg Holden's office was small and functional, the headquarters for his ongoing battle with all the fiscal and half the emotional problems of the International Ballet Theater. Today was a sandwich-at-desk day, like most working days. Greg and Boris Mogador, the ballet's creative director, and Dima Lubov were having a war conference. They had widely differing motives but one obvious enemy: Judith Winchester.

"Is very simple," said Dima, stirring his yogurt, "is proven fact. When Jenny and I dance together, people come. With de Lis, she has no real partner. With you, Dima has no real ballerina. Nadia, well, ultimately is not magical, Nadia and me. She is fine dancer. But not giving, understand? Not becoming a team. Nadia remains Nadia. Her partner remains furniture."

This was a long speech for Dima. That he was able to make it at all was a measure of how deeply he cared about having Jenny Hale brought into the International Ballet—over Judith Winchester's dead body, if necessary. He looked at his audience. Boris, Dima knew, loved the idea of having a Jenny-Dima combination to work with. Greg Holden was an unknown quantity. Dima had felt a certain coolness in the man, possibly because it had been Judith's idea to hire him away from de Lis.

Greg sipped his coffee. Boris grinned.

"How about that, for making headlines about the gala?" Boris was already deep in the preliminary-planning stages for Judith's gala, now less than a month away. "How," he added, "could she complain?"

"Here we sit," said Greg quietly, "acting as though that lady has us all by the balls. Well, I have no doubt she'd like to. But, gentlemen, the fact is, Mrs. Winchester has no official say about hiring—or firing—in this company. That's totally up to you, Boris, naturally subject to my approval."

Dima's eyes widened and narrowed. He looked at Greg Holden with new respect.

Greg took the last bite from his roast beef sandwich and another sip of coffee. "I have to tell you, Dima, that I wasn't too happy about her bringing you in the way she did. Not, you understand, because of you, but because of the way she did it. Going right over our heads. Well," Greg continued, smiling for the first time in the discussion, "we're pleased as hell to have you, Dima. You fit right in; some of the problems I anticipated—jealousies—just haven't happened. And I, for one, would be delighted to have Miss Hale join us. I don't know exactly how much we can offer her right now—"

"Please." Dima leaned forward intently. "Is not the most important thing, not for the moment, the money. I cannot speak for Jenny, but if you will have her, something can ultimately be worked out. Wonderful, it would be, to dance again with Jenny!"

"Boris?" Greg spoke to his creative director, but his eyes remained on Dima.

"If we can swing it, absolutely!"

"Then, Dima, I'll dig into the exchequer and see what we can come up with."

"Wonderful! I thank you."

The urchin who always lurked near the surface of Dimitri's most businesslike manner broke through now, bringing with him the well-known grin. The room was warmed by it; they all smiled. There was a sense of triumph in the air, and mischief, too, for they all felt they'd put one over on the dragon lady.

Greg Holden knew perfectly well there'd be trouble, maybe big trouble, from Judith. And with a sudden rush of relief he realized he didn't give a damn; it would be worth it just to show the old bitch she wasn't always going to have everything her way. The price, Greg know, of Jenny Hale's employment would be counted in other ways than just dollars and cents. Well and good. If Winchester wanted a fight, he was just the man to give it to her.

Greg leaned back in his desk chair, stretched, smiled again. He hadn't felt this good since leaving the aircraft business. Here was a real challenge, a chance to use his resourcefulness to the limit. It was a very good feeling. *Watch out, Winchester.*

Dima, in rehearsal clothes, stood up. But before he could leave, Boris had a question: "Tell me, Dima; can we be sure she'll do it?"

"Jenny," he said, smiling the thin, seraphic smile of a Donatello angel, "will be delighted." Then he bowed, the Kirov training surfacing reflexively, and left the office. And wondered if she really would go through with it.

Jenny was waiting in the apartment when he got there. She had moved back in the day after the cast came off. They kissed, had tea, sat by the fire. Dina took her hand. *You must be gentle,* said a voice that remembered how deeply he'd frightened her in de Lis' office, how terrified she must be at the prospect of leaving the Civic. "Today," he said, softly, "I speak to Boris, to Greg Holden."

"About me?" Her voice was quiet, too. It was as if the two of them were stepping very tentatively across ice that might be thinner than they knew.

"About us." Now he covered her hand in both of his hands. "Is madness if we are not together, dancing, *deushka.* Ultimately you must come to the International." He left his words hanging in the stillness and the flickering firelight, and for a moment it seemed that all the hope left in the world depended on her answer.

She leaned toward him, kissed his cheek. "I know," she said; "I know!" It came softer than whispering, but Dima knew her promise was forged in fires that could consume them both.

The next day Jenny called Sheldon Sylvester. And the day after that, Jenny knew she'd have to face de Lis. The ballet world was too small, too ridden with gossip to admit even the smallest delay. If Jenny didn't tell him, someone else would. She shuddered now, just thinking of it, remembering de Lis, remembering what Iris had said. It would be the scariest thing she'd ever done, and even the fact that Dima and his love and his partnering were waiting at the other end of the ordeal wouldn't make it any easier.

Sam Purcell hid his rising anger with an actor's skill, buried it under a seamless veneer of poise and presence. But the anger was there, building. Opportunity was showing a most unwelcome tendency these days to come knocking on the wrong door. And at the wrong time. He stood in the director's office, agreeing with what the old fool said.

"Yes, absolutely. Of course you're right. I can leave tomorrow. What do you think, a week?"

The director of the Central Intelligence Agency had long been in the habit of relying upon Sam to put out brushfires wherever they might spring up. And one had sprung up just yesterday, and in Singapore, that threatened to blow the entire Southeast Asian network all to tatters. The chief of station in Singapore had apparently defected. It wasn't certain, but it looked bad. The man had vanished, leaving not a trace. It was possible he was simply dead. He might have gone underground for reasons they had yet to learn. But the logical—dreaded—assumption was that he'd been recruited, gone over, taking with him all the details of the Asian operation: agents, logistics, plans and projections. In other words, disaster. They had to know for sure. And the only man the director trusted absolutely for an assignment of such awesome sensitivity was Sam Purcell. Very flattering. Sam clenched his fists and tried not to think of the situation in New York.

A week in Singapore was exactly what Sam Purcell didn't need. A week? More than a week, really. A full day's jet time just to get there and back. Well, he had to go; there was no avoiding it. The irritation faded in the face of the inevitable. He'd just have to act faster when he did get back; that was all there was to it. Much faster. Sam managed a smile and shook hands with the director and left the office. *Very dull,* he thought, looking at the conventionally furnished room. *When I move in, things will be different. Very different.* And he would move into the director's office; Sam could feel the certainty in his bones.

Alexander de Lis prowled the empty rehearsal hall, stalking the soul of a dance. The idea was there. It would be Jenny Hale's dance. The girl who fell. A parable of Icarus: the girl who flew too high. A pas de deux. A Liszt rhapsody. With amazing lifts! The girl would seem to be flying. And then the fall, brought to earth, broken. Struggling to rise. Faltering. Pathos! And the ending? De Lis wasn't sure about that. Tragic, more likely than not. Alone upon the stage, quivering, abandoned. Yes, exactly. Like the dying swan, only more contemporary, more psychological. More moving. She must enter flying, an entrance like no other. Perhaps a great leap from the wings. He turned, distracted; here was the girl now, ready to rehearse. And where had the time gone?

Alone with his vision, de Lis knew no time. Seven days to make the world was nonsense. The world would never be made, not on the day after eternity, nor any dance either, nor any created thing. For the creation must be continuous, fermenting, living.

He might be an old man—surely they said so—but no one was ever younger, more ready to invent, to mold, to change. Last week's dance or last year's was nothing compared to tomorrow's dance. Nothing was finished, or could be, or should be.

But here was the girl; here was little Jenny, she of the great tragic eyes. Yes, tragic. Why, he wondered, so tragic, after just last week getting out of her cast? Already, de Lis could tell, she was recovering most remarkably, better than he had dared hope. Suddenly remembering himself, he smiled. "Good afternoon, my dear. And how is the foot?"

"The foot seems fine. Thank you."

The pain showed in her eyes, but it was not physical pain. *Do it, damn it,* she told herself. *Do it. Tell him.* She took a deep breath. The breath escaped as a sigh. *Help! The worst he can do is kill me. Ballerina strangled in rehearsal hall. De Lis pleads justifiable homicide. A crime of passion, your Honor. The little bitch betrayed me.*

"Mr. de Lis, I'm leaving."

"You don't feel good, Jenny?"

"I mean, really leaving. The company. I'm very sorry, but I have to. Really." She forced herself to look at him. She felt herself growing smaller and smaller, and that gave her a bit of hope. Maybe she'd actually disappear, just vanish.

"You have to?" Alexander de Lis stood quietly in the big, empty room looking at this girl he had nurtured from childhood like some rare flower.

He looked at Jenny Hale and through her, beyond her and saw all the ghosts of all the young dancers he had trained and promoted and starred, who had left. Had to leave. The rehearsal hall filled with them, generations of brilliant young dancers, girls, boys, dancing, leaping, soaring, saying goodbye, some in tears, some in anger, but all saying good-bye. He looked at Jenny in a kind of quiet disbelief, as if from a great distance. "You have to." He repeated her words like a mantra. "You have to."

"I'm in love, Mr. de Lis. I can't help it."

"Ah, yes. Love." The intruder in his magic kingdom. They were always falling in love. It wasn't enough to love dancing. They must love each other. Love was the serpent in his garden, upsetter of well-laid plans, a smoldering fuse that led directly to the bomb of temperament.

Five times married and five times divorced, Alexander de Lis was in love with the idea of love. It could never be said that he was unsympathetic to its pleasures. But the fact of it, the uninvited arrival of the emotion itself, that was something else, something to be wary of, something to resist, avoid, deny. If only, he had often thought, there were a little pill that would take the place of love, an instant remedy for the awful itch, the yearning, the volcanic desires. Fat chance.

De Lis turned for a moment as if to walk away and then turned back. He reached out and touched Jenny's shoulder. It was quivering. The tears would not be long in coming. "And am I such a monster, Jenny, that it would be impossible to be in love and yet to dance for de Lis?"

"It's not that at all. Of course not. I can't bear being separated from Dima. That's all. It isn't you."

"Dima. Of course." It would be Dima. They were well matched. De Lis looked at Jenny with deepening regret. The girl who flew too high. She had flown so high, this one, that she would fly away entirely, and to the damned International. Always, it seemed, it was to the International, with their stars and their money and their fame. "I hope, my dear," he said with the smallest of smiles, "that you and Dima will be happy. How soon will you be leaving us?" He tried for a casual tone and nearly made it work.

"Two weeks. I can be flexible about that, if there's something you need me for. You know you can always call on me, Mr. de Lis. Anytime."

He could call on her, could he? Send an ambassador, perhaps? De Lis knew as he stood there that the girl had no idea of the arrogance in her words, in her offer. That she should make such an offer to Alexander de Lis!

"Thank you, my dear. That won't be necessary." Then he did turn and leave her. As he walked proudly out of the rehearsal hall, Jenny reached out one arm, as if to stop him. For she felt in that moment as though de Lis had left taking a big chunk of her life with him, and it would never, never be returned.

Jenny stood in the enormous empty hall like a stranger. It was as she had sneaked in through the back door and might be thrown out at any minute. How many miles had she danced on these polished boards? How many gallons of sweat, what thousands of pairs of toe shoes had she worn to tatters here, and all for Alex de Lis? When Jenny Hale left the Civic, she would leave her childhood behind in these sweaty halls.

Well, she'd done it! Actually faced the beast in his own lair, and come away unharmed. The strings had been cut, and she was still alive and unscathed! Alive anyway. She wasn't too sure about the rest. Foxy old de Lis wasn't going to give her the satisfaction of showing emotion. There had been no tearing of hair, no scene, no recriminations. They would be interior, whatever regrets, whatever anger de Lis might hold for her.

Jenny expected to feel relief. But all she felt was exhaustion. She felt tired, more tired than after a long solo performance. Well, it had been a long solo performance. Dima would be proud. That was what mattered. And they'd be together. Always. However long always might be.

Judith Winchester looked across her huge steel desk at Greg Holden, her eyes as cold and hard as steel itself. Greg had determined he wasn't going to justify himself to this hatchet-faced tyrant, whatever the provocation. She had called him in for a conference about the gala. He intended to keep it on that basis.

She came right to the point. "What's all this about the Hale girl? Have you gone to contract?"

"Signed yesterday. Dima's delighted."

That's it, play it from Lubov's point of view. Lubov was Judith's idea, let her bear the brunt of her protégé's request.

"I do wish, Greg, that you had asked me first." Judith smiled sweetly. *I'll bury him*, she thought. *I will see him buried*.

Greg was the agent of the thing Judith feared most: a coalition. Her scheme for running the International Ballet, her publishing empire or anything else she wanted to control was based on divided factions. Judith didn't really care a damn whether Jenny came or went. But the fact that Jenny's arrival signaled the formation of a team, a team that might work well together, that might take on a velocity of its own, beyond her control, within the company, was intolerable. Just when she had insinuated Dimitri into the company as a divisive factor! Just when the Oriental tour had gone so well, just when all her plans seemed to be coming true. No. It was not to be tolerated, not at all. Still, she smiled the smile of a lost little girl.

Greg waited for her to unsheath her dagger. "There really wasn't time," he said. "Dima had it all set up, and naturally, we were anxious to do anything that keeps him happy. It should be the making of the gala."

"And what about Nadia? Isn't she furious?"

"Nadia was born furious. She will be a furious old lady soon. And, let's face it, the partnership of Nadia and Dima isn't what we hoped it would be. Jenny and Dima will be a far hotter ticket."

"I hope you're right." Judith kept her voice light, but there was a threat in it. She was so used to the politics of intimidation that she often didn't even bother to hide the naked power that was never more than half an inch behind the mask of the moment. "Well, then," she said, all business, "enough of gossip. The gala's still on for Friday, March fourth, am I correct?" Of course, she was correct. She'd done the scheduling.

"Right. Boris is whipping up a new pas de trois for Dima and Machito and the Hale girl. If I can persuade Nadia to do something from *Swan Lake,* that ought to assuage her. And maybe one solo for her in the first act, her choosing, just so she feels loved."

"And all this can be done in three weeks?"

"It'll have to be. Sure. They're pros. Boris is more excited than I've ever seen him."

"How lovely," said Judith with her sweetest smile, "for Boris."

In a few minutes the interview was over. It hadn't, Greg knew, been necessary at all. A phone call would have done it. But Judith Winchester must go exploring, from time to time, in this jungle of her own creating. She was, Greg thought, checking her traps and snares. Testing him, seeing if he could be pushed around a little. Well, Mrs. Hatchet Face was barking up the wrong managing director. He stood up and took his leave, smiling contentedly, the smile of a craftsman who knows his work is well wrought.

The door closed behind him. Judith stood up and looked

out her windows. Then she turned and walked the length of the huge office, up to the Coromandel screens.

She opened the screen panel that concealed the miniature theater. Automatically the lights came up, and the music came on the stereo, the new music for the *Antony and Cleopatra* ballet. The tiny stage setting stood there in its stark magnificence. There had been an addition to the setting. The designer had added two little figures, carved to scale from some light wood.

Antony and Cleopatra stood on the temple porch, costumed, looking startlingly real in the artificial light. The music throbbed, wailed, sighed. Judith stood silent for a moment, then slowly, as if in a dream, she reached out with her right hand and picked up the little carved figure of Cleopatra. Her other hand came up, silently, automatically, and then she snapped the little figure in two, like a pretzel.

Like any minor Mafioso on the lam, Dave Loughlin had taken to carrying a pocketful of quarters and making his critical phone calls from obscure public phone booths. He stood in such a booth now, shivering with the late January cold, cursing the bureaucracy of the Central Intelligence Agency.

He had headquarters on the line, Sam's secretary—which one of those identically prune-faced bitches he wondered. And true to her code of "need-to-know," she was giving Dave a very hard time. "Look," said Dave, trying with all his will-power to keep from screaming at her, from ripping the damned phone out by its guts, "if you can't tell me where he is, can you say when he'll be available? It's really important."

"I am sorry, but we aren't allowed to give out such information." It was probably the sixth time the dumb broad had said that in less than ten minutes.

For a while there, Dave wondered if he had been plugged into a tape recording. And the maddening thing was that Sam might be right there, all the time, laughing, scheming his schemes. Something in Dave snapped at that moment; if he was cast in a mad comedy, why not play it like a comedy? "Could you give me the correct time, miss?"

"I am sorry, but we aren't allowed. . . ." Dave hung up, laughing, but it was an empty laugh. There was no mirth in it. Chances were Sam was out of town. On the loose. And where? And up to what? It might, of course, be official business. Innocent. But nothing to do with the Old Man smacked of innocence now.

From all the long years of hero worship, of suspecting nothing, Dave Loughlin's bourbon-dimmed instincts had done a slow, lumbering, but total about-face. He now looked twice, three times, at anything to do with Sam Purcell. But looking wasn't enough, not when you were dealing with the Old Man, the man who wrote the book. Dave left the icy phone booth and got himself a cup of steaming black coffee.

The round-the-clock surveillance of Dima Lubov continued. It was the finest surveillance money could buy, and the reports were detailed. But Dave was old-pro enough to know how little real protection this kind of clandestine surveillance offered. He couldn't stop people from going into Dima's apartment building; brownstone that it was, five other people lived there, had friends and servants and delivery people come and go. He couldn't cordon off the whole block. Or the whole of Lincoln Center. Or the whole damned island of Manhattan.

The only sure protection would be to put Lubov in protective custody. If the kid would stand for it, which Dave very much doubted. In any case, that would be complicated by the fact that Lubov wasn't a U.S. citizen yet. And protection against what? Dave still had no ironclad proof. There were two questions that needed answering, and fast: One, did Sam know he knew, and two, where the hell was Sam anyway?

Sam Purcell had always been a little larger than life from Dave's point of view. Now, in the ninety-nine percent certainty that Sam himself was behind the defector murders, the Old Man took on the magical powers of some ancient and implacable, and implacably evil god. An all-seeing, all-knowing god who could assume a thousand guises, who could come and go undetected, day or night, who answered to no higher authority than his own mad whim.

Ivan had been right. There was probably no one in all the world better suited, more strategically positioned to carry out this kind of scheme than Sam Purcell. That, Ivan had admitted, was what made him suspicious in the first place. Who but a very highly placed CIA man would have the tradecraft, the mobility, the imagination and the motive all at once, all at hand? Dave gulped his coffee as though he might never see another cup and looked at his watch. If he hustled, he could just make the eleven A.M. Eastern Airlines shuttle flight to

Washington. That would get him to headquarters by two. He'd wring the goddamned information out of them with his bare hands, and from the director himself, if necessary. And it was necessary. He'd find out where Sam had taken himself, and why, and for how long. And he'd find out this very day. At least he could do that much.

Nadia Beshanskaia lounged against the barre, a study in predatory grace, and watched the tiny figure of Jenny Hale approaching through a blue haze of cigarette smoke. Like many dancers, and contrary to all known rules of health and conditioning, Nadia was a chain-smoker, and of Gauloises.

So this was the famous Jenny, *the* new Giselle! Unconsciously, Nadia arched her throat a little higher, lest a wrinkle mar that famous line. *A perfect little match girl she looks,* thought Nadia with the beginning of a smile, *all bones, more sparrow than a woman, downright gaunt she looks, and those clothes! Even in rehearsal, one must have standards. That blue bathrobe looks like the Czar's own armies had marched across it. In retreat.*

The girl was coming up to her, shyly, about to be introduced by Boris. She might well be shy. She obviously had much to be shy about!

Nadia turned and smiled the smile of an hereditary monarch. She would be gracious. It was always better to start out graciously. It left them unprepared for what would come later. Boris made the introductions. "How lovely, Jenny," said Nadia, radiant with noblesse oblige, "we are delighted to have you with us." Nadia actually bent to kiss the girl.

Jenny murmured something pleasant and hoped her inclination to back away didn't show in her face. It was like some old fairy tale. In which she, Jenny Hale, was about to be offered the poisoned apple. Dima had warned her about the tempestuous Nadia and of the inevitable time when Jenny would feel the force of that tempest, as everyone else in the company had felt it.

"She is a lesson to every dancer, *deushka*," he'd said, "of what a dancer must not become, whatever the temptations. If the energy spent by Nadia upon playing the prima ballerina were to be spent creating ballet, ultimately she might have been the greatest ballerina in the world. Tragic. For is fact; Nadia can dance."

"I wonder why."

"Why does flea bite? Nadia is Nadia—always was, to hear Boris."

Dima could not be with her this first day at the International. He was having costume fittings for three new ballets. Jenny's arrival was such a sudden thing that the casting hadn't been set for her yet. The gala was the one sure thing they'd lined up for her so far. *Fair enough,* she thought; *take one thing at a time.* Boris had been very kind, fatherly almost, and Greg Holden was a pleasant man.

Judith Winchester hadn't set foot on the premises since her meeting with Greg two weeks before. One thing at a time. Today Jenny would simply take the basic International group class. Rehearsals would begin in earnest later in the week. So much to do, and fewer than three weeks to do it in! The pas de deux with Dima would be no problem; they'd pick something they both knew and loved, maybe the big one from the second act of *Giselle.*

But to work with Machito again; that sent her quivering. And in a new pas de trois, made specially for the three of them. Even after her short, sad affair with Machito had ended, Jenny felt no bitterness. He couldn't help being what he was: a card-carrying Don Juan.

Jenny liked Machito Ramirez, and was glad that Dima did, too. Already they'd had supper together at the apartment, made plans, laughed about de Lis. They were all, each in his own way, the de Lis Alumni Association, Jenny most of all. And for Jenny to laugh about her former mentor wasn't easy. But there were other things to laugh about: her rediscovery of Dima, her good luck in joining the International at three times her former salary—still a drop in the bucket compared to Dima's fabulous contract, but a fortune from Jenny's humble point of view. "Look at us," she said happily as Machito and Dima opened another bottle of Bordeaux, Machito holding the bottle while his friend tugged at the reluctant cork; "the Three Musketeers!" The pop of the cork punctuated her remark.

"Against the world!" Machito lifted his newly filled glass.

"Against Judith Winchester!" Dima clinked glasses with both of them.

"I," said Jenny, giggling, "don't want to be against anything. What are we for?"

"For us!" Machito's grin got broader.

"For dancing!" Dima raised his glass to the gods of dance.

"For tomorrow." Jenny said it quietly. For the first time in her life tomorrow meant something more than just the day after today.

Diana Leighton's Rolls-Royce was waiting, as usual, outside Greg's office. He climbed into the back seat and kissed her. "Beats hell out of taxis," he said, grinning, "where are we going?"

"To a simple supper at my house." Diana had never seen him so relaxed. She had brought back more than scrolls and carvings from her trip to Japan. She'd brought back the beginnings of an affair that—she hoped and at the same time was scared to hope—might be more than just another affair.

"A few hundred of your closest chums?"

Greg made no bones about satirizing the gaudier aspects of Diana's busy social life. She just laughed. It was one of the things he liked most about her, that laugh. Unforced, easy, deep. Some women giggled, and some women sneered. But very few women, in Greg Holden's experience, really knew how to laugh. Especially at themselves.

"Just us." She turned to him and winked broadly. "A star-studded cast."

"And you came all the way out of that wretched hovel you call home just to pick me up?"

"I had an errand. And it ain't wretched. People who live in glass penthouses shouldn't throw stones." Well she knew that penthouse, its view, its impersonal decor that she was half-afraid to tell Greg she hated, its big, well-used bed.

"I guess not. Anyway, thanks for the lift."

"Thank you for coming. How's it going with the gala?"

"Shaping up. We only get one week to rehearse in the New York State Theater, on the heels of the opera, so it's going to be a scramble at the end. But the gala will open the season with a splash, and if Judith turns the juice full on, we might even raise some money out of it." He sat back, rested his head against the supple amber calfskin and closed his eyes for a moment. "What bugs me," he said quietly, "is the god-damned seething politics of it all. It's like the court of Byzantium some days."

"And today was one of them?"

"Today was one of them. Imagine," he said, shaking his head and sitting up again, "Nadia in a snit over nothing. What she's really in a snit about is the fact that we've brought in Jenny Hale. At Dima's request, naturally, but it's a good request. Winchester's furious, sulking, and we can only wonder what she might have up her sleeve. Then there are the usual ordinary everyday traumas, like will the State Council for the Arts renew our subsidy, or will we have to go begging for an extra half million bucks on top of the two million we're already begging for. And where will we get it if Judith stays mad at us? It was a fun day at International Ballet Theater."

He looked at her and felt better already. It was dawning on Greg Holden that Diana was the first woman he'd met in years he really liked talking to. And it didn't hurt one bit that she was also beautiful, talented and great in the sack. He reached out and took her hand. It was waiting. "You," he said softly, "are very good therapy."

"It's all part of the service," she said, leaning over to kiss him. "Psychiatric advice, five cents." Her bearded Sikh driver wove the sumptuous machine through the tangle of New York's six-thirty traffic. A Mozart string quartet flowed lightly out of hidden stereo speakers and wrapped itself around them. "Sherry?" asked Diana, reaching for the mahogany, brass and crystal Edwardian fitted liquor cabinet.

"I think," he said softly, "that I'll just enjoy the view."

The view was Diana. They rode like that, in silence, bathed in Mozart and the awareness of affection very possibly building into something more than just affection, as the cream-colored Rolls went gliding through the dusk to Diana's house on Forty-Ninth Street.

Whoever had taken a knife to Fred Gordon was driven more by passion than professionalism. Sam Purcell looked down at the stinking, hacked-up corpse of his Singapore chief of station and wondered. Often it was a convenience to make a pro job look amateur. No matter, the man was truly dead, dead as it was possible to be, and in a condition not made more lovely by a week in a bog in the Singapore heat, in the company of the Singapore land crabs. But still and all, it *was* Fred Gordon, and dead, and now Sam could wind up here and get back to the bigger business awaiting him Stateside. Sam hadn't wasted the long flight out to Singapore. He had a calendar, and a program of the new season of the International Ballet Theater, and a plan. A foolproof plan.

He turned from the appalling wreckage of Fred Gordon

and walked back to the waiting Mercedes, discreet and black like half the official cars in Singapore. The driver bowed courteously as Sam climbed into the immense back seat. Davis, the second-in-command at Singapore, climbed in next to Sam, saying nothing, wearing the slightly greenish expression of someone fighting with all his willpower not to throw up. Interesting, the man's nausea. It was an indication. It was an indication that Davis had probably not been behind Gordon's death. Or that he was a better actor that Sam had reason to expect. No matter. The immediate problem out here was past.

Now came Lubov. Sam knew that the bulk of his plan would succeed—had succeeded already—without Lubov's death, or the death of Sergei Rosoff. But Sam was never one to tolerate loose threads or unfinished business. Killing Lubov, and soon, would drive the last nail into the coffin of detente! Sam smiled. The worldwide headlines that had joined in such a pleasing chorus of outrage at the discovery of the KGB plot to murder defectors had slowly collapsed of their own weight. Public outrage needed further fuel, and soon. The pot must be kept, if not boiling, at least simmering. Sam must consolidate his gains; the hawk must fly again; the moment must not be allowed to pass.

Other, weaker, less visionary men might take a rest now, might be content by this small success. Not Sam. Never Sam. Sam felt the power building in him, felt his influence extending right into the very corridors and conference rooms of the Kremlin itself. They'd learn! They'd learn a lesson they would never forget—that the world would never forget.

They would learn because he, Sam, would teach them. And if his lesson was a violent one, so be it. How astonished they had been, poor fools, the defectors on his list, how cheerfully they'd walked into his subtle snares. How un-Russian they became, flexing the wings of their newfound freedom. How quickly they threw off the ingrained habit of suspicion. How very stupid they were, how deserving of his punishment. Sam leaned back against the rich mouse-gray velour of the Mercedes' back compartment and permitted himself a small but delicious smile. And how little they knew, poor fools, that at least they went to their several deaths in a good and just cause! And what a shame that even today there were so few men of vision, to share his, Sam's vision of an America reborn, and revitalized, an America that stood tall once more, that could and would defend its hard-earned place in this scheming, evil, Communist-inspired world. There was simply no one he could talk to, no one with whom he could share his dream. Sam Purcell sighed the sigh of a prophet who knows he must walk alone, who knows that the only judge of heroes is history itself.

The black limousine sped through the outskirts of town. With luck, he could be on the three P.M. jet for London. Not a moment too soon, either. There was work to be done, work that only Sam Purcell could do, work that would be—in all due modesty—of some interest to future historians. Sam Purcell smiled and asked the driver to drive faster. Destiny was not a patient mistress.

Boris Mogador looked alarmed. Nadia hissing was more to be feared than Nadia ranting. This was a strange new Nadia. The screams, the operatic gestures, the threats and curses all were a matter of routine by now. This was Nadia deadly serious, stating facts, not demands. Although, naturally, they really were demands, and monstrously unreasonable at that. "It shall be a pas de quatre, *not* pas de trois. And that is that. And Nadia shall dance in it. You do not—*not*—give the best place on the program to this upstart. Now, Boris, this happens, or Nadia becomes very, very sick. Too sick to dance at all."

"But, Nadia, we've already begun—"

"You think I am blind? You will now unbegin. Begin over again."

"We've given you the whole sceond act of *Swan Lake*."

"And it will be swanless, Boris, unless you do as I say. That is final."

She turned and stormed out of the room.

Boris went instantly to Greg Holden, arbitrator of all such disputes. Secretly Boris hoped Greg would tell Nadia to take a flying fuck back to wherever she came from. Nadia was rapidly getting to be too much. In fact, Nadia was too much to begin with; she was quickly passing the limits of everyone's tolerance. Somewhere, somehow, there had to be a point of no return. As far as Boris was concerned, this was it. He said this to Greg, and Greg nodded in sympathy. For the instant Boris had hopes. Then Holden turned diplomat on him.

"I really think, Boris, that we've got to give in this time. I know it sounds weak, I know she's getting impossible, but we've got to think of the whole scene."

"Meaning?" Boris Mogador was thirty years out of Russia. But he could get very dark-humored and Russian when provoked. And he was provoked.

"Meaning Judith Winchester. She's just waiting for us to make some kind of mistake. If Nadia quits—for whatever reason—Judith will find a way to use it against us. Against me, anyway, but probably against you, too. To put it bluntly, we could both be looking for jobs."

Boris knew that Greg didn't need a job. But his own situation was far different. He lived on his income, and if he was sacked, it would be a serious hardship for him. And for Mrs. Boris. He thought of these things, and saw the wisdom in what Greg said, and hated both Nadia and Judith Winchester for lousing up his beautiful gala with their petty politics and tortured vanities. Boris threw up his hands in a gesture of despair quite worthy of Nadia herself. "What's the use?" he said with a wail, "what's the bloody use? I'll tell the kids."

"Thanks, Boris. Don't think I don't know how you feel. Will they be up in arms?"

"A little. But they're young. They're pros. It's only a one-shot. No, Gregory, it isn't that that makes Boris want to strangle that bitch. It's the bitch herself."

"Plural. Goes for me, too."

"Exactly. A pair of the finest bitches in bitchdom. Why us?"

Boris was smiling now. The dark moods never lasted long. He'd talk to Jenny and Dima and Machito, put the case as Greg had put it, and they'd understand. After all, those kids had all the glory yet to come. Nadia was clinging to the last sunset glow of her fame, shoring up her legend with odd bits of string, with timely dabs of glue. It would be easy to feel sorry for Nadia—if she weren't such a solid-gold piece of one hundred percent bitchery.

"Boris?" Greg had an afterthought.

"Yes?"

"Cheer up, pal. The good guys win in the end."

"Tell that," said Boris with a wicked Russian grin, "to Ivan the Terrible. You forget, my friend, that Boris is Russian. And all Russians know a great secret."

"Which is?"

"In the end, Greg, nobody wins."

He was gone before Greg could reply. *In the end,* thought Greg with a rueful smile, *Nadia gets her pas de quatre. And we? What do we get? A severe dose of the dread Winchester, more likely than not.* He thought of the dread Winchester and wondered if, anywhere, there was a cure for that very special ailment. If there was, it wasn't in this office, not today, not now.

The big panel truck pulled up in front of Dima Lubov's apartment house, and two workmen got out. They opened the front door with a passkey, then unloaded two large panels that looked like glass from the truck and carried them up the three flights of stairs to Dima's apartment.

Four hours later they left as quietly as they had come. Ten minutes after that Dave Loughlin's phone rang at the Delage Feather and Trimming Company. "Yes?" His voice was tense.

"The windows are in."

"And there's no trace, no trace at all?"

"Zero. He'll never know."

"Thanks, Billy." Dave Loughlin hung up the phone and sighed. It was the least he could do for the kid. The workmen had been operating under very special instructions. And the glass was not glass but Lexan, a superstrength, bulletproof material developed for the windshields of jet fighters.

There were just too many convenient rooftops across the street from the Lubov brownstone apartment that offered clear shots to any good marksman. Sam Purcell, Dave knew, was a superb shot who kept his skills polished at the CIA's rifle range twice a week. But even Lexan windows were a pathetic gesture compared to the thousand possible ways Dave could think of to eliminate the young Russian.

The same marksman who might have shot through the apartment window could just as easily pick off the kid when he went in or out of his front door. There was no way to prevent that, this side of chauffeuring Lubov around town in a tank. Dave looked helplessly at the stack of manila folders on his shabby desk. There were seven folders, and five of them were filled with information about dead defectors. The other two belonged to Dimitri Lubov and Sergei Rosoff, the only two remaining alive from the initial list. Rosoff had dropped out of sight—or had been eliminated and no one knew about it. And Lubov was a sitting duck. Or a dancing duck, which was even more vulnerable.

For the third time in three days Dave dialed the CIA head-quarters number in Virginia. Sam's prune-faced Secretary number one picked up the line. Dave's visit had jolted the bullshit out of her; she gave him straight answers now, was convinced Dave possessed that most desirable of all CIA characteristics, "need to know." The woman's voice was half-choked with her reluctance to divulge any information on any subject. If there were a way, thought Dave, for spoken words to wear bright-red top-secret stamps, this bimbo would be the first in line. "Mr. Purcell," she rasped, "is back in town, but he is not available at the moment. I'll tell him you called."

"Thanks. Thanks a lot."

Dave hung up the worn black circa 1945 telephone and looked at it with new animosity. The game was about to begin again. And Dave already knew he was playing against enormous odds.

"Nadia!" Judith Winchester smiled her best little-girl's-birthday smile. "How sweet of you to come, my dear." Judith rose from behind the immense steel desk and greeted her guest with a kiss. "We'll have a cozy little lunch, just the two of us, and then you can get back to rehearsal."

They sat on a low couch that faced a dazzling view of Manhattan through a north window wall, and a maid brought blond Dubonnet on the rocks with a twist of orange.

"Tchin-tchin!" said Nadia festively, raising her glass. "And how thoughtful of you to know my favorite drink."

Judith looked at her and smiled again. *She's aging faster than she knows,* thought Judith. *In a year or so it'll be a question of cosmetic surgery. And yet she claims to be thirty-nine. Well, so did Jack Benny.* Judith sipped the sweetish apertif. *But Nadia will be useful, possibly very useful. Given her natural inclinations, all I'll have to do is aim her in the right direction.* Nadia looked at the vast room with frank interest. She had never been in the inner sanctum before. Nadia wondered what Judith Winchester wanted. For as surely as Tchaikovsky had written *Nutcracker,* she was after something. And its price, Nadia calculated with the instincts of a born courtesan, would not be low.

Judith Winchester's ambitions did not include making the best-dressed lists. Her clothes were beautifully made but somehow not beautiful. There was something invulnerable about her clothes, as though they were made to last forever and would very likely be asked to; it was a look common to the ladies of the British royal family, a kind of militant dowdiness. Today, on her rather severely tailored Chanel-derived (but not Chanel) suit, Judith wore one of her mother's emeralds, a fat cabochon set in Art Deco pavé diamond lattices, with the specific intention of impressing Nadia.

Nadia was famous for her interest in jewelry. Judith had no interest in it whatever. Jewels were eternally beyond manipulation. Still, she knew the spell they could cast, and anything at all that could bring Nadia Beshanskaia more closely into her net was something that Judith considered worthwhile doing. She saw Nadia's hard eyes appraise the even harder emerald. *Burmese*, thought Nadia, *and perfect, too, with that magical blue undertone haunting the green.* Nadia had two such emeralds, though not so large, set as earrings. A maid appeared with luncheon: cold salmon mousse with cucumber salad and a domestic Pinot Chardonnay. For a few moments they traded girlish banalities, fencing; then Judith—characteristically—came straight to the point.

"Tell me, Nadia, about the little Hale creature." The way Judith spoke the word "creature" was a green light, Nadia knew, for any degree of slander. But Nadia was more clever than that. Nadia was, and this newspaper female had best not forget, one of the reigning ballerinas of the world, well able to afford gracious gestures to beginners.

Such gestures as Nadia actually made were superficial only; she felt newcomers should work and scheme as hard as she, Nadia, had done in her time, and still did.

"She has talent," said Nadia softly, almost as though she were speaking to herself: "and she has the dedication—the intensity—that is required. Her technique is of course only beginning to be what, with luck, it may become. Personally, privately, I know her not at all. She strikes me as perhaps a bit colorless."

There! Noncommittal. Erring on the side of kindness, maybe, just a little. But ladylike. Whatever Winchester was fishing for, she'd have to fish a little harder. Nadia tasted the salmon mousse. It might have been pink foam rubber.

"It was against my express wishes," said Judith, "that the girl was brought into the company." Judith looked at her guest, wondering when this vain and silly prima donna would get the hint.

"Well," said Nadia with a gracious laugh, "she does no harm. Dima seems to be in love with her, although one hardly understands why." *She wants*, thought Nadia with a little surge of apprehension, *me to murder the bitch.*

The interview wasn't going at all the way Judith had planned. Toying with a fork, she looked down at her plate, then directly at Nadia. She'd try a new, bolder tack. "The reason I didn't want her, Nadia, my dear, is that I think she was brought into the company on Greg Holden's specific orders in order to undermine you."

Nadia looked up, and Judith was secretly pleased to see the fear crystallizing in her eyes, which widened imperceptibly, by degrees, until they took on the startled and rather glassy look of the eyes of some woodland creature trapped in the headlights of an onrushing car. The message was sinking in.

"Just think, my dear." Judith leaned confidentially across the small table, girl to girl. "Holden is trying to take complete control of the company—business and creative. Boris is his creature. Boris, I know, will do whatever Holden asks. They want to set up their own team, Nadia, against me—against us. Only yesterday Greg was in here with a bunch of plans I simply won't repeat. It would upset you dreadfully."

"You aren't serious!" Nadia's worst fears were realized in Judith's accusations: fear of aging, of losing her talent, of being replaced by someone younger, more beautiful, a better dancer. *So it was happening! Just as she'd always known it would happen.* Nadia bit her lower lip to keep herself from saying something rash. She looked up at Judith. It was a very different look from the one she'd assumed earlier. It was an appeal.

Judith reached across the table and patted her hand comfortingly. "Now, darling, just don't worry. You don't think I'm going to let a stupid aircraft mechanic destroy the ballet company I love on some crazy whim?" Judith sat back and relaxed a little, enjoying the situation. She sipped from her untasted wineglass. "We girls have to stick together, Nadia. That's why I asked you up here today. I'm so glad you came."

"So," said Nadia in a voice so low it might have come out of a trance, "am I."

"If you could have heard"—Judith let her voice trail off provocatively—"but, you're nobody's fool, Nadia. You must have at the very least guessed? Why, they have a schedule.

It's like an invasion plan. They're going to take your best
roles, one after the other, and give them to that scheming
little bitch! Of course, they'll do it subtly—bit by bit. But if
we don't do something conclusive, Nadia, by this time next
year you'll practically be in the corps de ballet. Or out of the
company altogether."

"No!"

"But yes. I consider you the greatest ballerina of your generation, Nadia. To me, you're a poem when you dance.
That's why I wanted to keep Jenny Hale out of the International. I know, darling, that you and I have never exactly
been close friends, but you are a superb, irreplaceable artist!
On those grounds alone, I would fight, and fight hard for you.
But"—Judith paused, for breath, for effect—"there is another
reason. You aren't the only person that Holden man has a
grudge against. I can't think why, but he seems to have taken
some sort of dislike to me. After all I've done. What I think
is we have to find some way to get the Hale girl out of there
and to get Holden out right after her. Do you agree?"

"I . . . I suppose we must do something." Nadia was in
shock. She had lived for so long as a prisoner of her own
fears that this sudden evidence of their coming true was
violently upsetting. Nadia well knew she had enemies. In fact,
she rather enjoyed the scenes that made neutral people into
enemies. But this! This was something else altogether, something that must be dealt with.

Judith pressed an invisible buzzer, and a maid appeared to
take away their luncheon plates. Judith asked for coffee. "I
wish," she said when the maid reappeared with demitasse for
two, "that I had some brilliant plan. But I don't. Not yet. For
the moment, dear Nadia, the burden will have to be on you."

"On me? But what can I do?"

"Show her up for what she is—a scheming little bitch. Out-
dance her at the gala. Don't give her a chance. Fight for every role, demand more roles, better roles. I'll back you up,
whatever you do. Together we can fight this."

Nadia put down her coffee cup and stood to go. "Whatever
I can do, Mrs. Winchester, will be done. You have been most
kind. I thank you."

Judith stood, smiling, and kissed her terrified guest lightly
on the cheek. "Try not to worry, Nadia. Forewarned is
forearmed, don't forget. You'll show Jenny Hale what danc-

ing is all about, and you'll show her at the gala, where all the
world can see. After that, we'll have another little chat and
see what more can be done."

"Thank you," said Nadia in a small and frightened voice
as she fumbled for her purse and left the huge office. Judith
smiled at her retreating back. It had been a very useful
luncheon, if she did say so herself.

The silver-gray Mercedes sedan moved through the gray
morning mist like the ghost of luxury. Sam Purcell's private
automobile had a lot in common with its owner. The car was
quiet, swift and enormously precise. It also had a certain ano-
nymity; the gray Mercedes was not a car you'd easily remember. Sam drove skillfully and fast, but not fast enough to
arouse the interest of any radar-happy highway patrolman.
He thought of the package in the trunk of the car and
smiled.

He drove past the suburban sprawl of Washington, past the
piny-scrub fields and into the foothills of the Allegheny
Mountains. Sam turned off the highway after an hour and
wove his knowing way through a maze of ever-narrowing
country roads. At last the big chain fence told him he was
nearly there. He drove on a red-clay-dirt road for two miles
along the fence, then braked and swerved left at the deserted,
double-padlocked gate. The well-oiled padlocks responded
easily to his keys.

Sam drove through the big gate, stopped the car and pad-
locked the gate behind him. The clay-dirt road wound deep
into a pine woods with no apparent purpose. After a bit more
than a mile of woods the road threaded its way into a huge
clearing.

The fenced-in land was an old, abandoned U.S. Army Artillery practice range left over from World War II, which had
been retained for the exclusive use of the Technical Services
Division of the Central Intelligence Agency. Sam Purcell had
seen to it that the old range would be his alone on this gray
Monday morning in January. It was cold enough for snow,
but the snow hadn't come. Good. It was a good sign when
the small details began going your way, right from the beginning.

The old spotting tower stood tall in the empty field,
guardian of foxes and jackrabbits, of deer and the lonely
wind. The tower was big, solid and still sturdy thirty years af-

ter its abandonment. The tower was square and tapering, and you climbed it on steps that paralleled the squared-off tapering sides as they climbed. Sam was grateful for that, considering what he'd have to carry up those stairs. A ladder might have been risky. Sam trusted TSD, but only so far.

He stopped the car at the edge of the woods, maneuvering it under some feathery pine branches so that even in this totally fenced-in, isolated and secure retreat it would be tough to spot unless you were specifically looking for it. Habit. Sam grinned. He hadn't been tailed. That was sure. Sam would bet his life on that. In a way he *was* betting his life on it.

The artillery spotting tower had three platforms, boxed in at waist height. The first platform, Sam knew, was only twenty feet above the ground. Too low. The top level was two hundred feet: too high. But the middle level was within two feet of perfection. It was very nearly the same height above the ground as the fourth balcony of the New York State Theater at Lincoln Center was above the stage.

Sam walked to the tower, looked up and all around him—habit again, you never really knew—then he picked up a fallen stick, paced off forty-three steps, heel and toe, precisely the horizontal distance from the tower to the imaginary stage. Where the forty-third step ended, Sam Purcell drew a long, straight, line at right angles to the east face of the spotting tower. Sam drew the line for about thirty feet, turned and drew another line in the red dirt, parallel to the first, but about a foot farther away from the tower. Then he drew still a third line, at right angles to the two long lines, close to the tower. This marked the proscenium arch of the theater. The outside line was the actual edge of the stage. The inside line was his safety margin. From the short line marking the proscenium, Sam paced twelve steps, keeping carefully just inside the second of his two long lines. Then he stopped, turned to face the tower, bowed to the pine woods and smiled a thin and mirthless smile.

He took the stick and drew a circle around himself as he stood there. Sam moved three paces to his right and drew another circle in the dirt. Three paces beyond that he drew another. And another. The gala announcement had specified a pas de quatre. Sam couldn't be sure which position would belong to Dimitri Lubov. No matter. The range and the trajectory were all that really mattered. Last-minute adjustments were to be expected.

Satisfied with his strange hieroglyphics in the dirt, Sam walked briskly back to the Mercedes. Thank God there was no wind. He opened the car's trunk and carefully unwrapped the florist's box from its steel-mesh and asbestos-quilted demolition-squad blanket. Gently, handling the box like a newborn baby, Sam lifted it out of the trunk. Holding the long, green cardboard container in both hands, he walked back to the tower and climbed the stairs to the second level.

Kneeling slowly, Sam lowered the box to the floor of the landing. Only then did he open it.

Inside the florist's box were six identical bouquets of yellow tea roses, two dozen to the bunch. They were surrounded prettily with maidenhair fern and encased in old-fashioned paper-lace doilies. Around each bouquet was a bright-red silk ribbon with trailing ends.

Gingerly, like a surgeon choosing a scalpel, Sam picked up a bouquet from the left side of the box. He balanced it in one hand, then picked up another bouquet, this from the right side of the box. Yes. He had balanced the weights perfectly. Setting down the bouquet in his right hand, Sam advanced to the edge of the platform with the other bouquet. The deeply scratched lines were clearly visible below. And still, blessedly, there was no wind. Swinging his throwing arm a few times to get the rhythm, Sam scaled the bouquet down toward the red-clay "stage." It had just enough substance. Two dozen was definitely the right amount of flowers.

The bouquet sailed lazily through the chill January morning, turning over and over on itself, and finally landed just inside the nearest of the two long parallel lines defining the imaginary stage. Close, but not close enough. Sam reached for another dummy bouquet, reconsidered his trajectory, took a practice swing and hurled it toward the hypothetical stage. It felt better even as it left his hand. The ribbons were doing just what Sam had intended they do; they called attention to the flying flowers. At the end of a gala there would be hundreds of balletomanes flinging flowers on stage as the stars took their final bows. *Final*, thought Sam as he watched this second bouquet falling and turning toward the ground, *was the word for it.*

The second bouquet was right on the mark. It landed exactly in the middle of the first of Sam's circles. The ribbons floated gracefully as a kite's tail as the flowers fell; it would be noticed by the Russian boy, Sam was sure of it, a charming gesture, he'd think, to snatch the flying bouquet out of midair and present it to his ballerina. It was an impact-detonated explosive; the slightest pressure would set it off once the thrower released a hidden pin.

Satisfied with his trajectory, Sam reached for the bouquet on the right. He picked it up, examined it closely with the dedication of a born gardener seeking out Japanese beetles, then stuck one slim finger through the ferns and clicked a miniature switch. His hand swept back in the now-familiar swing and came smoothly forward. The yellow bouquet sailed prettily over the rough wooden barrier and somersaulted gracefully toward the stage drawn on the red Virginia dirt below.

It landed exactly where Sam intended, just to the left of the second dummy bouquet. But when this bouquet landed, it exploded with a satisfying, if muffled, roar. And where it hit a small crater appeared, perhaps a foot wide by six inches deep. This was a very precisely calculated charge. Sam had no intention of wiping out the entire International Ballet Theater's roster of stars. One would be more than enough, and the explosive within the slim green-painted metallic cone that stuffed the bottom of the yellow bouquet had been calculated to do just that, no more and no less.

Sam Purcell stood tall and stretched his chilly arms and smiled the broad, all-embracing smile of a contented man. He looked down at his handiwork with satisfaction. There were two more loaded bouquets ready in the florist's box. Carefully, deliberately, Sam threw them after the others. His control grew better. The second bomb and the third worked perfectly. He looked at the one remaining dummy bouquet and decided not to throw it. They were so pretty, the yellow roses. If he got back home before lunch, and put them in water, they'd probably last all week.

Sam climbed down from the tower and picked up all the debris he could find, sweeping it into a black plastic garbage can liner he'd brought for the purpose. Then he broke off a small pine branch and brushed away the lines he'd drawn in the dirt. The next rain would erase them entirely. Then, after loading the garbage bag and the one remaining dummy bouquet into the trunk of the Mercedes, Sam started the car and headed back toward his big old Georgian-style brick house on the outskirts of McLean, Virginia.

And as he drove, as the heat from the car's heating system

warmed him, Sam Purcell felt another, better kind of warmth come flushing through his lean body. It was the warmth of contentment, of satisfaction in the sure knowledge that a worthwhile project was coming to fruition, and soon, and entirely because of his foresight, his vision, his technical skills. It was the feeling all good workmen must have, Sam reflected, as they see a hard job coming together at last. It was a very American kind of feeling, a combination of courage and sweat and pure patriotism of the sort that wasn't fashionable anymore, except for what lingered on in a few of the old-timers, a few lonely, dedicated men like Sam Purcell. Sam smiled his tight little smile and stepped harder on the gas. Lubov, Sam felt, was as good as dead. Now it was Dave's turn, good old slow-thinking Dave, and his fat friend.

CHAPTER
❧ 13 ❧

Jenny and Dimitri lay back against a fortress of pillows watching *The Gay Divorcee* on late-night television. Dima was a late-blossoming TV fanatic, and of all the things he liked to watch, the old movies of Fred Astaire ranked first, second and third. Astaire was a cult figure for most of the younger ballet dancers, for they saw in his fluid movement, and his seamless choreography the touch of a master artist and a true pro; he made the impossible look effortless, and that is what ballet is all about.

Fred and Ginger were about to go into their famous dance to the music of "Night and Day." Dima and Jenny watched in silence, holding hands like teenagers, fascinated. When the lovely dance was over, he turned to her. "One take, *deushka*. He rehearsed for weeks. Weeks and weeks. Is stupendous."

"And Boris is giving us all of four days for the new pas de quatre. Is not stupendous." She giggled. "And I don't even have the benefit of Ginger's ostrich feathers."

It was Monday. The gala was Friday. Dima and Jenny had picked their own pas de deux for the first half of the program, *Corsaire*. They already knew it, it was one of Dima's favorites and it would present no problem for them. The new, hastily revised pas de quatre, now including Nadia, was something else. Boris had hoped for something spectacular in his first concept of a pas de trois for Jenny and Dima and Machito. Now, the basic compromise having been made, he'd settle for something attractive, something adequate. He had decided on three Chopin waltzes, on very simple white costumes, on trading drama and innovation for elegance and style. Jenny knew she'd shine in *Corsaire*. And she knew Boris was for her, that he'd make sure that she and Nadia were treated equally in the new dance. Yet still Jenny was apprehensive. She could feel the hostile vibrations from Nadia. She also felt the nervousness any sensitive beginner feels in a completely new environment.

A great deal of the routine in the International was reassuringly similar to the routine Jenny had grown up in, in the Civic Ballet. Classes, for instance, were very nearly the same here and probably everywhere, and conducted in French as everywhere. The sweat and the strain and the technical problems were the same. The attitude of most of the dancers was similar. But the Civic had no Nadia, no Judith, no unexplored emotional obstacle courses to trouble Jenny. Well, she had made her choice and didn't regret it. Still, the uneasiness stayed with her. Maybe it was going to be a permanent part of her life. Not even Dima's love, and reassurances, and physical presence seemed to put the tension to rest.

She looked at him. "Nadia," Jenny said quietly, "would like to murder me."

"Ultimately Nadia does in Nadia. Drowns in a sea of jealousy."

"When we're both onstage, in the pas de quatre, who's going to look at me when they can be looking at her?"

"That is what Nadia hopes. Her arrogance makes her blind, *deushka*. She will learn, to her sorrow, who they look at." Dima put his arm around her then, buried his head in the small warm hollow where Jenny's slender neck joined her shoulder. "You must not think of Nadia. Think of Jenny. Think of Jenny and Dima. Of tomorrow. For," he continued, pausing only to kiss her, "tomorrow has no Nadia in it. Nadia is the wicked witch who melts in the last act." And soon the thought of Nadia was melted by the act of love.

Sam had never counted the ways he knew to kill people. For Sam, the skills of dealing out death had long since passed from craft into art; he approached each new challenge as a painter might come to a fresh, blank canvas. The impulse might always be the same, but the method and the result allowed for infinite variety. Maybe it was the potential for creativity that fascinated Sam most: setting the stage, refining his timing, attending to all the dozens of details that divided art from manual labor. And always Sam kept the final picture firmly in mind, his effect as he intended the world to see it.

Sam had been thinking about Dave Loughlin's death, and Ivan's, too, for several days now. That it must be done was beyond question. The only problem was exactly how, precisely where and when. Even the "when" almost answered itself: very soon. Before the International Ballet's gala, Dave Loughlin must die, and Ivan with him.

The classic solution would have been to stage a shoot-out: Dave killing Ivan, who in turn would shoot Dave. Heroic agent gives his life in the eternal struggle against Communism. Sam liked the ring of it, but he knew too well how tough it would be to stage such an episode convincingly, and alone. Ivan was fair game; if he or any other KGB agent, in the country illegally, vanished, who could protest? Dave Loughlin was the real obstacle, Dave with his known position in the CIA, with his wife and kids on Staten Island, with his reputation for an almost boring integrity.

The shoot-out might be impossible, but Sam's fertile brain soon invented something just as good, and far easier to pull off alone. Having thought of the plan and an alternate, having checked and rechecked the possibilities for error, Sam Purcell leaned back in his leather wing chair and smiled. Tomorrow, Wednesday, he'd do it. Friday was the gala. It would all be over by the weekend. Maybe he could even get in some golf.

Nadia, thought Jenny Hale with uncharacteristic suspicion, *is being much too nice. She has to be up to something.* It was the second of their four days of rehearsal for the Chopin waltz pas de quatre. Nadia was being kind, charming, witty, generous in small ways. Nadia was being, in other words, absolutely unlike the Nadia the ballet world had known and hated for more than twenty years.

Still, the rehearsals were going well, the dance would be quite lovely, and why look a gift kindness in the mouth? Jenny watched the older woman now, as Nadia flirted charmingly with Machito, who—being Machito—flirted right back. Yes, it was all just a few degrees too perfect. Something had turned Nadia from Nadia into a candy-box cartoon of a gracious ballerina. It was not, Jenny sensed, a role in which Nadia found herself at ease.

Then the music started up again, and Jenny was too busy to think about anything beyond the complicated enchaînment that Boris had devised for her.

"There is no way," said Dave Loughlin with the utter certainly of one who has thought out a problem long and hard, "to make that theater secure. Even if we had unlimited police and security men—or even my own guys—we still couldn't do it. And never forget, old chum, we still don't have one scrap of real evidence that what we think might happen actually will happen." Dave and Ivan were having coffee in a drugstore on Broadway down from Lincoln Center.

"What about the gates they have at your airports these days to detect guns and so forth? They must be portable?"

"They'd never allow it, Ivan. That's be the same as closing down the theater. You've got to remember this—"

"Is a free country? Don't I know it, old buddy-roo. Free to have every dope fiend in the gutter clanking with handguns. Free to make sure murders have more rights and privileges than you do. This is a free country all right, Davey, old fart—especially if you're a crook."

"Ask our former President about that."

"We must stop the boy from dancing." Ivan had the Russian's inborn love of dancing; if Dima Lubov had been a plumber, Ivan's sympathy might not have had such a keen edge.

"You think he'd buy that?"

"No. But I think you should try."

"I'll try anything." Dave looked into the bottom of his coffee cup as though he were looking into his own grave. They sensed, but didn't know for sure, that Sam would be making his move soon. Dave had just come back from a meeting with the head security officer at the theater. The officer had been polite, interested and absolutely unable to do anything more than offer minimal cooperation. Now would anyone help, until Dave came up with some real evidence. There was an efficient plainclothes security staff on guard at every performance, and this would be augmented for the gala. A drop, Dave knew, in the bucket.

There was no question of searching the gala patrons; they'd be some of the fanciest people in the city, fancy and well connected and not about to tolerate crap like that. Especially on the grounds of no real evidence at all. Yes, they'd cooperate with any extra men Dave chose to bring in. As long as those men were in plain clothes and very discreet. Dave sensed the grudging quality of the man's offer and sympathized. It probably did sound wacky. Hell, it was wacky. Insane, to be specific. Dave sighed, and finished his coffee, and decided to pay a visit to Dima Lubov that same night.

Once again Sam Purcell was grateful for the CIA helicopter. He could never have risked taking the commercial shuttle to New York, not with the contents of his luggage being what they were: Three identical green cones from TSD would undoubtedly arouse suspicions, not to mention the two .38 caliber Walther automatics from his private stock of unregistered weapons. Sam stood on the landing pad in his old gray tweed topcoat, hatless in the wind, waiting for the chopper. It was one minute late. He waved at the pilot and ducked under the whirring rotors and climbed up the ladder, carrying only his worn attaché case and the Washington *Post*. It was always good to have something to read on the flight.

Dave Loughlin had taken a chance in not going through official channels in contacting Dima. He didn't want to alarm the whole ballet company. He didn't want to alarm the boy either, but that might be unavoidable. Disaster might be unavoidable, too, Dave thought as he rang Dima's doorbell that night at eight P.M. *How easy it is,* he thought, *the boy doesn't know me from Adam. I could be Sam. I could be anyone.* The buzzer rang. Dave let himself in and climbed the steps.

The boy opened the door wide and stood backlit in the beckoning frame; a perfect target, the kid was already dead. There hadn't even been a chain lock on the door. Dave repressed a shudder. "Mr. Lubov?"

"I am he."

The boy smiled. He looked about eighteen.

"I'm David Loughlin, Central Intelligence Agency."

"Yes. Come in." The boy stood back, and Dave walked into the room. No sign of the girl. It was a nice room, Dave thought, not fussy.

Lubov motioned Dave to a chair, took his coat, offered tea. Dave refused. The boy sat down. Blue jeans, scuffed cowboy boots, a dark, expensive-looking sweater. He might have been a casual-rich college kid. Anything but the world's hottest male dancer. Anything but a name on a murderer's death list.

"This is not really an official visit, Mr. Lubov." The boy's eyebrows raised slightly, inquiring. "But we have reason to believe. . . ." The official language rang falsely in Dave's ear as he spoke it. What must it sound like to Lubov, fresh from a country where police visits, official or not, were the stuff of nightmares? Ivan had briefed him well, but maybe not well enough. The boy listened politely, with no sign of fear or apprehension. "We have reason to believe that someone may try to harm you."

"Harm? What harm?"

"Did you know Gaia Muldovska?"

"I know who Gaia is—was. Not personally."

"Madame Muldovska was one of seven people whose names have been found on a certain list. All the names belong to well-known defectors from Russia. Of the seven names, five are dead. The list was planted on a KGB agent whose suicide was faked in Paris a few months ago."

"My name is on this list?" The deep-blue eyes got maybe a shade deeper, but they didn't blink or waver. The face didn't change.

"I'm afraid so. And we feel the trouble may not be over. What I hope to do—and again, please understand this is unofficial—is to get you to take a little holiday. Not to perform in public for a while."

"Is impossible." The boy smiled a thin, not very humorous smile. Dave suddenly realized what might be going through his mind.

"You come," Dimitri continued, "out of the night and tell me I am going to be killed, that I must stop dancing. I don't know who you are. Is impossible. Thank you in any case."

"You're in danger, Mr. Lubov."

"Dancers are always in danger. Is dangerous profession." The boy stood up, nervous, pacing. "Is possible you are right. Is possible you are not right. In any case, one must dance."

"You think this is some kind of a joke . . . a trick?" Dave heard his voice rising. He hadn't meant it to rise.

"Perhaps. Perhaps not. Ultimately it matters not. Ultimately Lubov must dance."

Dave stood up and reached for his wallet. The boy flinched just a little. *He thinks I'm pulling a gun. That's how stupid he is. If I'd been Sam, the kid would have been cooling ten minutes ago.* Dave got the worn billfold out and produced an identity card. Wordlessly he handed it to the boy.

"Is very beautiful."

"You don't believe it?"

"I am only slowly learning to read English. Please forgive.

In any case, does a paper make you right? Does it make me dead or not a dancer?"

"We're only trying to protect you."

"I am sure."

Suddenly Dave felt the anger rushing through him. It wasn't aimed at young Lubov, not necessarily; it was a pure hot wave of frustration at the whole goddamn situation. He felt helpless, and the helplessness itself fueled the anger. Dave suddenly bent down, pulled off his shoe and hurled it violently at the big brownstone window. Glass would have shattered. The heavy shoe hit with a sharp crack and bounced harmlessly off the Lexan pane. Dimitri Lubov watched in fascination. Dave hobbled to his shoe and put it back on. Then he stood up, the anger gone. "I'm sorry. I had to do something to show you—I mean business. That isn't glass, as you might guess. It's bulletproof, a special material. We had it installed two weeks ago. That's how worried we are."

"Thank you. Is good of you to care. I am not even a citizen. But still, I cannot stop dancing."

The boy shrugged, a small motion of his athlete's shoulders, and even though he might be shrugging his life away in that same gesture, Dave Loughlin knew he'd run into a brick wall—and a Russian brick wall at that. The boy had a kind of built-in gallantry, an offhand bravery that Dave had almost forgotten about. Lubov came up to Dave, touched his shoulder and smiled a gentle smile. Lubov was about five-six to Dave's six-one, and the kid looked younger than Dave's oldest boy, who'd be graduating from high school next June. But the strongest and the most philosophical man in that room wasn't Dave Loughlin.

"Please do not think, Mr. Laklan," said Dima softly, "that I am either stupid or suspicious. Is not that. But you ask what no real dancer can give. This threat, this harm—when will it happen?"

"I don't know."

"So ultimately, is not one night, one week, I must not dance, but perhaps I should be hiding forever?"

"I just can't answer that. Not forever."

"In a dancer's life forever comes faster than to most people. At—let us say—forty the prime is past. To lose one night is to lose something that disappears forever. I must live my life, while I live it, as a dancer. You understand this?"

"I understand." Dave felt the helplessness enveloping him

like a shroud. "Can I leave you an emergency phone number, where you can reach me anytime—should something unusual happen?"

"Of course."

"Here." Dave had set up a twenty-four-hour hot line and written down its number before the meeting.

Lubov took the card and looked at it for an instant, then looked at Dave. "Is only me on this list? Of the dancers, I mean. Not Jenny Hale?"

"Only you. She shouldn't be in danger." *Unless,* thought Dave, *Sam gets desperate, gets careless, wants a big spectacular last act.* "Whoever is doing this has been all too precise in the past."

"Precise." The boy smiled an unreadable smile. "I see. Thank you for trying to help, Mr. Laklan."

"Good luck." They shook hands. Dave turned and walked down the carpeted brownstone stairs, admiring the kid's guts in spite of the fact that Dimitri Lubov's very indifference to death might kill the boy. As he turned on the landing, a skinny young girl with huge gray eyes came up the stairs two at a time, looking like one of the Dead End Kids in her worn Navy-surplus pea jacket and knit woolen cap. Jenny Hale. Dave wondered if the Lubov kid would be able to keep his mouth shut, whether he'd spend the rest of the night telling the Hale child of the danger. She might be able to make him go into protective custody for a while. But no. Dave remembered the boy's calm eyes, the quiet determination in everything he had said. No, the boy wouldn't tell. And the girl wouldn't make him do anything he didn't feel like doing, not Jenny Hale or Cleopatra herself. Dave sighed and stepped out into the suddenly foggy January night, wondering as he walked to the waiting car if the twenty-four-year-old sensation of the International Ballet Theater were ever going to see twenty-five.

She was in the door and kissing himself just as he set the hot teapot on a trivet. "Who was that man?"

"A sad man, whom ultimately I could not help." Dima held her close and felt the warmth and strength in his own body enclosing the electric tension that raced through hers. Jenny sensed that this was something Dima didn't want to talk about. She was surprised when he added, "It was something about my citizenship. Defectors cannot simply go through the mill like other people."

"You'll get it."

"Yes, this is what he said. But perhaps it takes a bit longer." He kissed her again, and they sat down with their tea and talked of other things.

Sam Purcell checked into his apartment in the Beekman Tower Hotel Tuesday morning and spent most of the afternoon shopping. He got back to the hotel at three-forty-five, made tea in the little kitchenette, then reached for the telephone. Sam's first call was to a small but efficient theatrical booking agency. His second call was to the Delage Feather and Trimming Company.

Dave Loughlin answered the phone himself. "Yes?"

"Well, David, old sport," began a voice that knew it didn't have to identify itself, "maybe it's time we had a little chat about the Alfalfa sale. Do you agree?"

"I sure do." Dave tried to keep the fear out of his voice. He had known the summons would come sooner or later. In a way he was glad it was sooner. Whatever came of it. Anything was better than simply waiting, in the dark, fearing the worst. Or almost anything.

"I'm in town for a few days, Dave, and tomorrow morning looks pretty clean." Clean. That was another one of the old code words. A person, a situation, a safe house—anything uncluttered with menace was "clean." Dave wondered what the next morning's chances were of truly being clean. He stopped the ironic laugh while it was still building in his throat. Not funny, not funny at all, and definitely not clean.

"I am," said Dave heavily, "at your service." Redundant. And a lie at that. In the web Sam Purcell wove even lies were getting redundant, and death, and maybe even Dave's own feeble tries at stopping the slaughter. "Just say where and when."

"You know the little park at the United Nations?"

"Sure."

"Go in the main gate—the visitors' gate—on First Avenue at Forty-sixth street. Walk straight ahead down the steps, past that big Russian statue, the sword-into-plowshare bronze. Right up to the rail. Turn left. I'll be down at the end of the path, feeding sea gulls. Ten o'clock OK?"

"Ten's fine." Fine as things go for confrontation and maybe for death.

"I look forward to it. I may have thought of a solution to the whole alfalfa question."

"Congratulations." There was a click, not an answer.

Jessica Privet put down her teacup with a small, decisive click. Her companion merely smiled his serene, yet somehow mischievous smile. "I'm pushing sixty and no bargain, Gerald."

"It's time, my dear. There is a time for all things, and this is ours." He reached out and touched her hand, tentatively, a small boy's touch.

He's been widowed twelve years, she thought, *and for eleven of them he has been faithful to me. In return for nothing. Well, almost nothing.*

The Tuesday and Thursday afternoons hadn't really been nothing. At times, when Jenny was entirely absorbed in her dancing, when Clifford Hale had been driving her nearly frantic with worry and, yes, with the cold prospect of poverty, that, too, these afternoons at the rectory with Gerald Lanier had been a kind of salvation.

Many had been the times when the generous old-fashioned Anglican high tea had taken the edge off her hunger. And always, always the soul of generosity, there had been Gerald at the door when she left with a small paper sack of goodies for Jenny. And for this, he had asked nothing but her companionship.

Jessica would pour at the parish teas, would help him with lists and the small desperate politics of ladies' committees of the parish. With good deeds and good companionship and these quiet afternoons their small beginning of a friendship had slowly, slowly grown into something more than friendship, yet still, Jessica thought, less than love. And always, when she thought of Gerald Lanier, Privy thought of Jenny, then Jenny and Dima Lubov. There was love! She blinked and felt his hand. Such thoughts! And at her age. And at his! It was surely not love, this thing between them. And still, still, it was precious to her. She looked at Gerald, smiling, and thought: *He has never been to the apartment. We have never been out at night. He has never seen Jenny dance.*

"And would it be so terrible, Jessica, to be the bishop's wife?"

"Gerald! They did it!" She leaned across the old mahogany tea table and kissed his check. Not a lover's kiss, but deeply felt nonetheless. The vacancy had just come open, and Gerald had long been overdue for such an honor.

"So I am given to understand." His hand tightened on hers. "She doesn't need you so much now, Jessica. You have given what she needed, and more, and for all these years."

"While you waited. I couldn't help that. There was no one."

"What you did, my dear, was beautiful. It made me realize exactly what a treasure had popped up on my humble doorstep. But life is a moving river, Jessica, and we must move with it or, at the least, try to."

"Spoken like a bishop born to the cloth."

"Marry me, Jessica."

She looked at him. She, who had always prided herself on being resourceful, independent, beholden to no one. But that was a lie. She was beholden to Gerald Lanier. Had been, too, and for many a year. She looked at his face, such a good and good-natured face that she had come to take it for granted the way she might take a sunny day for granted. It was not a face that broke hearts or led armies. But it was a kind face, and intelligent, and it held a sense of fun and of discovery. And, Privy suddenly realized with more than a bit of a jolt, it held love. For a moment she could say nothing. The words were there, but they caught in her throat. And when they came out, they didn't come smoothly. "I . . . I'd be honored and very proud . . . to be your wife." Suddenly she was crying. And suddenly he had taken her in his arms and was kissing her, and the cold wall of the future melted into something warm and happy.

Ivan Sokolovny sipped the warm red wine and looked sadly at his old friend. "He will kill you."

"He might." As he said those words, Dave Loughlin got a surprise. The surprise was that he suddenly realized he didn't care. All he wanted to do was stop Sam Purcell, stop the killing. Any way he could. Whatever it cost. What was his life, that it should pain him so much to leave it? Dave thought of Effie and his four kids. They'd be all right. What kind of husband or father had he been lately anyway? His bride was bourbon whiskey, and his kids were turning into rebellious strangers. And Sam Purcell had to be stopped. If he, Dave

Loughlin, longtime patsy for the Old Man, didn't have the brains to do it, maybe—just maybe—he had the guts. And maybe tomorrow morning would tell about that. One way or the other. "He might," said Dave, again, as much to himself as to Ivan.

"Ten, he told you, at the UN park?"

"Yes. Ten. A.M."

"It's a setup, old chum, old fart. Davey the sitting duck. I'll have him staked out."

"No, you won't." Dave looked at Ivan. It was all there: the friendship, which Dave now knew to be true. And the despair—that was in Ivan's face now, too. He didn't expect to see Dave Loughlin alive again and wasn't even taking the trouble to hide that fact. "I've told you before, Ivan, Sam Purcell wrote the book. He'd spot you and take his ass away from there, and we wouldn't know which end was up."

"We don't really know that now, do we? And, Davey, while your faith in this man is a pure and touching thing, perhaps it is time you knew there are other books. That man didn't write all the books in the world. No one did."

Ivan left it at that; the subject was beginning to bore him. They paid the restaurant check—Ivan's treat—and walked out into the night.

Nadia's response to her interview with Judith Winchester had slowly evolved from raw shock through terror into a kind of numb confusion. She must do something, something demonstrable. Something against the little Hale creature. Judith's word: "creature."

Nadia was capable of violence; many a dish had been hurled by those slender hands, many a face had been slapped. But always in anger, always in the heat of the moment's passion. Nadia was capable of scheming, too; in fact it was perhaps her favorite occupation other than dancing. But the idea of deliberately sabotaging Jenny in some physical way was repellent to Nadia. Like every dancer, Nadia had heard the old stories of nineteenth-century rivalries in which the straps of costumes were cut through, broken glass secreted in toe shoes, itching powder substituted for talcum. But that was long ago, and if anything similar had happened lately, it would be news to Nadia Beshanskaia. And, she knew, the retribution for any such pranks would be sudden, legal and very public. No! There had to be another answer, another way to vanquish the threat of Jenny Hale without putting her own reputation in jeopardy.

Nadia finished dressing for rehearsal, a procedure very nearly as painstaking as dressing for the performance itself. Let the others come dragging into the hall any which way, no makeup on the girls, all in rags and tatters! Nadia would remain Nadia, perfectly groomed and with her wits about her. With all the force of her shrewd brain concentrating on one problem, the problem of effectively eliminating Jenny Hale from the International Ballet Theater.

It was a morning like every other morning in Dave Loughlin's brown-shingled two-family house on Staten Island. The kids were nearly late for school, too noisy, fighting among themselves over things Dave didn't understand or care about. The paint was flaking in the corner of the kitchen ceiling again, which meant the roof of the little kitchen extension he'd added on three years ago was leaking again, damn green wood the contractor used, and overcharged him in the bargain. Effie looked tired. As always. The toast was underdone. Dave wiped his mouth with a paper napkin—the cheapest grade; Effie could never bring herself to buy the better ones—stood up, grabbed his old brown tweed topcoat and kissed his wife on the forehead. Just like every day.

Only Dave Loughlin knew too well that this day was special. This was a day he very well might not come back from. He tried not to look Effie in the eye, fighting the fear he'd give something away. So he kissed her a little faster than usual, made a show of looking at his watch and rushed out of the house, narrowly missing disaster in the form of Judy's stray ice skate, which she'd left on the second of the three worn wooden front-porch steps. "And make that damned kid pick her skates up!" Dave yelled as he strode down the hill toward the ferry building, thinking as he walked that those would hardly do as the last words of a loving father to his family.

Dave got a second cup of coffee on the ferry and took the styrofoam container up front. The huge old ferryboat was only half-filled now, nine-fifteen, a bit after the regular nine-to-fiver's crush. The day matched his mood; it was cold and gray. The improbable towers of lower Manhattan came floating at him like so many big slate dominoes against a shirt-cardboard sky. And somewhere under that wet gray sky Sam Purcell was waiting, primed to kill, planning—what?

The ferry lurched to a halt in its berth, shuddered twice and opened its gates. Dave was among the first off. And he was running late; it was nearly quarter to ten, he'd have to take a cab. An empty yellow Checker came by instantly, so fast that Dave did a double take; could this be a setup by Sam? He didn't know the driver. Of course, he wouldn't know the driver, if Sam Purcell had set it up. The Old Man hadn't got to be the Old Man by using obvious assassins. Dave forced himself into the cab and gave the address.

The driver could really drive. That made Dave suspicious, too: your typical New York cabby was a spastic, psychotic speed freak and more often than not hardly able to read or write. Dave was all for hiring the handicapped, only not in jobs that risked people's lives. This kid could drive; he was quiet, clean-cut, straw-haired, polite. Very untypical. Looked a little like the Lubov boy. Dave got over wondering when the cabby was going to pull the gun, or the knife, or the switch that locked all the doors from the front. It didn't happen. The car flowed smoothly into the traffic of the FDR Drive. Dave grinned as the figures clicked up and up on the taxi meter; it'd be a four-fifty ride. On Sam Purcell. He imagined Sam signing the expense voucher, as he had signed so many in the past. If Dave lived to fill out the voucher.

He tried to remember the way his CIA insurance policy read, just what the death benefits were. Well, trust the good old Civil Service. It'd take care of Effie and the kids. There would be a cash settlement; Effie'd get his pension; there was mortgage insurance on the house; they could go right on living there; there'd be Social Security, a special fund for sending the kids to college—if the kids buckled down enough ever to get into college. *That's just great, Dave,* he told himself, *that is absolutely swell. Keep this up, and you'll talk yourself right into the grave.*

He shook his head like a big dog shaking off water, blinked his eyes and saw the UN Secretariat looming dead ahead, a huge sugar cube wrapped in black glass. In Dave's frame of mind it looked exactly like a great shiny tombstone.

The cab swung off the drive and turned right on First Avenue, glided past the shallow arc of the free world's flags, flapping wetly against the dull sky above, and pulled up at the Forty-Sixth Street visitor's entrance.

There were no tourists at the UN. The chartered buses of uncomprehending schoolchildren from the suburbs hadn't begun their daily migration. The snow that had barely dusted Staten Island had fallen more thickly on Manhattan, leaving a slushy inch, maybe an inch and a half on the granite terrace. Dave walked slowly across the terrace, slow and alone, conscious of himself as a target, moving but nevertheless a very good target indeed.

No one tried to stop his gentle progress toward the river. The guard at the gate stayed at the gate, a New York guard, well used to crazies. To his left Dave saw the huge horse's ass of a bad equestrian statue mounted on a tall rectangle of granite as gray as the sky, the horse and its nameless rider patinaed green and bleeding green onto the granite base. Dave wondered for the hundredth time whose statue it was, what tin hero galloped forever in place, sword raised, charging the cold, expensive luxury of the twin co-op towers of UN Plaza.

Dave crossed the big terrace and walked down the steps at the left. Two long allées of gravel edged with razor-cut boxwood ran parallel to the river. Halfway down the near allée a small yellow snow plow patiently chugged its way toward Dave, redundantly scraping the snow that was hardly deep enough to plow. Somewhere underneath this park, the busy FDR Drive spewed cars in and out of town, but its noise was muffled to a distant hum, and all Dave heard was the chuga-chuga of the plow and gulls, screaming. The river was gray, surly, threatening. As if Dave needed help feeling threatened. The path was virgin slush, unmarked by any footprints but the ones Dave made as he strode to the rail.

And there was Sam. Or, anyway, one tall lone individual in gray tweed standing just where Sam said he'd be, way down the river walk at the UN Plaza end of the park, standing at the rail with a brown paper bag, feeding sea gulls. Sam. The Old Man. Dave gave no sign, kept walking, slowly, head down, gloved hands at his sides, swinging to the laggard pace, feeling the weight of the revolver in his shoulder holster, far heavier than pounds or ounces, a gun he knew he'd probably never use on Sam.

Sam.

Dave walked the hundred and fifty yards as though they were the last mile. The luxury apartments rose disdainfully from behind the tall gray shape that was Sam Purcell. Ten o'clock in the morning. They'd be having their second cup of coffee, the ladies who lived in those hundred-thousand-dollar co-ops, the men, if there were men, having long gone off to Wall Street or the ad agency or wherever the money came from. And the women would be sleek, expensive women, nothing out of place, having their second cup of coffee and maybe phoning the florist about tonight's dinner party, or a girlfriend for a spot of gossip, or an employment agency about the new laundress, or the dean of Billy's school because he simply did not understand the boy's problem. And what would they see, those ladies, if they should deign to look out of their big plate-glass windows? Dave Loughlin dead in the slush with a brown paper bag next to him and the sea gulls gathering?

But they wouldn't look. They'd be casing their expensively filled closets now, the women, wondering what to wear to Caravelle or Lutece, wondering if the day was too gray for brown silk, wishing for lovers, moving a heavy silver picture frame two inches to the left. No, they wouldn't look. Nor would the thousand busy-beaver clerks and typists and interpreters of the United Nations be looking his way. It would be him, and Sam, and a few impartial sea gulls. Except maybe the gulls weren't so impartial. Sam, after all, was feeding them.

Dave was much closer now. Less than fifty yards. Sam was Sam, sure enough. Sam gave no sign. Tradecraft. Somewhere behind him, Dave felt the Soviet-donated statue of the huge naked blacksmith symbolically beating a sword into a plowshare, a hypocrite to his toes, Dave had always felt, silly green giant all Socialist Realism but for the coy, incongruous fig leaf, and who was to say the bastard wasn't whacking the plowshare into a sword? *I saved your fucking life, Sam.* Dave was almost within voice range now. It was suddenly very quiet. Even the chuga-chuga of the snow plow had coughed itself to silence. No sign was offered or taken.

Sam continued his gull feeding, reaching into the brown paper bag with an ungloved left hand, pulling out chunks of bread and tossing them in the air for the diving, soaring gulls. Left hand. Ungloved. Sam Purcell was left-handed. The way he was holding the bag, in his right hand, supporting it from below, Dave could tell there was weight to it. The weight of a gun? Of TSD's latest handy-dandy instant aerosol heart-attack spray? That would be typical of Sam, Dave knew. Tragic accident befalls loyal servant. *Overcome with shock*

*and grief, Effie dear, right before my eyes, and there was
nothing I could do. Thank you, Sam, I understand, he was a
good man, Sam, a good provider. I know, Effie.* Dave looked
at Sam Purcell. Sam turned now, turned toward Dave, looked
at him and through him and gave no sign of recognition. *It's
as if I'm dead already,* Dave thought. *As though I don't exist.*

Sam stood against the rail, exactly at the juncture of a secondary footpath with the main walkway that rimmed the
river. Dave walked closer and closer. *Say something, damn it,*
Dave told himself; *don't just let him do it to you without a
word. At least ask him why.* Words invented themselves in
Dave's throat like the bubbles in beer and disappeared as
mysteriously as they came. *Shall I say, "Don't shoot, Sam, it's
me, remember, Dave, your old pal, remember, who saved
your ass in Aix-la-Chapelle"?*

No words came. Dave watched, exactly as if he were
watching an old movie on television, as Sam slowly lifted the
brown paper bag and even more slowly, more deliberately,
slid his ungloved left hand into it. *He is going to do it,*
thought Dave. *He really is going to let me have it right here
and now, right in broad daylight, right in the fucking UN
Plaza.*

When the shots came, they had a special unreal quality,
too. Dave heard them before he saw the result.

The bag jumped in Sam's hand, twitched and burst and fell
to the slushy path in a confusion of torn paper and bloodstained bread. The miniature automatic pistol was so small
that at first Dave didn't notice it. Something flashed in Sam's
eyes. He twisted, pivoted and darted along the boxwood
hedge before the marksman had another chance to aim. In
seconds he had vanished into the evergreen shrubbery at the
far end of the park. *Follow him, damn it, use your silly gun,
the bastard tried to kill you.* But Dave Loughlin just stood
there, numb. *He moves damn well for a man his age,* Dave
thought idly, as the Old Man vanished into the bushes. He
still felt the basic unreality of the moment, felt detached, as if
none of this were really happening, especially not to him.

Ivan's voice snapped him out of the trance. Of course, it
had been Ivan. "How you sonsabitches ever won the war es-
capes me entirely." Ivan came lumbering up to his old friend,
a comical guardian angel disguised in the blue coveralls and

bright-orange slicker of a park attendant. "You OK, old fart?"

"I'm very OK, pal. Stupid, maybe, but OK. Thanks, Ivan. If thanks is what you say when somebody saves your life."

"It will do." Ivan clapped him on the shoulder, and suddenly Dave Loughlin felt alive again.

"I lost him, Ivan. Sorry about that."

"At least," said the Russian with a philosophical sigh, "now we know for sure. That-there warn't bubble gum the man was offering you." He indicated the bloodstained bag with its grisly contents.

Dave bent to pick up the gun, not bothering about fingerprints. That gun would never be entered into evidence. None of this would ever go the conventional route of justice in America. Where, exactly, it would go, Dave couldn't have said. They'd cross that bridge when they came to it.

"There's no point chasing the sonofabitch," Dave said absently. "There's a Forty-Seventh Street exit to the park. He's long gone."

"But wounded."

"Why didn't you kill him?" It had just dawned on Dave that Ivan had not taken the obvious option.

"Dead men," said Ivan with a thin smile, "tell no tales. To coin a phrase. And that motherfucker is going to tell lots and lots of tales, old fart, if your cousin Ivan has anything to say about it."

"You just acquired the majority vote, buddy. Can I buy you a drink?"

"I bet," said Ivan with a laugh, "you say that to all the boys in uniform."

"You have never looked lovelier, pal, believe it." Dave bent down to pick up the bloody bag and its contents. He threw the bag in a trash bin and pocketed the pistol and for the first time that morning felt glad that the expensive ladies in UN Plaza weren't looking out their expensive windows. The two men walked down the path, past the snow plow, toward the main exit. The plow, Dave noticed absently, was painted with a black sign that read: "United Nations #20." It should have read *lifesaver.*

"I think," said Ivan as they strolled past the blank-faced guard, "that we had better do a bit of the old rethinking."

"Yeah, and fast." Dave hailed a cab and they disappeared into the traffic on First Avenue.

CHAPTER
◄◄◄(14)►►►

The girl was twenty-six, but she might have been forty. She was dark, slender, about five-six, with the kind of elegantly overstated facial features that might have been Italian, or maybe Greek. The polo coat wasn't new, but it was well-made. She wore very little makeup over a wary expression. You never knew what kind of kook was going to try using the agency as a pimping machine. The Beekman Tower was a good enough address, and Sandra de Angelo could take care of herself, but still and all, you never knew.

She knocked on the door of 23B. It opened to reveal a tall man, deeply tanned, with a lot of blond hair going to gray, blue-tinted aviator-style eyeglasses and the kind of very expensive, too-shiny sports clothes that Sandra had learned to associate with the flashier breed of agents and producers from the West Coast. Or small-time New Yorkers who tried to cultivate that look.

He spoke quietly, a surprisingly cultivated voice. "Miss de Angelo?"

"That's me." Keep it noncommittal. The singing lessons had to be paid for somehow. The break would come, she knew it would. And in the meantime, bit parts and commercials and movie extra work paid the rent. The agency was good about that. Sandra was grateful for that. So when they'd mentioned this gig, that it was special, not a stage part, but some kind of private thing—escort service work, really, she'd agreed to check it out. Hell, why not? Trained as a singer, she concentrated on placing the man's voice.

"Come in," he said, "may I take your coat?" There was a tea wagon from room service with a coffee service for two. She sat down in the small but nicely furnished living room. It looked a lot friendlier than most hotels, less commercial. The

[345]

guy was maybe a little weird, but she'd hold off on that judgment. After all, it was his nickel. He offered her coffee, and she accepted with a smile. The guy had a little trouble pouring with his right hand; there was a bandage around the palm of his left hand, but if he was in pain, he didn't show it. When they both had coffee, he sat down in a club chair some distance away. "This is a rather special job, Miss de Angelo, and I don't know how much they may have told you about it."

"Not a lot, just that it wasn't a commercial or a stage role."

"What I'm hiring you to do—if you'll accept—is to have supper with me on Friday and go on to the gala at the International Ballet."

He sipped his coffee and gauged her reaction through the blue lenses of his aviator glasses. Noncommittal.

"I have reserved a box. The reason is private—personal, may I say—but what I want is for us to be seen by a certain lady who will be there. I want it to seem that we are deeply in love. Only"—and he laughed, a low, chuckling laugh—"in public, please be assured. You will be in evening dress, covered in furs, very elegant. I, in black tie—as many of the patrons will be for the gala. We will laugh, hold hands, behave like young lovers. You see, Miss de Angelo, why I need an actress."

"I get the picture." She smiled. It was weird, all right, but harmless. The poor guy had probably had a falling-out with his wife. "About the clothes. . . ." Sandra didn't own an evening gown, let alone furs.

"I was hoping," said Sam Purcell with a smile, "that we could go shopping this afternoon. The furs can be rented; we'll do that, too. As for jewelry, we'll see what the gown requires. You have no problems, then, I take it?"

"Sounds like fun . . . Mr. Reynard."

"Call me Charles . . . Sandra."

"Charles."

"Now then," he said cheerfully, standing up, "do you think Bendel's or Bergdorf's?"

"Bendel's," she said instantly, although Sandra de Angelo had never really been in a position to choose before today.

The man who called himself Charles Reynard helped Sandra into her coat and put on his own flashy brown leather

trench coat and a fake-rustic Irish tweed floppy hat. The left
hand hurt damnably, throbbed with pain, but that wasn't going to alter the well-laid plans of Sam Purcell, not by one
inch. The bullet had come as a surprise, and the surprise was
a warning. Sam would be even more careful now. And bolder
at the same time. And the plan would continue on schedule,
no matter what.

In a life that had held more than its share of frustration,
Dave Loughlin never felt so helpless as he did that Thursday
afternoon in January. Ivan had made him a gift of Sam Purcell, and he'd blown it. For once, Sam had been outfoxed. It
wouldn't happen twice. Dave's chances of living out the week
were shrinking every second. And he was just about helpless
protecting the Lubov kid at the gala.

Dave had scraped the bottom of his resources and was able
to come up with six men. Six among more than two thousand
patrons of the ballet. Six men among five balconies and the
orchestra of that giant theater. And the regular security force
maintaining a polite, but firm, policy of noninvolvement.

Dave's men would be in plain clothes—black tie—and
they'd have small hand-held walkie-talkies. And only their
powers of observation stood between the Lubov kid and
whatever Sam had planned. If what Sam planned was
scheduled to happen at the gala after all.

Dave was sure of three things, and three things only: that
Sam would be working alone, that he'd work fast and that he
wouldn't miss. And after Lubov would come Dave's turn. So
this gambit was going to put old Dave Loughlin back in the
big picture again! This was going to be like the old days. The
old days were a Girl Scout picnic compared to this. In the
old days good was good and bad was bad, and you didn't
have to be Sigmund Freud to tell the difference. Dave sighed.
He'd have to call Effie, tell her he wouldn't be home for a
couple of days, go buy some clothes, rent a tux. Shit. On top
of everything else, he had to put on a penguin suit! Some
days you just ought to roll over and stay in bed.

Every time Dave thought about how carefully and completely he'd been set up, his anger grew. Sam had instructed
him to keep the investigation absolutely to himself, on the
very believable grounds that since they had no idea who was
behind the killings, since it might be anybody at all, even
someone within the agency, secrecy was the best policy. The

result of Sam's policy was that there was no one Dave could turn to. Even Sam's enemies would have a hard time swallowing this crazy story. Dave knew that if he weren't living it, he'd laugh at the idea. But Dave wasn't laughing now. Dave was fighting mad, and his anger had the edge of fear on it.

Jenny had a different dressing room now, but they were all so much the same, on the stage level of the New York State Theater, that it might have been the one she'd had the night she'd danced that first *Giselle* with the Civic. Less than a year ago! And how many lifetimes it seemed. Like all performing days, this Friday, the gala day, would be spent almost entirely inside the huge theater, class, rehearsal, fitting, warm-up, makeup, dressing and so on. There was always a special electricity in the air on gala days. The crowd itself was special and expecting the best of the best. Spirits that were high to begin with were somehow tuned up, nearly to the danger point. There was something a little devil-may-care about it all, a sense that almost anything might happen.

Jenny wouldn't be twenty-one for nearly a year. Yet tonight, somehow, she felt old, as though she'd seen it all. The gala excitement carried with it a special tension. Nadia continued to send out unconvincing signals of kindness and affection.

Boris had been preoccupied in rehearsals, as though the new pas de quatre were somehow not living up to what he'd hoped for, and even Dima seemed a bit withdrawn these last few days, maybe a Russian mood building, and if it were, Jenny vowed, she'd learn how to deal with it, she wouldn't let it affect her as she had in the past. Only Machito remained Machito, happy as any porpoise at high tide, bouncy, irrepressible, making them laugh whether they wanted to or not. And thank God for that.

Jenny looked at her two freshly pressed costumes hanging ready from the stark, utilitarian brass hook: colorful for *Corsaire;* simple, white and almost Grecian for the pas de quatre. It would be a good contrast, good for Dima, good for her.

Boris Mogador was no de Lis, nor did he try to be. Boris' choreography was simpler, more superficially charming, less psychological, less avant-garde. The International brought in guest choreographers all the time, and Boris' main function was simply to hold the artistic balance of the company, to run classes and the school and to orchestrate the season's program. It was a role that suited him perfectly, and the company was happier for the fact that he never tried to play God.

Jenny couldn't give a name to what was bothering her. It was nothing specific, but a kind of general underlying tension that set her on edge, something beyond opening-night jitters. *Corsaire,* after all, she had known for years. Probably she could have danced it in her sleep. And Boris' new pas de quatre was fun; it might not change the history of ballet, but it would match the gala mood. It would be pretty, a crowd pleaser. It would send them home happy they'd shelled out the hundred bucks a seat for the orchestra and first ring. Then why did she feel this way?

Jenny showered and changed into the *Corsaire* costume, throwing her afternoon's peach-colored leotard into the laundry bag and carefully hanging up the peach-silk scarf. Even the scarf had lost its magical powers; it was just another scarf now, not a talisman against demons, not a special mark of favor from the gods. She smiled at the thought and wondered about de Lis. Would he be in that gala audience tonight? Somehow she thought not. Jenny pulled on the bright *Corsaire* costume, flexed and examined her pink satin toe shoes and began the ancient ritual of mummifying her toes in cotton wool and Kleenex. Then came the Elmer's Glue on the bottom of the shoes, just to make sure they stayed where they belonged, the firmly laced ribbons, the final touch of makeup.

She sat back on the stiff little stool and surveyed the result. Not bad; at least she wouldn't frighten anyone. A knock sounded firmly on the door, and Jenny said, "Come in," knowing it was Dima.

There he stood, her Corsaire, very dashing with his overstated eye makeup, bowing and holding out a bouquet of violets. It was almost a ritual now, on opening nights: the violets if violets were to be found, otherwise small white roses. "For Giselle, with the compliments of Albrecht."

There were other flowers: a mixed bouquet from Privy, who had specially said she wanted to invite Jenny and Dima for supper after the gala; she had something to tell them. Jenny wondered what, but she was too busy to dwell on it. There was a small joke cactus plant from Iris Dowling with a card that said, *"Merde."*

Jenny thanked Dima and blew him a kiss; anything more

would wreck his makeup or her own. They walked out of the dressing room together to warm up, Jenny in her lucky leg warmers.

"Seen Nadia?" she asked softly.

"I have not had that pleasure since this morning."

"That female is up to something."

"Ultimately the Nadias of the world are *always* up to something. Is not to worry." He squeezed her hand, and they walked backstage to a small rehearsal room with a barre. Then they began their own individual warm-up exercises and were lost in concentration. The backstage intercom announced, "Fifteen minutes to curtain. Fifteen minutes to curtain." Jenny warmed up with pliés, tendus, lifted her arms in port de bras.

The gala was divided into two long acts; the first opened with a big, full-cast version of the second act of *Swan Lake*, featuring Nadia. Then came Jenny and Dima in *Corsaire*. Then intermission. Then two short pas de deux, followed by Nadia, Machito, Jenny and Dima in the finale, Boris' new pas de quatre.

The noise level backstage rose as the clock inched closer to curtain time. A flock of white swan-maidens surrounded them.

Suddenly there was Nadia herself, the white swan of Act II, serene, gracious, her huge dark eyes radiant with a bright crystalline dazzle. Nadia smiled a bit distantly, bowed her head slightly at Dima, turned to Jenny and said, "Good luck, child."

Jenny smiled shyly. "Thank you, Nadia."

She couldn't bring herself to say *merde* to Nadia. *Merde* was for friends. But maybe she'd been too suspicious. Maybe Nadia was turning over a new leaf.

Jenny went back to her exercises and thought about Nadia no more.

Dave Loughlin faced this night with the agonizing frustration of knowing he'd done everything he could do, and that it wasn't enough. He'd planned with Ivan, gone over diagrams of the great theater, the backstage arrangements, the cellars, the office and rehearsal space and the auditorium itself. A hundred people wouldn't have been sufficient. He had six, plus himself, plus Ivan. Against . . . what? Dave sighed and scanned the theater with a hyperalert gaze that saw the whole place as one big ticking time bomb and every man, woman and child in it a suspect.

The New York State Theater blazed gold into the purple January night. The gala curtain time was eight, and now at half past seven the early comers were just beginning to trickle in. The orchestra and first ring, Dave knew, would be almost exclusively black-tie, the glitter set, the hundred-dollar-a-seat folks, who probably wrote the whole thing off against some corporation or charity. The four other balconies held the true balletomanes, a very motley lot from what little Dave had seen of them, all ages, sizes, colors and degrees of affluence. Perfect for anyone who wanted to slip in disguised.

Dave stood on the mezzanine level, at the bend in the great travertine staircase, a vantage point from which he could survey the entire entrance to the theater. He held a small black Sony walkie-talkie, and there was another CIA man far across the enormous lobby at the top of the twin of Dave's staircase. Ivan was backstage, dressed as a grip. Five other CIA men were scattered through the house. Ivan had offered to ring in some of his own people, but that was a little too tricky for Dave, even now, even as desperate as they were.

If I were Sam Purcell, how would I disguise myself? It was a very interesting question, and Dave had so many answers he could hardly think straight.

Seven-forty. The crowd was building now, and the excitement was building with it.

Suppose he just walks in, bold as brass, undisguised? I've no authority to arrest the man. None at all. And no evidence except the word of a KGB agent who just happens to be in the country under false pretenses, and no doubt with a pretty fancy record of his own, if it came to that. Which it might. Dave knew these things, knew that Sam would have considered all of them and that Sam would have a plan, maybe several plans. The aborted hit at the UN park was very typical of Sam Purcell. Simple and bold and fast. *If I were going to hit Lubov, how would I do it? Let me count the ways. In a crowd. For maximum publicity impact, now that the so-called conspiracy was public knowledge? Turn the heat up a little; the KGB killings had been out of the headlines for a couple of months now; the fire could use a little stoking.* Dave's instinct told him tonight was the night. Dave's instinct had been wrong plenty of times. Including this morning.

He looked at his watch: quarter of eight.

You could get seated after the curtain was up; Dave had checked on that. That would be one way to sneak in. He'd have to stay right where he was for a good half hour into the program. Six men to cover thousands of potential Purcells, plus all backstage. Like bailing out the ocean.

Some damned exotic crowd, this was. Dave's work hardly ever involved anything fancier than some minor embassy clerk dipping into the code room for free samples now and then, or some rough stuff on the docks, or tedious tracing of people who weren't what their passports claimed they were. He looked down at this glittering mob, swelling into a river of affluence and merriment now, the sleek women, some of them no doubt his invisible friends of the morning, the ladies of UN Plaza, the confident older men pretending to enjoy the scene, men whose culture-hungry wives had dragged them away from the club or the television tonight. Then there were the chic young ones, impossibly skinny girls with Garbo faces and haunted eyes on the arms of boys who looked as though they lived in advertisements for Saks Fifth Avenue. *Only in New York, New York,* thought Dave as they flowed past him, the air around them laden with subtle perfumes, famous names and the gentle explosion of well-bred laughter. These were the sleek ones, the hundred-dollar-a-head ones.

The others came surging in with the haste and fervor of crusaders, in totally different uniforms, motley, shaggy of hair, rough of tweed, serious of mien, obviously disdaining the posh usurpers in black tie as dilettantes who had earned no right to their privileged seats in the temple of dance. There were thousands of them. They came carrying flowers, green cloth book bags, huge purses for men and women, a million places to hide a gun, a bomb, a spray of poison.

Ten to eight.

It seemed as though a final surge of balletgoers was building, a flood tide of humanity moving with the special intensity a tide develops just before it turns. Dave saw the tall blond man and his mistress. There was no doubt she was his mistress. First, there was the sable coat. It was not the kind of coat you gave your daughter for getting all A's at Bryn Mawr. Then there was the woman herself, exotic, Latin-looking, passionate, theatrical, stunning in no jewelry and a blood-red velvet gown to the floor. And the way she clung to the tall, suntanned man, a New York-effete man in his blue aviator glasses and lion's-mane hair, not a kid, but obviously getting his, and regularly, and in satisfying doses. The broad—Dave did not consider her a lady—was carrying a big bunch of yellow roses with a flagrant scarlet ribbon around the stem. Laughing, touching her man on the cheek, very much in love. New York, New York.

And where was Sam Purcell?

The lovers walked slowly across the lobby and up the stairs at the other end. *Of course,* thought Dave. *Two hundred bucks in seats alone, and he'll never miss it.* The crowd thinned. There was a wave of applause from the auditorium. The haunting swan theme from *Swan Lake* filled the theater. The curtain was going up. And still, Dave Loughlin stayed where he was. Sam Purcell would show up sometime. And Dave was going to be ready when he did.

Nadia had never danced better. The intensity of the emotion she had focused on Jenny Hale now went into making her white swan something the audience would never forget. Odette, the princess transformed into a swan, came magically to life as Tchaikovsky's beguiling swan theme carried her to romantic doom. Hers was a studied performance, but there was fire in it, too: Nadia made herself into a spirit caught forever between earth and heaven and torn forever between the attractions of each. The audience loved it. Jenny Hale, watching from the wings, still doing her warm-up exercises, loved it, too, and forgot any doubts she had about Nadia. Whatever else she might be, Nadia was an artist, and for that one could forgive a lot. The curtain came down; Nadia was called back for six curtain calls.

Now it was Jenny's turn, and Dima's.

The curtain stayed down for a few minutes while the magic forest of *Swan Lake* was exchanged for the neutral background for the excerpted pas de deux from *Le Corsaire.* The dance was quick and flashy, with dramatic solos for both of them; Jenny found herself enjoying it thoroughly. To be onstage with Dima again was one cause for rejoicing. As he soared and vaulted in the famous Lubov defiance of gravity, hanging in midair with the proud proprietorship of one who owns a long-term lease on the airspace over Lincoln Center, Jenny caught his enthusiasm and added it to her own.

The pas de deux was rather short, a curtain ringer-downer, calculated to end the first portion of the gala on an upbeat note of triumph. It did just that. The audience roared, cheered, clapped their hands sore. They could have coaxed more than the six curtain calls they took, but Jenny could sense Dima thinking about Nadia's six calls. Diplomacy triumphed, and in any case they had to change for the final pas de quartre.

High in the blackness of a battery of lights to the left of the stage and behind the proscenium, Ivan Sokolovay crouched in discomfort and muttered unheard curses in gutter Russian. It was an impossible situation. He admired Lubov's courage and hated the boy's guts at the same time. The sense of utter helplessness only made the frustration worse. Ivan was a stranger, beyond the law, fighting, just this once, on the side of the angels. And absolutely impotent!

From his light-stand Ivan could survey almost the entire backstage area. If anyone tried to sneak up on young Lubov from the wings, Ivan would be able to stop that. If. And there was one of Dave's men roving about back there, too. Equally helpless. Equally unsure of what to watch out for. Dave hadn't even been able to level with his own people; it was just too farfetched, they'd probably have him locked up for a loony, and who would blame them? You simply didn't make accusations like that against the deputy director of CIA unless you had him by the ass. And they didn't have Purcell by anything.

Intermission. Probably not much would happen during intermission. The boy onstage was a perfect target. One bullet, well aimed, would do. Once again, Ivan's appraising eyes raked the vasty gloom backstage. Anyone could be lurking anywhere. There were a thousand places to hide, and darkness to help, and plenty of stagehands and corps de ballet kids churning about to add to the confusion.

Ivan thought of his little dacha. He wondered who they'd give it to next, after he flubbed this assignment. It was not a pretty thought.

Judith Winchester sat in her box like royalty, surrounded by a carefully chosen coterie of powerful men and their women. It was going beautifully, her gala. She thought of it as hers, just as she thought of the entire company as hers. Nadia had been delightful as the Swan Queen. Dima Lubov outdid himself in *Corsaire*. Even the Hale creature was acceptable, although Judith had altered her original plans for

Jenny not one whit. It simply remained to be seen how Nadia would implement those plans. That she would do so, Judith had no doubt at all.

It was strange for Diana to sit with Greg Holden in his house seats in the orchestra, watching her former lover write dance history in midair with that seemingly casual élan that had become Dima's trademark.

How effortless he made it look! And with Jenny Hale, too. They were together, Diana knew, and she felt no regret at all. In fact, she wished them well. *How right they look together*, Diana thought, watching them dance with her well-trained decorator's eye. They had just enough difference in look and in style to make an interesting pair, yet somehow— like all perfect pairs—they contrived to be the same, molded from the same spirit.

She turned to look at Greg. He was leaning forward a little, intent on the dancing. A good man, a fine man, a solid, serious, funny, lovable man. There was something permanent about Greg Holden that appealed to Diana profoundly. She smiled, and reached for his hand, and squeezed it. Solid. That was the word for Greg Holden.

Dave prowled the mezzanine of the great theater like a team of bloodhounds and found nothing to alarm him. Maybe he was wrong after all. Maybe Sam would choose another day. Maybe Sam would wait until he'd eliminated Dave himself, and Ivan, too. Who knew what evidence Sam might have cooked up and planted about Dave and Ivan? Sam Purcell would never have to justify the elimination of someone like Dave Loughlin. Not likely! Dave repressed a shudder of fear and disgust and turned to stalk his way back down the length of the huge mezzanine, past all the glittering hundred-dollar-a-seaters, past the bar, from one of those huge over-blown, unborn-looking shiny-white Nadelman sculptures to the other. With every step Dave felt more useless.

They gathered in the wings, Nadia and Machito on the left of the stage, Jenny and Dima Lubov on the right. The simple costumes were identical: white leotards for the men, white tights and simple white tunics for the women. The backdrop was a cloth of dull silver. Boris had chosen four Chopin waltzes, each no more than five minutes long, each with a different theme and tempo. The first was rather slow, dreamy, young. The second evolved around a merry peasant theme. The third was dark and passionate, and the concluding waltz was regal, measured, very grand. They built; they were well chosen; they would allow a wide range of emotion in the dancers.

The first chords struck up. They made their entrances simultaneously, tentatively, the men leading the women, for this was a dance of young love awakening. The men led the women into the waltz, took their hands, knelt, rose and waltzed. The waltz melted from the classic, formal step with which Boris had begun it into something much more fluid, with the two couples crisscrossing the stage in elegant pattern upon pattern.

Dancing the second act of *Swan Lake* had taken more out of Nadia than she realized. It had been a hard decision for her, whether or not to risk it. In the end it was her fear of Jenny that turned the scale, and it was Nadia's fear of Jenny that led her to overact her role now, in the newest pas de quatre that was only a pas de quatre because she, Nadia, had insisted on being included.

In the first of the four waltzes Nadia reacted unconsciously, making her gestures just a little broader than they needed to be, holding certain poses just a fraction of a beat longer than necessary, doing anything that might show herself to best advantage. After all, was she not Nadia? Was she not the real prima ballerina of the International, in fact, if not in official policy? And was she not far more beautiful than the little Hale creature, and far, far more skillful as a dancer? These were Nadia's thoughts as the first waltz ended and the second began.

Now she intensified her scene stealing. Nadia would rule this stage, and no presumptuous Yankee waif of a Jenny Hale was going to intrude! Nadia built from the occasional gesture broadened to more calculated, more self-indulgent movements, prolonging an extension here, accelerating a tempo there, confusing Machito a little, now flinging an arm dangerously across Jenny's face, causing Jenny to jerk back in a highly ungraceful motion. Let the Hale creature take care! She would defy Nadia at her peril.

Now it became obvious to Jenny and Dima and Machito exactly what was happening. Soon the more knowledgeable balletomanes in the audience caught on, too, and tensed in their seats for what might turn into a good old-fashioned battle-royal.

Now Jenny was in Dima's arms, spinning. "Did you see that?" she hissed through her smile? "She practically hit me!"

He lifted her in a smooth elevation and, when his back was to the audience for a second, answered, "I saw. Beware." They were trapped out onstage, and at Nadia's mercy, imprisoned by the spotlights and their own sense of professionalism as effectively as by any iron bars.

The dance continued.

Nadia had a new sense of power now. Her moves got bolder, more brazen, and she began enjoying herself for the first time this evening, for the first time, truly, since her luncheon with Judith Winchester. Nadia lost all regard for Boris's carefully wrought choreography, lost all consideration for Machito's gallant partnering, thought only of new ways to outshine Jenny.

Only in the third waltz did Machito find a chance to do something about Nadia. This was a dark, throbbing passionate waltz, more like Liszt than Chopin, and Boris had ended it with a great series of supported lifts and spins for the women. In the first of these lifts, Nadia came prancing across the stage and flew through the air into Machito's arms. As he held her aloft, Machito smiled his radiant Latin smile and murmured quite distinctly under the smile, "Cut it out this minute, or I drop you, bitch!" Nadia froze. The tone of his voice left no doubt that he really would drop her. Ballerinas were dropped by accident from time to time, and Nadia knew the results could be disastrous. The music throbbed on, Machito's cue to let her down, but still, he held her in the steel-trap grip of his long arms. "You'll stop?"

Her smile remained radiant for all the world to see. "I stop."

Slowly, a monument to grace and gallantry, Machito lowered her to the stage. The dance continued. The two couples crossed and recrossed the stage. When Machito passed Jenny, he winked. She winked back. *The Three Musketeers strike again,* thought Jenny, and she had to make a firm effort not to laugh right there onstage.

Jenny had never known a trick like Nadia's. There might be jealousies, rivalries, even hatred in ballet, but it was always kept backstage. To hog the choreography as Nadia had done was unheard of. Jenny wondered what she had done to make Nadia take such a foolish, and publicly foolish, chance.

Maschito's threat had cooled Nadia's antics. Possibly not a
dozen people in the audience had a real idea of what had
happened. The final waltz resounded in its regal cadences,
something that might be played at a coronation ball, building,
stately, very elegant.

The last bars came crashing to a climax. The curtain came
down in a thunderstorm of applause. Dave Loughlin stood
nervously at the side of the left-hand aisle in the orchestra,
sweating freely, feeling the pistol in its shoulder holster,
knowing he would use it if the chance only came.

In a box on the first ring Sandra de Angelo sat smiling,
wondering who the lucky woman was that Charles Reynard
had gone to see, taking the yellow bouquet with him. The
former flame, no doubt, the lady who was meant to be jealous of Sandra de Angelo. What the hell, a hundred bucks and
a good French supper and a chance to wear sable with all the
bigwigs. Not bad at all. Sandra threw her head back and
laughed and clapped as the curtain rose to reveal the four
star dancers, bowing.

Dave shifted his weight, looking from left to right, wondering, waiting, helpless.

Onstage the choreography had left Machito at the far left
of the stage, then Nadia, then Dima, then Jenny. Jenny made
her reverence, and smiled, and was glad to have Dima between her and whatever menace Nadia might be cooking up.
The boys bowed to the audience, to their partners; an assistant manager in black tie came out with huge bouquets for
both of the ballerinas, identical sheaves of red roses. Jenny
pulled one rose from the bunch and gave it to Dima, who
smiled and knelt and kissed her hand. This had been done ten
thousand times, for generations, in all the ballet theaters of
the world, and the audience loved it every time.

Nadia repeated the performance, and Machito's grin was
more derisive than grateful as he took the rose. *If it has
thorns,* he thought, *I bet they're poisoned.* Still, he smiled and
took the rose. The curtain rose and fell and rose again, five
times, six times, a dozen. Now the flowers began their customary rain onto the stage.

Fans came crowding down the aisles, hundreds of them,
jampacked, bearing flowers, clicking cameras, and flowers

came hailing out of the darkness above, from all levels of the great theater. The four dancers stood there, bathing in the warm waves of adoration, smiling over the ache of their strained muscles, giving the patrons what they came for, putting the finishing touch on the first gala of the new season.

Nadia seethed. To be humiliated by this Puerto Rican peasant, and right there onstage, so publicly! Her resentment of Machito and his threat was capped only by her renewed fury at Jenny Hale. She was the cause of it all! It was Jenny's fault, Nadia's disgrace. Well, Jenny Hale hadn't heard the end of it, not by a long shot. Nadia smiled and seethed. The curtain rose and fell.

It was on the fourteenth curtain call, with the orchestra thinning out and all but the most devout of the balletomanes trickling toward the exits, that Nadia spotted the big yellow bouquet as it came sailing down from the fourth balcony, trailing scarlet ribbons as it fell.

The bouquet came spinning gently through the air, and the distance it fell was so great it seemed to Nadia to be falling in slow motion. It tumbled end over end gently, like something underwater. And it seemed to be coming right toward her. *One last chance*, thought Nadia, *for one more dramatic gesture, and let them think what they will*. The flowers were probably for her anyway. As the bouquet came tumbling toward the stage, more toward Dima, really, Nadia made her move.

Smiling radiantly, the smile of a young girl in love, and with no visible preparation, Nadia propelled herself into the air, extended her left arm and caught the yellow roses as they fell, drawing the bouquet toward her face in the same instinctive gesture.

TSD had done its work well. The bomb exploded in that instant, taking half of Nadia Beshanskaia's head with it. Jenny and Dima and Machito were hurled to the stage as the applause turned to screaming. Jenny blacked out then, aware only of a burning sensation on her leg.

Sandra de Angelo watched the yellow bouquet come sailing out of the darkness. She couldn't tell exactly where it came from, but high up, very high, and on the right. The auditorium was still dark, still ringing with applause. Five red rectangles were stacked in the darkness, one over the other, marking the five exits from the balconies. They glowed balefully, like animal's eyes reflecting firelight. There was something faintly ominous about them. Sandra wondered where her escort had gone, why he'd choose this moment to throw the flowers. Maybe one of the ballerinas was his girlfriend! Sandra watched the bouquet floating lazily down from the fifth balcony, turning in the air, trailing the scarlet ribbons like some exotic tropical fish gliding through a night sea. She saw Nadia smile, the flash of recognition, saw Nadia leap for the bouquet—it was for her then!—and watched in terror as the lovely flowers turned to death right there on stage. Her first instinct was to run. Sandra pulled the rented sable close about her, touching it like a talisman to make sure that this part of the dream—nightmare—was real. It was all too real. She watched the panic in the orchestra, the confusion on-stage, with the shocked detachment of someone viewing an old disaster newsreel on television. *They're dying out there!* Then she began to cry.

In the orchestra pit one yellow rose lay incongruously on a grand piano, its soft yellow petals spattered with blood. On-stage the scarlet ribbons of Sam's bouquet mingled with the lifeless blood of Nadia.

The longest day Dave Loughlin could remember was turning into the longest night of his life.

The instant the bomb went off the New York State Theater's own security men went into action, smoothly, efficiently, but too late. The curtain came down; Nadia's body was covered and removed; the three other dancers were treated. Lubov and the other boy were in shock, but uninjured, and the Hale girl had a shallow cut on her left leg, nothing serious. The exits were watched, a few possible suspects detained and searched, but it was useless. They found nothing.

Then came the city police and their endless questions, most of which Dave couldn't answer, not then, not there. Ivan, by prearrangement, vanished into the night. The whole theater was searched front and back, top to bottom. There were a million places to hide, and nothing was found in any of them.

Dave was about to leave the theatre at three-thirty when the police captain in charge motioned him into a small room behind the ticket counter. There sat Sandra de Angelo, calm but tense, the sable gathered tightly around her in the smoky room as if to ward off evil. She told her story, told them where they could reach her, of the room in the Beekman

Tower, the rented fur, the tall man's story, the yellow roses. Dave felt sorry for the girl, and sorrier for himself. Of course. Trust the Old Man. Sam knew they'd have been banking on his working alone. As he'd worked alone in every other murder. Well, the hopelessness weighed down on Dave with the brutal reality of an avalanche. He didn't dare go home now. For all he knew Sam would be waiting, staking out his house, maybe somehow endangering Effie and the kids. And Dave had no authority, even now, to broadcast an alert. Who'd believe him? Who'd take Dave Loughlin's word over Sam's? He thanked the girl, and let her go. Sam's unvouchered slush fund might just have bought her a sable coat. That wouldn't be the weirdest thing Sam's fund had purchased.

It was a trucker's café far downtown on the West Side, near the warehouses and the entrance to the Holland Tunnel. Ivan had a booth in a corner and a plate of uneaten eggs and sausage in front of him when Dave finally made the rendezvous at four-fifteen on Saturday morning. Dave lowered his big tired body into the opposite seat and said nothing for a minute or two. It felt good just to sit, to be quiet, not to think.

Ivan sipped coffee well laced with cream. "Even the eagle," said Ivan, "must one day go home to roost."

Terrific. Dandy. Just what Dave needed, a few more of Ivan's Khrushchev-retread folk metaphors. "And a stitch in time saves nine, don't forget that one."

"Truly, old fart, you may lose your sense of humor, but take care not to lose also your powers of reasoning." Ivan grinned. "Where, Davey, does the bastard live?"

Dave looked at his old friend, and blinked, and grinned.

The burning pain was gone now, replaced by a dull throbbing. Jenny opened her eyes and saw Privy with a man she didn't know, an older man. He had a nice face, the older man. Maybe a doctor.

"My darling," said Privy softly, "how do you feel? We've been so worried."

"A little woozy. What happened?"

Dima's voice answered. "Someone threw a bomb at the stage, *deushka*." He took her hand.

She was lying on a massage table backstage, with a blanket thrown over her costume. Jenny turned to look at Dima,

smiled, looked him up and down and saw that he was uninjured. "And Machito?"

"He is fine."

"Nadia?"

"She is . . . not well. She is dead from the bomb."

The pressure of Dima's hand intensified. She thought it was
to reassure her. It was because in that instant Dima had decided that Jenny would never learn, at least not from him,
that the bomb had been meant for Dimitri Lubov.

"God. Poor . . . thing."

As usual, Privy took charge. Jenny felt well enough to get
up and change, and, late as it was, they'd still go back to the
Fifth Avenue apartment for supper. *Good heavens, the young
people must be starving, don't you agree, Gerald?* Gerald
agreed.

It was the interference by the Russian that determined Sam
Purcell's final course of action. It would have been the Russian, naturally; Sam knew Dave Loughlin would never have
had the cunning to infiltrate the UN park like that or the
quickness of reflexes to shoot so fast and so well. But the
Russian had written his obituary with that bullet. Sam could
feel it tingling yet in his left hand; lucky the fat little Commie hadn't shattered bones.

Sam's plan was simple, like all the best plans. It was really—if you stretched a point—Phase II of Sam's original program. Which had been nothing less than taking the usual
precautions when a local chief of station had been recruited.
Today, tired as he was, Sam would drive the few miles to
headquarters and put out two alerts: one for Dave Loughlin,
one for Ivan Sokolovny. And they'd be silver alerts, international, stop-at-nothing, shoot-to-kill alerts. They'd get Loughlin. Loughlin would, weakly, stupidly, kill himself rather than
face questioning. As for Ivan? With luck, Ivan would be
killed in the capturing. Silver alerts tended to do that.

All these thoughts came to Sam as he showered in the
green marble shower stall of his large, imitation Southern
Colonial house at the outskirts of McLean, Virginia. He'd left
the damned ballet theater just as the Beshanskaia bitch made
her vain, stupid leap for the bouquet. Still, Sam had thought,
as the elevator raced him to the lobby floor while the panic
exploded in the auditorium, it would have its publicity value.
They'd know the menace was still stalking the defectors. It

wouldn't be a total loss. Sam's rented car had been waiting on a side street behind Lincoln Center. He'd been through the Lincoln Tunnel and heading south before midnight. By four on Saturday morning he'd dropped the rented car and picked up his own gray Mercedes in a public lot in Arlington. And half an hour after that Sam Purcell had been sound asleep in his own big four-poster bed.

And when his alarm clock went off at eight-thirty, Sam Purcell felt as refreshed as though he'd spent the last two days on a Caribbean cruise. After the shower, he shaved carefully and put on his Saturday-casual, go-to-the-office clothes, an old tweed jacket over tan cavalry-twill trousers and a tattersall shirt of tissue-weight wool. A foulard scarf knotted loosely at his throat completed the picture.

Sam went downstairs to make coffee and breakfast. January was far from the best time in the Virginia countryside, but the day was bright, and Sam felt the inner glow of one who knows a long, hard job is nearly finished.

He ate his scrambled eggs and toast, had a second cup of Blue Mountain coffee, neatly stacked the dishes, pan and cup in the dishwasher, pulled on a lightweight trench coat and suede gloves and walked down the flagstone path to the detached, fake Jeffersonian, old-brick-with-white-shutters garage.

The air smelled of damp and pine needles and a fickle promise of spring. He pushed the hidden button that activated the electronic garage doors. The gray Mercedes gleamed softly from the murky interior of Sam's garage. Trust the Krauts for a decent paint job; they made everything as though it might be called on to invade Belgium at any moment. Sam rather liked that; it appealed to his sense of fitness. He hadn't bothered to lock the car's door.

Sam slid across the black leather seat and fastened the seat belt. Then he turned the key. The engine coughed, chugged, gasped and failed to catch fire. Damn. He'd flooded it again.

Sam sat back and waited for one minute exactly. Then he turned the starter key again, this time pressing the accelerator all the way to the floor. Sometimes that helped. But once again he got the chugging, choking, gasping. Maybe some damn thing was caught in the fuel pump. That had happened once. No, hell, it was just flooded. He turned off the key and

sat back again. It was stuffy in the closed car. Or maybe he
was more tired than he had thought.

Sam put his head back against the headrest for just a moment, then jerked forward and remembered to look at his
watch. Goddamn! Nearly five minutes had passed. He was
tired. Still, it had to be done. This was not an alert he'd like
to put out on the telephone. Once again he turned the key,
turned it too far this time, so that it made a weird grinding
sound. Turned it properly, slowly, with some effort. Pushed
the accelerator to the floor again. Heard the damned cough-
ing again. Shit! Sam could hear his own heavy breathing
now. It was stuffy in here. Ought to have the damned garage
ventilated, you never knew, there was always a chance of
leaking carbon monoxide. He'd open the window. Maybe
take a stroll, let the engine flooding evaporate for a few
minutes, anyway the window, open the window. Sam could
see the window. It was right there on top of the door where
the Krauts had thoughtfully placed it. And the crank, the
crank was there too, just where it always had been, well then,
why was it such a damned effort to reach the thing, all right,
that's better, at least he'd gotten his hand on it, no—wait—
slipped off, up, OK, on again, now turn. The effort of turning
the window crank seemed enormous, like lifting huge rocks,
but still, Sam made the effort. It was on the second turn that
he slumped forward and struck the horn button with his forehead. But by then Sam Purcell hardly even heard the shriek
of the tortured horn.

The howling Mercedes horn was cut short almost as soon
as it began.

"He's out." Dave Loughlin, incongruous in a one-day beard
and a very wrinkled dinner jacket, expertly flicked back Sam
Purcell's eyelid. Ivan's bag of tricks had worked and worked
well. The flat cushion of gas with its slow-release nozzle had
slid undetectably under the driver's seat. It contained, Ivan
said, a very sophisticated first cousin of Sodium Pentothal,
odorless and quick, but guaranteed not to be fatal. "One
cushion equals three hours," said Ivan, "and three hours is
more than we need." In fewer than five minutes they had
Sam trussed hand to foot and tucked him on the floor of the
back seat under his own raincoat. Then Dave did a minute's
worth of tinkering under the Mercedes' hood, and they drove
off into the bright Saturday morning.

It was a rather pale and apprehensive Jenny who sat across from Jessica Privet in the seldom-used dining room of Clifford Hale's apartment on Saturday night.

The table looked lovely; there were flowers and four tall candles and the best glasses for red wine. Privy had outdone herself with the food, too: hot leek soup with cream, a roast of veal with brown mushroom sauce, spinach puree baked with noodles and cheese and, for dessert, Jenny's childhood favorite, rum-custard trifle.

"I feel," said Privy over coffee, "just a bit silly."

"After all that's happened tonight, darling," Jenny answered with her first real smile, "it's a wonder any of us can feel at all."

"I think what she means is this." Gerald Lanier's voice was usually gentle, but he had a lifetime of training speaking from the pulpit, and when he wanted to project, he projected. What he projected now was love. "Jessica has done me the honor to say she'll marry me."

"Privy!" Jenny was on her feet and kissing Jessica Privet, who uncharacteristically blushed.

Dima followed Jenny's footsteps and kissed Privy, too. "Is very happy news," said Dima, turning to the about-to-be-bishop. "Congratulations." Then he turned to Jenny and put his arm around her. "Why," he asked softly, "on so happy an occasion, are you crying?"

The gray Mercedes kept exactly to the fifty-five-miles-per-hour speed limit all the way to Dulles International Airport in Maryland. The trip took an hour and a half, and there were times when Dave Loughlin thought he'd never make it. Slowly, as he drove, Dave overcame the vast exhaustion of the last forty-eight hours, the tensions of the last several weeks. He got a kind of second wind, which experience told him couldn't last. Still, it was better than the desperate final edge of tiredness that he'd felt just a few hours before. They drove almost in silence. Dave knew their destination, but he did not know the reason why. At last, around half past ten, they began seeing signs directing them to the airport.

"Twice," said Dave dully, "you've passed up chances of killing him."

"And told you why." Whatever Ivan felt, he wasn't elaborating on it for Dave's benefit.

"Yeah. But who's going to buy a confession delivered by

you guys? I mean, you're fairly well known as cookers of confessions."

"We cry of the wolf once too often? Maybe, old fart, maybe. But one thing we know: after this there will be no more killings, *nyet*?" The old-movie accent wavered in and out of focus as Ivan grew wearier and wearier. Dave knew just how he felt.

"Please God." It came out as a sigh, but it was meant as a prayer. Dave wondered how long it had been since he'd prayed. And for what and to whom.

"It won't be my decision, old buddy-roo. But an educated guess tells me that this gentleman in the back seat is going to have a long and useful career—in cold storage."

"Siberia?" Somehow the thought amused Dave, who thought of the silk curtains and the China tea and the two grim secretaries.

"Really, Davey, you see too many movies. No, by golly, something quiet in the hills beyond Moscow, something perhaps with a view—through bars, naturally—of the birch groves. Not Siberia, not by a long shot."

"And why?"

" 'Give me a lever,' said your philosopher, and I don't mean Comrade Khrushchev, 'and I shall move the earth.' " Ivan permitted himself a chuckle and began to sound more like the old Ivan. "It seems to me that Mr. Sam Purcell is going to be a lever. Maybe our biggest. How many times, Davey, does one wish for a believable reason to say, *'All right, youse guys, drop your guns, we got da place surrounded'*? If we have Mr. Purcell on ice, we got da place surrounded. Simple, perhaps, but it has worked in the past—and for your side, too."

Dave said nothing for a moment but simply drove at his steady, legal speed and let that sink in. He cleared his throat and said quietly, "You know, Ivan, for a high-living Commie KGB agent with the morals of a scorpion in heat, you make a lot of sense. One thing's sure: I could never make it stick in this country, not in my organization. He's too damn smart, too well connected; he'd have me in the loony bin, or worse, before I could so much as holler."

"Exactly."

"Not only that, the sonofabitch hates you guys so much it'd be hard to think of better punishment for him than to spend the rest of his days with you."

"We're really lots of fun, when you give us a chance."

"Right on." It was only then that Dave laughed, long and loud. The car passed in through the main gates of Dulles International Airport, then turned left toward the cargo-loading area. Dave drove more slowly now, at Ivan's direction, past the main cargo area and onto a little-used dirt track that seemed to circle the landing field itself.

Huge jets landed and took off nearby, and Dave hoped their altimeters were all in perfect working order. The gray Mercedes made its stately way along the dirt track, trailing dry winter dust, and finally pulled up to an improvised-looking prefab tin cargo shed at the edge of one long lone runway. The shed looked deserted, but there was a huge Aeroflot jet parked a few hundred yards down the runway. "The joys," murmured Ivan, "of diplomatic immunity. Our buddy-pal back there will go out of the country—so to speak—in the CD pouch."

Dave braked to a halt by the shed's side door. Instantly three men in tan jumpsuits appeared. Ivan spoke softly to them in Russian. They nodded, opened the back door of the Mercedes, lifted the unconscious form of Sam Purcell gently from the floor and carried him into the shed. "A medical emergency, it seems to me." Ivan spoke with such sympathy that Dave had to look twice before he caught the twinkle in that familiar eye. "Our pal will be on a stretcher and heavily bandaged and more efficiently sedated before our great silver bird takes off." Ivan looked at his big Rolex, a comical figure still in the uniform of a stagehand at the New York State Theater. "Which will be in less than an hour. You are sure, Davey, old fart, that I can't recruit you?"

"Effie would never understand."

Ivan solemnly reached out his hand and took Dave's hand. "We'll have to stop meeting like this, old fart."

"Once every thirty years." Dave grinned. "It doesn't seem like thirty years."

"More like a lifetime, dummy." Underneath the banter the two tired men shared something they could not give a name to, something rare and fragile, especially for Dave and Ivan, especially in their line of work. What they shared was trust, and they each, unconsciously, prolonged the moment of parting because they knew how seldom this happened, how unlikely it was ever to happen again.

"Thanks for everything, Ivan."

"It was nothing, old sport, nothing." Old sport. Sam's words. He'd never hear them from Sam Purcell again.

"Saving my life was something."

"If one values life." Dave Loughlin valued his life more in this instant than he had for many years. But he didn't—couldn't—say that to Ivan.

"Is there an extra sack in that dacha of yours, buddy?"

"And girls who know the way there. Anytime, pardner."

A uniformed pilot walked silently out of the shed toward the plane, followed by another uniformed pilot carrying two clipboards. Copilot. Dave stood next to the car looking at Ivan, waiting for he knew not what. The sun was warmer now, the sky still the same dense blue that had followed the dawn. Dave looked at his watch, noticed the dinner jacket, laughed. "I must look like a drunk home from a spree."

Ivan grinned. "It was some spree, all right. My expense account will never forget it."

Dave wondered who'd be signing his expense account now or if he'd have one to sign. There was going to be a lot of tall explaining to do, and Dave had no idea at all if he'd be believed. Already, though the blur of his weariness, Dave could imagine the scene. They'd try to cover it all up; it would be far too compromising for the CIA to admit its deputy director could have reached such a deadly level of instability undetected. And maybe Ivan's bosses would want to play it that way, too, to give themselves even more leverage. The more Sam's activities were covered up, the greater the impact when they'd be revealed. If they were ever revealed. Dave looked at Ivan and smiled and realized that it didn't matter. It didn't matter one damn.

Two stretcher-bearers walked out of the tin hut, carrying a bandaged form under a rough wool blanket. They walked smoothly, steadily, as if carrying eggs. Sam Purcell was going on his last assignment. Dave watched until the stretcher had been lifted onto the Aeroflot jet. Then he walked up to Ivan and put his hand on the man's shoulder. "Some things don't change, pal. Remember that." Then he turned and got into the gray Mercedes and drove very fast back to the main gate of the airport.

Bishop Gerald Lanier's voice seemed to belong to the cool air and calm, stately arches of his gray-stone Gothic chapel. The voice was never loud, never shrill, yet it carried to the farthest cranny of the church. Possibly, Jenny thought, because it was so very silent.

"Unto you, O Lord," said Gerald, "we commend the soul of Nadia Beshanskaia, she who has been taken from us so young, she who has given the world so much beauty. . . ."

She gave, thought Jenny, *and she took.*

Nadia had left no will, no family, no loved one to mourn her. So here they were, the greater family of ballet, almost the whole International, and many others, here for the memorial service that Gerald had so kindly volunteered to give. To live, to dance, to die without friends! Instinctively Jenny reached for Dima's hand where he stood hatless by her side. *I want to be a dancer because dancers make people happy.*

There had been no dirge for Nadia. The swan theme from *Swan Lake* had sounded odd, at first, played on the organ in this vaulted chapel. But still and all, it was a song of melancholy, of passing. So they had played the swan theme, slowly, as the mourners filed into the pews. And they would play it again, Jenny knew, when the service was over. Which would be soon because it was a performance day after all; they had to get back to class, to rehearsal, to fittings.

Still taking warmth from Dima's hand, she looked slowly around her. There stood Privy, proudly, belonging to all this now, partly to the ballet world, but more a part of Gerald, and his church, and his good works. And there, down front—naturally!—Judith Winchester in black and black-veiled hat, the picture of a crow in deep mourning, all midnight and angles, with two young men, some sort of flunkies, it was written all over them, flanking her like royalty. Well, she was royalty, of a sort, and good luck to her. Even de Lis was there, impeccable in dark blue, cream shirt, black tie. Who knew more about mourning than a Russian of the old school?

Jenny wondered if he'd seen her, if he'd speak. She hadn't seen Alexander de Lis since she'd left the Civic. He'd speak or he wouldn't speak. Suddenly Jenny realized how little it mattered. Machito was there, tall and pale, grave in a very dark suit, for once almost expressionless. That his last words to Nadia had been a threat, a curse! That wasn't a good memory, no matter how much she'd done to deserve the threat, the curse. Jenny didn't have to look at Dimitri. She sensed him, his strength, warmth, vitality, his hand in her hand; they had no need for looking.

Gerald's euology came to its graceful finish. There would be no burial; Nadia had been cremated. They all recited the Lord's Prayer for Nadia, and as the prayer ended, the organ began again, muted at first, then growing in strength, the swan theme again, building, until all the mourners found their way out of the chapel and into the dull winter noon. Jenny knew that Privy would be waiting for her Gerald, so she kissed Privy and passed on, still hand in hand with Dima.

The swan theme kept playing in the nearly empty chapel, and they could hear it sliding along the vaulted roof and down the reeded pillars as they left. They walked down the seven stone stairs to Seventy-eighth Street. Jenny hardly noticed, as she brushed passed it, the cream-colored Rolls-Royce of Diana Leighton. It seemed that many things had died with Nadia, jealousy among them.

They walked, Dima leading, his impatience building as cab after cab went by but never an empty one, until they came to Fifth Avenue. It was a quarter to one. Suddenly he let go of her hand and leaped into the street like a goat, dodging a bus, popping up on the other side, waving happily, the captured cab tamely marking time at his side. Jenny ran. He was sitting in the big back seat of the old Checker as she slid in. His laughter filled the compartment, and even though Jenny didn't quite know what the joke was, she soon joined in. But not before giving the address: "Lincoln Center, please." She turned to Dima, giggling.

He kissed her, lightly, a laughing kiss. "If we are not to make fools," said Dima, wearing his best urchin grin, "ultimately we must rehearse."

"The pas de deux?" She knew the answer.

"The pas de deux." The taxi nosed into the midday traffic, gathering speed.

They danced that night, and for many more nights. After one of their performances Simon Bridge wrote these words in his dance column:

A time may come when I will be old, and alone, and the wind will chill me more than it does now. Then my heart will be warmed because I'll remember that once I saw them dance, saw Jenny Hale and Dimitri Lubov set the night on fire with the startling eloquence of the music that lives in their bodies, their souls. It is for this special magic that we are irreversibly in debt to dancers everywhere, for they pluck beauty out of vacant space and lay it at our feet, the gift of grace.

About the Author

Tom Murphy, a graduate of Harvard, began his career as an Intelligence Analyst for the G-2 of Berlin Command in Germany. When he returned to America, Mr. Murphy went to work in advertising, eventually becoming Vice President and Creative Supervisor at the J. Walter Thompson Company. Currently, he holds the same position at Bozell & Jacobs, and, in his spare time, is a dealer in art and antiquities. Mr. Murphy is also the author of SKY HIGH.

More Big Bestsellers from SIGNET

☐ **MARATHON: The Pursuit of the Presidency 1972-1976** by Jules Witcover. (#E8034—$2.95)

☐ **THE RULING PASSION** by Shaun Herron.
(#E8042—$2.25)

☐ **THE WHORE-MOTHER** by Shaun Herron.
(#W5854—$1.50)

☐ **CONSTANTINE CAY** by Catherine Dillon.
(#J8307—$1.95)

☐ **WHITE FIRES BURNING** by Catherine Dillon.
(#J8281—$1.95)

☐ **THE WHITE KHAN** by Catherine Dillon.
(#J8043—$1.95)*

☐ **KID ANDREW CODY AND JULIE SPARROW** by Tony Curtis. (#E8010—$2.25)*

☐ **WINTER FIRE** by Susannah Leigh. (#E8011—$2.25)*

☐ **THE MESSENGER** by Mona Williams. (#J8012—$1.95)

☐ **FEAR OF FLYING** by Erica Jong. (#E7970—$2.25)

☐ **HOW TO SAVE YOUR OWN LIFE** by Erica Jong.
(#E7959—$2.50)*

☐ **MISTRESS OF DESIRE** by Rochelle Larkin.
(#E7964—$2.25)*

☐ **THE QUEEN AND THE GYPSY** by Constance Heaven.
(#J7965—$1.95)

☐ **TORCH SONG** by Anne Roiphe. (#J7901—$1.95)

☐ **OPERATION URANIUM SHIP** by Dennis Eisenberg, Eli Landau, and Menaham Portugali. (#E8001—$1.75)

☐ **NIXON VS. NIXON** by Dr. David Abrahamsen.
(#E7902—$2.25)

☐ **ISLAND OF THE WINDS** by Athena Dallas-Damis.
(#J7905—$1.95)

☐ **THE SHINING** by Stephen King. (#E7872—$2.50)

☐ **OAKHURST** by Walter Reed Johnson. (#J7874—$1.95)

☐ **FRENCH KISS** by Mark Logan. (#J7876—$1.95)

*Prices slightly higher in Canada

Have You Read These SIGNET Bestsellers?

☐ **COMA by Robin Cook.** (#E8202—$2.50)

☐ **MISTRESS OF DARKNESS by Christopher Nicole.**
(#J7782—$1.95)

☐ **DESIRES OF THY HEART by Joan Carroll Cruz.**
(#J7738—$1.95)

☐ **CALDO LARGO by Earl Thompson.** (#E7737—$2.25)

☐ **A GARDEN OF SAND by Earl Thompson.**
(#E8039—$2.50)

☐ **TATTOO by Earl Thompson.** (#E8038—$2.50)

☐ **THE ACCURSED by Paul Boorstin.** (#E7745—$1.75)

☐ **ALYX by Lolah Burford.** (#J7640—$1.95)

☐ **MAC LYON by Lolah Burford.** (#J7773—$1.95)

☐ **THE RICH ARE WITH YOU ALWAYS by Malcolm Macdonald.** (#E7682—$2.25)

☐ **THE WORLD FROM ROUGH STONES by Malcolm Macdonald.** (#J6891—$1.95)

☐ **CLANDARA by Evelyn Anthony.** (#J8064—$1.95)

☐ **THE FRENCH BRIDE by Evelyn Anthony.**
(#J7683—$1.95)

☐ **THE PERSIAN PRICE by Evelyn Anthony.**
(#J7254—$1.95)

☐ **TELL ME EVERYTHING by Marie Brenner.**
(#J7685—$1.95)

☐ **DEVERON HALL by Velda Johnston.** (#E8018—$1.75)

☐ **THE FRENCHMAN by Velda Johnston.**
(#W7519—$1.50)

☐ **A ROOM WITH DARK MIRRORS by Velda Johnston.**
(#W7143—$1.50)

☐ **FIRST, YOU CRY by Betty Rollin.** (#J7641—$1.95)

REMEMBER IT DOESN'T GROW ON TREES

ENERGY CONSERVATION -
IT'S YOUR CHANCE TO SAVE, AMERICA

Department of Energy, Washington, D.C.